Civil Society and Government

Civil Society and Government

Edited by
Nancy L. Rosenblum and
Robert C. Post

PRINCETON UNIVERSITY PRESS, PRINCETON AND OXFORD

Copyright © 2002 by Princeton University Press
Published by Princeton University Press, 41 William Street,
Princeton, New Jersey 08540
In the United Kingdom: Princeton University Press, 3 Market Place,
Woodstock, Oxfordshire OX20 1SY
All Right Reserved

Library of Congress Cataloging-in-Publication Data

Civil society and government / edited by Nancy L. Rosenblum and
Robert C. Post.
    p. cm. — (Ethikon series in comparative ethics)
Includes index.
ISBN 0-691-08801-2 (alk. paper)—ISBN 0-691-08802-0 (pbk. : alk. paper)
    1. Civil society. 2. State, The.   I. Rosenblum, Nancy L., 1947–
II. Post, Robert C.   III. Series.

JC336 .C5645 2002
301—dc21   2001050010

British Library Cataloging-in-Publication Data is available

This book has been composed in Janson

Printed on acid-free paper. ∞

www.pup.princeton.edu

Printed in the United States of America

10 9 8 7 6 5 4 3 2 1

10 9 8 7 6 5 4 3 2 1
(Pbk.)

CONTENTS

ACKNOWLEDGMENTS

THE TRUSTEES of the Ethikon Institute join with Philip Valera, president, and Carole Pateman, series editor, in thanking all who contributed to the dialogue project that resulted in this book. We are especially indebted to the Ahmanson Foundation and its trustees, Robert F. Erburu and Lee Walcott, who provided major support for the project, and to other important donors, including the Carrie Estelle Doheny Foundation, Joan Palevsky, and the Sidney Stern Memorial Trust.

Special thanks are due to Nancy L. Rosenblum and Robert Post for taking on the challenging task of editing this volume.

In addition to the authors' contributions, the project and its results were greatly enhanced by the active participation of other dialogue partners: Brian Barry, Richard Madsen, and Tracy B. Strong, many of whose ideas have also found their way into this book.

Finally, we also thank Ann Himmelberger Wald, editor in chief, and Ian Malcolm, our editor, at Princeton University Press, for their valuable guidance and continuing support.

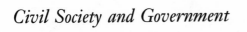

Civil Society and Government

Introduction

Robert C. Post and Nancy L. Rosenblum

CIVIL SOCIETY is so often invoked in so many contexts that it has acquired a strikingly plastic moral and political valence. The recent renaissance of the term began with anticommunist dissent in Eastern Europe, which gave civil society its association with opposition movements and a "parallel polis" to the state. But the term has been endlessly invoked since that time. In the United States, where "civil society" has become a staple of both academic and political discourse, its ideological orientation runs the entire partisan spectrum; we can identify social democrats, grass-rooters, neo-Tocquevilleans, centrists, conservatives of many stripes, libertarians, multiculturalists, and civic republicans.

There are also vastly disparate understandings of the relationship between civil society and government. Civil society is alternately viewed as a source of legitimacy and stability for government and as a source of resistance against arbitrary, oppressive, and overweening government. Civil society is sometimes conceived as a spontaneous growth, prior to and independent of government, and sometimes as dependent on government for legal structure, robust recognition, or outright fiscal support. Civil society is described both as developing in partnership with government and as substituting for the failings of government. Prescriptions for privatization, devolution, and "subsidiarity" can arise from faith in communalism or in voluntarism, or from a loss of faith in the justice or efficacy of government.

This volume portrays the relation between civil society and government as seen from a variety of perspectives in political theory. Our compass is not exhaustive, but it is unusually inclusive. These essays discuss civil society and government from the point of view of classical liberalism, egalitarian liberalism, critical theory, feminism, natural law theory, Judaism, Catholicism and Protestantism, Islam and Confucianism. Our goal is comparative; we wish to provide the materials for assessing how theorists from diverse political and religious traditions understand the relationship between civil society and government.

The concept of civil society is historically bounded, and it is not an organizing concept in every tradition. Where the concept is alien, we have instead inquired into the functional equivalents, if any, to oppositions like those between state and society, citizenship and membership. The essays have been organized topically, according to six basic inquiries:

BOUNDARIES: In terms of function and consequences, does it matter where the line is drawn between civil society and the state?

NEEDS: Do civil society and the state need each other? If so, what does civil society need from the state? What does the state need from civil society? What are the particular values they impart to one another?

LIABILITIES: Do civil society and the state pose liabilities for each other? If so, what liabilities does civil society pose for the state? What liabilities does the state pose for civil society? How are these liabilities to be contained?

GROUPS AND INDIVIDUALS: In what contexts and/or under what conditions, should government interact with individuals (*a*) directly? (*b*) indirectly through communal associations? In general, what factors should determine the appropriate arrangements?

CITIZENSHIP: In moral rather than strictly legal terms, what are the prerogatives of citizenship? What are its duties? What, if anything, is the role of civil society in forming good citizens?

CONFLICT: How are conflicting demands of citizenship and membership in the non-governmental associations of civil society to be handled?

By organizing each essay topically, we have tried to make comparisons among cultures and traditions accessible. Mindful that theoretical perspectives are not internally uniform, we have included critical responses to each account.

In this introduction we propose to focus primarily on the first topic, on the boundary between civil society and government. We will not address the descriptive question of how state entities may be empirically distinguished from their private counterparts. We will instead discuss the normative question of how this boundary should be conceived and why it matters.

To say that the boundary between civil society and government is located differently in diverse political regimes and that its purposes are justified differently by various political, moral, and religious theories is just the beginning. Within any given state, the boundary is shifting in practice; it responds to the ongoing contingencies of political experience. The history of political thought shows that it is ceaselessly contested. We have only to think of the varying kinds and degrees of separation of church and state, or of the range of feminist challenges to articulations of a public/private divide, to get a sense of this.

   Nonetheless, contemporary political theories distinguish between
ernment and civil society, and they identify a boundary between them,
even if it is not fixed. What resources do we have for understanding the
constant postulation of some boundary between civil society and government, on the one hand, and the variability of its location, purpose, and
justification, on the other?
   We propose a general theoretical proposition about the boundary
between civil society and government. To employ the usual spatial metaphor, civil society is the realm of social life which, when viewed from the
perspective of government, is characterized by plural and particularist
identities. Government, by contrast, is an inclusive sphere, which, when
viewed from the perspective of civil society, is characterized by overarching public norms made and enforced by official institutions. Civil society
is a zone of freedom for individuals to associate with others and for
groups to shape their norms, articulate their purposes, and determine for
themselves the internal structure of group authority and identity. Government is a domain of common purpose and identity.
   In the remainder of this introduction, we shall explore the many implications that follow from this seemingly simple theoretical proposition,
and we shall indicate how they may be used to frame the questions discussed in the essays collected in this volume.

CIVIL SOCIETY

   The elements of civil society range from groups based on religion and
ethnicity to more fluid voluntary associations organized around ideology,
professionalism, social activities or the pursuit of money, status, interest,
or power. They range from circles of friends, which Humboldt described
as the condition for cultivating "beautiful individuality," to single-pur-
pose political advocacy groups. Civil society also includes communities,
like formally organized religious settlements, with their implication of
primary socialization, strong attachment, and common history and
expectations. Civil society harbors cultural institutions of all kinds, from
the deep, constitutive practices of a cultural group with a common language and history, to the wildly eclectic popular culture of self-help
groups in the United States. From many perspectives, the family counts
as an element of civil society; it is the premier mediating, moralizing
institution. These essays demonstrate that the purposes of association
and their personal meanings for members are as various as human needs
and imagination. The value of association is as encompassing as the value
of liberty.
   In saying that civil society is the realm of pluralism, we are endorsing
Isaiah Berlin's observation of the historicity of human nature, his notion

that human identities cannot be other than local and particular, and his belief that this diversity is not transitory. Civil society is not a residue on the way to a unified state in which citizenship eclipses other aspects of belonging, or on the way to a cosmopolitan order in which universality is our essence. Pluralism has a normative as well as a descriptive dimension.

The substantive content of group purposes and the internal organization of associational life are as various and malleable as human creativity. From any given perspective, the groups that are singled out as shaping the nature of civil society will depend on theoretical commitments. There is sharp dispute, for example, on the question of whether market institutions should be included in the concept of civil society. From our perspective, however, this dispute can be framed as turning on the degree to which market institutions are seen as contributing to the formation of the identities of their participants or, by contrast, as primarily engaged in instrumental or strategic action that objectifies or alienates these participants.[1]

With respect to those aspects of associational life that are pertinent to identity formation, we would stress that a key variable is the degree and manner in which the diverse groups that make up civil society are open and permeable. The structure of pluralism is of great significance. We can in fact range pluralist societies along a spectrum from fluid to rigidly segmented.

From a number of perspectives, the "ideal type" of civil society is identified with voluntary association, meaning that membership is consensual and exit possible without loss of status or public rights and benefits. Escape from hereditary and ascriptive attachments (or their willing affirmation) and the ceaseless formation of new associations for every conceivable purpose mark this type of civil society. There are few obstacles to the proliferation of groups through creation or schism.

A defining characteristic of civil society in this view is the capacity of individuals to move freely among groups and to shift involvement among them. So long as this capacity realistically obtains, even traditionalist or "functionally traditionalist" associations serve to underscore individualism, voluntarism, self-construction, and self-expression.

Another crucial aspect of a fluid civil society is that men and women typically join more than one group; membership is plural. Group identifications overlap and conflict. Beyond having a pluralist structure, then, a fluid civil society affords individuals *the experience* of pluralism.

The significance of civil society is not exhausted by its meaning for individuals. Self-expression and self-development are not the only justifications for groups. Even in fluid civil societies, some associations are not voluntary or chosen. As a matter of moral psychology, belonging is often a matter of assent rather than consent. This is sometimes true, although not always, with religion; it is truer for race, or indeed for any ascriptive trait that a given society singles out as especially valued or despised. One of the principal purposes of association is pursuit of "recognition" by minority groups. The aim is to get symbolic and distributive signs of the group's status, exhibitions of public respect for the group's unique differences.[2]

Many perspectives challenge individualist, voluntarist accounts of civil society that give priority to personal autonomy. They substitute accounts of civil society in which the openness of groups and shifting involvements among them is less important than the capacity of groups to endow persons with stable and enduring identities. In such circumstances, civil society is not fluid, but segmented. It is comprised of deeply embedded spheres or orders, classes, or cultural groups, or corporations that are closed and that restrict membership—whether by ascriptive traits or status. Membership is not a matter of contribution, merit, or active joining, but of a person's general characteristics. Groups may claim individuals as their own and attribute obligations to them regardless of subjective identification or participation in a cultural "way of life." From these perspectives, identification with a group is not psychological—and not (or not only) a matter of subjective affiliation expressed through affirmative membership—but objective. Indeed, presumptive identity trumps personal identification, and presumptive identity is oriented to the collective identity of presumably integral groups and communities.

In segmented societies, groups are more inclined to see membership as mutually exclusive and to be hostile to the idea of plural identities and multiple, overlapping memberships. Groups and communities inevitably experience internal divisions over authority and over the interpretation of norms and purposes, but those who value a segmented vision of civil society believe that conflicts should be resolved internally, insulated from government intervention and from the influence of other powerful and intrusive socially dominant groups.

Some civil societies verge toward the segmented because of the power and authority of tradition and because of the relative weakness of social forces encouraging to social mobility and voluntary association. But the character of legal regulation is also important for the fluidity of civil society. The law can range from ascribing to people group identity to actively suppressing all forms of group rights, with a myriad of intermediate positions. Those who wish to use the law to maintain social segmentation employ a "politics of recognition" whose goal goes beyond public respect, and beyond the degree of self-government afforded voluntary associations in relatively liberal societies. Rather, the goal is to secure a group's legal and political authority over members and over the distribution of public goods. The associations of civil society claim authority over personal status law and even criminal law as it pertains to group members.

Within civil society, then, there are inequalities of rights and responsibilities and resources. These differentials subsist between groups and within groups. In segmented civil societies with codified membership and authority that controls the distribution of important rights and benefits, these inequalities are entrenched. We have only to think of the status and opportunities of women in hierarchic religious communities governed by religious laws and courts. Where civil society is segmented and association ascriptive or closed, the critical questions are whether government codifies communal identities and deals directly with group authorities and corporate communities rather than directly with individuals on the basis of universal norms, and for what purposes.

Political theory has continuously shifted between envisioning civil society as fluid and as segmented. It oscillates between imagining persons within civil society as possessing identities circumscribed by singular cultures, religions, and autonomous communities, and imagining persons as autonomous individuals who are members of diverse arrays of primarily voluntary associations.

In practice, however, fluid and segmented civil societies exist on a continuum. Voluntary and ascriptive associations, open and closed groups, coexist in any given civil society in different proportions. The identities constituted by and affirmed in groups develop out of history and available norms and social forms; we all come from somewhere, and we begin making decisions within the options we know. But identity is not exhausted by history; individuals are not "radically situated." If our points of origin provide us personally and collectively with an initial source of meaning, they are not the sum or stopping place for meaningfulness in our lives. Ascriptive identity is not the whole of identity, either phenomenologically or morally, if for no other reason than that recognized contributions to associations, not objective belonging, are an essential part of self-respect.

Within civil society, individual well-being is tied to, and understood to be tied to, the well-being and independence of groups. But this means that it is also connected to the self-government of associations, with struggles for control over the group's authority, membership, internal rules, and purposes. Thus if associations are constitutive, they are not wholly constitutive. Every component of civil society, even hermetic separatist communities, are permeable to the influence of other groups, to overarching public culture, to influences from abroad, and to the ceaseless invention of novel values and social forms.

This suggests that segmentation within civil society must have limits. The freedom that produces pluralist associations must be prized and enforced. Some allowance for multiplicity of memberships and some possibility of shifting participation by individuals among at least some social and political groups is always a defining characteristic of civil society. When that sphere of freedom is too constricted, the capacity to shape and sustain associations that provide the structure of personal and collective life is choked off. It is one thing to give precedence to affirmation of the group over members' freedom to join and leave; it is another thing to erect very costly obstacles to exit that make membership effectively inalienable. Where freedom of association is truncated, civil society fragments into an aggregate of unalterable ascriptive attachments defined by heredity, tribal identity, race, ethnicity, or caste. A pluralist society that affords autonomy only to particularist groups and not to individuals loses its normative standing as a civil society.

Civil society is not merely plural; it is also particularist. Within civil society identity is always specific. Identity springs from contingencies of socialization and from choice; it is not the product of a single and unified design. It comes from participation in particular groups and associations, and is not imposed uniformly upon all by the state.

Every form of civil society recognizes that groups and associations are not coterminous with the state. Groups and associations need not be sovereign to flourish. They are *jurisgenerative*, and their members are subject to authoritative norms and practices. But their goods and services—from burial societies to education—are distributed only to members. They are "partial publics" that acknowledge the distinction between member and citizen. Within civil society, therefore, membership is diverse *and* particular.

It is not necessary, however, that each such group or association understand itself as particularist. Sometimes groups and associations within civil society conceive themselves as the bearers of universal truths, which all ought to acknowledge. Groups and associations may seek to use the state to impose their truths. If they were to succeed, however, and if the conformity required by their vision were extensive enough, the viability of civil society would be mortally threatened. The grip of the state can impose a uniformity fatal to pluralism.

The persistence of civil society, therefore, depends upon a complex equilibrium among diverse groups and associations. The power to deploy the state in the service of group identity must be reasonably diffused among competing associations. Or groups and associations must implicitly agree, however grudgingly, to compete for adherents through persuasion rather than through legal compulsion. Or there must be implicit understandings about the limits of the state's ability to impose uniformity. However this equilibrium is maintained, the upshot will be that civil society will remain, from the perspective of the state, a domain of partial and particular identities. Particularism marks the boundary that separates civil society from the state.

GOVERNMENT

Associations proliferate and assume their structures in part in response to law, to the various provisions of corporate, tax, tort, or constitutional law that create the framework within which associations define their purposes and carry out their activities. Groups and the experiences groups make possible are partially shaped by these forms.

The legal framework is the means by which government performs its civilizing role of transforming arrant pluralism into civil society. The "civil" in civil society is not exhausted by civility. Most fundamentally, society is civil when it is not subject to militarism, violence, and the will to domination on the part of particularist groups. Government is the agency responsible for controlling private armies and private oppression. It sets limits to the authority of associations over their members and outsiders, and protects against at least the worst oppression by private authorities. It enforces rules for settling disputes and looks for ways of diminishing hostility and enabling coordination and alliances among groups. Without government, the result is anarchy, private oppression, or the private engrossment of collective resources.[3] Neither individual rights nor the rights of collectivities are meaningful without the enforcement of law. This implies that limited government must be distinguished from weak government.

It is the responsibility of government to provide groups and associations with sufficient public goods and entitlements to commit them to publicly imposed order and cooperation.[4] At a minimum these benefits must include civil peace and the distribution of certain rights. At a maximum they might include public funding for parochial education and cultural reproduction, support for services to group members, and public recognition of group identity.

Government must also establish an appropriate legal framework for formalizing and securing associations.[5] Often this is done through the concept of legal personhood. Government assigns individuals and corporations *enforceable* civil and political rights; legal status as a person signifies the capacity to enter contracts, form agreements, own property, and to form associations for these and other purposes. Civil society is inconceivable absent a reasonably stable structure of civil law, which is a vehicle for particularism.

Government, finally, is a collective agent whose identity and purpose transcends the instrumental. In contrast to the pluralism and particularism of civil society, government may be defined as standing for inclusive public norms and common identity. Through an overarching public political culture embodied in institutions and perpetuated through many forms of public education, direct and indirect, government articulates and sustains shared ground. It claims authoritatively to represent common interests. The substance of common political identity is variable, as is its capacity to attract the commitment of groups and the identification of citizens. It may consist of democratic norms of individual autonomy and equal and universal civil and political rights, or of public norms identified with a national culture ("American" or "French"), or of established religion and the secular norms that complement it. But in every case, government claims to embody the fundamental nature of a polity.

Common political identity is made manifest not only in formal institutions, but also in public rituals and monuments.[6] It is cultivated through public education and proselytizing of various kinds. It is made effective by strategies of inclusion. All governments claiming to represent common interests must serve, if not every interest, then every group and association capable of challenging its stability and legitimacy, every element of civil society whose cooperation is needed. Common identity requires that these benefits be palpable and appreciated, that cooperation be general. And this demands a minimal degree of fairness—of public justification for the distribution of rights and benefits and costs. In this sense, Michael Walzer contends, every state is to some degree a welfare state.

The claim of government to represent the common good and the common identity is of course entirely putative. It is the everyday stuff of politics to expose this kind of claim as merely masking the particular interests of specific groups or associations. Under the conditions of diversity characteristic of civil societies, it is most improbable that there is any single common identity, and of course any vision of the common good is always *somebody's* vision.

What is at issue with respect to this kind of claim, therefore, is the right to speak in the name of a common good and identity. The right is authorized by whatever structures of legitimacy sustain the state. But it is from the perspective of the particularism of civil society that this right acquires meaning, for the common good is that which purports to transcend particularism. This contrast between the common good and the particular is expressed in the distinction between citizen and member.

If membership expresses particular commitments of discrete groups and associations, citizenship reflects the overarching norms of a government. For the pluralism of civil society to persist, these norms must be limited. They must not radically preempt or displace the possibilities of membership. It follows that the scope of citizenship must have intrinsic limitations.[7]

In fact citizenship in a modern state, even in a liberal democracy with its positive norms of public respect and avenues of effective participation, is often circumscribed. In the absence of external threats, citizenship is typically invoked only with respect to a restricted number of political occasions, instrumental and ritualistic, open to citizens regardless of merit, like voting, jury duty, or military service. Often participation in these occasions is not mandatory. Citizens are presumptively equal, and for this reason birthright citizenship has nothing to do with individual merit or ability. While in many contexts citizenship can be a source of pride and identity, citizenship does not ordinarily serve within quotidian domestic politics as a principal source of self-respect.

Exclusion from citizenship is demeaning, of course, an injurious mark of public disrespect, but inclusion per se does not have the opposite, positive significance. Although citizenship can call up the disposition to participate through one's own acts and energy, industry and skill, in the same ways that membership in private associations can summon these dispositions, it normally does not. Most frequently these dispositions are instead cultivated, exhibited, and appreciated through the associations of civil society, where contributions are suitably fitted to individuals' capacities and wants.

The development of a full and rich personality thus ordinarily draws upon participation in civil society. The philosopher Hegel, for whom "the creation of civil society [is] the achievement of the modern world," explained this best. *The Philosophy of Right* teaches that civil society must be seen against the historical background of alienation and a falling off from original social unity. But at the same time as civil society disconnects individuals from traditionalist moorings, it is the "tremendous power" that draws individuals into itself, provides them with a "second family," and reorients them. "The sanctity of marriage and the dignity of Corporation membership are the two fixed points round which the unorganized atoms of civil society revolve." What Hegel called the corporation—meaning economic organizations, religious bodies, learned societies, and so on—is the principal "ethical entity" that provides members rank and dignity, and "work of a public character over and above their private business . . . which the modern state does not always provide."[8]

CONCEPTUALIZING THE BOUNDARY BETWEEN GOVERNMENT AND CIVIL SOCIETY

Against this background, how, then, are we to conceive the boundary between government and civil society? The boundary functions to set civil society and government in productive tension. It defines the pluralism and particularism of civil society in opposition to the inclusive and overarching norms of government. Push the boundary too far in the direction of government, and civil society can wither away. Push the boundary too far in the direction of civil society, and government can collapse into anarchic disorder. Yet civil society requires government to survive, and government, at least democratic government, draws deeply from the strengths of civil society. The location of the boundary is a matter of judgment, which means that it is subject to perennial dispute and contestation. It has no single correct or fixed position, but moves with contingencies of history, tradition, culture, and politics.

Wherever the distinction between civil society and government is marked, however, there must always exist a boundary between them, because each is defined in opposition to the other. Government fails if it embodies merely particularist values. A police officer betrays his office if he does not treat citizens equally, but gives favor to members of his own group. Government must have reasonably independent police and courts, as well as an impartial administrative apparatus. If religious authorities establish theocratic rule; if ethnic or religious groups hold sway and deny civil and political rights to members of other groups; if government is captured by (or is itself) a dominant economic interest; if the common good is conflated with, and understood to be conflated with, particularist goods, government ceases to sustain civil society.

Without independence from civil society, government cannot protect basic rights or well-being. The associations of civil society mirror, reinforce, and actively create social inequalities of all kinds, with the accompanying enmity and rivalry. Government must be able to intervene to set bounds, to enforce basic requirements of peace, order, civil equality, and so forth. Government cannot perform even these minimal tasks if we assume that government "independence" is, like "impartial government," a ruse or an impossibility. Government's claim that it is not simply the mirror and agent of the most powerful forces in society must be credible.[9]

Conversely, civil society must be independent of government. The divide between civil society and government sets off civil society as *nongovernmental*: that is, as distinct from the official, coercive, political apparatus. In this limited sense the distinction between civil society and government corresponds to the split between private and public, where the term "public" is understood to signify "official" government entities. Associations in civil society must speak in their own name; they do not have the authority "officially" to speak in the name of the common good.

In contrast to government, civil society must remain particular and plural. Whether or not membership in the associations of civil society is wholly voluntarist and best conceived as unfettered individual choice rather than inherited or ascriptive, it is not, with the important exception of the family, mandated by public law. To the extent that groups and associations are authorized by government to exercise coercive legal authority over their own members or outsiders, the domain of civil society begins to lose its character. The internal laws of groups may be powerful, command obedience, and regulate members' lives in minute ways, but members must be able to exit from associations. There are frequently material and psychological costs to disassociation, of course, but the promise is that membership status does not determine civil standing or vital civil and political rights. A background of general civil laws of contract, property, marriage, and so on, allows people, particularly women, to disassociate from the authority and restrictive personal laws of specific religious and ethnic groups.[10]

The analytic distinction between civil society and government has functional implications. As we have stressed, civil society cannot persist if government does not actively intervene to maintain civil order and personal legal rights. But civil society also requires government to abstain from interventions that undermine pluralism. The very origin of civil society is inseparable from the theory and practice of limited government. Totalitarianism is its antithesis; so is authoritarian repression of self-organized groups and any form of paternalistic regime that does not provide space for autonomous associational life.

Members of groups within civil society must experience themselves as normally free from official repression and from regulation that conscripts their identities, membership, and self-government. Civil society is unintelligible without defined limits both to the means government can legitimately use to regulate groups and to the justifications that count in such regulation. Associations must be free from intervention that undermines their singular purposes and activities, inhibits self-definition, chills expression, or threatens viability. To the extent these limits are transgressed, civil society is endangered.

Accommodating Civil Society and Government: From Congruence to Modus Vivendi

There is an obvious tension, however, between a government that aspires to speak in the accents of a common good and identity and a civil society that encourages pluralism and particularism. Unless citizens actually have common values and beliefs, how can government possibly function? This question has led theorists from a variety of perspectives to argue that the internal lives of groups should be closely regulated to conform to public values and common principles of justice. They advocate what Rosenblum has called the "logic of congruence."

Advocates of congruence fear that the multiplication of intermediate institutions does not mediate but balkanizes public life. They are apprehensive that plural associations and groups amplify self-interest, encourage arrant interest-group politics, exaggerate cultural egocentrism, and defy government. What is needed, in their view, is a strong assertion of public values and policies designed to loosen the hold of particular affiliations, so that members will be empowered to look beyond their groups and to identify themselves as members of the larger political community. The "logic of congruence" envisions civil society as reflecting common values and practices "all the way down."

Congruence is often advocated with regard to the egalitarian norms of liberal democracy. The claim is that the internal lives of associations should mirror public norms of equality, nondiscrimination, due process, and so on. In the United States, for example, norms of equality and due process have been imposed on vast areas of social life, even on small, informal associations. Antidiscrimination law, for instance, requires most groups to admit unwanted members. By this means the government compels association.

Until recently, the principal rationale for such law was equality of opportunity. Regulation of groups was deemed necessary to redress past discrimination and to underwrite necessary economic advancement. But such regulation is now also defended on the grounds of moral education. Antidiscrimination law is seen by some as a means by which a tutelary government teaches egalitarian values. Such instruction is necessary because groups that discriminate in "private" will cultivate dispositions in their members that are antagonistic to public egalitarian commitments. If government depends upon the dispositions formed through membership in groups, then "a crucial task of educational statecraft is to foster a healthy structure of group life."[11]

Taken too far, however, this logic of moral education potentially trespasses across the boundary that separates civil society from government. It invites state institutions to colonize social life in the name of progressive public ideals. It follows the same logic as contemporary proposals to democratize the family by enacting statutes requiring partners to share domestic chores and income, or to democratize religion by requiring churches to ordain women or gay priests as a condition of receiving the tax status of a charitable organization.

Advocates of congruence properly note that the boundary between government and civil society should not be overdrawn or mechanically interpreted. Every government uses law to define and educate its citizens. When a state creates rights to sue for defamation or invasion of privacy, for example, it uses law to protect common values and to safeguard a certain common ideal of personality.[12] The riotous plurality of demo-

cratic civil society subsists upon a substrate of common values and identity that is legally fostered and enforced.

The question of congruence is therefore one of degree. To the extent
that the common values established by law are too thick, to the extent
that the common identity protected by law is too pervasive, civil society
will suffer. The degree of appropriate uniformity will depend upon many
factors, including the antecedent cultural homogeneity within a society
and the particular domain of civil society that is subject to regulation.
The aspiration for thick and pervasive congruence will be more damaging to a truly heterogeneous society than to a culturally homogeneous
one; and we are far more tolerant of intrusive moral regulation of the
marketplace than of religious institutions.

The question of congruence is also one of kind. Government has many
means by which to create congruence. It can do so by direct legal regulation, by asserting its rights as a coercive sovereign. But it can also exercise its capacities as educator, patron, sponsor, employer, and owner.
There are important differences between legally mandating churches to
ordain women and refusing to extend tax benefits to churches that
acknowledge only male priests. The latter alters the "terms, conditions,
and public status" of groups, thus enabling groups to choose the terms of
their accommodation to public values.[13] On the other hand, the powerful
inducements of governmental largesse can be exceedingly seductive; it
can exemplify aggressive state "capture" of independent groups and create a climate of passive clientelism.[14] The impact of government action
on the particularism and plurality of civil society must always be kept in
mind.

Congruence represents only one possible form of the accommodation
between civil society and government. Advocates of civil society may care
more for the conditions of independent associational life than they do for
the conditions that reinforce overarching norms and that incline groups
to contribute to governmental efforts to maintain political stability. They
may be content if vigorous independent associations exhibit only a minimal commitment to public order. Recognizing that common norms
impose costs on the purposes and internal culture of many groups, they
may lobby for exceptions to general laws and special accommodations for
group autonomy.

If advocates of congruence desire that common norms be inculcated all
the way down, those partial to civil society argue that public life can be
sustained by a modus vivendi among competitive groups, or by an "overlapping consensus" in which elements of civil society bring their own
distinct principled reasons for cooperation to bear in justifying government. The hope is that individuals qua group members can wear their
citizenship lightly and avoid testing whether their primary loyalty is to

their particular group or to a common public life. This does not nec
sarily indicate that government is weak; within limits, it may prov
justifiable compromise between civil society and strong government.

In evaluating how government and civil society may be accommodated, therefore, we can place congruence and modus vivendi along a
spectrum. To the extent that civil society flourishes and evidences general
agreement about significant public values, greater degrees of congruence
can be tolerated. But to the extent that civil society is less open and more
segmented, with deep social divisions based on class or status, modus
vivendi may as a practical matter be all that is attainable. If a genuinely
inclusive public identity is fragile and government resources limited,
modus vivendi is a real achievement and a reasonable accommodation to
civil society.

Civil Society and Democracy

Democratic values are relevant to the goal of securing a proper accommodation between civil society and government. This is because democracy turns on the value of self-government, of a people ruling themselves.
Implicit in this value is the distinction between a people and the state
that represents them. This distinction is lost if a state merely programs
persons in its own image, as, for example, in Aldous Huxley's *Brave New
World*. Implicit in democracy, therefore, is a boundary between state and
persons that is analogous to the boundary between state and civil society.

Although all states, including democratic states, contribute in multiple
ways to the identity of their citizens, the independence of persons within
democracies is typically marked sociologically and politically by the independent institutions and associations of civil society. This implies that the
logic of congruence is bounded by democratic values, as well as by those
of civil society. Even the most stalwart advocates of strong democracy
would acknowledge that values and identity derive significantly from
sources that reach beyond public norms like democracy or social justice.
Most persons care intensely about matters that are the exclusive business
of groups in civil society. Our interests, convictions, cultural, religious
and sexual identities, status, salvation, exhibition of competence, exhilarating rivalries may have nothing to do with citizenship or the state.
Democratic accountability is importantly measured by a state's responsiveness to these independent concerns.

Consider, for example, Hannah Arendt's analysis of the Nazi and the
Stalinist regimes. The origins of totalitarianism, Arendt argued, lay in
the weakening of secondary groups and associations. The defining characteristic of totalitarianism is the combination of "atomistic individualism" with techniques of terror. The absence of social buffers between

individuals and the state makes persons vulnerable to ferocious mobilization and extinction. Totalitarianism can be understood as the end point of unremitting congruence.

For close to half a century this view of civil society has been exploited by political theorists who describe what they perceive as conditions of growing atomism and privatism and raise the specter (not always apt) of totalitarianism. Theorists like François Furet pronounce the continuity between the Jacobin heritage of the Revolution and French "statism," and warn of the "matrix of totalitarianism."[15] American theorists portray the "megastructures" of American government as hostile to healthy pluralism. They claim that government erodes the independent life of groups and associations directly by official regulation, subsidy, and control, and indirectly by monopolizing social functions and displacing secondary institutions. It is said that overbearing government has transformed the United States into a "mass society" and that the revival of civil society is necessary to transfer "meaning and value to the megastructures of public order."[16] Recapturing the density of association life has been deemed a necessary protection against atomism and its invitation to an antidemocratic totalitarianism.

Whatever the accuracy of these various diagnoses, they have in common the assumption that democracy depends on the activities of particularist, self-determining associations of civil society, where independent commitments, interests, and voices are developed. They express the insight that civil society is the precondition for democratic decision making, whether democracy is conceived as deliberation or as interest group pluralism, and that this is true even if the goal of democracy is to transcend particularism and arrive at uncoerced agreement or a common will. They stress that democratic values will be imperiled if congruence is pursued too comprehensively or too vigorously.

Political theory since World War II has also stressed the complementary insight, however, that democracy presupposes citizens who come genuinely to identify with the state as "their" representative. This perspective has important implications for pursuing modus vivendi as an acceptable model of the relationship between civil society and government within democracies. To the extent that democracy presupposes the forging of a genuine common will, a mere modus vivendi must be ruled out as an option for accommodating civil society and government.

This perspective is implicit in the work of many theorists who stress that civil society is vital to the efforts of a democratic government to achieve consensus by building structures of "interpenetration" between government and interest groups for making and implementing public policy. Associations are crucial to governance, particularly to the delivery of public services, even where they have no formal role and are best described as social or civic rather than political groups. In the United States, churches and neighborhood groups, ethnic associations and civic charities, as well as for-profit organizations, share responsibility for addressing social needs with local, state, and federal governments in everything from housing to crime control.

This should not be conceived as pure voluntarism; groups may be neither an alternative to public provision nor unsupported by the state. Catholic Charities, the Boys and Girls Clubs, tenants' advocates, literacy centers, immigrant support services, after-school youth centers, family planning clinics, and innumerable others have been publicly subsidized. Lester Salamon calls this partnership between government and civil society "third party government."[17] At its essence, such interpenetration forges genuinely common commitments that underwrite a democratic allegiance and legitimacy far removed from a modus vivendi.

This analysis suggests that democratic states must pursue a logic that avoids the extremes of congruence and modus vivendi. A legitimate democratic state neither mechanically reproduces its citizens nor rules merely by default. Whatever compromise between these extremes is ultimately reached, political theory since World War II has stressed that the independent groups and associations of civil society will perform at least three functions that have special importance for democracies.

The first is to serve as a center of collective political resistance against capricious and oppressive government. This aspect of civil society received particular emphasis in the struggle against Soviet imperialism. "Civil society" entered the political lexicon of Central and Eastern Europe as an oppositional idea. Because it was imperative to break free from party dictatorship and because overt political opposition was ineffective, even suicidal, the principal resistance to centralized authority became associated with intellectual and cultural circles. Civil society signaled the ability to eke out some portion of negative liberty: "Let me be, leave me alone, don't try to tell me how to live."[18] Civil society referred initially to an underground "parallel polis" of groups attending to ostensibly nonpolitical affairs.

Poland's Solidarity came to epitomize civil society as a seedbed of more active human rights claims and dissident movements.[19] As communist regimes collapsed, trade unions, professional organizations, churches, and political parties were prized as "a living society in which public life and activities originating 'from below' are possible." "The social self-organization of society" became an ideal.[20] In the enthusiasm of the moment, however, it was forgotten that civil society and government are complementary and that they require each other, so that some actually proposed civil society as a substitute for government. For our purposes, however, it is sufficient to stress the ways in which civil society functioned to counterbalance oppressive and antidemocratic state actions.

A second function civil society performs for democracy is to organize people for democratic participation. There is nothing mysterious or organicist about this. Experience tells us quite a bit about the unpredictable origin and course of political participation. Groups that engage in political advocacy and agenda setting are not always formed initially for political purposes; their politicization is contingent and unpredictable. Group life is transformative. Thus when American jeremiahs interpret low voter turnout as a crisis of democracy, they see association as a resource for revivifying participation. They search for substitutes for groups like trade unions that were once strong, often looking to "new social movements" to counterbalance entrenched interests and alter political agendas. Government initiatives are propelled by the mobilization of feminists and environmentalists, taxpayers and consumers, student groups and the politically organized elderly. Political parties are of course a key association, but all kinds of groups expose political arbitrariness and corruption and hold officials accountable by agitating outside of formal political arenas.

It would be a mistake, however, to imagine that civil society is a guarantee for successful democratic mobilization. Freedom of association may be a necessary condition for responsive and accountable democratic institutions, but it is not a sufficient condition. Not all "interests" find their way into "interest groups" and effective political representation. Groups may be too dispersed and trivial to set agendas and effectively energize democratic politics.[21] Individuals and groups may lack the resources for organization. The very pluralism of civil society can be politically intimidating. Jürgen Habermas observes that instead of creating strong new public identities, pluralization can produce a sense of "impotence in the face of an impenetrable systemic complexity."[22] Others caution that if politicized groups are too many and too strong, a "hyperpluralist" crush can create crises of ungovernability.[23]

A third function civil society performs for democracy concerns socialization into the political values necessary for self-government. Many political theorists conceive civil society as the "seedbed of virtue." The governing assumption is that associations inculcate civic virtues and constructive dispositions like sociability and trust. They understand this socialization to spill over into public life. The phrase "mediating institutions" is meant to capture this idea. The thought is that the sense of cooperation and shared responsibility generated by associations produce "social networks" and "virtuous cycles" of trust on an ever-expanding scale. Civil society is said to provide participatory, egalitarian experiences that foster the disposition to care for others. The moral dispositions and "social capital" generated within groups are deemed invaluable for the conduct of democracy.

This point, however, can easily be overstated. Not all associations provide exemplary education. Certain groups cater to dark emotional needs and amplify selfish interests. They may even inculcate in members antisocial dispositions like snobbery or ethnic hatred, dispositions that Madison's "mischiefs of faction" do not begin to encompass. In the face of such patently uncivil associations, theorists either define civil society in terms of benign formative associations, omitting vicious and incongruent groups from the start, or they assign government a stern tutorial and regulative role, invoking the logic of congruence.

We can conclude from this analysis that civil society is no guarantee of democracy, but it is necessary for democracy and can serve important democratic functions. A flourishing pluralistic civil society and strong democratic government are reciprocally supportive.

Perspectives on Civil Society

The conception of civil society that we have sought to develop in this introduction is unmistakably a product of Western culture and institutions. It not only presupposes characteristically occidental social and governmental structures, but it draws upon a long intellectual history of attempting to comprehend the normative implications of these structures.

This history is most vividly displayed in the essays in this volume discussing natural law and Christianity. Both natural law perspectives and Christianity have over the millenniums sought to endow evolving occidental social structures with normative political significance. Within the natural law tradition, as Fred D. Miller demonstrates, this significance can vary from imagining society as "an organism with government as its head" to envisioning individuals as endowed with inalienable rights. All natural law theories are committed to explicating the social implications of human nature, and this commitment creates a certain strain when confronted by the particularism of modern civil society. Indeed, as William M. Sullivan observes, influential Stoic contributions to natural law stressed the universalism of transcendent values "available through 'right reason,'" which they contrasted to the particularism, the *ius gentium*, of specific states.

This attribution of universal value to extragovernmental sources heavily influenced early Christian thinking. John A Coleman's essay traces the efforts of modern Catholic thought to reconcile the transcendent truth of the church to the particularism of contemporary civil society. The principle of subsidiarity does yeoman's service in this context. Unresolved tensions about how Christianity can accommodate the pluralism and particularism of civil society are at the root of Max L. Stackhouse's advocacy of "the 'federal-covenantal' view, most fully articulated by the Reform tradition," as distinct from "the 'hierarchical-subsidiarity' view, most fully articulated by the Roman Catholic tradition."

From the vantage of these historical traditions, the various contemporary perspectives on the relationship of government to civil society that are represented in this volume—classical liberalism, liberal egalitarianism, critical theory, and feminism—all seem remarkably similar. All accept the basic notion that the state speaks for the common good, while participants in civil society engage in enterprises that are plural and particular. All accept the interdependence of civil society and the state, while at the same time recognizing the potential danger that each holds for the other. These contemporary perspectives differ from each other largely in matters of emphasis and focus.

It is "almost definitive" of classical liberalism, as Steven Scalet and David Schmidtz characterize it, to be simultaneously driven by a fear of the potential abuse of state power and a complementary passion for voluntarism. These very practical apprehensions profoundly influence the ways in which classical liberalism conceives the appropriate relationship between government and civil society, as the comments of Tom G. Palmer illustrate.

Liberal egalitarianism, by contrast, seems to be guided as much by a profound commitment to certain ideals, like justice and equality, as by practical concerns. Will Kymlicka's essay exemplifies how liberal egalitarians reason backward from the attainment of these ideals to conclusions about how the state ought to relate to civil society. Kymlicka concludes that equality requires the state to reach deeply into the socialization processes of civil society. William A. Galston, however, cautions that such intervention may come only at the price of undermining the independent and equally important value of liberty.

Critical theory, as explained by Kenneth Baynes, is less concerned with the achievement of specific values than with the complex dialectical processes by which values can be clarified and legitimized in modern society. Critical theory explores the preconditions for such legitimation. It especially focuses on the question of how the particularities of civil society can be transmuted into the common values necessary to sustain state action, and how state action can in turn sustain civil society's capacity to create undistorted and legitimate values. Stephen K. White's comment emphasizes that historically critical theory was not always satisfied with such abstract structural analysis, but focused also on the "lived experience of suffering on the part of the disadvantaged segments of the population."

Feminism is quite attentive to such experience. More than any of the other contemporary perspectives, feminism purports to speak for a substantive political perspective—its paramount concern is gender equality.

As Rosenblum notes, feminists may differ on a myriad of strategic and tactical questions, but they all embrace the task of "patrolling the civil society/government boundary" so as to nourish and support the lives of women. Susan Okin's commentary confirms the deep ways in which this substantive orientation informs and illuminates feminism's understanding of the relationship between government and civil society. Like other essays in this section, Rosenblum's looks ahead to perspectives marked by more profound disjunctures between equal citizenship and the laws of groups, between bounded government and civil society.

The differences between classical liberalism, liberal egalitarianism, critical theory, and feminism, which loom so large in the contemporary theoretical landscape, dwindle almost to insignificance when these perspectives are compared to the Confucian tradition explored by Peter Nosco. If modern conceptions of civil society presuppose that persons move between distinct and inconsistent roles, the Confucian imagination pictures society as an "organic" whole. This unitary order rules out any vision of the social world as resting agonistically on an endless opposition between the particularism of a civil society and the universalism of the state. Henry Rosemont thus concludes that "the question of drawing boundaries between civil society and the state is not a meaningful one for classical Confucians."

A similar point can be made about Jewish perspectives on civil society, as developed by Noam J. Zohar. Questions of particularity and pluralism simply have no internal traction within the biblical and medieval Jewish tradition, where Torah is supreme law and the state is an alien threat to the covenental community. Zohar describes the minority Jewish community in larger states as analogous to elements of civil society. This history of semiautonomous communities in exile, recognized as minorities but not as full citizens, has had a formative effect on the modern state of Israel, Zohar argues, where there is an uneasy equipose between the public system of justice for all citizens and private law, which requires individuals to be legal subjects of a particular religious group and assigns rights and duties on the basis of membership. But the question, as David Biale points out, is whether such categories can "work" in the context of a contemporary state with a fully modernized economy.

As John Kelsay explains, the analogue to civil society/government in classical and modern Islam is the idea of "complementarity" between religious and government authorities, the 'ulama/khilafat relation. From Islamic perspectives, the tie between Muslim status and citizenship is pervasive. The elements of civil society recognized as legitimate and autonomous are more constrained than in any Lockean or Hegelian account. Although religious authority is loosely structured so that there is a plurality of Muslim "groups," professional and business classes do not yet have secure liberties, and there is, for example, little freedom for voluntary association in Iran. The boundaries between government and social groups are defended principally in terms set by the ʿulama as guardians of Islamic law and by governors worried about the sectarian potential of religion. While arguing for the importance of the distinction between society and state, Farhad Kazemi underscores ongoing contention over the applicability of "civil society" to Islamic societies. He sets it in the context of questions of state authority and exclusionary norms with regard to religious minorities and women—part of a larger debate about the congruence of Islam, civil society, and democracy.

The conceptual dissonance underlined by these essays is of obvious political importance. As globalization spreads Western institutions throughout the world, the question of how these institutions will be received assumes increased significance. The essays in this volume on classical liberalism, liberal egalitarianism, critical theory, feminism, natural law, and Christianity illustrate the family of meanings that civil society has received in the West. But the essays addressing Confucianism, Judaism, and Islam query whether and how these meanings can be transposed to radically different traditions. David Biale, for example, points to the anomaly of ultrareligious groups in Israel seeking to participate in a modern state using a conceptual framework derived from a biblical and medieval past. John Kelsay observes that moves to impose gender equality by government from above are depicted as anti-Islam and as a threat to the traditional role of religious leaders. He predicts that changes will come mainly from within religious institutions. Globalization can only magnify the extent and reach of such anomalies. The essays in this volume are intended to provide a framework within which the diffusion, adoption, or imposition of Western concepts and social structures can be analyzed and understood.

The volume concludes with a comprehensive overview by Richard B. Miller. Miller explores how distinct perspectives on civil society and government conceive the question of human flourishing. He asks "whether the attitudes and practices that materialize in civil society are civil and civilizing, and how we are to distinguish civilizing attitudes and practices from those that are not." He usefully summarizes how different perspectives understand the proper role of the state in promoting human flourishing.

Conclusion

Our own view of these questions, which we have tried to defend in this introduction, is that freedom of association is an independent good, whose value can be realized only within a flourishing civil society. Perhaps that is why the concept of "civil society" is almost always used with positive import. Civil society is the "chicken soup" of the social sciences.[24] The valence is invariably positive, despite the enduring array of manifestly uncivil societies, hateful associations, and private despotisms. It is not too much to say that "civil society" is the locus of what there is of utopianism in contemporary political thought.

In the flush of this utopianism, it is sometimes assumed that civil society can substitute for government. But, as we have tried to make clear, civil society and government are complementary constructions. Civil society cannot exist without government, and democratic governments cannot exist without civil society. The difficulty, however, is that government and civil society represent discrete values that are conceptually exclusive. There is thus enormous tension over the boundary between civil society and government. The resolution of this tension—the determination of *which* elements of civil society are salient for political resistance, democratic participation, or effective governance, or exactly *how* government may secure and promote civil society—is of course contingent and contestable.

That is why nothing is more important than comparative political theory and a keen historical sensibility in getting right the dangers and the opportunities. The diverse normative and historical perspectives offered in this volume are meant to be an informative and useful means of sharpening our judgment in these matters.

NOTES

1. This is not the way that the participants in this dispute would characterize the question, but compare the moral understanding of the market in Adam Smith. See too Albert O. Hirschman, *The Passions and the Interests: Political Arguments for Capitalism before Its Triumph* (Princeton: Princeton University Press, 1977).

2. We note, however, that ascriptive belonging to an inchoate ethnic or racial group—better described as an objectively identifiable population—does not entail membership in an organized association, and undifferentiated populations are not properly speaking components of civil society except insofar as they are organized into actual groups. This is the theme of Nancy L. Rosenblum, "Repairing the Empty Politics of Recognition," in *Membership and Morals: The Personal Uses of Pluralism in America* (Princeton: Princeton University Press, 1998).

3. See Stephen Holmes, *Passions and Constraint* (Chicago: University of Chicago Press, 1995).

4. See Stephen Holmes and Cass R. Sunstein, *The Cost of Rights* (New York: W. W. Norton Co., 1999).

5. On the relationship between civil society and law, see Martin Krygier, "Virtuous Circles: Antipodean Reflections on Power, Institutions, and Civil Society," *East European Politics and Societies* 11, no. 1 (Winter 1997): 36–88.

6. See Sanford Levinson, *Written in Stone: Public Monuments in Changing Societies* (Durham, N.C.: Duke University Press, 1998).

7. See Robert Post, "Between Democracy and Community: The Legal Constitution of Social Form," *NOMOS* 35 ("Democratic Community") (1993): 175–77.

8. G. W. F. Hegel, *Philosophy of Right* (Oxford: Oxford University Press, 1952), p. 266 addition to ¶182; p. 148 ¶238; p. 276 ¶238; p. 452; p. 133 ¶207; p. 278 ¶255.

9. See for example Iris Marion Young, "Impartiality and the Civic Public," in *Feminism as Critique: On the Politics of Gender*, ed. Seyla Benhabib and Drucilla Cornell (Minneapolis: University of Minnesota Press, 1987). This parallels the argument in moral philosophy that moral reasoning cannot transcend particularist perspectives. Cf. Seyla Benhabib's revision of Jürgen Habermas in "The Generalized and the Concrete Other," in Benhabib, *Situating the Self* (New York: Routledge, 1992), 148–77.

10. The importance of this fact is brought out by comparative studies of legal systems and the civil standing of women. See essays by Martha Nussbaum and Carol Weisbrod in Nancy L. Rosenblum, ed., *Obligations of Citizenship and Demands of Faith: Religious Accommodation in Pluralist Democracies* (Princeton: Princeton University Press, 2000).

11. Steven Macedo "Community, Diversity, and Civic Education: Toward a Liberal Political Science of Group Life," *Social Philosohy and Policy Foundation* 13, no. 1 (1996): 264, 250.

12. See, e.g., Robert Post, *Constitutional Domains: Democracy, Community, Management* (Cambridge: Harvard University Press, 1995).

13. Joshua Cohen and Joel Rogers, "Secondary Associations and Democratic Governance," *Politics and Society* 20 (1992): 393–472.

14. John Gray, "Totalitarianism, Reform and Civil Society," in *Post Liberalism: Studies in Political Thought* (New York: Routledge, 1993), 157.

15. Francois Furet, *Interpreting the French Revolution*, trans. E. Forster (Cambridge: Cambridge University Press, 1981), 180.

16. Peter Berger and Richard Neuhaus, *To Empower People: The Role of Mediating Structures in Public Policy* (Washington, D.C.: American Enterprise Institute, 1977), 6, 3, 41.

17. Lester Salamon, *Partners in Public Service: Government Nonprofit Relations in the Modern Welfare State* (Baltimore: Johns Hopkins University Press, 1995). There is ample confirmation that in the United States the growth of government has been a spur to the growth of the voluntary sector.

18. Cited in John Keane, ed., *Civil Society and the State: New European Perspectives* (London: Verso, 1988), 5.

19. For theorists of Latin American politics, too, civil society is commonly said to harbor pockets of resistance to party and military dictatorship.

20. Jan Simsa in H. Gordon Skilling, "Parallel Polis, or an Independent Society in Central and Eastern Europe: An Inquiry," *Social Research* 55, no. 1–2 (1988): 245; Vaclav Benda, cited in ibid., 218.

21. Michael Walzer, "Constitutional Rights and the Shape of Civil Society," in *The Constitution of the People*, ed. Robert E. Calvert (Lawrence: University Press of Kansas, 1991), 123–25.

22. Jürgen Habermas, "Further Reflections on the Public Sphere," in *Habermas and the Public Sphere*, ed. Craig Calhoun (Cambridge: MIT Press, 1992), 453–56.

23. Claude Lefort, to take a recent example, argues that the recent French sympathy for fluid groups will overwhelm the capacity of government and administrative experts to respond in an orderly fashion as arbiter of the social contract in *Ecrire: A l'epreuve du politique* (Paris: Calmann Levy, 1992), 71, cited in Cheryl Welch, "Tocqueville and the New Europe" (manuscript).

24. As Eric Uslaner says of trust, it is the "chicken soup" of the social sciences. See *The Moral Foundations of Trust* (Cambridge: Cambridge University Press, 2002), 1. The exception is Marxist thought and early critical theorists; see White's response to Baynes, below.

State, Civil Society, and Classical Liberalism

Steven Scalet and David Schmidtz

What Is Classical Liberalism?

Classical liberalism's central concern is, and always has been, the interface between civil society and government. Should governments have a mandate to do whatever it would be good to do? Should citizens have an unbounded obligation to comply with whatever demands government chooses to impose? May government usurp functions already performed by civil society, undermining civil society's ability to perform those functions on its own? Classical liberals say no. Classical liberals are committed to civil and economic liberties, and to limited government.

Classical liberals have drawn inspiration from various philosophical and religious traditions: Aristotle, Kant, natural law, utilitarianism, and Christianity, to name some of the most obvious. Some classical liberals defend the minimal state because they believe only a minimal state can protect our natural rights without violating those same rights. Others defend the minimal state because they believe the test of civil society, and the state, is whether it helps people flourish. The most classic of classical liberals—John Locke, David Hume, Adam Smith—were also classical utilitarians, as were Benjamin Constant and Wilhelm von Humboldt on the Continent.[1] To say they were classical utilitarians is to say that although they believed in individual rights, they treated rights as a natural product of their vision of a flourishing society, not as an external constraint upon it. In their eyes, people have the rights they do because those are the rights that society and state must respect if citizens are to flourish.[2]

However, as the variety of classical liberalism's philosophical sources may suggest, classical liberalism is not itself a foundational philosophical theory. The heart of classical liberalism is a simple policy prescription: Nurture voluntary associations. Limit the size and, more importantly, the scope of government. So long as the state provides a basic rule of law that steers people away from destructive or parasitic ways of life and in the direction of productive ways of life, society runs itself. If you want people to flourish, let them run their own lives.

Classical liberals see government as properly an agent of the community, appointed by the community to provide the community with governance. *Civil society* is the community that delegates authority to government, and civil society is the body within which ultimate authority resides. Civil society retains the right to dismiss those whom it hires to provide it with governance. In this sense, classical liberals typically use the term *civil society* to refer to anything *but* government: businesses, schools, clubs, unions, media, churches, charities, libraries, and any other nongovernmental forms of organization through which a community's members relate to each other. Civil society on this view is a cluster concept. It refers to a cluster of things that bear a family resemblance to each other but share no common essence, apart from being nongovernmental forms of association.[3]

John Locke contrasted civil society not with government but with a (Lockean) state of nature. The question he confronted was whether civil society, understood as government-ordered society, was justifiable. He thought it was, especially to resolve instabilities that arise when there is no overarching authority to resolve disputes impartially and peacefully. Locke believed we need government—limited government.

The issue today, though, is not about limited government versus the state of nature but limited government versus unlimited government. This issue is twofold. First, does government have the right to pursue any worthy goal whatever, or is its appropriate job description more limited? Second, are there limits on what means government may employ in its pursuit of worthy goals? Hobbes typically is classified as an absolutist because he believed there were no moral limits on *means*. However, the legitimate *goals* of Hobbes's Leviathan are roughly those of the "night watchman" state. Many liberal egalitarians think government is unlimited in the first sense, insofar as they would give it the power to pursue the entire range of the modern liberal agenda (hoping it would remain limited in the sense of there being limits on the extent to which that power will be used for other purposes instead).[4] Classical liberals think of government as having a far more restricted mandate. To some extent, they disagree with modern liberals about what constitutes a worthy goal, but beyond that, they reject the view that government is an all-purpose vehicle for pursuing worthy goals. Classical liberals think that while we all have a plethora of worthy goals, there are relatively few goals that it is the government's job to realize. For example, classical liberals would say the idea that government generally should take over the production and distribution of food is absurd, just as absurd as the idea that we should turn to WalMart for national defense.[5]

In keeping with the focus of this volume, we will understand civil society as a form or, rather, forms of social organization that contrast with government-imposed organization. In any case, we need some such marker for conceptually separating communities from the states that provide communities with governance. Loren Lomasky defines civil society as "the realm of voluntary association that stands between individuals (and perhaps their families) and the state."[6] Classical liberals tend to think of the private and nongovernmental public sectors as jointly constituting society's voluntary sector. They want government functions to be returned to this voluntary sector wherever possible. Yet classical liberals must acknowledge that the array of civil associations standing between family and state are not necessarily voluntary. (For that matter, neither is the family.) Businesses, schools, clubs, unions, media, churches, charities, libraries: there is something presumptively but not necessarily voluntary about those ways of gathering.

Also hinted at in Lomasky's definition is the idea that we may or may not include the family as part of civil society. The question of classification is not important. What is important is to understand the family's place in the classical liberal agenda. The agenda evolved over centuries, and appropriately so. Classical liberals warned us against abuses of power latent in the institution of monarchy. They warned us against a prospect of majority tyranny that emerged with the flowering of democracy. Classical liberals such as Mary Wollstonecraft and William Godwin were at the forefront of suffrage and civil rights movements, and warned us (in keeping with their categorical rejection of censorship) that such movements can evolve into tyrannies of political correctness. Classical liberals have not been at the forefront of discussions about injustice within the family. But there is nothing intrinsic to classical liberalism that would make it unsympathetic to such investigations. Feminism developed against a background of theories of equality, but it also developed as a philosophy of liberation, and to that extent feminists and classical liberals are fellow travelers. Unlike conservatives, classical liberals do not lament the decline of the traditional patriarchal family. Feminism is essentially liberal, but it does not stand or fall with liberal egalitarianism.

Classical liberals definitely think of markets as parts of civil society, and this is not merely a matter of arbitrary classification. Those who see markets as classical liberals do—as places where people voluntarily congregate to exchange products of their labor for mutual benefit—will see markets as at the heart of civil society. They believe trade is a central part of our moral education; it is part (albeit only a part) of the process by which people become civilized. In contrast, those who see markets as places where villains come to exploit the unwary will see the issue very differently, and will object to the valorization implied by categorizing markets as organs of civil society.

That said, it is worth stressing that the market is not the only (or even the main) thing classical liberals care about. It merely is the focus forced upon classical liberals by the intellectual tide of the twentieth century. As socialists around the world destroyed markets, and as liberal egalitarians applauded or at best refused to criticize such destruction, classical liberals had to assume responsibility for the market's defense. It is that recent course of events that has resulted in classical liberals coming to be seen as champions of markets above all else. Traditionally, it is a different form of unlimited government—monarchy rather than socialism—that has been classical liberalism's main foe. Robert Heilbroner recently said, "The battle between capitalism and communism is over. Capitalism won." Perhaps he is right. More certainly, we may say the battle between liberalism and monarchy is over. Liberalism won. Indeed, the latter victory was so complete that it no longer occurs to us to celebrate it.

In the realm of civil liberties—freedoms of speech, religion, and conscience—classical liberalism has been triumphant. Classical liberal positions on civil liberties became orthodox, and remain so within the liberal community as a whole. Of course, the battle for civil liberties will never be over, for there will always be new forms of censorship and repression to fight against. Still, classical liberalism's success in this realm is stunning. Only within the realm of economic liberties has classical liberalism failed to become a conventional view, resisting the modern liberal impulse to superimpose large regulatory government upon what classical liberals think of as a realm of voluntary exchange.

Classical liberals have been champions of democracy.[7] But they recognize that democracy is not utopia. Compared to monarchy, democracy is a move toward voluntarism, but how voluntary democracy turns out to be in practice is a contingent matter. Likewise, civil society, including the market, tends to be a realm of free association, but how much freedom it affords in practice, and how well it promotes flourishing, is a contingent matter. In order for civil society to be and to remain, as much as possible, a realm of truly voluntary association, what does civil society need from the state, and vice versa? What liabilities do these different forms of organization pose for each other, and for citizens? Do they—should they—impose limits on each other?

This chapter considers how classical liberals might respond. At the risk of belaboring the point, our assignment here is to set out the rudiments of a classical liberal view. We do not defend that view here, except insofar as we try to state it as sympathetically as we can. Moreover, we are conscious of the limitations of our broad-brush approach. We describe a general view of civil society and government, inevitably missing points that would emerge from discussion of particular civil societies, particular governments, and the unique personalities that circulate among them. For all that, though, the general view remains distinctive.

BOUNDARIES

We have discussed the distinction between civil society and government in conceptual terms. In terms of function and consequences, does it matter where we draw the line between civil society and the state? The straightforward classical liberal answer is: Yes, it surely does matter. Civil society has needs and poses liabilities, as does the state. Classical liberals want boundaries that contain the liabilities, especially those associated with being governed by a state. From a classical liberal perspective, the government's proper role is to help construct and enforce the rules of a cooperative game in which (if all goes well) people win by helping each other win. Civil society supplies the players and more or less defines a field of opportunities. Government provides the referee, trying to deter those who would seek to win at the expense of other players.

Yet, this view may somehow seem too thin. Why should government be bounded by its role as an impartial referee, when it could actively be identifying the "good guys" and helping them win? A classical liberal will reply: But does it not matter that the power to help the good guys inevitably goes to those who are best at convincing government officials to take their side? Does it not matter that this ability inevitably tracks money and political connections rather than the property of actually being one of the good guys?

Classical liberals like Loren Lomasky tend to feel (not without reason) that the extrapolitical realm is where we have a chance to be free. Communitarians like Charles Taylor worry (not without reason) that the extrapolitical realm can be too free, thereby limiting our ability to make decisions as a community about what our community should look like. Therein lies a contrast and a crucial boundary-setting issue. Where communitarians *identify* community with the realm of political decision making, classical liberals tend to see politics as an *alien intrusion*, something that converts us from a peaceful community into Hobbesian factions trying to impose our political will on the community as a whole, lest someone else's will be imposed upon us.

In one respect, classical liberals are great optimists. They believe great things happen when people take it upon themselves to stand or fall according to their own merit. They believe that in a free society people are not only willing to help each other; they believe that in a free society people love to help each other—that freely helping others, including bringing to market products that other people want and need, is one of life's greatest joys.

In another sense, classical liberals are profoundly pessimistic. They believe people can be utterly vicious when given power over one another or when made to feel vulnerable to one another.[8] When bureaucrats take themselves to have a mandate to run other people's lives, as if citizens were pawns on a chessboard, bureaucrats become frustrated and outraged when the pawns do not act as they are supposed to. At that point bureaucrats start caring less about pawns' welfare and start caring more about augmenting their power over pawns. The means—the power to run other people's lives—becomes the end. Classical liberals believe anyone who expects anything else from government bureaucrats will as a rule be disappointed. (No one denies that something analogous, albeit on a smaller scale, can happen with midmanagement bureaucracy within large companies.)

A modern welfare liberal envisions government as a machine that would fully implement his or her political agenda, if only it had enough power. When classical liberals think of government, though, they envision a dangerous servant and a terrible master. They see it as obvious that government, even democratic government, does not do what voters want. It does not do what liberal academics or even politicians want. It is a bureaucracy. Human productivity disappears in a haze of filling out forms, standing in line, being put on hold, lobbying, lawyering, tax sheltering, outright bribery, and simply giving up. In real life, even people who *run* governments find government endlessly frustrating.[9]

John Stuart Mill (generally regarded as a transitional figure between classical and modern liberalism) eventually realized that switching from monarchy to democracy did not solve the problem with government: that is, the problem of a citizen's being subject to the arbitrary will of other people. Unlimited democracy is no solution to the problem with unlimited monarchy. The solution is truly limited government, one whose aims are limited to doing what it reasonably can do to ensure that the community is and remains a place where people are not subject to one another's arbitrary will.

Classical liberals should not deny that it is possible for institutions of civil society to be oppressive, but they believe government has a liability that civil society does not; namely, government has an inherently expansionist dynamic. Limited government does not tend to stay limited. It tends to grow. Government programs create revenue streams. The streams are profitable in the first instance for government employees. Thus, it becomes imperative to employees that these streams of revenue not dry up. In turn, it becomes imperative that problems meant to be solved by these revenue streams get bigger, not smaller.[10] Most classical liberals find it easy to believe we would be unsafe without government, but find it much harder to believe we are or ever will be safe *from* government. Some problems have no solution. One such problem is the problem of ensuring that government will be powerful enough to protect us from ourselves and from foreign aggressors without itself becoming a threat. We may need for our governments to have significant power, yet the more power they have, the more they can and will abuse.

Both the optimism and the pessimism are integral to the classical liberal view. Indeed, we might view them as almost definitive: A classical liberal is characteristically optimistic about the ability of a free society to run itself and pessimistic about the competence and goodwill of government bureaucrats; a modern liberal is characteristically less optimistic about the former and less pessimistic about the latter. Thus, classical liberals insist on small government, while modern liberals want their governments big.

There is, of course, another reason why modern liberals embrace big government where classical liberals reject it. Liberal egalitarians generally embrace the classical liberal position on equal and expansive civil liberties but conjoin it to a commitment to equalizing economic opportunities, and perhaps outcomes as well. Thus, their political agenda is far more expansive and aggressive than that of classical liberalism. Classical liberals deny that justice requires any particular distribution of economic goods. Civil society does not guarantee any particular distribution, but classical liberals have no problem with that.

Of course, classical liberals are in favor of vertical mobility, to say the least, but they are uneasy about endorsing a political commitment to equal opportunity as a platform for government interference. All too often, such interference makes it harder rather than easier for people to move.

What State and Civil Society Need from Each Other

Do state and civil society need each other? Here is a simple answer, acceptable in principle to classical liberals: Civil society needs the state because only the state can provide public goods. Conversely, the state needs civil society because the state is not competent as a direct producer of ordinary private goods. Ideally, the state induces efficient production and distribution of private goods by securing a framework that encourages productive competition within the private sector.

Classical liberals will want to qualify this answer, though, for they will note that it is false that only the state can provide public goods. Classical liberals think there are few public goods that the state can provide at acceptable cost, and even fewer public goods that only the state can provide at acceptable cost. Classical liberals also say it is an error to assume that if government is providing something, that something must be a public good. Government officials are in a position to buy things with other people's money, and it just seems crazy to think they'll use that power only to solve our most important problems in the most cost-effective way.

To be sure, there are public goods that citizens truly need. We may need national defense, and the state may be the right organization to provide it. But it is an increasingly well documented error to think government is or must be society's only provider of public goods in general. Healthy civil societies have rich histories of providing themselves with whatever public goods their citizens deemed important, unless and until government took over. By the same token, although some think the state is the only thing keeping communities intact, classical liberals will say that, historically, it has always been the case that we organize ourselves spontaneously, unless a totalitarian government stops us. We organize as the need arises. We always have, since long before there was any such thing as what we now call the state.[11] As Loren Lomasky playfully but accurately observes, humans may be atoms, but they are everywhere found in molecules.[12] Classical liberals say the legacy of free association is community, not atomic isolation.

Classical liberals will stress that government is not the only game in town, and that both government and citizens need to understand this fact. When government sees civil society as an independent source of moral authority, the stage is set for a relationship that can benefit citizens. In contrast, when government thinks of its will as necessarily rather than contingently expressing the general will, such that any dissenter automatically becomes an enemy of "the people," the stage is set for humanity's most notoriously vicious acts of repression and exploitation. Charles Taylor, although by no means a classical liberal, seems to concur when he acknowledges that "[a] strange and horrifying reversal has taken place, whereby an idea whose roots lie in a prepolitical concept of society can now justify the total subjection of life to an enterprise of political transformation. And in less spectacular form, the power of the state has often been enhanced by its self-definition as an instrument of the national will."[13] From a classical liberal perspective, the state needs to acknowledge that it is not "the people." It needs to understand that there are boundaries. It needs civil society to keep it honest.

Classical liberals will insist that the state cannot carry the burden of maintaining a healthy culture and a healthy citizenry.[14] States help to meet needs by fostering civil society's ability to meet needs. We are learning something from the new economies of Eastern Europe about civil society's role as the ultimate engine of long-run prosperity. Market orders are never merely market orders.[15] They exist in virtue of coexisting—existing with a larger civil society of diverse and less inclusive but more intimate groups. A market order is hospitable to nonmarket suborders of civil society in a way central planners can never be. The efficacy of markets in facilitating human flourishing depends on the legal and cultural frameworks that induce people to work in mutually advantageous ways. Thus, to some extent, good markets presuppose good government. Crucially, though, good government may in turn presuppose good markets and good culture to some extent, for it is the culture that produces the political decision makers.

Part of the problem in Central Europe is that it lost its culture of productivity. Over generations, the idea of entrepreneurship came to be associated not with productivity but with using political means to capture streams of revenue. Central Europeans have a common saying that translates as He who does not steal, steals from his children. It now seems unsurprising that, in the aftermath of Soviet socialism's fall, entrepreneurship often took the form of stealing government property and selling it on the black market. It would seem the most successful European economies are those that have been able to recall the rule of law, together with a model of entrepreneurship that includes the idea of its citizens being productive, as opposed merely to using political pull for personal gain.

People in general flourish—entrepreneurs make people around them, not just themselves, better off—by being actively engaged in civil society, understood as including the marketplace. Civil society enables people to take responsibility for their lives and to develop meaningful social roles. States enforce conditions that make possible this flourishing. States are the background for this flourishing; civil associations are the foreground. Classical liberals believe responsibility for making life worthwhile ultimately lies with ordinary citizens, not with the state.

A final thought: Citizens need to be able to respect their government. Blind faith is bad, but optimism and high expectations are good.[16] Cynicism does not impose discipline on government, but high expectations might. In South Africa, circa 1999, there is great optimism about the future, despite the past, and while it is hardly clear what the future holds, it is clear that the pervasive goodwill and faith and the patient persistence of its black population is currently South Africa's greatest asset. When one returns from South Africa to the United States, though, the relative pessimism of black and white youth alike is striking. There are attitudes whose inculcation damages those who internalize them. The attitude that government is fundamentally evil may be one of them.[17] Classical liberals, though, typically are willing and able to walk a fine line here, warning against the abuses of ever-expanding government, yet remaining optimistic that appropriately limited government can be good government. Classical liberals are not anarchists.

LIABILITIES

Do civil society and the state pose liabilities for each other? If so, how might these liabilities be contained? A straightforward answer is that power corrupts, and the power of the state everywhere has a notably reliable history of attracting and fostering corruption. People need a civil society able to hold the state in awe, and thereby contain the liability that goes with having a government.

A more nuanced classical liberal answer would in turn temper the optimism about civil society. Like governments, civil associations are capable of bigotry, corruption, and other systematic evils. The state can contain these evils, or it can serve as the vehicle that lets them run wild. Government can contain associations that undermine civil society's tendency toward voluntarism, even while itself standing as the preeminent threat to the tendency toward voluntarism.

Related to classical liberalism is a current of thought sometimes called left-libertarianism.[18] Left-libertarians (as we use the term) say government is indeed a threat to our liberty and for that reason should be small, other things equal. But other things are not equal. *Any* large organization is a concentration of power, and thus any large organization threatens our liberty. Accordingly, left-libertarians insist that government must be empowered to contain other concentrations of power, likely to emerge over time. Self-described left-libertarian Ellen Willis says, "At best the contemporary left, with few exceptions, defends particular liberties and challenges particular repressive laws and policies while ignoring the structures of unfreedom built into institutions like the state, the corporation, the family, and the church. At worst it attacks 'excessive' liberty as a mere extension of capitalist individualism. . . . Most leftists are uncritically statist, merely complaining that the government is controlled by the wrong people."[19]

There is no point in denying the legitimacy of left-libertarian concerns about the threat posed by big business. However, we ought to be realistic about what this threat means in practice. Large corporations have done deplorable things, but when it comes to perpetrating large-scale tragedies, most classical liberals will say the history of corporations is nothing compared to the history of governments. This is not to say we should be complacent about dangers posed by large corporations. The point is simply that creating more state power for the purpose of reining in corporate power can easily be a cure that is worse than the disease.

Needless to say, civil society need not be innocuous. Left-libertarians will insist, and classical liberals will concede, that organized religions in particular are forces for good in some measure, perhaps a large measure, but they can be a threat as well. Classical liberals will say the threat posed by big business may not be trivial in an absolute sense, but history has revealed that it surely is trivial in comparison to that posed by church or state.[20] Communitarians deplore the disintegration of civil society they see as following from the freedom of individual atoms to detach themselves from oppressive molecules and float away in search of a better deal. By contrast, the left-libertarian worry is not that civil society is too weak but rather that civil associations, especially the church, remain (or could once again become) too strong. Be that as it may, classical liberals hold that if you look at the history of occasions when liberal civil societies were in danger of being obliterated, the threat came almost always from governments, occasionally from organized religion, and never from corporations.

Classical liberals hope we finally have learned from painful experience that the welfare state has a terrible social capital problem. It undermines institutions of civil society through which poor people prosper in the long run, and it cannot replace those institutions. The welfare state responds to problems of poverty by replacing long-term solutions with short-term solutions. This is a matter of evidence, and classical liberals believe the evidence is in. Yet, some advocate government programs that crowd out institutions of civil society in part precisely because they endorse this crowding out.[21] Thus, Robert Goodin says civil society is a ninety-year-old parent upstairs driving her grown children crazy as she becomes increasingly bitter about her dependence on them. Civil society is being financially unable to leave an abusive husband. Civil society is being stifled by meddlesome (or worse, racist) neighbors and oppressive religious conformism. Goodin sees civil society as a problem to which the welfare state is the solution. He thinks the "atomism" that communitarians deplore ought to be welcomed.[22]

Civil society is at best imperfect, and always will be. Undoubtedly, civil society and the state can and in some places do correct and contain each other. Civil society may also be an obstacle to an activist, progressive government, because it will moderate and resist attempts to impose rapid revolutionary change. It seems fair to say civil society in the United States has been gradual in its embracing of racial and gender equality. Sometimes it has been slow to change despite government efforts; other times it has been slow precisely because it had to work against government efforts on *behalf* of segregation, preferential treatment, and so on. The Jim Crow laws are a notorious example.[23] For better or worse, civil society curbs the power of the state to dictate how people will live. A decentralized society makes the work of progressive governments, and repressive governments, more difficult. Such decentralization by no means guarantees that we will flourish, but nothing can do that. What it can do, classical liberals believe, is give us a better chance. On balance, classical liberals view the curbing of state power as overwhelmingly to the advantage of citizens in general.

CENTRAL to a proper understanding of the respective liabilities posed by state and civil society are the various ways in which state and civil society tend to merge in practice. Within a society are structures whose emergence, evolution, and ongoing function is influenced by their interaction with the government. In particular, many institutions are to varying degrees subsidized by, but not administered by, the state. Civil society and the state interpenetrate each other. For example, systems of education are intermediate institutions between family and state. But many schools are state funded, making them at once an organ of both state and civil society. These more or less blurry boundaries between state and civil society change over time, so that, for example, health care services once private are now, for better or worse, the business of government.

Corporatism is the idea that the blurring of boundaries between civil society and the state is desirable. Charles Taylor extols the virtues of corporatist culture, where civil institutions merge with the state and lose their separate identities, and boundaries are for practical purposes obliterated. He says, "The really successful economies in the late twentieth century are resolutely corporatist, for instance, Germany and Japan."[24] As government and business merge and form partnerships, industrial policy will be determined not in a piecemeal and chaotic way but rather by government ministries staffed by political appointees and working closely with business leaders. Such ministries frame policy for entire industries, thereby avoiding wasteful competition, setting and maintaining prices at rational levels, and so forth. So the story goes.

But proponents of corporatism can no longer ignore the fact that civil society can stop short of a nation's borders and also can extend beyond them. Commerce is increasingly global in scope.[25] De facto power increasingly is devolving into private and corporate hands. States have increasingly limited power to set interest rates, currency exchange rates, and so on. Civil society is more than one thing. It has a variety of boundaries, but in any case its boundaries are rapidly evolving, and the boundaries of the state are becoming less relevant. We are naturally frightened by change, of course. Still, classical liberals tend to be confident that these changes will on the whole be for the better. Classical liberals are not conservative.

Corporatist thinking is becoming increasingly obsolete as civil society leaves national boundaries behind. From a classical liberal perspective, corporatism is an attempt to remake a society in the image of the *Titanic*. In theory, the thing is unsinkable; in practice, it is ponderous, blind, and eventually paralyzed as decision makers get increasingly out of touch with workplaces and marketplaces where the action is, and increasingly fall under control of people who (to put it mildly) are not committed to acting in the community's interest. The ability to cope with or even perceive changing tides is lost. When people are attempting to make decisions for whole sectors of the economy, there are no small mistakes. There are only disasters, followed by coverups and bailouts, all on a titanic scale. The ongoing crash of Japan, Incorporated, now in its second decade, is no fluke.

Classical liberals champion what corporatists repudiate: the free movement of people and capital across national boundaries. Competitive and innovative businesses migrate to areas where government is less meddlesome, while less competitive and less innovative businesses welcome and indeed clamor for government assistance in regulating their respective industries. In actual practice, the result of corporatism is an unholy alliance between government and the worst of private industry.

Classical liberals want functions usurped by government over the past century to be returned to the voluntary sector, but they also believe there no longer is a truly voluntary sector when civil associations merge with government. We agree with Nancy Rosenblum that, at least in the West, when institutions of civil society have decayed, it most recently has been government subsidies rather than government repression that have been doing the most damage.

Classical liberals believe the core functions of a minimal state are the best examples of where government/civil society partnership is relatively benign: armed forces, police forces, courts. Obviously, these functions are liable to abuse, but they are less likely to be abused in a society that gives its government a tightly limited mandate, rather than a general mandate to do whatever it thinks is worth doing. A minimal state is the state most likely to do its patient no harm.

GROUPS AND INDIVIDUALS

When should government interact directly with individuals as opposed to indirectly through communal associations? The straightforward classical liberal answer, historically, has been to insist that the state recognize and respect individuals as such. Classical liberals have been very suspicious of group rights.

But the straightforward answer may in some respects be dated. Lately, feminists have expressed a related concern when criticizing states for recognizing the family as a private sphere within which states have limited license to meddle. Feminists distrust the distinction between private and public spheres because they worry that the distinction is a license to abuse women within the so-called private sphere.[26] Those who defend group rights are vulnerable to a version of the feminist critique, for they are defending new instances of what appear to be the same distinction between private and public. To recognize a group's right to organize itself according to its own principles can be tantamount to licensing a group's leadership to abuse rank-and-file members. Thus, Quebec has asserted its right to sovereignty within its domain. Indian tribes within Quebec have repudiated that right, asserting a sovereign right to secede from Quebec if Quebec should secede from Canada. Meanwhile, members of the Indian tribes, female members in particular, have warned Canada it had better not neglect to protect them as individuals against the abuse permitted by tribal custom.

It would seem what we need today is balance. To recognize a group's right to treat its internal relations as a private matter is to liberate members of that group from government interference, which is good. But that benefit comes at the cost of making group members more vulnerable to fellow members. Will Kymlicka distinguishes between a minority group's freedom from external interference and its freedom to suppress internal dissent. As a liberal, he defends the former but not the latter.[27] The problem, of course, is figuring out how to do the former without ipso facto doing the latter. As Kymlicka notes, to prohibit internal suppression often would amount to qualifying rights "in such a way that they no longer correspond to the real aims of minority groups."[28] A classical liberal might agree that a government ought to be guided by the need to manage that trade-off to the best advantage of individual members. We wish this were a mere platitude, but it is not. On the contrary, those who endorse "politics of identity" insist that government's objective should be to act on behalf of (favored) groups rather than on behalf of group members considered as individuals.

In principle, classical liberals celebrate the idea of ethnic identity. In principle, ethnic diversity makes the world a more intellectually and culturally vibrant and creative place. Moreover, ethnic groups are among the preeminent providers of civil society. They can order their internal relations in a way that facilitates internal monitoring and feedback, and enforcement of social norms. Ideally, society would look like this: it would be notably multicultural. People would be proud of their own cultural heritage, and would be delighted to live in a society that exposed them to people whose backgrounds were very different. They would view cultural differences as intrinsically fascinating and practically enriching. They would feel some commitment to preserving what is best in their own heritage, but not at a cost of providing their children with anything less than maximal freedom of choice. Their vision, rather, would be that their children would grow up multicultural, autonomously returning to the fold as young adults, having developed an informed appreciation for the larger society that enables their culture and other cultures to flourish side by side.

That is the dream. Is it even remotely realistic? One thing seems sure: It will not come about by force. It will happen only where people can be confident that, first, other cultures are not a threat, and, second, that interaction with other cultures is a positive opportunity for enrichment: financial, spiritual, aesthetic, and so forth. The classical liberal commitment to genuinely voluntary association is the bottom line here. There is no guarantee of happy results when government interacts directly with individuals to the extent of trying to ensure that they have a meaningful right to exit, but government must take this risk. Government must do it for the sake of the principle of (individual) voluntarism, and for the sake of the possibilities for human flourishing that go with voluntarism. To that extent, citizenship has to trump membership.

There is a second kind of group-versus-individual arena within which the commitment to voluntarism is tested, for there is an issue of voluntarism not only within groups, but between them. Classical liberals want to live in a society that not only facilitates reasonable diversity, but also reasonable integration. What does it take to induce members to venture beyond the confines of their own ethnic groups, and to do so without fear? Are there circumstances where a kind of integration that is healthy for individuals will occur if and only if the process is set in motion initially by force? This is in part an empirical question. Classical liberals will consider it unlikely, although they may acknowledge the possibility. The thing to avoid, though—the thing that is a recipe for the antithesis of peaceful integration—is acting so as to create a perception that government is sponsoring one group at another group's expense.[29]

CITIZENSHIP: PREROGATIVES AND DUTIES

What are the prerogatives and duties of citizenship? What is the role of civil society in forming good citizens? Is there a straightforward classical liberal answer here? There seem to be two, and they seem to contradict each other. (Perhaps that just goes to say that classical liberals are not all of one mind. Or perhaps it is hard not to be swayed by each answer in turn, incompatible though they may be.) The first answer: Keep government out of communities as much as possible. Let communities develop spontaneously, forming new generations of citizens as they will, with whatever mutual understandings of rights and duties they are going to have. Such groups will not be politically correct, but then a genuine liberal hates the idea of political correctness anyway.

The second answer is that this kind of neutrality is a utopian mirage.[30]

If a liberal society really cares about liberalism and wants to sustain itself as a liberal society, it needs to do what it takes to make sure children get an education that prepares them for life in mainstream liberal society. If those children grow up and autonomously opt to return to their fundamentalist roots, that is perfectly fine. But their parents have no right to deprive children of the intellectual and psychological tools for autonomously choosing what kind of lives they want to live.

Part of the point of liberal freedom is to enable people autonomously to join communities that make them more than merely free. Conservatives have reservations about liberal society's failure to actively promote their own particular conservative conception of the good life, but there is a reason why those very same conservatives choose to live in free societies. It is liberal societies, and only liberal societies, that make it safe to be the kind of conservatives they want to be. It is free societies, not authoritarian regimes, that make possible the autonomous embracing of thicker communites that flourish as a matter of fact within free societies.

However, those thick communities in some cases can become a liability from the viewpoint of liberal citizenship, which raises the question of whether we need to take steps to ensure that children receive an education that equips them for citizenship in a liberal society. Perhaps letting people raise their children as they see fit is incompatible with what we need to do to promote liberal society.

We want children to grow up free and autonomous. We also want people to be able to participate willingly in thicker social and spiritual communities. Thus, any liberal has a hard choice to make when a government has to decide whether to interfere with parents' rights to exercise their judgment in deciding how best to raise their children. This point brings us back to the topic of group rights: Jehovah's Witnesses who try to deny their children life-saving blood transfusions are not villains. When governments intervene to overrule parents, they are not protecting children against criminals. In the parents' eyes, a person's soul resides in the person's blood. Polluting the blood pollutes the soul, thereby robbing their child of a chance at the afterlife. (Jehovah's Witnesses do not believe in hell. When the "unsaved" die, they simply die.) Perhaps we can dismiss such beliefs as ridiculous. But even so, it should be obvious that there is something painfully illiberal about state interference in such cases.

Similarly, if a fundamentalist community decides that secular liberal education is a destroyer of souls, not to mention a repudiation of fundamentalist culture, and if it undertakes to provide an education that (in our eyes) deliberately stunts the children, then we have a problem. Should we stand silent, tacitly accepting the parents' illiberal commitment to preventing their children from acquiring the tools to freely choose among alternative ways of life? Or should we force-feed their children a liberal education? If we do, we tacitly repudiate their parents' way of life. Perhaps we tacitly repudiate our own as well. After all, we're liberals. We're supposed to stand for freedom of choice.

From a classical liberal perspective, the genius of civil society resides prominently in its tendency toward voluntarism, and this commitment toward voluntarism implies limits on both the prerogatives and the duties that go with citizenship. Perhaps we should think of the right to raise one's children by one's own lights as a prerogative grounded in the presumption that children will one day have a meaningful opportunity to make their own choices. So, we could say the presumption that grounds the right also ground the limits of that right. In other words, parents do not have a right to raise their children in a way that renders the presumption false. Instead, parents have a right to prepare their children as best they can for membership in liberal society (which need not rule out preparing their children to autonomously embrace fundamentalism), but they have no right to try to render their children incapable of such membership. If parents try to do the latter, then it is not the fault of liberal society if its only options, interference and noninterference, are both awful.

Most people find fulfillment in their families and communities, but those who do not are free to seek alternative associations to which they can make a more satisfying contribution.[31] Critics sometimes seem to say liberal neutrality (resolving not to use state coercion to dictate the shape of civil society) is a denigration of civil society. However, Lomasky suggests precisely the opposite—namely, that a classical liberal willingness to let civil society evolve according to its own logic is in fact an expression of profound appreciation for civil society.[32] It is a vote of confidence in the bonds and associations freely formed through civil association.

But this vote of confidence is not blind faith. Classical liberals are aware that while civil society can be a wonderful thing, it is not necessarily so. Although they regard the tendency toward voluntarism as uncontroversially good, they realize that civil association's tendency toward voluntarism is not guaranteed. There may sometimes be things a state could do, or even things a state needs to do, to secure or augment that tendency.

But it is so very easy to do too much. A civil association is a response to a challenge, as is the feeling of solidarity that infuses organizations that develop in response to a challenge. The shape taken by civil society depends in part on the particular set of challenges to which it is a response. Social capital accumulates in response to challenges. Take away the challenge that creates the proximate need for some aspect of civil society, and that aspect of civil society withers away. Thick community is not something that grows out of bowling leagues. It grows out of people coming together when stakes are high and when it is up to them to get the job done. When government does not trust them to get the job done and takes over, community cannot survive. In short, necessity is the mother of solidarity.

Those with communitarian conservative leanings might find that worrisome. We might worry (as classical liberals have not) that as life in market society becomes ever easier, civil society becomes ever more attenuated. There is less of a challenge in response to which civil society can take shape. A classical liberal might claim that if the withering away of civil society is a genuine problem, then people will respond by taking steps to preserve it. There is some truth in that; it is a robust feature of human nature that we seek what we take to be best for us.

Unfortunately, it is an equally robust feature of human nature that we seek what is easiest. The trouble is, what is best and what is easiest can be two different things. Thus communitarian conservatives are afraid to put their faith in voluntarism, for they see that we are capable of laziness and procrastination even when we know perfectly well that we need to take action. Television makes it easier for us to lead passive and solitary lives. Being a "couch potato" is not a good life, but it is easy, which for many people makes it an attractive alternative to the effort and emotional risk involved in trying to be social. Civil society might wither away not because it has no value, but rather because the kind of value it has to communitarians is not the kind of value that drives people to take action. Communitarian conservatives will say such freedom threatens to undermine the traditions and values that underlie a true community.

Classical liberals, though, understand that there are no guarantees. Society will evolve, like it or not. Wherever there is evolution, there is something decaying and being left behind. We will, of course, lament what we are losing even as we take for granted what we are gaining. (Some people think the middle and lower classes have not prospered in market society. That is preposterous. Our life expectancy is three decades longer than it would have been if we had been born a mere century earlier.) We are only human. Nothing in this world can guarantee that we will be happy. Nevertheless, classical liberals claim to have a genuine response to these worries, a program that in actual practice works to strengthen civil society rather than to replace it with the state. As Lomasky says, "A liberal order can be viewed as the standing wager that people who guide their own projects rather than consign these to the putative wisdom of technocrats, benevolent despots, and philosopher-kings will do better than their more coddled cousins. And like any genuine wager, it is one that can be lost."[33]

CONFLICTS: COMPETING DEMANDS OF CITIZENS AND MEMBERS

How are conflicting demands of citizenship and community membership to be handled? In her essay for this volume, Nancy Rosenblum wisely answers, "Handled by whom?" The answer to her question may depend on the particular conflict, but presumably the general answer is that this should be a matter of individual conscience wherever practicable. It is, in turn, incumbent upon government to cooperate in defining a conception of citizenship's demands that leaves room for people to devote the bulk of their attention to their lives as community members rather than as state citizens.

Real conflict is often between different groups within civil society rather than between civil society and the state. Moreover, some conflicts are good. Letting unions and management work out their differences among themselves can lead to better workplaces and better products. Top-down impositions by the state tend to put a lid on conflict rather than let the involved parties resolve conflict in a productive way.

Government has to take responsibility for trying to work with communities rather than against them. Classical liberals insist that agents of the government must avoid thinking of themselves as the community's heart and soul and must realize that others may have ample reason to view them as unwelcome guests. Such agents ought to practice respect just as visitors to a foreign country ought to practice respect. They ought to understand that the demands they place on citizens do not always trump the demands communities place on members, and do not always trump the demands that groups within civil society place on each other.[34]

Opportunities to cooperate for mutual advantage do not always translate into mutually advantageous outcomes, but classical liberals are confident that good things come from limiting opportunities for people to profit at others' expense, and from creating opportunities for people to secure their own advantage in mutually advantageous ways. Classical liberals see decentralized decision making, combined with robust exit rights, and limited government as our best hope for living good lives. Nurture civil associations. Keep governments limited. This is their vision.

NOTES

WE THANK the Earhart Foundation for supporting Scalet's research on the larger project of which his contribution to this article is a part. We also are deeply grateful to the participants in the Ethikon Conference in Santa Fe, whose contributions have been enormous

We are especially grateful to our official reactor, Tom Palmer, for contributions that go beyond anything we would describe simply as helpful suggestions. Were his comments not being published separately in this volume, we would have felt bound (as well as honored) to list him as a coauthor.

1. Of course, to call someone a classical utilitarian (or a classical liberal, for that matter) is to focus on only one aspect of that person's thought. Locke in particular was strongly influenced by the natural law tradition.

2. The classical utilitarian element in Locke's work emerges from a natural law perspective according to which the earth was given to us by God for the purpose of preserving humankind, and God's purpose binds us accordingly. See Fred D. Miller, Jr., "Natural Law, Civil Society, and Government," in this volume.

3. Elsewhere in this volume, Stephen White criticizes the classical liberal perspective for "reifying" the concept of civil society. There is some truth to White's accusation. It is a problem, although it may not be a problem only for classical liberals. Actually, it would seem a problem for anyone put in the awkward position of having to talk about civil society (for example) as if it were an entity with an essence. We try as best we can to minimize the problem by noting up front that civil society is not a natural kind, and above all by not assuming that any given civil association must by definition be strictly voluntary. We realize, though, that minimizing the problem is not the same as solving it.

4. But see William Galston's reaction to Will Kymlicka, in this volume. Galston insists that there may be claims of liberty that restrict the power of the state to act—even in the name of bolstering core public institutions, practices, and beliefs.

5. We do not mean to say such ideas have never been taken seriously. There have of course been countries where people did indeed think of toothpaste provision as a government responsibility (and where, consequently, toothpaste was not readily available).

6. Loren Lomasky, "Classical Liberalism and Civil Society," in *Alternative Conceptions of Civil Society*, ed. Simone Chambers and Will Kymlicka (Princeton: Princeton University Press, forthcoming). Lomasky's definition might seem to suggest that civil society is contained within a state's borders, but as we discuss below, nongovernmental forms of association increasingly tend to stretch beyond national boundaries. We assume Lomasky would agree.

7. See Stephen Holmes, "The Secret History of Self-Interest," in *Beyond Self-Interest*, ed. Jane Mansbridge (Chicago: University of Chicago Press, 1990), 267–86.

8. We have in mind here vulnerability to each other's political influence, but the point might be extended to personal relationships in which people are not, or feel they are not, free to leave.

9. A reporter once asked Bill Clinton what surprised him the most about his first two years as U.S. president. Clinton answered that his biggest surprise was finding out how little power a president has.

10. A good example concerns how incredibly seldom the Environmental Protection Agency actually uses Superfund money to clean up designated Superfund sites. See Todd Zywicki, "Environmental Externalities and Political Externalities: The Political Economy of Environmental Law," in *The Common Law and the*

Environment, ed. by Roger Meiners and Andrew Morriss (Lanham, Md.: Rowman and Littlefield, 1999).

11. See Christopher Morris, *An Essay On the Modern State* (Cambridge: Cambridge University Press, 1998).

12. Lomasky, "Classical Liberalism and Civil Society."

13. Charles Taylor, *Philosophical Arguments* (Cambridge: Harvard University Press, 1995).

14. Developing China is not blind to these realities, Xu Xinhai, an official in Shanghai's Communist Party, told a *New York Times* reporter, "We encourage people to take responsibility in building a civil society. Our central aim now is to support economic development, not interfere in people's personal lives" (June 22, 1998).

15. Lomasky, "Classical Liberalism and Civil Society."

16. Francis Fukuyama, *Trust: The Social Virtues and the Creation of Prosperity* (New York: Simon and Schuster, 1995).

17. This point was made by David Luban at a Liberty Fund conference on David Schmidtz and Robert E. Goodin's *Social Welfare and Individual Responsibility* (New York: Cambridge University Press, 1998) in Alexandria in the summer of 1998.

18. The label is catchy, and quite a few authors have appropriated it to describe positions that have nothing in common with libertarianism or classical liberalism. We are using the term in Ellen Willis's sense (see n. 19), as discussed below. Like libertarianism, what Willis calls left-libertarianism is recognizably a departure from classical liberalism, starting from common roots.

19. See Ellen Willis, "Their Libertarianism—and Ours," *Dissent* (Fall 1997): 111–18.

20. See Lomasky, "Classical Liberalism and Civil Society."

21. See Fred Siegel, "Planned Disaster," *New Democrat* (November/December 1996): 14–18.

22. See part 2 of Schmidtz and Goodin, *Social Welfare and Individual Responsibility*.

23. Several papers by David E. Bernstein are instructive: "Licensing Laws: A Historical Example of the Use of Government Regulatory Power against African-Americans," *San Diego Law Review* 31 (1994): 89–104; "The Law and Economics of Post–Civil War Restrictions on Interstate Migration by African-Americans," *Texas Law Review* 76 (1998): 781–847; "Roots of the Underclass: The Decline of Laissez-Faire Jurisprudence and the Rise of Racist Labor Legislation," *American University Law Review* 43 (1993): 85–138. See also Jennifer Roback's classic paper "The Political Economy of Segregation: The Case of Segregated Streetcars," *Journal of Economic History* 46 (1986): 893–918.

24. Taylor, *Philosophical Arguments*, 207.

25. The point is pursued in Steve Scalet's doctoral dissertation, "Justice, Liberalism, and Responsibility" (Tucson: University of Arizona, 1999).

26. See especially Susan Moller Okin, *Justice, Gender, and the Family* (New York: Basic Books, 1989).

27. See Will Kymlicka, *Multicultural Citizenship: A Liberal Theory of Minority*

Rights (Oxford: Clarendon Press, 1995), 37. See also Chandran Kukathas, "Multi-culturalism as Fairness: Will Kymlicka's *Multicultual Citizenship*," *Journal of Political Philosophy* 5 (1997): 406–27.

28. Kymlicka, *Multicultural Citizenship*, 153.

29. See Jennifer Roback's discussion of government enforcement of ethnic economic cartels in "Racism as Rent Seeking," *Economic Inquiry* 27 (1989): 661–81.

Here as elsewhere, we are mindful of Tom Palmer's reaction (in this volume), and indeed agree with it. People sometimes seem to think their sheer impatience is justification enough for advocating force. People sometimes seem to think it is okay for them to advocate forced racial segregation (or integration, as the case may be) so long as their liberal egalitarian credentials are otherwise intact. See Palmer's comments on a proposal of Brian Barry's to restrict interstate movement by blacks. How could anyone *avoid* seeing such policies as sponsoring one group at another group's expense?

30. For a critique of the idea of grounding liberal neutrality in skepticism about our ability to assess the relative merits of differing conceptions of the good, see Steve Scalet, "Liberalism, Skepticism, and Neutrality: Making Do without Doubt," *Journal of Value Inquiry* 34:207–25.

31. Lomasky, "Classical Liberalism and Civil Society," 7, reaches a similar conclusion.

32. ibid., 9.

33. Ibid., 14.

34. Contract law might be viewed as a legal tool for facilitating the process by which different parties within civil society codify and enforce reciprocally acknowledged demands, thereby making those demands more secure, if all goes well.

Classical Liberalism and Civil Society: Definitions, History, and Relations

Tom G. Palmer

CLASSICAL LIBERALISM has been so successful in so many ways that it is often taken for granted. Indeed as Fareed Zakaria has pointed out,

> Classical liberalism, we are told, has passed from the scene. If so, its epitaph will read as does Sir Christopher Wren's, engraved on his monument at St. Paul's Cathedral: "Si monumentum requiris, circumspice." If you are searching for a monument, look around. Consider the world we live in—secular, scientific, democratic, middle class. Whether you like it or not, it is a world made by liberalism. Over the last two hundred years, liberalism (with its powerful ally, capitalism) has destroyed an order that had dominated human society for two millennia—that of authority, religion, custom, land, and kings. From its birthplace in Europe, liberalism spread to the United States and is now busily remaking most of Asia.[1]

Naturally, the consequence is that the greatest disputes about policy take place at the margins. But debates about principles often go toward the core, rather than remaining on the margins. Differing conceptions of rights and justice, for example, are often at great variance, and if consistently carried out would lead to dramatically different policy outcomes. So while critics of classical liberalism—whether communitarians, welfare-state liberals, socialists, nationalists, or other collectivists—may offer what seem marginal changes from classical liberal policies, their core principles, if consistently carried through, could lead effectively to the elimination of liberal principles, policies, and practices.

In this essay I offer a defense of the classical liberal conception of civil society, followed by several suggestions for alternative classical liberal approaches to such central problems as distributive justice, corporate (or group) rights, and the relationship between liberalism, democracy, and popular consent.

DEFINITIONS OF CIVIL SOCIETY

Definitions matter, for a number of reasons. The definition of civil society is one of the more important problems in moral, social, and political thought. One answer is simply to stipulate how one will use the term, but, as logicians insist, whether stipulative definitions "are clear or unclear, advantageous or disadvantageous, or the like, are factual questions."[2] Steven Scalet and David Schmidtz deal straightforwardly with this very thorny problem, by stipulating that

> [c]ivil society is that community . . . [that] delegates authority to government, and is the body within which ultimate authority resides. Civil society retains the right to dismiss those whom it hires to provide it with governance. In this sense, classical liberals typically use the term "civil society" to refer to anything *but* government; businesses, schools, clubs, unions, media, churches, charities, libraries, and any other nongovernmental forms of organization through which a community's members relate to each other. Civil society is in this sense a cluster concept. It refers to a cluster of things that bear a family resemblance to each other but share no common essence, apart from being nongovernmental forms of association.[3]

Scalet and Schmidtz did not have the space in their contribution to this volume to defend their definition of civil society, to show why it is clear and advantageous, so the task falls to me. Their definition is superior to most common contemporary competing definitions because it is both consistent with a very long tradition, and therefore with most usage of the term, and because it satisfies the criteria of a good definition in ways that other proposed definitions do not.

Will Kymlicka, in his contribution to this volume, stipulates that by civil society he intends "Associational Life," which he distinguishes from "The State" and from "The Economy." The state can at least be understood as an organization, but seeing "The Economy" in this way reveals a socialist understanding of human interaction. It excludes from civil society all of the many forms of association (partnerships, cooperatives, stock markets, unions, joint-stock companies, etc., etc.) organized for purposes of mutual benefit, all of which are lumped together and reified, converted into an entity known as "The Economy." This is a particularly striking example of an increasingly common trend of defining civil society as a "third sector" of society. For example, the social democratic theorist Benjamin Barber in his recent book on civil society defines civil society as "a 'third sector' (the other two are the state and the market) that mediates between our specific individuality as economic producers and consumers and our abstract collectivity as members of a sovereign people."[4] Barber recognizes his divergence from historical usage but defends his ahistorical and purely stipulative account on the grounds that the term *civil society*'s "lively history no more determines or limits the ideal of civil society in political discussion today than Smith's eighteenth-century account of laissez-faire liberalism determines or limits modern debates about global market economics. We all depend on intellectual history, but this does not mean that we must constantly engage in it."[5] The last point is fair enough, but it hardly licenses us simply to make up new meanings for a term or to make spurious appeals to grammar, as in "less inclusive groups certainly qualify as generically social, but if they are to count as part of a rigorously defined democratic *civil* society they need to be more than that. Otherwise, the modifier 'civil' loses its meaning."[6] The "civil" in civil society does not distinguish the civil parts of a society from the uncivil parts, but civil societies from uncivil societies— for example, from states of nature or from societies ruled by totalitarian states or based on rigid caste distinctions. Words and concepts have histories, and simply stipulating that one will use a term in a way entirely different from—indeed incompatible with—previous uses, in order to legitimate certain ideological goals, is misleading and unacceptable. In contrast, the use of the term by Scalet and Schmidtz comports well with historical usage, has the advantage of distinguishing institutions and practices in useful ways and in terms of appropriate categories, and serves as a foundation for the pursuit of ideas about justice, rather than as part of a conclusion.

ORIGINS OF CIVIL SOCIETY

The notion of civil society arose from the cities of Europe and was historically used to describe the new kind of life emerging there from about the eleventh century onward. It was the way of life of a particular order of society. As the church asserted its independence from the secular powers, the burghers of the cities asserted their independence from both.[7] The knightly order and the orders of the church had their peculiar characteristics, and so did the order of the burghers that began to take definite form in the eleventh century. The foundation of the way of life of the burghers was commerce, in the forms of both trade and manufacturing. In contrast with the hierarchical and coercive orders of the feudality and the hierarchical and mystical orders of the church, commercial orders tended to equality, liberty, and rationality. As Henri Pirenne noted, of the needs of the order of civil society, "the most indispensable was personal liberty. Without liberty, that is to say, without the power to come and go, to do business, to sell goods, a power not enjoyed by serfdom, trade was impossible."[8]

Max Weber saw the conception of the burgher as a member of an association endowed with rights and privileges as characteristic of occidental city life. In contrasting the cities of western Europe with other urban conglomerations on the Eurasian landmass, he observed,

Most importantly, the associational character of the city and the concept of a *burgher* (as contrasted to the man from the countryside) never developed at all or existed only in rudiments. The Chinese townsman was legally a member of his sib and hence of his native village, where the temple of his ancestor-cult stood and with which he carefully upheld his association. Similarly, the Russian member of a village community who earned his living in the city remained a "peasant" in the eyes of the law. The Indian townsman was, in addition, a member of his caste.[9]

The citizens of the towns built strong walls to protect themselves from the various armed bands—including the princes and knights of the feudal orders, as well as their less-settled cousins, the Viking raiders and pirates. Within the walls they created social and legal bonds through the publicly sworn ritual oaths of the burghers. John of Viterbo (ca. 1250) even went so far as to invent an etymology of the term *civitas*:

A city is called the liberty of citizens or the immunity of inhabitants. . . . [F]or that reason walls were built to provide help for the inhabitants. . . . "City" means "you dwell safe from violence" (*Civitas, id est "Ci(tra) vi(m)(habi)tas"*). For residence is without violence, because the ruler of the city will protect the lowliest men lest they suffer injury from the more powerful, since "we cannot be equal with those more powerful" (*Digest* 4.7.3). Again, "no one must be unjustly treated on account of the power of his adversary . . . " (*Digest* 1.1.19). Again, since the home (*domus*) is for each person a most secure refuge and shelter, no one should be taken therefrom against their will; nor is it reasonable that anyone in a town should be compelled by violent fear and so on (*Digest* 2.4.18 and 2.4.1). Again [the city] is truly called a place of immunity, because its inhabitants are guarded by its walls and towers and protected in it from their enemies and foes.[10]

In very many cases the cities of Europe were built on historically well documented (not merely hypothetical) social contracts. Harold Berman, drawing on the account in the *Domesday Book of Ipswich*, describes the act of oath taking in the town of Ipswich, England:

[O]n Thursday, June 29, 1200, the whole community of the town assembled in the churchyard of St. Mary at the Tower. They proceeded to elect, with one voice, two bailiffs, who were sworn to keep the office of provost, and four coroners, who were sworn to keep the pleas of the crown and to handle other matters affecting the crown in the town "and to see to it that the aforesaid bailiffs justly and lawfully treat the poor as well as the rich." . . . On Sunday, July 2, the bailiffs and the coroners, with the assent of the community, appointed four men of each parish of the borough, and they elected the twelve capital portmen. (Understandably, the two bailiffs and four coroners were among those elected.) After they were sworn faithfully to govern the borough and maintain its liberties, and justly to render the judgments of the courts "without respect to any person," all the townsmen stretched forth their hands toward the "Book" (the Gospels) and with one voice solemnly swore to obey and assist, with their bodies and their goods, the bailiffs, coroners, and every one of the capital portmen in safeguarding the borough, its new charter, its liberties and customs, in all places against all persons, the royal power excepted, "according to their ability, so far as they ought justly and rationally to do."[11]

The legal relations among the inhabitants of such places were normally governed by contract, rather than status; they were the quintessential "social order in which all these relations arise from the free agreement of individuals" described by Henry Sumner Maine.[12] This was clear and obvious to all in the many cases in which the cities and towns were founded, rather than simply there from time immemorial. As contractually formed legal associations, cities had a juridical existence.[13] The principle that "city air makes one free after the lapse of a year and a day," a recognized privilege of Bremen from 1186 and of Lübeck from 1188,[14] was quite widely recognized throughout Europe. In the "Customs of Newcastle-Upon-Tyne in the Time of Henry I, 1068–1135" we find stated, "If a villein come to reside in the borough, and shall remain as a burgess in the borough for a year and a day, he shall thereafter remain there, unless there was a previous agreement between him and lord for him to remain there for a certain time."[15]

These associations were known by many different terms, but two came into wide usage to describe the legal status of such associations: the Germanic *burgenses* and the Latin *civitas*.[16] As Hans Planitz notes, "The expression burgenses was at first used only if the city was not a civitas, and civitas was at first only the old episcopal seat ('Bischofsstadt')."[17] Both terms and their derivatives—*bürgerlich*/bourgeois and civil—have come down to the present age and are used interchangeably. The advantage of the former is its obvious connection with city life—with the burgh (retained in English as borough and in such names as Canterbury and Pittsburgh)—and the advantage of the latter is its obvious connection with a way of comporting oneself—with civility. Civil society is the society of those who live in a certain kind of relation. From its origins as a particular order of the wider world of human relationships, civil society has so grown that it has displaced the feudal and ecclesiastical orders as claimant to the status of all-encompassing or universal order or, as we might say today, as the default or background order. The growth of commerce and of the associated commercial and scientific mentality had brought in its wake pluralism, which had undermined the claims of the church to universality in practice, and equality, which had made both pointless and odious the privileges of "noble" birth.[18]

The unique characteristics of the order of civil society include individual liberty, peace, and equality before the law. Individuality and personal
liberty developed along with civil society. In Antony Black's words,

> Civil society . . . was the beneficiary of the enhanced value now ascribed to the
> individual: the sacred was becoming identified with the human, personality was
> beginning to be seen as the only human entity with absolute value. . . . The
> crucial point about both guilds and communes was that here individuation and
> association went hand in hand. One achieved liberty by belonging to this kind
> of group. Citizens, merchants, and artisans pursued their own individual goals
> by banding together under oath.[19]

Peace and personal security were central values. As Pirenne remarks,
in the midst of widespread violence and predation, the medieval commune was a peace association: "The burghers were essentially a group of
homines pacis—men of peace. The peace of the city (*pax villae*) was at the
same time the law of the city (*lex villae*)."[20]

Legal equality and the rule of law developed in civil society. Antony
Black describes the basic values of civil society as follows:

> [F]irst, personal security in the sense of freedom from the arbitrary passions of
> others, and freedom from domination in general. This involves freedom (or
> security) of the person from violence, and of private property from arbitrary
> seizure. But these, it would appear, can only be maintained if legal process is
> credibly and successfully enforced as an alternative to physical force, in settle-
> ment of disagreements, and in redressing wrongs committed by violence. This
> leads to the notion of legal rights (whether or not so called), both in the sense
> of the right to sue in court on equal terms with everyone else—legal equality—
> and in the sense of claims, for example to property, recognized and upheld by
> law.[21]

A central part of the growth of equal legal rights was toleration of
nonviolent beliefs and behaviors. Benedict de Spinoza observed of the
civil society of his native city,

> The city of Amsterdam reaps the fruit of this freedom in its own great prosper-
> ity and in the admiration of all other people. For in this most flourishing state,
> and most splendid city, men of every nation and religion live together in the
> greatest harmony, and ask no questions before trusting their goods to a fellow-
> citizen, save whether he be rich or poor, and whether he generally act honestly,
> or the reverse. His religion and sect are considered of no importance; for it has
> no effect before the judges in gaining or losing a cause, and there is no sect so
> despised that its followers, provided that they harm no one, pay every man his
> due, and live uprightly, are deprived of the protection of the magisterial
> authority.[22]

Civil society rests on a foundation of fundamental equality and liberty, a legal foundation. This explains the use of the term to refer to both the various "private" contractual associations often associated with civil society—corporations, associations, unions, partnerships, clubs, churches, and so on—and the common use of the term to refer to the entire complex set of arrangements governed by a legal order. James Harrington used the term *civil society* to refer to the people governed by a common set of laws, or government, rather than by the arbitrary will of rulers: "Government (to define it *de jure* or according to ancient prudence) is an art whereby a civil society of men is instituted and preserved upon the foundation of common right or interest, or (to follow Aristotle and Livy) it is the empire of laws and not of men."[23]

The better-known John Locke uses "civil society" interchangeably with "political society" to refer to the relationship among those who form one body politic, which has the power to choose one government.[24] Thus,

> [t]he only way whereby any one divests himself of his Natural Liberty, and *puts on the bonds of Civil Society* is by agreeing with other Men to joyn and unite into a Community, for their comfortable, safe, and peaceable living one amongst another, in a secure Enjoyment of their Properties, and a greater Security against any that are not of it. This any number of Men may do, because it injures not the Freedom of the rest; they are left as they were in the Liberty of the State of Nature. When any number of Men have so *consented to make one Community* or Government, they are thereby presently incorporated, and make *one Body Politick*, wherein the *Majority* have a Right to act and conclude the rest.[25]

As such, a civil society or a body politic is distinguished from its government, from the body of people to whom the civil society may delegate its powers of enforcing and executing the laws. Unlike many later writers, Locke does not make the mistake of confusing the group to whom the members of civil society delegate certain powers with civil society as a whole.[26] The appropriate relationship between civil society and government is that of principal and agent, as understood in most normal contractual relationships. Although civil society might be referred to as an institution, as the term is used to refer to the "institutions" of property and marriage, it is not an organization. Government is both an institution in the sense that civil society and marriage are institutions *and* it is an organization to which the members of the civil society may entrust certain powers. The difference is important and helpful to delineate the rightful authority of government and its rightful limits.

Thus, civil society refers first and foremost to a kind of legal relationship among persons.[27] Above all, it is a relationship in which each is in possession of what is properly her own, of her property, or right. Fundamental rights—clustered around property in one's person—are equal for all. The concept of subjective right emerged and developed along with civil society.[28] Immanuel Kant identifies as a condition of civil society a well-defined understanding of *mine* and *thine*, which in turn requires that all are equally subject to the same known law:

> Now, with respect to an external and contingent possession, a unilateral Will cannot serve as a coercive law for everyone, since that would be a violation of freedom in accordance with universal laws. Therefore, only a Will binding everyone else—that is, a collective, universal (common), and powerful Will—is the kind of Will that can provide the guarantee required. The condition of being subject to general external (that is, public) legislation that is backed by power is the civil society. Accordingly, a thing can be externally yours or mine only in a civil society.[29]

Civil society is a kind of social order based on a particular kind of legal foundation. This legal foundation is not the civil society itself, but civil society can hardly be conceived, much less realized, in its absence. The social order made possible by a legal foundation of equal and compossible individual rights[30] protected by limited government admits of complexity far exceeding the power of the human intellect to design or control; what is important for the enterprise of defining civil society is not what particular forms it may happen to take, what organizations or associations its members form, or what religion they profess, but that the infinite complexity and variability of which civil society is capable rests on a set of fairly simple rules.[31] Religious associations, business enterprises, self-help and mutual-aid societies, intellectual and scientific unions, and many other forms of association must conform to the rule of law, but within the rather wide parameters set by Kant's conditions an infinite variety is possible. The satisfactions of life in society rest on a foundation of well-defined legal rights protected by government, but the satisfactions of human life in society are provided by the peaceful interactions of free citizens.[32] As the influential classical liberal Benjamin Constant noted in his 1819 speech "On the Liberty of the Ancients Compared with That of the Moderns,"

> The holders of authority . . . are so ready to spare us all sort of troubles, except those of obeying and paying! They will say to us: what, in the end, is the aim of your efforts, the motive of your labours, the object of all your hopes? Is it not happiness? Well, leave this happiness to us and we shall give it to you. No, Sirs, we must not leave it to them. No matter how touching such a tender commitment may be, let us ask the authorities to keep within their limits. Let them

confine themselves to being just. We shall assume the responsibility of being happy for ourselves.[33]

CIVIL SOCIETY AND MOTIVATION

Some philosophers, however, came to identify the social order of civil society principally with a particular kind of activity or motivation, rather than with the legal order that Locke, Kant, and others agreed was its foundation. Thus, G. W. F. Hegel asserted that "individuals in their capacity as burghers are private persons whose end is their own interest" and characterized civil society (*bürgerliche Gesellschaft*) as "the battle-ground where everyone's individual private interest meets everyone else's."[34] Hegel thus identified civil society not merely with a legal order, but also with a kind of partial and selfish motivation. Karl Marx followed Hegel in identifying this legal relationship with a particular motivation when he argued in "On the Jewish Question" that "the so-called *rights of man*, as distinct from the *rights of the citizen*, are simply the rights of a *member of civil society*, that is, of egoistic man, of man separated from other men and from the community."[35] Further, "the right of property is . . . the right to enoy one's fortune and to dispose of it as one will; without regard for other men and independently of society. It is the right of self-interest. This individual libety, and its application, form the basis of civil society. It leads every man to see in other men, not the *realization*, but rather the *limitation* of his own liberty."[36]

Benjamin Barber and others share this view of a rights-based society as one of solitariness and selfishness. In Barber's words, "Rights secure our negative liberty, but since they are often claimed against others, they entail being left alone."[37] Barber decries "the atmosphere of solitariness and greed that surrounds markets."[38] Most recent attempts in the United States (at least) to come to grips with civil society have taken the same tack of focusing on motivation, but remarkably they have simply flipped Hegel and Marx on their heads by identifying civil society exclusively with *non*-profit enterprises and activities. Thus, civil society is typically identified as that sector of society "between state and market," as Barber did in a passage quoted earlier. The conservative thinker Don Eberly has written of

> a departure from our current obsession with either the state or the market as instruments for social progress. Civil society is a different sphere. It is an inter-mediary sector, where private individuals join voluntarily in associations that operate neither on the principle of coercion, nor entirely on the principle of

rational self-interest. In fact, the modus operandi of life in civil society gives expression to the pursuit of the common good, where actions are animated by a spirit of trust and collaboration.[39]

Definitions of civil society as "between state and market" or as a "third sector" have at least two serious defects: first, they represent a break from the long tradition of understanding civil society, generating confusion rather than illumination; second, to the extent that they identify the state with coercive power and the market with self-interest, they divide up the various possible forms of interaction in terms of nonexclusive categories. Coercion is a way of treating others, while self-interest is a motivation. One can coerce others for self-interested motives (robbers and politicians do this quite regularly) or for altruistic motives (the theory of righteous persecution behind the Spanish Inquisition, for example, ostensibly justi- fied breaking people on the wheel for their own good, not for the good of the inquisitors). One can interact voluntarily with others for self-inter- ested reasons (as merchants typically do when selling us products) or for altruistic reasons (as pious missionaries do). Motivations and behavior can also be mixed in a wide variety of ways. Attempts to define civil society as self-interested (in contrast to government?) or as neither state nor market fail to do what good definitions ought to do: to mark out a part of reality in a way that helps us to increase our understanding.

Thus, we return to the problem of definition: civil society is that kind of human interaction made possible by equality of rights that are pro- tected by institutions/organizations that exercise delegated, enumerated, and thus limited powers, such that those members of civil society not tied to one another by kinship, friendship, love, faith, or even geographical proximity can nonetheless interact in a "civil" manner. Civil society includes religious orders (monasteries, convents, mosques, synagogues, temples, church hierarchies, and circles of believers), business enterprises (including individual proprietorships, family enterprises, partnerships, joint-stock corporations, cooperatives, and other forms of enterprise), labor associations (including unions and a wide range of associations now less commonly found as compulsory unionism and welfare statism have narrowed the range available to employees), and the clubs, associations, neighborhood groups, bowling leagues, kaffeeklatsches, and the like that have been the topic of so much discussion lately. No one of these associa- tions, and certainly not the state, need exhaust the personalities of the members of civil society. One may simultaneously be a Muslim and a businessperson who does business with nonbelievers as well as believers, a member of the Parent-Teacher Association and a member of a jazz group that meets every Wednesday at a local club. By resigning from any one of these associations one does not become a traitor to the entire civil society, an outcast, a pariah. This was recognized clearly by Otto von Gierke in his classic study of the law of association: "Our present system of association, which resembles a great number of infinitely intersecting circles, rests on the possibility of belonging with one part, one aspect of one's individuality, perhaps with only one closely defined part of one's range of ability, to one organization, and with others to others."[40]

Ernest Gellner, in his book *Conditions of Liberty: Civil Society and Its Rivals*, termed this feature of civil society modularity, in contrast to atomism:

> There are firms which produce, advertise, and market modular furniture. The point about such furniture is that it comes in bits which are agglutinative: you can buy one bit which will function on its own, but when your needs, income or space available augment, you can buy another bit. It will fit in with the one acquired previously, and the whole thing will still have a coherence, aesthetically and technically. You can combine and recombine the bits at will. . . . What genuine Civil Society really requires is not modular furniture, but modular man.[41]

Gellner's point is that in civil society one can form attachments of one's own choosing; one can recombine them in new ways; and one can withdraw from them without thereby withdrawing from the civil society as an order of relations, as would be the case in a little gatherer/hunter band or perhaps a primitive society, at least, as they are conceived by organicists.

What makes this dazzling complexity and wide range of voluntary human association possible is liberty in the enjoyment of one's "civil rights," a term that has been degraded in meaning in recent years. From a term for the wide range of rights enjoyed by those in civil societies, "civil rights" has come in the United States to be used almost solely to refer to immunity from discrimination, while "civil liberties" has come to refer to a narrow—albeit important—set of rights, typically those of greatest importance to intellectuals. In a gathering of intellectuals there is often wide agreement to extend freedom primarily (or even only) to what intellectuals do—speak and write—just as in a gathering of farmers a consensus might be found to limit freedom to what farmers do. Limiting civil rights to those involved in speaking or writing is a dangerous and selfish conceit. It is only rarely criticized, but then, criticism is almost by definition the exclusive product of intellectuals.[42]

So much in defense of Scalet and Schmidtz's definition of civil society, which they do not arbitrarily restrict to the churches, bowling leagues, and kaffeeklatsches that have been the subject of so much attention lately.

DISTRIBUTIVE JUSTICE

Scalet and Schmidtz assert that "classical liberals deny that justice requires any particular distribution of economic goods." The truth of the statement depends on what they mean by "economic goods," but the ambiguity in the term could lead readers to think that distributive justice plays no role in classical liberal theories of justice. In fact, there is in most classical liberal approaches a very robust theory of distributive justice at their foundation—namely, the right of each individual (under normal circumstances, at least) to have jurisdiction over one and only one body—her own. Most liberals have seen legitimate property in estate as in some way derived from or related to property in one's person.[43] This is a theme not only in the familiar works of Locke, but in the works of many other protoliberal and liberal thinkers, who considered property in one's person as the moral and legal implication of a recognition of human moral agency. Marsilius of Padua noted in 1324,

> This term "ownership" [*dominium*] is used to refer to the human will or freedom in itself with its organic executive or motive power unimpeded. For it is through these that we are capable of certain acts and their opposites. It is for this reason too that man alone among the animals is said to have ownership or control of his acts; this control belongs to him by nature, it is not acquired through an act of will or choice.[44]

This is not the place to set out an entire theory of distributive justice in holdings, but a short sketch of the relationship between property in one's person and property in estate may prove suggestive. Locke uses the metaphor of labor-mixing to refer both to "whatsoever then he removes out of the State that Nature hath provided, and left it in" and to "the first gathering";[45] what both of these have in common is that they involve taking possession. And, as Tony Honoré points out, "The right to possess, namely to have exclusive physical control of a thing, or to have such control as the nature of the thing admits, is the foundation on which the whole superstructure of ownership rests."[46] In order for naturally occurring resources to be useful at all, to provide even nourishment, as Locke notes, "there must of necessity be a means *to appropriate* them some way or other before they can be of any use, or at all beneficial to any particular Man."[47] They must be capable of being possessed, and they must actually *be* possessed before they can yield any benefit to anyone.

If persons have property in their persons and the right to appropriate naturally occurring objects through the right of first possession (which right is compatible with a wide variety of forms of property holding), then they have those rights normally considered under the rubric of the right to exchange, that is, the right mutually to abandon their property in objects (conditional on the abandonment by the other party of property in the goods title to which will be exchanged) and then to acquire property in new objects. If that is so, then they have the right to benefit from such exchanges and to enjoy the increased value that motivated the exchange and that would not be called into existence in the first place without the anticipation of enjoying such increased value. Although considered diachronically there is no "distribution" of property, for there is no consciously directed distributive power, at any moment we can account for holdings according to the following abstractly formulated principle of "distributive justice": "From each according to what he chooses to do, to each according to what he makes for himself (perhaps with the contracted aid of others) and what others choose to do for him and choose to give him of what they've been given previously (under this maxim) and haven't yet expended or transferred."[48]

The question is not, then, whether there is a classical liberal theory of distributive justice, but at what point it is invoked and what relationship it has to commutative justice. (Many contemporary theories of distributive justice in effect swallow up commutative justice into distributive justice, which has led some classical liberals to deny distributive justice entirely, rather than to see distributive justice and corrective justice in their proper relationship to each other.)

Thus, the overall "distribution" is not the result of the carrying out of any particular plan. Patterned theories, in contrast, face serious problems of implementation, for even if some set of distributions were to be preferred, it may very well be that attempts to secure them directly by legal means are self-defeating.[49] There has been much controversy over the actual effects of welfare states on their populations, for example, whether they encourage the dependence and growth of an underclass or rescue the poorest of the poor from even worse circumstances.[50] What seems clear is that the growth of coerced transfer payments is inversely related to the propensity of people to transfer wealth voluntarily on grounds of need.[51] In addition, political manipulation of welfare-state benefits may very well accentuate inequalities, rather than diminish them.[52] Attempts to generate equality of wealth by means of legal coercion may, in fact, merely generate greater inequality, as the experience of the socialist countries demonstrated so clearly. After all, as F. A. Hayek warned us in *The Road to Serfdom* in 1944, in order to diminish inequalities in wealth, we must endow some with the legal power to bring this about, and they will therefore no longer be equal in power to the rest of us. And, given the normal motivations of most people, it does not take long for that inequality in legal power to be translated into inequality of wealth. As Snowball discovered in George Orwell's story *Animal Farm*, all animals are equal, but some are more equal than others.

BOUNDARIES

Scalet and Schmidtz quite correctly identify the classical liberal contribution to political theory as its focus on limited government, rather than (as classical liberals are often accused of preferring) "weak" government. The size of government is not the primary concern of classical liberals; its limits are. Limited governments tend to be small relative to unlimited governments. They also note that "classical liberals have been champions of democracy." The two issues—limited government and democracy—have traditionally been linked together in classical liberal thought by the theory of constitutionalism, which limits the powers of majorities no less than of minorities.

The principal difference between the institutions of civil society and the institutions of government is that the latter are inherently endowed with coercive powers. As Scalet and Schmidtz note, "One can say 'No, thanks' to the church (when it does not have the power of the state behind it), but when government bureaucrats think up more forms for small businesspeople to fill out, there is nothing to do but either hire another lawyer or give up and shut up." Precisely, but it should be made clear just why one can say "No, thanks," to the church but not to the state: the state has guns and the power to kill people. State actors claim legitimacy for their acts when they do use violence against people. They aspire to a monopoly over violence. As Benjamin Barber notes, after insisting for many pages that the term *civil society* be limited to his "third sector," between state and market, "Democratic central government is, in other words, civil society organized for common action. It is civil society when it picks up its law code and straps on its pistol and, legitimized and authorized by its popular mandate, becomes the sovereign."[53] Constitutional limits on power—on people with pistols—are among the greatest accomplishments of the classical liberal tradition.

Constitutionalism is one of classical liberalism's principal inheritances from the Whig tradition. As Thomas Jefferson noted in the Kentucky Resolutions of 1798, "Free government is founded in jealousy, not in confidence; it is jealousy and not confidence which prescribes limited constitutions, to bind down those whom we are obliged to trust with power."[54] Here it seems that I disagree with Scalet and Schmidtz when they write that "believing government is fundamentally evil may be one of those attitudes [whose inculcation damages those who internalize them]." Deep distrust of those with the power to imprison and kill their fellow citizens seems quite appropriate to me, and is certainly a central element of the Whiggish cultures that have been the most fertile soil for individual liberty.

The American attempt to impose limits on government included:

- explicit constitutional limitations on power (in the forms of an enumeration in the Constitution of the United States of those powers delegated to government, thus reserving all others to the people; explicit prohibitions on exercises of power; and in the Ninth and Tenth Amendments, which state that "[t]he enumeration in the Constitution of certain rights shall not be construed to deny or disparage others retained by the people" and that "[t]he powers not delegated to the United States by the Constitution, nor prohibited by it to the States, are reserved to the States respectively, or to the people");
- and a citizenship distrustful of power, jealous of its rights, and willing to exercise those rights to restrain power.

The reading of the American Constitution as one of enumerated powers and unenumerated rights is both a more plausible reading of the text and of its history and is consistent with the traditional understanding of civil society that Scalet and Schmidtz advance. Civil society may delegate certain powers to government, but only those powers that individuals have may be so delegated. As the Declaration of Independence asserts:

> That to secure these Rights, Governments are instituted among Men, deriving their Just Powers from the Consent of the Governed, that whenever any Form of Government becomes destructive of these Ends, it is the Right of the People to alter or to abolish it, and to institute new Government, laying its Foundation on such Principles, and organizing its Powers in such Form, as to them shall seem most likely to effect their Safety and Happiness.

Only *just* powers may be delegated to government. Since individuals do not have the right to expropriate the possessions of others, enslave others, or threaten others with bodily harm for their peaceful religious practices, romantic attachments, or pharmacological preferences, then government cannot have a right to nationalize property, conscript soldiers or hospital orderlies, or enforce victimless crime laws. Government's legitimate powers are necessarily limited to those powers and only those powers that the people can and do delegate to it. I know of no clearer or more concise statement of the classical liberal theory of the relationship between civil society and the state than the Declaration of Independence of the American colonies.

GROUPS

Classical liberals are, in general, moral and political individualists.[55] Historically, they have insisted that the state recognize and respect individuals as such. Classical liberals have been very suspicious of group rights and have tended to view them as, at best, mere compromises that may be necessary to ensure greater stability of liberal political structures and thereby respect for individual rights. Examples would be federalism, in which political rights are often highly unequal (electors in Nebraska and in California have differently weighted electoral influences on the United States Senate and on the selection of presidents), and transitional regimes, in which corporate bodies are given veto powers over policies that might be harmful to them (examples would be the compromise of 1867 that created the dual monarchy in Austria and the recent transition to greater democracy in South Africa). These are, however, practical political matters of achieving stability in the face of often greatly conflicting interests; they are practical remedies intended to avoid far worse dangers, rather than statements of what is in principle desirable. In general, classical liberals believe that only individuals have moral rights and that justifiable legal and moral rights should be traceable back to individual moral agents.[56]

Classical liberals have typically emphasized the distinction beween private and public realms. But making such distinctions does not necessarily determine the limits to legitimate legal intervention. For example, some feminists have criticized the treatment of the family as a private sphere within which the magistrates have little or no authority to intervene; such private spheres may in fact harbor gross violations of the rights of women, and these violations of rights may merit intervention by legal authorities. Insofar as their concern is with the rights of women as individual persons, these concerns are perfectly consonant with those of classical liberalism.[57]

More generally, however, a variety of political theorists have insisted, sometimes in the name of defending individual autonomy and dignity, that the appropriate bearers of rights may not be individuals, but groups.[58] Or they may argue that although the bearers of rights are in every case individuals, the individual members of different groups should be accorded different rights.[59] Those groups—typically ascriptive, rather than voluntary, associations—may have rights over the individuals that make them up, or rights to special treatment by the wider community (as contrasted to other groups), or some combination of these. This approach represents a direct reversal of the classical liberal movement to replace the Law of Persons with the Law of Contract as the primary law governing human interactions.[60]

Will Kymlicka has defended a version of group rights on the grounds that such group rights may be necessary to undergird the cultural infrastructure that alone can make individual autonomy possible.[61] Others have advanced additional arguments for group rights, often on grounds of collective responsibilities or political "realism."[62] Group rights may take the form of entitlements as against other groups in the wider society or rights of the group as against members of the same group, or both.[63] Both approaches are recipes for social conflict.[64]

Such approaches do not clearly distinguish between *interests* and *rights*.[65] Both individuals and groups, whether voluntary or ascriptive, may have well defined interests, but classical liberals do not generally equate interests directly with rights, and for very good reasons.

Modern welfare-state liberals have tended more and more toward endorsing an "interest theory" of rights, in which the interests of persons are held to be the grounds for holding others under duties.[66] One of the interest theory's most noted exponents cheerfully admits that, so construed, rights have "a dynamical character."[67] They change in ways that are unknown and even unknowable to the holders of rights and obligations. Further, as another welfare-state liberal also cheerfully admits, "if rights are understood along the lines of the Interest Theory propounded by Joseph Raz, then conflicts of rights should be regarded as more or less inevitable."[68] Since interests conflict, rights will conflict under the increasingly dominant modern "liberal" approach. That is a very serious problem, for if Sam and Cathy both have "rights" that clash, then the determination of which of them should be allowed to exercise the right must be made on the ground of something other than right. Further, such theories also generate conflicting duties. Matthew H. Kramer, another defender of the interest theory of rights, glosses the problems of conflict generated by such theories as follows:

> Unlike a duty to do φ and a liberty to abstain from doing φ, a duty to do φ and a duty to abstain from doing φ are not starkly contradictory. They are in conflict rather than in contradiction. Though the fulfillment of either one must rule out the fulfillment of the other, the existence of either one does not in any way preclude the existence of the other. This non-contradictoriness is one main feature of jural logic (with its categories of "permissibility," "impermissibility," and "obligatoriness") that prevents it from being collapsed into modal logic (with its categories of "possibility," "impossibility," and "necessity").[69]

That is to say, the two statements are not logically contradictory; only the fulfillment of the duties they enjoin is impossible. (Some) logicians may be comforted by such remarks, but those with conflicting legally enforceable duties or rights probably will not be. Experience shows that political power and influence, not to mention simple force and violence, come readily to mind as likely solutions to such conflicts, which—by stipulation—cannot be resolved on the basis of right. The interest theory of rights actually tends to undermine rights and the rule of law as the characteristic feature of the legal order.[70] James Madison seemed to have had the theories of Raz, Waldron, and Kramer in mind—with their "dynamical" rights and obligations and conflicts of rights and duties—when he stated in *Federalist* number 62,

> It poisons the blessings of liberty itself. It will be of little avail to the people that the laws are made by men of their own choice if the laws be so voluminous that they cannot be read, or so incoherent that they cannot be understood; if they be repealed or revised before they are promulgated, or undergo such incessant changes that no man, who knows what the law is today, can guess what it will be tomorrow. Law is defined to be a rule of action; but how can that be a rule, which is little known, and less fixed?[71]

Positing "dynamical" group rights makes matters even worse, for as group interests conflict, so will group rights, and there will be no means to resolve such conflicts on the basis of right (for the rights are already in conflict), meaning that groups will resort to other means to pursue their conflicting interests/rights. The prospect is decidedly unsettling for the stability of a liberal constitutional order. It is a recipe for tearing civil society asunder through intergroup warfare. Attention to the common good becomes more difficult, if not impossible, for by stipulation there no longer is any good that is actually common to all groups. Not surprisingly, the history of systems of group rights has been one of conflict—often very violent—rather than of peaceful cooperation. Indeed, something remarkably like the system of differential rights that Kymlicka endorses has already been tried in Europe and was criticized by the influential Hungarian classical liberal Josef Eötvös, who was a major participant in the revolution of 1848 and subsequent political developments in central Europe, as well as a learned writer on the problems of nationality. With apologies for the difficulties of translating a German text that was translated from Hungarian, I offer his very telling criticism of Kymlicka's proposals, published in 1865:

> The particular nationality may demand a separate territory to rule in order to secure its freedom. It may further demand the codification in law of its sphere of rights in a way that grants the rights of each single person regarding the use of his national language, not as something to which he is entitled as an individual, but rather as a member of a specific nationality. Moreover, it may be demanded that the offices of the country be divided up according to nationality, and that in particular areas only members of a certain nationality should be eligible for office. In short, there may be a movement that started in the name of freedom and equality, and afterwards everyone demands only privileges and endeavors that those privileges be as plentiful as possible. All those things described are truly not new, and everyone who knows history knows how in times past the various religious confessions stepped forth under the

same pretext and with the same demands against the others. The protection of one confession from oppression by the others and the abolition of the occasions for friction through the determination of the spheres of the rights of all the particular confessions: those were the reasons that then motivated the demands of the particular confessions, just as now they motivate the demands of the particular nations. In Catholic countries, Protestants were assigned to their own territories and particular fortresses were equipped, which served as weapons depots for the religion. Moreover, it was determined what number of individuals of every confession were allowed to run for a particular office, and what part of the city council should consist of members of one or of another confession. And what was the result of all these rules and measures in those places where the solution of the religious question was sought in this way? What else, besides never-ending frictions between different confessions, the suppression of those who were a minority in a particular territory, and unbounded intolerance on the side with the opportunity to express it. And, as a consequence of all this, it led to a bloody war lasting centuries, which shattered the most powerful states, brought about a not-yet-healed cleavage in one of the greatest nations of Europe and everywhere hindered the advance of civilization! In some states the conflict was bloodier, in others it resulted in complete suppression of one confession. In all states where complete suppression did not occur reconciliation among the confessions was sought by creating laws that determined the spheres of rights and the privileges of each confession. The consequence was the same, namely, the citizens of each such country, segregated according to confessions, stood in hostility against one another. The more numerous and the more detailed the laws intended to protect the confessions were, the less peace and harmony were achieved.

The newer age has followed different paths in this regard. Instead of special spheres of rights and privileges for each confession, the principle of freedom of belief was established, according to which confessional diversity is without any influence on the rights of individual citizens. It was recognized that, about the question of to which confession each individual is to belong, only his own conscience is to be decisive; that the maintenance and dissemination of every religion is to be left to the zeal of the individuals; that no other responsibility falls to the law, than to protect everyone in the enjoyment of his freedom—and to the extent that this principle was consistently applied, the religious question has been solved.[72]

Individuals have many interests that are best served by being members of groups. Groups, too, may have interests. But neither consideration justifies eliminating the principle that all are equal before the law and substituting for this one principle—one of the greatest accomplishments of civilization—a variety of regimes of differential rights. The pursuit of both individual and group interests should be undertaken solely through voluntary associations within the confines of a system of equal fundamental individual rights.

Some may ask, what guarantees that individual rights will be respected by the groups within which individuals associate? That is a misguided question, for life simply contains no guarantees. What can be meaningfully discussed is likelihood or probability, and what makes it more likely than not that the rights and dignity of members will be respected is the right of exit. Most modern states recognize a right of exit from the territory of the state, which is better than restricting exit, but such territorial-exit rights still set the cost of exit from the state extremely high, for one must then also exit from *all* of one's other associations in civil society. In contrast, exit from any particular association of civil society does not normally mean exit from all associations. A particularly promising approach offered by some classical liberals has been what we might call the right of "internal exit." Wilhelm von Humboldt pointed out the danger of giving projects to an institution that exercises deadly force, and then added,

> Nothing would be left to the unconsenting but to withdraw from the community in order to escape jurisdiction, and prevent the further application of a majority suffrage to their individual cases. And yet this is almost impossible when we reflect that to withdraw from the social body means the same as withdrawing from the State. Furthermore, it is better to enter into separate unions in specific associations, than to contract them generally for unspecified future contingencies.[73]

Along the same lines, Herbert Spencer proposed a "right to ignore the state" in his influential work *Social Statics*.[74] A more concrete set of proposals for "personal autonomy" was developed in central Europe to deal with the severe problems of national conflicts. Eötvös proposed that conflicts over nationality could be diminished by limiting state authority and collective choice and leaving as much of social life to voluntary association as possible.[75] Others who followed in his footsteps proposed that nationality be made a matter of personal choice, to be registered by government. This idea of "personal autonomy" was proposed in the late years of the Austro-Hungarian monarchy and in the Austrian republic by the "Austro-Marxists" Otto Bauer and Karl Renner, who recognized that over matters of religion, language, and culture collective choice could only generate conflict. Their Marxism led them to believe that "economic relations" would be harmonious after such affairs were made matters of collective choice (they might be forgiven for thinking that before socialism was actually tried), but their knowledge of religious, linguistic, and cultural conflicts convinced them, as it had Eötvös, that personal choice was the key to peace and harmony.[76]

Unfortunately, the trend among welfare-state liberals in recent years has instead been to restrict even exit from and entry into the territory of a state. Yael Tamir, in her recent work *Liberal Nationalism*, invokes the classical liberal prescription of freedom of trade and travel as a reductio ad absurdum, a theory so bizarre that no serious person could entertain it.[77]

Will Kymlicka notes that citizenship itself is "an inherently group-differentiated notion" and states that "[u]nless one is willing to accept either a single world-government or completely open borders between states—and very few liberal theorists have endorsed either of these—then distributing rights and benefits on the basis of citizenship is to treat people differentially on the basis of their group membership."[78] Freedom of travel and freedom of trade were once characteristic liberal positions, and it is profoundly sad that protectionism, guard dogs, and barbed wire are now endorsed by self-described "liberals." Brian Barry, apparently unaware that his proposal for restriction of the interstate mobility of African Americans had already been put into practice under Jim Crow, characteristically asserted without either evidence or argument that

> [a] counterfactual America combining state-level controls over immigration and strong federal policies to bring economic development to the South while ensuring legal and political rights to the Blacks would surely be a better one than that which actually exists. And that is, in broad terms, the formula that I advocate for the world as a whole.[79]

Barry seems unaware that such restrictions existed, that they were a major part of the state-enforced Jim Crow system, and that they were justified on the grounds of the well-being of African Americans themselves, for without them, "a wicked and corrupt agent" could "come into a community and at the dead hour of midnight, by promises and persuasions, induce an ignorant and wholly irresponsible (financially speaking) population to leave their peaceful homes and thereby disrupt the labor conditions."[80] In pursuit of social justice Barry would have suspended the rights of African Americans to move from state to state in search of better work and higher pay (he makes no mention of Caucasian statist British professors who emigrate from London to New York in search of better work and higher pay), and currently he seeks to implement such a system of restrictions on movement on a global scale. (Again, Brian Barry is himself presumably exempted from such restrictions; after all, all animals are equal, but some are more equal than others.)

The issue of freedom of movement is made all the more acute by the fact that upon entering the territory of a welfare state, one typically acquires a wide range of positive entitlements. The consequence of this is that emigrants are likely to be viewed as parasites or freeloaders by the citizens of the welfare state they have entered. (The existence of differential rights for citizens/insiders and for foreigners/outsiders is a particular case of differential group-based rights. It is objectionable on liberal grounds and has shown itself to be a powerful source of hatred, envy, resentment, racism, xenophobia, and brutal violence.) Accordingly, all welfare states have restrictions on immigration and effectively generate antiforeigner movements. If restrictions on freedom of movement are the logical conclusion of welfare-state liberalism (and a number of welfare-state liberals have followed the implications of adherence to the welfare state in precisely that direction), then there are good reasons for modern liberals to reject both group rights and the interest theory of rights behind them and to return to the classical liberal conception of rights and of the proper relation of individuals to groups.

In general, what should determine the appropriate relations among individuals, groups, and the state is consent. Individuals consent to form voluntary associations, on the basis of common interests; those voluntary associations interact with other associations and with individuals on the basis of mutual consent; and governments derive "their just powers from the Consent of the Governed," in the words of the American Declaration of Independence.

Individuals may consent to form voluntary groups through which to advance their common interests. In consenting to pool their assets, they may also create fictive persons (e.g., corporations), which may have legal relations with individuals, other corporations, and states. They may even be bearers of legal responsibility and may assume collective responsibility on behalf of their members. But for classical liberals such fictive persons should be founded on the consent of the materially and numerically individuated persons who are their members, rather than ascription.

Classical liberals insist that, under normal circumstances, at least, the liberty of the individual human being is the highest political end. It is not the end or goal of life itself, but the condition that makes the ends of life most likely to be attained.

NOTES

1. Fareed Zakaria, "The 20 Percent Philosophy," *Public Interest*, no. 129 (Fall 1997): 96–101, 101.

2. Irving Copi, *Introduction to Logic*, 6th ed. (New York: Macmillan Publishing, 1982), 150.

3. Compare Reinhard Bendix, *Kings or People: Power and the Mandate to Rule* (Berkeley and Los Angeles: University of California Press, 1978), 523: "*civil society* refers to all institutions in which individuals can pursue common interests without detailed direction or interference from the government." Bendix continues,

"Western European regimes and Japan possessed civil societies because they had inherited a tradition of local privileges or liberties; Russia did not enjoy a comparable inheritance."

4. Benjamin Barber, *A Place for Us: How to Make Society Civil and Democracy Strong* (New York: Hill and Wang, 1998), 4.

5. Ibid., 13.

6. Ibid., 53.

7. The great distinction between Latin Christendom and the inheritors of the Byzantine tradition is undoubtedly the relative independence of the church from the state. For the developments in Latin Christendom, see Harold Berman's account of the Gregorian Reformation, which proceeded on the basis of the slogan of the "freedom of the church." "Gregorian Reformation," in *Law and Revolution: The Formation of the Western Legal Tradition* (Cambridge: Harvard University Press, 1983), esp. chap. 2, "The Origin of the Western Legal Tradition in the Papal Revolution," 85–119. For a collection of the relevant historical documents, see Brian Tierney, *The Crisis of Church and State, 1050–1300* (Toronto: University of Toronto Press, 1988). For a learned description of Byzantine theories of church-state relations and their impact on later Eastern European politics, see Francis Dvornik, "Byzantine Political Ideas in Kievan Russia," *Dumbarton Oaks Papers*, nos. 9 and 10 (Cambridge: Harvard University Press, 1956), 73–121; and *The Slavs in European History and Civilization* (New Brunswick, N.J.: Rutgers University Press, 1962), 369–76.

8. Henri Pirenne, *Economic and Social History of Medieval Europe* (New York: Harcourt Brace Jovanovich, 1937), 50. This association of civil society with city life has been known for a long time. See Adam Smith, *An Inquiry into the Nature and Causes of the Wealth of Nations* (Indianapolis, Ind.: Liberty Fund, 1981), esp. vol. 1, bk. 3, chap. 3, "Of the Rise and Progress of Cities and Towns, after the Fall of the Roman Empire," pp. 397–410.

9. Max Weber, *Economy and Society: An Outline of Interpretive Sociology*, ed. Guenther Roth and Claus Wittich (Berkeley and Los Angeles: University of California Press, 1978), 2:1227.

10. Quoted in Antony Black, *Guilds and Civil Society in European Political Thought from the Twelfth Century to the Present* (Ithaca: Cornell University Press, 1984), 38. (The references in the text are to the codification of Roman law known as the *Digest of Justinian*.) Brunetto Latini (ca. 1260) described how cities grew: "it came in the end to the point where those who wanted to live by their own law and escape the force of evildoers grouped themselves together in one place and under one government. Thence they began to build houses and establish towns (*viles*) and fortresses, and enclose them with walls and ditches. Thence they began to establish customs and law and rights (*drois*) which should be common to all the burghers (*borgois*) of the town" (39). An illuminating account of the slow growth of a city, as defined by its fortifications, can be found in Paul Strait, *Cologne in the Twelfth Century* (Gainesville: University Presses of Florida, 1974), 30–36. Cologne's status as an old Roman city and an episcopal seat distinguishes it in various ways from the new cities of Europe, but the identification of the city walls with the freedom of the city and the security of the citizens was a common factor.

11. Berman, *Law and Revolution*, 383–84.

12. Henry Sumner Maine, *Ancient Law* (1861; reprint, Gloucester, Mass.: Peter Smith, 1970), 163.

13. As Berman observed, "The new European cities and towns of the eleventh and twelfth centuries were also legal associations, in the sense that each was held together by a common urban legal consciousness and by distinctive urban legal institutions. In fact, it was by a legal act, usually the granting of a charter, that most of the European cities and towns came into being; they did not simply emerge but were *founded*. Moreover, the charter would almost invariably establish the basic 'liberties' of citizens, usually including substantial rights of self-government" (*Law and Revolution*, 362).

14. Hans Planitz, *Die Deutsche Stadt im Mittelalter: Von der Römerzeit bis zu den Zünftkämpfen* (Graz und Köln: Böhlau, 1954), 117.

15. In John H. Mundy and Peter Riesenberg, *The Medieval Town* (Princeton: D. Van Nostrand, 1958), 138.

16. Antony Black lists the following names used to designate "the early town community": "*civitas, commune, communitas, universitas civium/burgensium, urbani, burgensis populus, universi cives*, and the vernacular *commune* (French and Italian), *Gemeinde, burgh*." Black, *Guilds and Civil Society*, 49.

17. Planitz, *Die Deutsche Stadt im Mittelalter*, 100.

18. As Thomas Paine noted, "The patriots in France have discovered in good time that rank and dignity in society must take a new ground. The old one has fallen through. It must now take the substantial ground of character instead of the chimerical ground of titles." In *The Rights of Man*, pt. 1, in *Thomas Paine: Political Writings*, ed. Bruce Kuklick (1791; reprint, Cambridge: Cambridge University Press, 1989), 90.

19. Black, *Guilds and Civil Society*, 65.

20. Henri Pirenne, *Medieval Cities: Their Origins and the Revival of Trade* (Princeton: Princeton University Press, 1974), 200.

21. Black, *Guilds and Civil Society*, 32.

22. Benedict de Spinoza, *A Theologico-Political Treatise*, trans. R.H.M. Elwes (New York: Dover Publications, 1951), 264. The burghers of the Netherlands were pioneers of religious toleration, as Geoffrey Parker noted regarding the attempts by the king of Spain to reorganize the bishoprics of the Netherlands and, in the process, to appoint resident inquisitors: "There was violent opposition to this measure from the magistrates of Antwerp (Antwerp was to be one of the new sees) on the grounds that the inquisition was contrary to the privileges of Brabant and that, more specifically, so many heretics came to Antwerp to trade that its prosperity would be ruined if a resident inquisition were introduced." *The Dutch Revolt* (New York: Penguin Books, 1988), 47. Compare also the observations on the London Stock Exchange by Voltaire: "Go into the Exchange in London, that place more venerable than many a court, and you will see representatives of all the nations assembled there for the profit of mankind. There the Jew, the Mahometan, and the Christian deal with one another as if they were of the same religion, and reserve the name of infidel for those who go bankrupt." Voltaire, "On the Presbyterians," in *"Candide" and Philosophical Letters* (New York: Modern Library, 1992), 141.

23. James Harrington, *The Commonwealth of Oceana* (1656), in *The Common-*

wealth of Oceana and A System of Politics, ed. J. G. A. Pocock (Cambridge: Cambridge University Press, 1992), 8. Further, "[a] commonwealth is but a civil society of men" (23).

24. Locke does not maintain, however, that civil society or political society is the source of all obligation: "The Promises and Bargains for Truck, *&c.* between the two Men in the Desert Island, mentioned by *Garcilasso De la vega*, in his History of *Peru*, between a *Swiss* and an *Indian*, in the Woods of *America*, are binding to them, though they are perfectly in a state of nature, in reference to one another. For Truth and keeping of Faith belongs to Men, as Men, and not as Members of Society." John Locke, *Two Treatises of Government*, ed. Peter Laslett (Cambridge: Cambridge University Press, 1988), bk. 2, sec.14, p. 277.

25. Ibid., bk. 2, sec.95, p. 330–31. Algernon Sidney, at about the same time, criticized the patriarchal theory of political power, noting that "for politick signifying no more in Greek, than civil in Latin, 'tis evident there could be no civil power, where there was no civil society; and there could be none between him [Adam] and his children, because a civil society is composed of equals, and fortified by mutual compacts, which could not be between him and his children." *Discourses Concerning Government*, ed. Thomas G. West (Indianapolis, Ind.: Liberty Fund, 1990), 88. In a Boston election sermon of 1762, Abraham Williams pointed out to his listeners that "[t]he End and Design of civil Society and Government, from this view of it's Origin, must be to secure the Rights and Properties of it's Members, and promote their Welfare; or, in the Apostle's words, that Men may lead quiet and peaceable Lives in Godliness and Honesty." "An Election Sermon," in *American Political Writing during the Founding Era, 1760–1805*, vol. 1, ed. Charles S. Hyneman and Donald S. Lutz (Indianapolis, Ind.: Liberty Press, 1983), 6.

26. One particularly confused commentator writes as follows of the United States of America: "The United States, which, in contrast to both Eastern and Western Europe, has always lacked a coherent concept of the state, has traditionally been presented as a model of civil society. Yet in the closing decades of the twentieth century the adequacy of this model is increasingly being questioned" Adam B. Seligman, *The Idea of Civil Society* (Princeton: Princeton University Press, 1992), 9. The author seems to think that a constitutional republic grounded on a written constitution that specifies enumerated powers and provides explicit limits on state power "lacks a coherent concept of the state."

27. This seems to be the general approach of Adam Ferguson in his rich and complex *Essay on the History of Civil Society* (1767; reprint, Cambridge: Cambridge University Press, 1995), in which he connects the rise of civil society with the emergence of property, and therefore of improvement and of civility.

28. See the historical treatment of these interconnected developments in Brian Tierney, *The Idea of Natural Rights* (Atlanta, Ga.: Scholars Press, 1998).

29. Immanuel Kant, *The Metaphysical Elements of Justice*, trans. J. Ladd (New York: Macmillan, 1985), 65. Kant defined "external proprietary rights" explicitly in terms of equal rights: "A thing is externally mine if it is something outside me which is such that any interference with my using it as I please would constitute an injury to me (a violation of my freedom, a freedom that can coexist with the freedom of everyone in accordance with a universal law)" (55). The latter condi-

tion is equivalent to the condition of "compossibility" described in Hillel Steiner, *An Essay on Rights* (Oxford: Blackwell, 1994).

30. In Kant's words, "Every action is just [right] that in itself or in its maxim is such that the freedom of the will of each can coexist together with the freedom of everyone in accordance with a universal law" *The Metaphysical Elements of Justice*, 35). Or as John Locke noted in the seventh of his *Essays on the Laws of Nature*, in *Political Essays*, ed. Mark Goldie (Cambridge: Cambridge University Press, 1997), "The duties of life are not at variance with one another, nor do they arm men against one another—a result which, secondly, follows of necessity from the preceding assumption, for upon it men were, as they say, by the law of nature in a state of war; so all society is abolished and all trust, which is the bond of society" (132).

31. See Richard Epstein, *Simple Rules for a Complex World* (Cambridge: Harvard University Press, 1995), for an updated restatement of this thesis.

32. This theme is developed in classical liberal terms in Wilhelm von Humboldt's treatment of civil society, *The Limits of State Action* (Indianapolis, Ind.: Liberty Fund, 1993), esp. chap. 3, "On the Solicitude of the State for the Positive Welfare of the Citizen." Humboldt's views are well described in in George G. Iggers, "The Political Theory of Voluntary Association in Early-Nineteenth-Century German Thought," in *Voluntary Associations: A Study of Groups in Free Societies*, ed. D. B. Robertson (Richmond, Va.: John Knox Press, 1966).

33. Benjamin Constant, *Political Writings*, ed. Biancamaria Fontana (Cambridge: Cambridge University Press, 1988), 326. As Wilhelm von Humboldt noted, it is "the free cooperation of the members of the nation which secures all those benefits for which men longed when they formed themselves into society." *The Limits of State Action*, 137.

34. G. W. F. Hegel, *The Philosophy of Right*, trans. T. M. Knox (Oxford: Oxford University Press, 1977), 124, 189.

35. In *Karl Marx: Early Writings*, trans. and ed. T. B. Bottomore (New York: McGraw-Hill Books, 1964), 24.

36. Ibid., 25.

37. Benjamin Barber, *A Place for Us*, 121.

38. Ibid., 65. Here Barber follows many in identifying classical liberalism with greed and selfishness, grossly distorting the simple insight of Adam Smith and others that self-interest rightly understood can be generally beneficial when, but only when, institutions are properly ordered. Smith and other liberal economists did not argue that all motivations are selfish, nor that societies that enjoy free markets are selfish societies, nor that self-interest is only present in free societies. For a correction, see Stephen Holmes, "The Secret History of Self-Interest," in *Passions and Constraint: On the Theory of Liberal Democracy* (Chicago: University of Chicago Press, 1995).

39. Don Eberly, "The New Demands of Citizenship," *Policy Review* (January–February 1996): 30–31.

40. Otto von Gierke, *Community in Historical Perspective*, trans. Mary Fischer, ed. Antony Black (Cambridge: Cambridge University Press, 1990), 23.

41. Ernest Gellner, *Conditions of Liberty: Civil Society and Its Rivals* (New York: Penguin Books, 1994), 97. Clearly, only an academic would describe the furniture sold in Ikea stores as "agglutinative."

42. As Vasily Grossman wrote, based on his experiences as a subject of a state that attempted to eradicate civil society entirely and to integrate all human interactions into the organization of the state, freedom must mean freedom for all kinds of endeavor: "I used to think that freedom was freedom of speech, freedom of the press, freedom of conscience. But freedom is the whole life of everyone. Here is what it amounts to: you have to have the right to sow what you wish to, to make shoes or coats, to bake into bread the flour ground from the grain you have sown, and to sell it or not sell it as you wish; for the lathe operator, the steelworker, and the artist it's a matter of being able to live as you wish and work as you wish and not as they order you to. And in our country there is no freedom—not for those who write books nor for those who sow grain nor for those who make shoes." *Forever Flowing* (New York: Harper and Row, 1986), 99.

43. For a denial of the relationship, see G. A. Cohen, *Self-Ownership, Freedom, and Equality* (Cambridge: Cambridge University Press, 1995). Cohen's account is fraught with confusion; see my "G. A. Cohen on Freedom and Equality," *Critical Review* (Summer 1998) for a catalog of these errors and a response to his claims.

44. Marsilius of Padua, *The Defender of the Peace: The Defensor Pacis*, trans. Alan Gewirth (New York: Harper and Row, 1956), discourse 2, chap. 12, 13, p. 192. Francisco de Vitoria, who studied in Paris and was probably influenced by Marsilian thought, noted in his defense of the rights of the American Indians, "If . . . brutes have no dominion over their own actions, they can have no dominion over other things." In "On the American Indians [*De Indis*]," in *Francisco de Vitoria: Political Writings*, ed. Anthony Pagden and Jeremy Lawrance (Cambridge: Cambridge University Press, 1991), 248.

45. Locke, *Two Treatises of Government*, bk. 2 sec.27, p. 288, and sec.28, p. 288.

46. Tony Honoré, "Ownership," in *Making Law Bind: Essays Legal and Philosophical* (Oxford: Oxford University Press, 1987), p. 166. This is the basic claim of John XXII in his bull of 1323, *Ad Conditorem*. See Tierney, *The Idea of Natural Rights*, esp. 93–97.

47. Locke, *Two Treatises of Government*, bk. 2, sec.26, pp. 286–87.

48. Robert Nozick, *Anarchy, State, and Utopia* (New York: Basic Books, 1974), 160.

49. On self-defeating theories generally see Derek Parfit, *Reasons and Persons* (Oxford: Oxford University Press, 1986).

50. The current debate in the United States was sparked largely by the extensive empirical studies of Charles Murray, *Losing Ground: American Social Policy, 1950–1980* (New York: Basic Books, 1984).

51. For a recent example, see the story of the attempts to encourage French people to help their less fortunate compatriots during a very cold winter, Charles Trueheart, "Can Winter Blast Melt Cold Parisian Hearts?" *Washington Post*, November 27, 1998, A39: "According to one recent study, the French citizen gives, on average, approximately 0.15 percent of his annual taxable income to nonprofit organizations. The figure in next-door Germany, according to the same study, is twice that. In the United States, it is eight times larger—about 1.2 percent of income." The issue is debated in David Schmidtz and Robert E. Goodin, *Social Welfare and Individual Responsibility* (Cambridge: Cambridge University Press, 1998). For a perspective from moral philosophy, see Tibor Machan,

Generosity: Virtue in Civil Society (Washington, D.C.: Cato Institute, 1998). Similarly, state financial support for churches, such as those in Germany and Sweden, demonstrably undercuts church participation, in comparison with voluntary support for churches, such as those in the United States. See Laurence R. Iannacone, Roger Finke, and Rodney Stark, "Deregulating Religion: The Economics of Church and State," *Economic Inquiry* 35 (April 1997): 350–64. For a history of the displacement of mutual aid by the welfare state, see David T. Beito, *From Mutual Aid to the Welfare State: Fraternal Societies and Social Services, 1890–1967* (Chapel Hill: University of North Carolina Press, 2000).

52. This problem was exemplified in a front-page article in the *Washington Post*, "5 D.C. Employees Charged: Only 10 of 400 New Rent Vouchers Issued since 1990 Didn't Involve Bribery, Probe Finds," by Cindy Loose, April 13, 1994, A1: "The city employees are accused of using their positions 'to prey upon the most vulnerable members in our community,' [U.S. Attorney Eric H. Holder, Jr.] said at a joint news conference of federal and city officials. 'Not only did they allegedly demand bribe money from those people least able to afford it, they also displaced from the housing list those who were rightfully entitled to government-subsidized housing and were playing by the rules,' Holder said."

53. Barber, *A Place for Us*, 62.

54. Thomas Jefferson, "The Kentucky Resolutions," in *The Portable Thomas Jefferson*, ed. Merrill D. Peterson (New York: Penguin Books, 1977), pp. 287–88.

55. For a correction of communitarian mischaracterizations of liberal individualism, see Tom G. Palmer, "Myths of Individualism," *Policy Report*, 17, no. 5 (September/October 1996) (http://www.cato.org/pubs/policy—report/cpr-18n5-1.html).

56. The problem of the fictive person who is a rights bearer, such as the church or the business corporation, has been addressed in a variety of ways in the history of jurisprudence. In general, classical liberals have seen such fictive persons as creatures of contract among rights-bearing individual persons. See Antony Black, "Society and the Individual from the Middle Ages to Rousseau: Philosophy, Jurisprudence, and Constitutional Theory," *History of Political Theory* 1, no. 2 (June 1980): 145–66, and, for a contractual view of the business corporation, see Ronald Coase, *The Firm, the Market, and the Law* (Chicago: University of Chicago Press, 1988); Ronald Coase, "The Institutional Structure of Production," *American Economic Review* 82 (September 1992), and Robert Hessen, *In Defense of the Corporation* (Stanford, Calif.: Hoover Institution Press, 1979).

57. Thus, the recognition that there may be rape within marriage would not be construed by classical liberals as an assault on the family, but as a vindication of one of the inalienable rights of individuals who choose to marry.

58. This issue is carefully discussed in Andrew Vincent, "Can Groups Be Persons?" *Review of Metaphysics* 42, no. 4 (June 1989): 687–714.

59. This is the approach of Will Kymlicka in *Multicultural Citizenship* (Oxford: Clarendon Press, 1995). Despite his insistence that the rights he defends are rights of individuals, Kymlicka rather consistently defers to groups as such, with such references as what "they wanted," "the historical preference of these groups," and so on. To determine the interests and therefore the rights of the individual members of the groups, he defers to the leaders (often self-appointed)

of those groups; it is thus the group that determines the rights of individuals, and thus the groups that are the repository of the power to award rights.

60. This is a central theme of Henry Sumner Maine's *Ancient Law*, 163–65. The retrograde motion from the Law of Contract to the Law of Persons in contemporary America is well described in Tom Bethell, *The Noblest Triumph: Property and Prosperity through the Ages* (New York: St. Martin's Press, 1998).

61. See Will Kymlicka, *Liberalism, Community, and Culture* (Oxford: Oxford University Press, 1989), 164: "Liberal values require both individual freedom of choice and a secure cultural context from which individuals can make their choices."

62. For an approach based on an examination of some common beliefs about group responsibility (e.g., collective responsibility) and state powers, see Vernon Van Dyke, "Collective Entities and Moral Rights: Problems in Liberal-Democratic Thought," in *Group Rights: Perspectives since 1900*, ed. Julia Stapleton (Bristol: Thommes Press, 1995), 180–200.

63. Will Kymlicka endorses only the former, namely, entitlements to benefits from the larger group, and opposes the group's right to restrict the activities of its own members ("Protecting people from changes in the character of their culture can't be viewed as protecting their ability to choose." *Liberalism, Community and Culture*, 167), but cannot help sliding toward the latter: "the viability of Indian communities depends on coercively restricting the mobility, residence, and political rights of both Indians and non-Indians" (146). Vernon Van Dyke also endorses both: "Where a country or people is sovereign, the right to preserve a culture is a legal right; at least, sovereign states are free to adopt laws designed to preserve a culture." "Collective Entities and Moral Rights," 186.

64. For some examples of such conflicts between ascriptive groups, see Donald L. Horowitz, *Ethnic Groups in Conflict* (Berkeley and Los Angeles: University of California Press, 1985), esp. chap. 5, "Group Entitlement and the Sources of Conflict," 185–228.

65. This is a central insight of Chandran Kukathas's critique of group rights: see "Are There Any Cultural Rights?" *Political Theory* 20, no. 1 (February 1992): 105–39. See also Will Kymlicka, "The Rights of Minority Cultures," *Political Theory* 20, no. 1 (February 1992): 140–46; and Chandran Kukathas, "Cultural Rights Again: A Rejoinder to Kymlicka," *Political Theory* 20, no. 4 (November 1992): 674–80. See also the critique of Kymlicka's theory by Anthony de Jasay "Liberty, Rights, and the Standing of Groups," chap. 11 in *Against Politics: On Government, Anarchy, and Order* (London: Routledge, 1997), esp. 232–34. Jasay notes that Kymlicka turns liberalism on its head by presupposing in his theory of rights that "actions must be expressly permitted in order not to be taken to be forbidden" (232).

66. See Joseph Raz, *The Morality of Freedom* (Oxford: Oxford University Press), 166: "'X has a right' if and only if X can have rights, and, other things being equal, an aspect of X's well-being (his interest) is a sufficient reason for holding some other person(s) to be under a duty."

67. Ibid., 185.

68. Jeremy Waldron, "Rights in Conflict," in *Liberal Rights: Collected Papers, 1981–1991* (Cambridge: Cambridge University Press, 1993), 203. For an exam-

ination of the differences between the interest theory of rights and the more traditional liberal choice theory, as exemplified in legal cases, see John Hasnas, "From Cannibalism to Caesareans: Two Conceptions of Fundamental Rights," *Northwestern University Law Review* 89, no. 3 (Spring 1995): 900–941.

69. Matthew H. Kramer, "Rights without Trimmings," in *A Debate Over Rights: Philosophical Enquiries*, ed. Matthew H. Kramer, N. E. Simmonds, and Hillel Steiner (Oxford: Clarendon Press, 1998), 19.

70. See also the similar treatment of rights in Stephen Holmes and Cass R. Sunstein, *The Cost of Rights: Why Liberty Depends on Taxes* (New York: W. W. Norton, 1999). According to Holmes and Sunstein, "an interest qualifies as a right when an effective legal system treats it as such by using collective resources to defend it" (17). Their theory generates an extraordinary logical chaos, as I show in my review in the *Cato Journal* 19, no. 2 (Fall 1999) (http://www.cato.org/pubs/journal/cj19n2/cj19n2.html).

71. James Madison, Alexander Hamilton, and John Jay, *The Federalist Papers*, ed. Isaac Kramnick (1788; reprint, New York: Penguin Books, 1987), no. 62, p. 368.

72. Josef Freiherrn von Eötvös, *Die Nationalitätenfrage*, trans. from the Hungarian to German by Dr. Max Falk (Pest: Verlag von Moritz Ráth, 1865), 145–47. The liberal political economist Ludwig von Mises stated in 1919, following the catastrophe of the Great War, "Whoever wants peace among nations must seek to limit the state and its influence most strictly." *Nation, State, and Economy: Contributions to the Politics and History of Our Time* (New York: New York University Press, 1983), 77.

73. Wilhelm von Humboldt, *The Limits of State Action*, p. 36.

74. Herbert Spencer, *Social Statics* (1850; reprint, New York: Robert Schalkenbach Foundation, 1995).

75. See Eötvös's treatment of the relationship between what he called the "ruling ideas of the nineteenth century": freedom, equality, and nationality. As he observed, the three were in contradiction; therefore, if these ideas were to be realized, one among them had to be made the dominant one. Eötvös defended freedom as the idea to which the others would be made to conform. See his two-volume work *Der Einfluss der herrschenden Ideen des 19. Jahrhunderts auf den Staat* (trans. by the author from the original Hungarian; Leipzig: F. U. Brockhaus, 1854).

76. See Otto Bauer, *Die Nationalitätenfrage und Die Sozialdemokratie*, in Dr. Max Adler and Dr. Rudolf Hilferding, Herausgeber, *Marx Studien: Blätter zur Theorie und Politik der Wissenschaftlichen Sozialismus*, Zweiter Band (Wien: Verlag der Wiener Volksbuchhandlung, 1924); Karl Renner, *Das Selbstbestimmungsrecht der Nationen: In besonderer Anwendung auf Oesterreich* (Leipzig und Wien: Franz Deuticke, 1918); and the descriptions in Robert A. Kann, *The Multinational Empire: Nationalism and National Reform in the Habsburg Monarchy, 1848–1918*, vol. 2, *Empire Reform*, esp. 154–78.

77. Yael Tamir, *Liberal Nationalism* (Princeton: Princeton University Press, 1993). Utilizing a quotation from Bruce Ackerman's *Social Justice in a Liberal State*, Tamir notes, "If liberal theory is unable to justify a situation in which 'noncitizens must depend upon the policy choices of *citizens* if they are to acquire

rights on their own behalf,' it should advocate that barriers be pulled down and allow the market to control immigration" (127). Only after a few paragraphs does it dawn on a classical liberal reader that this is not an invocation of a traditional liberal policy prescription, but a reductio ad absurdum.

78. Kymlicka, *Multicultural Citizenship*, 124.

79. Brian Barry, "The Quest for Consistency: A Sceptical View," in *Free Movement: Ethical Issues in the Transnational Migration of People and of Money*, ed. Brian Barry and Robert E. Goodin (University Park: Pennsylvania State University Press, 1992), 284–85.

80. These are the words of Colonel Butler, who prosecuted emigrant agent R. A. "Peg Leg" William for violating Georgia's emigrant-agent law. In David E. Bernstein, "The Law and Economics of Post–Civil War Restrictions on Interstate Migration by African-Americans," *Texas Law Review* 76, no. 4 (March 1998): 809, 781–847.

Civil Society and Government:
A Liberal-Egalitarian Perspective

Will Kymlicka

As THE NAME suggests, liberal egalitarianism attempts to combine two important ideas or principles: a liberal commitment to individual freedom of choice; and an egalitarian commitment to eliminating disadvantages in the distribution of resources and opportunities. It is this latter commitment to social justice that distinguishes liberal egalitarianism from its more right-wing libertarian counterpart.

Needless to say, it is a source of ongoing controversy whether or how these two principles can be reconciled in a single theory. My own preferred account of liberal egalitarianism rests on the following basic idea: inequalities due to people's choices about the good life, such as their choices about effort, risk, savings, or consumption, are permissible; but inequalities due to circumstances beyond people's control, such as their natural talents or the race or class they were born into, should be remedied or compensated. Since liberal egalitarians value individual freedom, people must be free to make different choices about the good life, and be held responsible for the costs of these choices. But people should not suffer as a result of brute luck about their social position or place in the "natural lottery."[1]

In the rest of this chapter, I will take this particular conception of liberal egalitarianism, sometimes known as the "equality-of-resources" view of liberal equality, as my starting point. However, I should emphasize that "liberal egalitarianism" names a family of theories, not all of which would share this rather demanding conception of distributive justice. There is enormous political and theoretical space between the libertarian commitment to a minimal state that rejects any obligation to rectify undeserved inequalities and the demanding form of liberal egalitarianism that requires rectifying all involuntary disadvantages. Indeed, the vast majority of liberal theorists and practitioners fall somewhere in between these two poles. And many of these in-between liberals can plausibly be categorized as liberal egalitarians. They are egalitarian both in the sense of accepting an important role for the state in redistributing resources to ensure some measure of equality of opportunity, even if not equality of resources, and in the deeper sense that they appeal to the basic moral equality of persons. William Galston, Michael Walzer, and Mickey Kaus are all recent examples of liberals who appeal to a robust notion of the equal moral status of human beings, and who insist that the state must treat its citizens as equals, but who deny that this requires equality of resources.[2]

A comprehensive survey of liberal egalitarianism would need to examine these and other "in-between" liberal theorists. However, I will focus my attention in this chapter on the equality-of-resources version of liberal egalitarianism, for three reasons. First, it is the view I find most compelling, and with which I am most familiar. Second, much of the important work on theories of justice in the last twenty years has been within this equality-of-resources framework. I am thinking here of the work of Ronald Dworkin, Richard Arneson, Amartya Sen, G. A. Cohen, Eric Rakowski, John Roemer, and others.[3] While this form of liberal egalitarianism remains relatively weak in real-world politics, it has quickly become a dominant trend within contemporary liberal political philosophy. Third, and most importantly, this left-liberal conception of equality of resources provides the sharpest possible contrast to the right-wing libertarian view, and hence helps stake out the boundaries of the liberal tradition. As I hope to show throughout this chapter, the left-liberal commitment to a strong form of distributive justice not only requires that the *state* play a more active role in securing justice than libertarians would allow, but it also requires *civil society* to play a more active role. This means that left-liberal egalitarians, more so than other "in-between" liberals, will require a systematically different conception of civil society than that offered by libertarians.

For the rest of the chapter, therefore, when I talk about liberal egalitarians, I will be referring to the equality-of-resources version of liberal egalitarianism, as reflected in the work of Dworkin, Sen, Cohen, Roemer, and others. It is rooted, as I noted earlier, in a commitment to individual freedom and social justice. This twin commitment has important implications for how we conceive of the relationship between civil society and government. On first glance, it might seem that the distinction between state and civil society maps onto the two parts of the liberal-egalitarian ideal: social justice is secured by the state, through such things as public health care, public education, redistributive taxation, and other aspects of the welfare state; individual freedom is secured in civil society, through participation in voluntary market transactions and voluntary associations. The state ensures that everyone has a fair share of rights and resources; individuals then deploy their rights and resources in civil society.

There is some truth in this simple picture of social justice in the public institutions of the state and of individual freedom in the private associations of civil society. But as always, reality is more complicated. In particular, what this picture leaves out is the crucial role of citizenship and civic responsibilities in a liberal-egalitarian theory.

Some people would argue that the exercise of citizenship is itself an important arena of individual freedom: that we achieve freedom not only in civic associations, but also through political participation. This is typically a republican conception, rather than a liberal one, but it is not entirely foreign to the liberal tradition.[4]

My main concern, however, is with the role of citizenship in ensuring social justice. Minimally, a liberal-democratic state can secure justice only if citizens vote for political parties that will pursue just policies. So it is not only the state that must be concerned with social justice; individual citizens must also share this concern, at least in their voting behavior. But the concern with social justice must go beyond voting: it must also regulate some of our behavior in civil society. A just society requires citizens not only to support and obey just laws, but also to exercise judgment and civility in their personal choices and associational life.

I will argue that once we recognize the importance of citizenship in securing social justice, we require a more complex and nuanced view of the relationship between civil society and government. After a brief terminological section, I will begin by considering what citizenship means in modern democratic societies, and what sorts of capacities and dispositions it requires. I hope to show that liberal-democratic citizenship is more complicated than is often realized, and that even "minimal" conceptions of citizenship impose significant obligations and constraints on individual and group behavior. I will then discuss how civil society relates to citizenship, so conceived.

BOUNDARIES

There are endless debates about how to define civil society, and how to distinguish it from other aspects or spheres of society. People argue about whether the economy, for example, should be included in civil society, or the family. For the purposes of this chapter, we can distinguish four broad categories:

#1. The State, which can further be broken down into
    (a) the system of representative democracy, including the electoral system, the legislative process, and political parties;
    (b) state administration, including courts, schools, welfare agencies, the army and police, and the like.
#2. Associational Life, which can further be broken down into

(a) public interest groups participating in democratic debate and public discourse, including NGOs (nongovernmental organizations) and social movements, in which citizens attempt to address each other on issues of public concern and to change public opinion;

(b) private associations (artistic groups, recreational groups, many religious groups) in which people associate with other like-minded people to pursue particular conceptions of the good.

#3. The Economy

#4. The Family

Needless to say, these are crude distinctions, with many gray or overlapping areas. The distinction between #2a and #2b in particular is blurry. Many churches, for example, engage in public debate, and have specific associations or committees devoted to this purpose, while they also contain other associations or committees that are devoted solely to helping church members or to developing their way of life. (They may also branch out into commercial activities, and so partly fall under #3 as well). There are many similar cases of overlap.[5] But I think that most people have some intuitive sense of these distinctive aspects of life.

Which of these qualify as "civil society"? In one sense, this question is unimportant. The important question, from a liberal-egalitarian perspective, is what role each plays in securing or threatening values of social justice and individual freedom. Whether or not we call something part of civil society should not affect our evaluation of its impact on liberal-egalitarian values.

However, for the purposes of this chapter, we need at least a working definition of civil society. Most people would agree that civil society excludes #1, but beyond that there is little agreement, and these disagreements often reflect underlying theoretical differences. For example, some people wish to connect the notion of civil society with an underlying theory of the "public sphere." Such people are likely to focus on #2a (and perhaps the outer edges of #1b), since these define the "public space" in which citizens can participate in public debate and the formation of a public interest. Indeed, according to the Habermasian tradition, the very notions of "a public" and "public opinion," needed for democratic legitimation, depend on the existence of participation in such public associations. For theorists who are concerned above all with discovering the conditions of a deliberative democracy, there is a tendency to define civil society in terms of its functioning as a public sphere, and to ignore or dismiss associations that are merely private in orientation.[6]

Others have the opposite inclination to define civil society in terms of an underlying notion of the "private sphere." Such people are likely to define civil society in terms of #2b (and perhaps #3 and #4 as well), since these define the spaces where we associate for private and personal purposes. These are "private" spaces in the sense that they are neither part of nor addressed to the state.

There are diverse motives for defining civil society in terms of a broader notion of the "private sphere." Libertarians, for example, emphasize the possibility and desirability of self-organizing spheres that are genuinely independent of the state. The market is often viewed as the most important such sphere for libertarians, but they wish to embed their theory of a self-organizing market inside a larger theory of a self-organizing society. Libertarians are inclined to define civil society in terms of private associations, and to ignore or be skeptical about associations involved in political advocacy.[7]

So there is a common tendency to define the boundaries of civil society in terms of some prior and underlying idea of a public sphere or a private sphere. However, such theory-laden definitions leave out important parts of our everyday notion of civil society, which surely includes both public interest organizations and private associations. Moreover, as we shall see, both public and private associations play an important role in achieving liberal egalitarian values, and so it is important to examine how both relate to the state.

In this paper, therefore, I will use the term *civil society* to include associational life in both its public (#2a) and private (#2b) forms. I hope that this definition is more in line with our commonsense views about civil society than those definitions which focus exclusively on either public or private associations. I will also include the economy (#3) in my discussion. What all of these have in common—and what distinguishes them from both the state and the family—is that they involve a large degree of voluntary interaction with people who are not intimates, and who may indeed be anonymous strangers. This is unlike the state (where the treatment of strangers is codified in legal rules) and unlike the family (where we interact with intimates, rather than strangers).[8] I emphasize the fact of freedom of interaction with nonintimates because I believe that how individuals choose to exercise this freedom has a profound effect on the ability of a society to achieve goals of social justice. From a liberal-egalitarian point of view, therefore, a central challenge of civil society is to ensure that people exercise their freedom of association in a way that promotes, or at least does not inhibit, the achievement of social justice.

To explain this challenge, however, we need to flesh out the relationship between liberal-egalitarian justice and citizenship. As I will try to show in the next section, the demanding conception of distributive justice endorsed by liberal egalitarians entails a demanding conception of the duties and virtues of citizenship, and this in turn has implications for the function and regulation of civil society. To understand the special role that civil society plays in a liberal-egalitarian theory, we must first consider the role that citizenship plays.[9]

CITIZENSHIP

Until recently, most liberal-egalitarian theorists have focused almost exclusively on the responsibilities of public institutions. In particular, they have tried to define a set of rights and fair shares that should be guaranteed by the state to all citizens, and to identify the public institutions that can secure these claims of justice. According to Rawls, justice is the "first virtue" of public institutions,[10] and the first task of liberal egalitarians was to determine what these just institutions would look like. They have paid much less attention to the responsibilities of citizens.

But it is increasingly clear that the justice of a modern democracy depends not only on its "basic structure,"[11] but also on the qualities and attitudes of its citizens: for example, their sense of identity and the way they view potentially competing forms of national, regional, ethnic, or religious identities; their ability to tolerate and work together with others who are different from themselves; their desire to participate in the political process in order to promote the public good and hold political authorities accountable; their willingness to show self-restraint and exercise personal responsibility in their economic demands and in personal choices that affect their health and the environment. Without citizens who possess these qualities, democracies become difficult to govern, even unstable.[12]

This was not obvious to many classical liberals, who believed that a liberal democracy could function effectively even in the absence of an especially virtuous citizenry, by the creation of checks and balances. Institutional and procedural devices such as the separation of powers, a bicameral legislature, and federalism would all serve to block would-be oppressors. Even if each person pursued her own self-interest, without regard for justice, one set of private interests would check another set of private interests. Kant, for example, thought that the problem of good government "can be solved even for a race of devils."[13] However, it has become clear that procedural-institutional mechanisms to balance self-interest are not enough, and that some level of civic virtue and public-spiritedness is required if justice is to be achieved and maintained.

Consider the many ways that public policy relies on responsible personal lifestyle decisions: the state will be unable to provide adequate health care if citizens do not act responsibly with respect to their own health, in terms of maintaining a healthy diet, exercising regularly, and limiting their consumption of liquor and tobacco; the state will be unable to meet the needs of children, the elderly, or the disabled if citizens do not agree to share this responsibility by providing some care for their relatives; the state cannot protect the environment if citizens are unwilling to reduce, reuse, and recycle in their own consumer choices; the ability of the government to regulate the economy can be undermined if citizens borrow immoderate amounts or demand excessive increases in salary; attempts to create a fairer society will flounder if citizens are chronically intolerant of difference and generally lacking in a sense of justice. Without cooperation and self-restraint in these areas, "the ability of liberal societies to function successfully progressively diminishes."[14]

In short, we need "a fuller, richer and yet more subtle understanding and practice of citizenship," because "what the state needs from the citizenry cannot be secured by coercion, but only cooperation and self-restraint in the exercise of private power."[15] Yet there is growing fear that the civility and public-spiritedness of citizens of liberal democracies may be in serious decline.[16]

Certain virtues are needed in virtually any political order, whether it is liberal and democratic or not. These would include general virtues, such as courage and law-abidingness, as well as economic virtues, such as the capacity to delay self-gratification or to adapt to economic and technological change.[17] But there are also certain virtues that are distinctive to a liberal democracy, and it is these I wish to focus on.

One such distinctive virtue is public-spiritedness, including the ability to evaluate the performance of those in office and the willingness to engage in public discourse about matters of public policy. These are perhaps the most distinctive aspects of citizenship in a liberal democracy, since they are precisely what distinguish "citizens" within a democracy from the "subjects" of an authoritarian regime.

The need to question authority arises in part from the fact that citizens in a representative democracy elect representatives who govern in their name. Hence an important responsibility of citizens is to monitor those officials and judge their conduct. The need to engage in public discourse arises from the fact that the decisions of government in a democracy should be made publicly, through free and open discussion. But the virtue of public discourse is not just the willingness to participate in politics or to make one's views known. Rather, as William Galston notes, it "includes the willingness to listen seriously to a range of views which, given the diversity of liberal societies, will include ideas the listener is bound to find strange and even obnoxious. The virtue of political discourse also includes the willingness to set forth one's own views intelligibly and candidly as the basis for a politics of persuasion rather than manipulation or coercion."[18]

Stephen Macedo calls this the virtue of "public reasonableness." Liberal citizens must give reasons for their political demands, not just state preferences or make threats. Moreover, these reasons must be "public" reasons, in the sense that they are capable of persuading people of different faiths and nationalities. Hence it is not enough to invoke Scripture or tradition.[19] Liberal citizens must justify their political demands in terms that fellow citizens can understand and accept as consistent with their status as free and equal citizens. It requires a conscientious effort to distinguish those beliefs that are matters of private faith from those that are capable of public defense, and to see how issues look from the point of view of those with differing religious commitments and cultural backgrounds. This is a stringent requirement that many religious groups find difficult to accept.

The virtue of public reasonableness is less relevant for citizens who do not wish to participate in political affairs, and there will always be a portion of the population who have little or no desire to be politically active. Some people will find their greatest joys and projects in other areas of life, including the family, or the arts, or religion. A liberal democracy must respect such diverse conceptions of the good life, and should not compel people to adopt a conception of the good life that privileges political participation as the source of meaning or satisfaction.[20] For these more or less apolitical people, the virtue of public reasonableness may be less important.

Some commentators would argue that most people in contemporary democracies will fall into this apolitical camp—that meaningful political participation is almost inevitably confined to elites. According to T. H. McLaughlin, this is one of the important points of division between "minimal" and "maximal" conceptions of citizenship. On the minimal view, citizenship for most people primarily involves passive respect for laws, not the active exercise of political rights. By contrast, maximal conceptions of democracy insist that a true democracy, or that political justice, must aim for more widespread participation.[21]

Justice clearly requires that all have the opportunity to become active citizens, if they so choose, which means eliminating any economic or social barriers to the participation of disadvantaged groups, such as women, the poor, racial and ethnic minorities, and the like. But whether we should encourage all individuals to choose to be active political participants is another matter. Whether active citizenship should be encouraged depends, in part, on the level of injustice in society.[22] To have a sense of justice does not simply mean that we do not actively harm or exploit others. It also involves the duty to prevent injustice by creating and upholding just institutions. So if there is a serious injustice in our society that can be rectified only by political action, then citizens should recognize an obligation to protest against that injustice. Or if our political institutions are no longer functioning, perhaps due to excessive levels of apathy or to the abuse of power, then citizens have an obligation to protect these institutions from being undermined. They should not sit passively by while injustices are committed or democratic institutions collapse, in the hope that others will step in. Everyone should do her fair share to create and uphold just institutions.[23]

The extent of injustice and the health of political institutions will vary from society to society. In some times and places, though perhaps only in rare and fortunate circumstances, our natural duty of justice will not require us to participate actively. Where a society is basically well ordered and its institutions healthy, individuals should be free to follow their own conceptions of the good, even if these give little or no weight to political participation.

So there will be times and places where minimal citizenship is all we can or should require. And for minimal citizens, the stringent demands of "public reasonableness" will be less significant. But even here, the requirements of liberal citizenship are by no means trivial. The obligations of minimal citizenship are often described in purely negative terms—that is, the obligation not to break the law and not to harm others or restrict their rights and liberties. Minimal citizenship, in short, is often seen as simply requiring noninterference with others.

But that ignores one of the most basic requirements of liberal citizenship: the virtue of "civility" or "decency." This is a virtue that even the most minimal citizen must learn, since it applies not only to political activity, but also—indeed, primarily—to our actions in everyday life, on the street, in neighborhood shops, and in the diverse institutions and forums of civil society.

Civility refers to the way we treat nonintimates with whom we come into face-to-face contact. To understand civility, it is helpful to compare it with the related requirement of nondiscrimination. The legal prohibition on discrimination initially applied only to government actions. Government laws and policies that discriminate against people on the basis of race or gender have gradually been struck down in Western democracies, since they violate the basic liberal commitment to equality of opportunity. But it has become clear that whether individuals have genuinely equal opportunity depends not only on government actions, but also on the actions of institutions within civil society—corporations, schools, stores, landlords, and so forth. If people are repeatedly discriminated against by prejudiced shop owners or real estate agents, they will be denied equal citizenship, even if the state itself does not discriminate. Hence legal requirements of nondiscrimination have increasingly been applied to "private" firms and associations.

This extension of nondiscrimination from government to civil society has been resisted by many libertarians. They deny that the state has the right or responsibility to restrict people's property rights in order to promote equal opportunity.[24] It is also resisted by those who see society as simply a modus vivendi among diverse social and cultural groups, each of whom should be free to discriminate as it pleases.[25]

But for liberal egalitarians, the state has an obligation to remove injustice, not only in its own actions, but throughout the "basic structure" of society, wherever it has a "profound and pervasive" effect on people's life chances.[26] And there is no question that discrimination by employers, merchants, and landlords can have a profound effect on people's opportunities. Antidiscrimination laws, therefore, are a necessary precondition for achieving the sort of distributive justice that liberal egalitarians endorse.

This extension of nondiscrimination to civil society is not just a shift in the scale of liberal norms; it also involves a radical extension in the obligations of liberal citizenship, for the obligation to treat people as equal citizens now applies to the most common, everyday decisions of individuals. It is no longer permissible for businesses to refuse to hire black employees, or to refuse to serve black customers, or to segregate their black employees or customers. But not just that; the norms of nondiscrimination entail that it is impermissible for businesses to ignore their black customers or treat them rudely, although it is not always possible to legally enforce this. Businesses must in effect make blacks feel welcome, just as if they were whites. Blacks must, in short, be treated with *civility*. The same applies to the way citizens treat each other in schools or recreational associations, even in private clubs.

For liberal egalitarians, this sort of civility is the logical extension of nondiscrimination, but it now extends into the very hearts and minds of citizens. Liberal citizens must learn to interact in everyday settings on an equal basis with people for whom they might harbor prejudice.

The extent to which this requirement of civility can (or should) be legally enforced is limited. It is easier to compel businesses to be nondiscriminatory in hiring than to compel them to treat black customers with civility. But the recent spread of laws and regulations against sexual and racial harassment, both in society generally and within schools and businesses, can be seen as an attempt to ensure a level of civility, since they include forms of offensive speech as well as physical intimidation, And while it is obviously impossible to compel civility between citizens in less formal settings—for example, whether whites smile or scowl at an Asian family in the neighborhood park—liberal-egalitarian citizenship nonetheless requires this sort of civility.

It is easy to trivialize this requirement of civility as being simply "good manners." Philip Rieff, for example, dismisses the insistence on civility as a superficial facade that simply hides a deeper indifference to the needs of others. As he puts it, "We have long known what 'equality' means in

American culture: it means . . . a smile fixed to the face, demanding you return a smile."[27] John Murray Cuddihy views civility as the imposition of a Protestant (and bourgeois) sense of "good taste" on other religious groups. He argues that Catholics and Jews (and now Muslims) have had to abandon their conception of true faith, which required the public expression of contempt for other religions, to conform to this "religion of civility."

It is true that liberal societies have reinforced, and thereby partially conflated, the moral obligation of civility with an aesthetic conception of "good manners." For example, the expectation of civility is sometimes used to discourage the sort of forceful protest that may be needed for an oppressed group to be heard. For a disadvantaged group to "make a scene" is often seen as "in bad taste." This sort of exaggerated emphasis on good manners can be used to promote servility. Appropriate civility does not mean smiling at others no matter how badly they treat you, as if oppressed groups should be nice to their oppressors. Rather, it means treating others as equals on the condition that they extend the same recognition to you.[28] While there is some overlap between civility and a more general politeness, they are nonetheless distinct—civility involves upholding norms of equality within the public life of a society, including civil society, and thereby upholding essential liberal values.[29]

Liberal egalitarianism, therefore, entails a robust conception of citizenship, one that involves a significant range of civic virtues. It requires that a substantial number of citizens be willing to participate politically, and that they do so in a publicly reasonable way. It also requires that all citizens, even the apathetic ones, exhibit a minimal level of decency and civility in their everyday behavior.

To be sure, this is not as robust a notion of citizenship as the republican one, which views citizenship as our highest or most valuable identity. On a liberal-egalitarian view, as we have seen, political participation (and civility) are not defended as goods in themselves, but as preconditions for the creation and maintenance of a just society. Nonetheless, the liberal-egalitarian conception of citizenship can be a demanding one. Moreover, its demands can often conflict not only with people's natural inclinations and prejudices, but also with their deep-seated convictions and cultural traditions. There is nothing natural about the requirements of public reason or about the duty to act civilly toward people one views as immoral or damned.

WHAT THE STATE NEEDS FROM CIVIL SOCIETY

It is important, therefore, to ask where liberal citizens learn these virtues. Where do individuals acquire both the capacity for citizenship and the motivation to act in a just and civil manner? So far as I can tell, there is no well-established answer to this question in the liberal-egalitarian tradition. It is only recently that liberal egalitarians have broadened their focus from institutions to citizenship, and much work remains to be done in fleshing out a liberal-egalitarian theory of citizenship. In particular, most of the work to date has focused on identifying the sorts of capacities and dispositions required for liberal citizenship, and less attention has been paid to the further question of how these capacities and dispositions are developed.

However, this question has been more thoroughly addressed by other theoretical traditions, and liberal egalitarians can draw upon their answers. If we examine other traditions, we can find theorists arguing that each of the four spheres I listed in the "Boundaries" section is the key "seedbed of virtue." To oversimplify, we can say that libertarians tend to look to the market, communitarians look to (nonprofit) public and private associations, some schools of feminism look to the family, and republicans look to the democratic process itself. To my mind, liberal egalitarians can learn something from all of these answers, without relying exclusively or uncritically on any one of them.

Let me briefly consider the role that each of these can play as schools of citizenship, starting with the market. Theorists of the "New Right" often praise the market as a school of virtue. Many Thatcher/Reagan reforms of the 1980s aimed to extend the scope of markets in people's lives—through freer trade, deregulation, tax cuts, the weakening of trade unions, and the reduction of welfare benefits—in part in order to teach people the virtues of initiative and self-reliance. Moreover, markets are said to encourage civility since companies that refuse to hire black employees, for example, or to serve black customers will be at a competitive disadvantage.

However, from a liberal-egalitarian point of view, the limits of the market as a school of civic virtue are clear. Many market deregulations have arguably made possible an era of unprecedented greed and economic irresponsibility, as evidenced by the savings-and-loan and junk bond scandals in the United States. Markets teach initiative, but not a sense of justice or social responsibility.[30] And so long as a sizable portion of the population harbors prejudices toward certain groups, then some businesses will have an economic incentive to serve that market, by creating goods and services that exclude these groups. In any event, it is difficult to see how the market can teach those civic virtues specific to political participation and dialogue—for example, the virtue of public reasonableness.

Some republican theorists argue that political participation itself will teach people responsibility and toleration. As Adrian Oldfield notes, these theorists place their faith in the activity of participation "as the means whereby individuals may become accustomed to perform the duties of citizenship. Political participation enlarges the minds of individuals, familiarizes them with interests which lie beyond the immediacy of personal circumstance and environment, and encourages them to acknowledge that public concerns are the proper ones to which they should pay attention."[31]

Here again, liberal egalitarians will see this faith in the educative function of political participation as overly optimistic. Political participation is important, but we must also ensure that citizens participate responsibly—that is, in a public-spirited, rather than self-interested or prejudiced, way.[32] Empowered citizens may use their power irresponsibly by pushing for benefits and entitlements they cannot ultimately afford; or by voting themselves tax breaks and slashing assistance to the needy; or by "seeking scapegoats in the indolence of the poor, the strangeness of ethnic minorities, or the insolence and irresponsibility of modern women."[33] It is true that successful political participation requires the ability to create coalitions, which encourages a partial development of the virtues of justice and public reasonableness. No one can hope to succeed in political life if she makes no effort to listen to or accommodate the needs and views of others. But in many cases, a winning coalition can be built that ignores the claims of marginalized groups. Indeed, if a significant portion of the population is prejudiced, then ignoring or attacking such groups may be the best route to political success.

Feminist theorists of "maternal citizenship" focus on the family, and mothering in particular, as the school of responsibility and virtue. According to Jean Elshtain and Sara Ruddick, mothering teaches women about the responsibility to conserve life and protect the vulnerable. For example, mothering involves a "metaphysical attitude" of "holding," which gives priority to the protection of existing relationships over the acquisition of new benefits.[34] If women had a more central role in political decision making, the virtues learned from mothering would have a significant impact on decisions about war, for example, or the environment.

However, from a liberal-egalitarian point of view, it is doubtful that mothering would promote all of the attributes or virtues of citizenship. Would maternal attitudes such as "holding" promote democratic values such as "active citizenship, self-government, egalitarianism, and the exercise of freedom"?[35] As Mary Dietz puts it, "An enlightened despotism, a welfare-state, a single-party bureaucracy and a democratic republic may all respect mothers, protect children's lives and show compassion for the vulnerable."[36] Indeed, Susan Okin argues that the family is often "a school of despotism" that teaches male dominance over women, and that liberal-egalitarian citizenship requires unlearning the lessons of the family.[37]

This leaves us with the public and private associations of civil society. Many communitarians emphasize the necessity of civility and self-restraint to a healthy democracy, but deny that either the market or political participation is sufficient to teach these virtues. Instead, it is in the voluntary organizations of civil society—churches, unions, ethnic associations, cooperatives, environmental groups, neighborhood associations, support groups, charities—that we learn the virtues of mutual obligation. As Walzer puts it, "The civility that makes democratic politics possible can only be learned in the associational networks" of civil society.[38]

Because these groups are voluntary, failure to live up to the responsibilities that come with them is usually met simply with disapproval, rather than legal punishment. Yet because the disapproval comes from friends, colleagues, or comrades, it is in many ways a more powerful incentive to act responsibly than is punishment by an impersonal state. It is in the associations of civil society that "human character, competence, and capacity for citizenship are formed," for it is here that we internalize the idea of personal responsibility and mutual obligation, and learn the voluntary self-restraint that is essential to truly responsible citizenship.[39] It follows, therefore, that one of the first obligations of citizenship is to participate in civil society. As Walzer notes, "Join the association of your choice" is "not a slogan to rally political militants, and yet that is what civil society requires."[40]

The communitarian claim that the associations of civil society are the "seedbed of civic virtue"[41] is essentially an empirical claim, for which there is little hard evidence one way or the other.[42] But here again, liberal egalitarians are likely to be skeptical. It may be in the neighborhood that we learn to be good neighbors, but neighborhood associations also teach people to operate on the NIMBY (not in my backyard) principle when it comes to the location of group homes or public works. Similarly, ethnic groups often teach prejudice against other races, and churches often teach deference to authority and intolerance of other faiths. Indeed, it would be quite unreasonable to expect churches to teach the virtue of public reasonableness. Public reasonableness is essential in political debate, but is unnecessary and sometimes undesirable in the private sphere. It would be absurd to ask churchgoers to abstain from appealing to Scripture in deciding how to run their church.

From a liberal-egalitarian point of view, then, we cannot rely exclusively on the market, the family, or the associations of civil society to teach civic virtue. All of these can play a useful role in forming democratic citizens, but all have serious limitations in this regard. In particular, people will not automatically learn to engage in public discourse or to question authority, in any of these spheres, since these spheres are often held together by private discourse and respect for authority.

So liberal egalitarians are unlikely to be satisfied with existing answers to the question of teaching citizenship. What then is the alternative? As I said earlier, there is no clear answer to this question in the liberal-egalitarian tradition, at least at the theoretical level. But in practice, we can perhaps discern a distinctively liberal-egalitarian answer. Liberal egalitarians, in practice, have often assumed that the appropriate "school of citizenship" is precisely schools: that is, the system of public education. Schools must teach children how to engage in the kind of critical reasoning and moral perspective that defines public reasonableness. Indeed, the promotion of these sorts of virtues was one of the fundamental justifications for making education mandatory within Western democracies.

This answer is not without its own problems, to which I will return below. But most liberal egalitarians, I think, would say that some form of common education is needed to supplement, and perhaps to correct, the lessons learned in the market, family, and civil society. None of these spheres can teach all of the needed virtues, and may indeed inculcate vices rather than virtues, and the system of public schools provides a kind of insurance policy against the gaps and failings of other social spheres.

Of course, schools do not exist in isolation from the rest of society, and it is a mistake to suppose that all the social ills can be resolved through more or better public education. (This may indeed be a mistake to which liberal egalitarians have historically been prone, but I think there is greater awareness now of the limitations of public education.) Lessons learned in school will not have much impact or resonance if they do not connect with the lessons learned in the market, family, and civil society. Ideally, there would be a certain congruence between these spheres. But whether or how we can make sure that these lessons coincide, to at least some degree, is obviously a difficult and unresolved question, both in theory and practice. I will return to this question in the "Liabilities" section below.

What Civil Society Needs from the State

So far, I have been examining the question of what the state needs from civil society. But we can also turn the question around, and ask what civil society needs from the state. Here the answer, from a liberal-egalitarian perspective, is perhaps clearer. In the first instance, the state must provide a legal framework that enables people to associate. By this I mean not just freedom of speech and assembly, although these are essential, but also the right of groups to officially incorporate themselves, own or rent property, collect income, and pay taxes, and so on. This may seem trivial, but the significance of this has become very clear in Eastern/Central Europe, where NGOs have been effectively crippled in many countries because of the lack of a legal framework that would allow them to incorporate.

This sort of a legal framework makes associational life possible in principle, but liberal egalitarians will also want to make sure that all citizens have an equal opportunity to participate in civil society. That is, they will want to make sure that no one is de facto excluded from associational life as a result of poverty, ignorance, discrimination, or harassment. Of course, this is already implicit in the more general liberal-egalitarian commitment to remedying involuntary disadvantages, but liberal egalitarians will be particularly concerned to rectify those disadvantages that create de facto exclusion from civil society. According to Walzer, this is the most damaging form of inequality.[43]

In short, just as the state needs civil society to help form responsible citizens, so too civil society needs the state to provide a stable legal framework of association and a fair distribution of the resources citizens need to participate in associational life. Under ideal circumstances, we can hope for a mutually reinforcing interaction between state and civil society: a thriving civil society produces the citizens who support the policies that support a thriving civil society.

LIABILITIES

Unfortunately, in reality, the interaction between civil society and the state is more conflictual. As we have seen, the state cannot safely rely on the associations of civil society to serve as a seedbed of virtue. As a result, there may be a temptation on the part of the state to intervene in associations to make them more reliable schools of citizenship. As Nancy Rosenblum puts it in her chapter of this volume, there may be a temptation to reconstruct associations from "gentle seedbeds of virtue" into "bootcamps of citizenship."[44] Rosenblum is discussing a trend among feminist theorists, but we can see the same dynamic among some liberal-egalitarian theorists.[45]

For example, Walzer recognizes that in actually existing civil societies, many associations do not teach the virtues of democratic citizenship. As he puts it, people are "trapped in one or another subordinate relationship, where the 'civility' they learned was deferential rather than independent and active." In these circumstances, he says, we have to "reconstruct" the associational network "under new conditions of freedom and equality." Similarly, when the activities of some associations "are narrowly conceived, partial and particularist," then "they need political correction." Walzer calls his view "critical associationalism" to signify that the associations of civil society may need to be reformed in the light of principles of citizenship.[46]

If the government were to adopt this aim too enthusiastically, it would become a threat to civil society. It would be a mistake, and a misuse of power, for governments to try to reconstruct churches, for example, to make them more internally democratic or to make sure that their members learn to be critical rather than deferential. (In any event, reconstructing churches to make them more internally democratic might start to undermine their essentially uncoerced and voluntary character, which is what supposedly made them the seedbeds of civic virtue.)

It asks too much of voluntary associations to expect or require that they become the main school for, or a small-scale replica of, democratic citizenship. While these associations may indirectly teach civic virtue, that is not their raison d'être. The reason why people join churches or ethnic organizations is not to learn civic virtue. It is rather to honor certain values and enjoy certain human goods, and these motives may have little to do with the promotion of citizenship. To expect priests to organize the internal life of their groups so as to maximally promote citizenship is to ignore why these groups exist in the first place. (Some associations, like the Boy Scouts, are designed to promote citizenship, but they are the exception, not the rule.)

However, this is not to say that liberal egalitarians can be indifferent to the internal life of associations. Just as the state can be a threat to civil society, so too associations can be a threat to a liberal state. It is one thing if associations fail to teach civic virtues, but quite another if they actively undermine a sense of justice, and yet another if they themselves are profoundly unjust.

Consider the former rule of the Jaycees excluding women from becoming members of the group.[47] In such a case, liberal egalitarians will likely have two distinct worries. The first is that the practice of discrimination within a particular association will not only fail to develop a sense of justice, but will in fact erode it, so that people who learn to discriminate in these private contexts will also be more likely to discriminate in other, more public contexts. If businessmen in the Jaycees feel uncomfortable sitting beside women in their club, will they feel comfortable working beside women in the office?

It is asking too much to expect that joining the Jaycees makes people better citizens than they otherwise would be—that is, to expect the Jaycees to be a positive seedbed of virtue. But it is a worry if membership in the Jaycees has a clear tendency to make people worse citizens than they otherwise would be—for example, more likely to discriminate in the workplace against women.

The second worry is that the discriminatory practice may itself be a serious injustice. The Jaycees' refusal to admit or accept women into their group may deny them an important opportunity. In some towns, membership in the Jaycees is vital to economic or political advancement.

Under these conditions, liberal egalitarians are likely to want to do something to "reconstruct" associations, not to make them a better school of virtue, but rather to uphold the principle of equal citizenship and fair equality of opportunity.[48] As I noted earlier, genuine equality of opportunity requires not only freedom from discrimination by the state, but also freedom from discrimination by employers, landlords, stores, and the like. The principle that nondiscrimination should be imposed on certain economic associations is now well established (although some libertarians still dispute it). But the extent to which nondiscrimination should be imposed on noneconomic associations, like the Jaycees, remains very controversial.

The Jaycees is just one of many such cases. Consider Catholic Church rules excluding women from being priests; Boy Scout rules prohibiting gays from being troop leaders; restrictive covenants prohibiting the sale of property to blacks; rules prohibiting gay groups from participating in Saint Patrick's Day parades; New Orleans Mardi Gras club rules excluding blacks; and so on.

WHERE these sorts of discriminatory practices are widespread in civil society, liberal equality is very difficult to achieve. An individual case may seem insignificant, yet the larger web of exclusions may be profoundly damaging, particularly when they exclude groups that have historically been seen as second-class citizens, and have been denied their civil and political rights. Under these circumstances, exclusion from associations in civil society can reinforce the stigmatized status of disadvantaged groups.

Liberal egalitarians will disagree among themselves about how to respond to these cases. Few will want to intervene to force all associations to be "liberal all the way down",[49] but they disagree about how far down liberal equality should go, and what the state should do to encourage or require such reforms. Responses range from moral criticism (for example, the government can publicly chastise golf clubs that exclude blacks) to withdrawal of financial subsidies (for example, the government can say that universities or churches which discriminate against women or blacks will not receive public funding or will lose their tax-exempt status, or both); to outright legal intervention to stop the discriminatory practice (for example, the government might take the Jaycees to court to force them to accept women members).

These cases help expose some of the competing principles and conflicting pressures within liberal egalitarianism. On the one hand, its commitment to a strongly egalitarian conception of distributive justice requires attending to people's opportunities within civil society, and also requires attending to the conditions that nurture a sense of justice in citizens. These considerations seem to push liberal egalitarians in the direction of what Rosenblum calls the "logic of congruence": the view that associations ideally should mirror liberal-democratic values of freedom and equality "all the way down," so as to eliminate inequalities within civil society and to inculcate a sense of justice.

On the other hand, liberal egalitarianism's commitment to individual freedom puts great weight on freedom of association as a central vehicle by which people pursue their conceptions of the good life. Attempts to impose a logic of congruence would undermine the liberal character of liberal egalitarianism. Moreover, the question of when discriminatory practices within a private association genuinely affect people's opportunities is difficult to gauge. In some small towns, membership in the Jaycees may be a virtual prerequisite for economic success, but in most large towns it probably has no significant effect.

It is even more difficult to gauge how participating in these discriminatory practices affects people's underlying dispositions towards justice and tolerance. There is little reliable evidence about whether, or under what conditions, the desire to discriminate in private associations leads to discrimination in other settings.[50] Indeed, as Rosenblum notes, from the point of view of learning good citizenship, a person may be better off participating in an association than being solitary and alienated. Alienated loners may be more prone to hate and discrimination than are people who feel a sense of belonging and respect as members of exclusionary groups. For some people, the alternative to participation in illiberal associations is not participation in flourishing liberal associations, but rather anomie, criminality, or drug addiction. Relatedly, membership in illiberal groups may strengthen some citizenship virtues, such as hard work, care for one's health, and economic self-sufficiency, even if it does little to promote public reasonableness or civility. The virtues of citizenship are diverse, and it may be that diverse kinds of association are needed to promote them. Focusing exclusively on the negative impact of an association with respect to one virtue, such as civility, may blind us to its positive impact on other virtues. Finally, the impact of a particular association on an individual's dispositions will depend on the role it plays within that person's larger pattern of associational life. Membership in an illiberal group is more threatening to liberal virtues if it is a permanent and all-encompassing commitment that excludes membership in other groups, than if it is a temporary or limited membership that coexists with many other shifting identities and memberships. To assess this, we need to look beyond the formal rules or practices of the group to the dynamics of individual membership: how often do individuals join and leave, how many other groups do they belong to, and so on. Viewed in this way, illiberal groups can have a benign, even positive impact on the civic dispositions of the particular individuals who pass through them.[51]

Given these many reasons to be skeptical of the "logic of congruence," liberal egalitarians have not adopted as a general goal the reconstruction of associations along liberal lines. But they will still insist that discrimination in civil society can be a threat, and that the threat is sufficiently great under some conditions to warrant some level of intervention in civil society. Where to draw this line is an unresolved issue for liberal egalitarians. A theory that is unwilling to intervene in acts of private discrimination, even when there is clear evidence that these acts create significant inequality in life chances, might be a liberal theory, but it will not be a liberal-*egalitarian* theory. Conversely, a theory that is willing to intervene in any and all cases of private discrimination, even without evidence of any significant impact on people's life chances, might be an egalitarian theory, but it will not be a *liberal*-egalitarian theory.

GROUPS AND INDIVIDUALS

Liberal egalitarians are open-minded as to whether or when the government should deal directly with individuals or via groups. As always, the underlying principles are respect for individual freedom and social justice, but these can be achieved both by individual- and group-based policies.

Let me look at one example: the case of schooling. I noted earlier that liberal egalitarians are likely to give schools an important role in citizenship education, and have been strong supporters of the public school system, in which each individual child is taught in state-run educational institutions. Indeed, the arguments of the previous section have, if anything, clarified the importance of public schools in inculcating civic virtue. If we cannot expect or require associations in general to be congruent with liberal values—if we must tolerate considerable incongruence between associational norms and liberal principles—then public schools become even more important as the likely site of civic education.

This raises questions about the role of separate schools in a liberal democracy, particularly religious schools. Various religious groups have sought to establish separate schools, partly in order to teach their religious doctrine, but also to reduce the exposure of their children to the members of other religious groups. Most liberal states have accepted this demand, as a way of respecting parental rights and religious freedom, but have insisted that such schools teach a core curriculum, including citizenship education.

Does this compromise position—separate schools with a common core curriculum—provide the appropriate sort of citizenship education? Such schools are obviously capable of teaching basic facts about government. But as I noted earlier, citizenship education is not simply a matter of knowledge of political institutions and constitutional principles. It is also a matter of how we think about and behave toward others, particularly those who differ from us in their race, religion, gender, class, and the like. Liberal citizenship requires cultivating the habit of civility and the capacity for public reasonableness in our interaction with others. Indeed, it is precisely these habits and capacities that most need to be learned in schools, for they are unlikely to be learned in smaller groups or associations, like the family, neighborhood, or church, which tend to be homogenous in their ethnocultural backgrounds and religious beliefs.

Some critics worry that it may be difficult for some separate religious schools to provide an adequate education in either civility or public reasonableness, particularly if their students have a homogenous ethnic and social background, for these virtues are not only, or even primarily, learned through the explicit curriculum. For example, common schools teach civility not just by telling students to be nice, but also by insisting that students sit beside students of different races and religions, and cooperate with them on school projects or sports teams.[52] Similarly, common schools teach public reasonableness not only by telling students that there are a plurality of religious views in the world, but that reasonable people disagree on the merits of these views. They also create the social circumstances whereby students can see the reasonableness of these disagreements. It is not enough to simply tell students that the majority of the people in the world do not share their religion. So long as one is surrounded by people who share one's faith, one may still succumb to the temptation to think that everyone who rejects one's religion is somehow illogical or depraved. To learn public reasonableness, students must come to know and understand people who are reasonable and decent and humane but who do not share their religion. Only in this way can students learn how personal faith differs from public reasonableness, and where to draw that line. This sort of learning requires the presence within a classroom of people with varying ethnocultural and religious backgrounds.[53]

In these ways, religious schools may be limited in their capacity to provide an adequate citizenship education. Of course, it is important not to idealize common schools, which suffer their own deficiencies, or to exaggerate the homogeneity of religious schools. For example, while common schools in North America typically contain a diversity of religions, they are more segregated than religious schools by class, race, and academic talent.[54] Yet divisions of class and race are equally important obstacles to civility and public reasonableness as religious divisions. Indeed, one could argue that the greatest failure of liberal citizenship in the United States is not the division between religious groups, but the increasing desire of middle-class whites to distance themselves (both physically and emotionally) from inner-city blacks, or the poor more generally.

In terms of teaching students how to have a public dialogue with the disadvantaged, religious schools may well do better than a common school in the suburbs full of well-off (but religiously diverse) whites.[55]

Moreover, it is important to distinguish temporary or transitional separate schooling from permanent separation. The requirements of liberal citizenship suggest that common schooling is highly desirable at some point in the educational process. But there is no reason why the entire process should be integrated. Indeed, there are good reasons for thinking that some children may do best by having their early schooling in separate schools, beside others who share their background, before moving into a common school later in the process. For example, this may be true of historically disadvantaged groups who can best develop their self-esteem in an environment free of prejudice.[56] More generally, schooling within a particular ethnocultural or religious setting may provide virtues unavailable within the common schools. If common schools do a better job promoting public reasonableness, separate schools may do better at providing children with a clear sense of what it is to have a stable sense of the good. They may provide a better environment for developing the capacity for in-depth engagement with a particular cultural tradition, and for loyalty and commitment to particular projects and relationships. There is more than one starting point from which children can learn liberal citizenship.[57]

The requirement of common schools—even if limited to the later stages of children's education—will be rejected by some religious groups who insist on keeping their children separate and apart from the rest of society. Should a liberal state impose integrated common schools, in the name of citizenship education? In answering this, it is worth distinguishing two kinds of religious groups that might seek exemption from common schooling. Some groups, like the Amish, voluntarily isolate themselves from the larger society, and avoid participating in either politics or the mainstream institutions of civil society. They do not vote, or hire employees, or attempt to influence public policy (except where a proposed policy would jeopardize their isolation), and seek only to be left alone. Since they do not participate in either politics or civil society, it is less urgent that they learn the virtues of civility and public reasonableness. Jeff Spinner calls the Amish "partial citizens," and he argues that because they have relinquished the right to participate in politics and civil society, they can also be absolved of the responsibilities which accompany that right, including the responsibility to learn and practice civility and public reasonableness.[58] Hence he supports their right to withdraw their children from school at the age of fourteen, before they would have to learn about the larger society or interact with non-Amish children. Assuming that such groups are small and sincerely committed to their self-imposed isolation, they pose no threat to the practice of liberal citizenship in society generally.[59] Such groups should not be encouraged, since they accept no responsibility to work together with other citizens to solve the country's injustices and problems. They are free riders, in a sense, benefiting from a stable liberal order that they do nothing to help maintain.[60] But a liberal state can afford a few such free riders.[61]

By contrast, other religious groups seeking exemption from integrated schools are active participants in both civil society and politics, and seek to influence public policy generally. This would include fundamentalist Christians in the United States or Muslims in Britain. In these cases, one could argue that, having chosen to exercise their rights as full citizens, they must accept the sort of education needed to promote responsible citizenship, including the obligation to attend common schools at some point in the educational process.

Here again, liberal egalitarians will disagree about the appropriate solution. They will disagree about what amount of common schooling is best; and even if they agree about this, they may still disagree about how to achieve it: for example, should a certain amount of common schooling be mandatory, or should there instead be financial incentives or penalties to support common schools and limit parochial schools?[62]

As I said earlier, there is no clear-cut rule for such cases, and liberal egalitarians are (or should be) open-minded about the role of ethnic, religious, or other associations in the provision of public goods and services, like education, health care, or social services.[63]

CONFLICT

The most obvious and familiar way to distinguish liberal egalitarianism from libertarianism is that the former gives a more significant role to the state in the securing of justice. But as I have tried to show, this enhanced role for the state also entails a more robust and demanding conception of the individual citizen. Citizens in a liberal egalitarian society should have a strong sense of justice, a capacity for public reasonableness, and a disposition toward civility. And this in turn entails a more demanding role for civil society: the associations of civil society must help develop such citizens (or at any rate must not inhibit their development), and must themselves abide by certain principles of civility and justice.[64]

In this way, civil society is both more important to, and also more of a threat to, liberal egalitarianism than to libertarianism. And, as we have seen, this creates many potential conflicts between the state and civil society. In particular, associations may fail to inculcate (or they may even actively undermine) civic virtues and a sense of justice; they may also themselves create injustice through discriminatory practices.

I have already suggested in the previous two sections how liberal egalitarians are likely to deal with such conflicts. They will try to determine the impact of the particular association or associational practice on both fair opportunity and individual freedom, and if one or both of these values is seriously harmed, then liberal egalitarians will try to identify the minimally disruptive way to remedy the problem.

If possible, noncoercive means will be used (for example, conducting public education campaigns to promote tolerance and civility; withholding tax breaks or government contracts to groups whose discriminatory practices create significant inequalities). If noncoercive means are inadequate, and if the potential injustice is great, then legal prohibition of the discriminatory practice may be required. But even here, the goal would be to change the practice in a way that leaves intact as much as possible the objectives of the group. For example, the state will regulate a church-owned commercial business to ensure that women are not discriminated against in employment, but will not prevent the same church from refusing to appoint women as priests or from preaching that women should stay in the home. The fact that a particular commercial activity of a church needs to be regulated to protect women's rights is not a reason to regulate all of the church's activities, let alone to regulate its religious doctrine or religious services. The goal is to protect disadvantaged groups from widespread discrimination in employment while preserving as much as possible the freedom of individuals to associate with other like-minded individuals to express and pursue a shared way of life.

The resulting decisions tend to be pragmatic and open-minded or, if you prefer, ad hoc and arbitrary. Any attempt to more rigorously enforce norms of equality and good citizenship within associations would be inconsistent with the liberal commitment to freedom; any attempt to exempt associations entirely from norms of nondiscrimination and liberal citizenship would be inconsistent with the egalitarian commitment to social justice. This is the constant tightrope that liberal egalitarians must walk. Since there is no magic formula for balancing these two commitments, questions about intervention in civil society will remain hotly debated and unresolved issues, even among liberal egalitarians themselves.

This may seem like a rather vague and disappointing conclusion, and one would wish for more concrete guidance about how these conflicts will be resolved. However, we are still at a very early stage in this debate, and it may be premature to expect greater precision in our theories. It is important to remember that until the 1960s, the state itself was still engaged in explicit discrimination against women, homosexuals, racial minorities, and so on. Many liberals hoped and assumed that the end of state-sponsored discrimination would lead to genuine equality of opportunity. It took several years for society to realize that removing state discrimination is insufficient if pervasive discrimination remains in civil society. So it is only in the last two decades that liberal egalitarians have started to systematically think about the role of civil society in ensuring liberal justice.[65]

There is another reason why liberal egalitarians have said so little about these conflicts. They have shared what Rosenblum calls the "liberal expectancy": the hope that the public structures and principles of a liberal democracy will exert a kind of gravitational pull on the associations of civil society. Liberals hope and expect that ethnic, religious, and cultural associations will, over time, voluntarily adjust their practices and beliefs to bring them more in line with the public principles of liberalism, which will reduce the "incongruence" between associational norms and liberal principles.[66] On this optimistic view, state intervention is rarely required to "correct" the practices of associations, since these practices will over time be reinterpreted by the group itself to bring them into greater congruence with liberal norms.

There is considerable evidence for this liberal expectancy. As I noted earlier, it is striking how most religious groups in America have become liberalized and "protestantized," gradually incorporating norms of individual freedom, tolerance, and sexual equality into their own self-understandings. The same is largely true of most immigrant groups: over a generation or two, perhaps even sooner, they abandon any thought of maintaining illiberal practices that continue to thrive in their countries of origin.

As a result, many liberal egalitarians hoped that conflicts between state and civil society would be limited and temporary. However, it is now clear that this was too optimistic. There are some forms of discrimination and incivility in civil society—racism most prominent among them—that seem to resist the liberal expectancy. Even as racial barriers fall within one type of civic association (for example, service clubs), new groups seem to emerge to reinstate these racial barriers (for example, gated communities). The gravitational pull of liberal equality on associations has proven too weak, or at least too slow, to serve as a reliable mechanism for dealing with injustices in civil society.

In short, it is only in the last two decades that liberal egalitarians have realized the full significance of discrimination in civil society for liberal justice, and the limits of the liberal expectancy regarding the voluntary reforms of associations. However, these issues are now at the forefront of liberal egalitarian theorizing, and we can hope that a more systematic approach to civil society will emerge in the near future.[67]

NOTES

1. Classic expositions of this conception of liberal equality are John Rawls, *A Theory of Justice* (London: Oxford University Press, 1971); Ronald Dworkin, "What Is Equality? Part I: Equality of Welfare; Part II: Equality of Resources," *Philosophy and Public Affairs* 10, nos. 3 and 4 (1981): 185–246, 283–345. For a more detailed explication of this conception of liberal egalitarianism, see my *Contemporary Political Philosophy* (Oxford: Oxford University Press, 1990), chap. 2.

2. See William Galston, *Justice and the Human Good* (Chicago: University of Chicago Press, 1980); Michael Walzer, *Spheres of Justice* (Oxford: Blackwell, 1983); Mickey Kaus, *The End of Equality* (New York: Basic Books, 1992).

3. This basic approach has been developed and refined in various ways. See, in particular, Richard Arneson's account of "equality of opportunity for welfare," "Equality and Equal Opportunity for Welfare" *Philosophical Studies* 56 (1988): 77–93; Richard Arneson, "Liberalism, Distributive Subjectivism, and Equal Opportunity for Welfare," *Philosophy and Public Affairs* 19 (1990): 159–94; G. A. Cohen's account of "equality of access to advantage," "On the Currency of Egalitarian Justice," *Ethics* 99 (1989): 906–44; G. A. Cohen, "Incentives, Inequality, and Community," in *The Tanner Lectures on Human Values*, vol. 13, ed. G. B. Peterson (Salt Lake City: University of Utah Press, 1992); G. A. Cohen, "Equality of What? On Welfare, Goods, and Capabilities," in *The Quality of Life*, ed. Martha Nussbaum and Amartya Sen (Oxford: Oxford University Press, 1993); Amartya Sen's account of "equality of capabilities," "Equality of What?" in *The Tanner Lectures on Human Values*, vol. 1, ed. S. McMurrin (Salt Lake City: University of Utah Press, 1980); Amartya Sen "Rights and Capabilities," in *Morality and Objectivity*, ed. T. Honderich (London: Routledge and Kegan Paul, 1985); Erik Rakowski's account of "equality of fortune," *Equal Justice* (Oxford: Oxford University Press, 1993); and John Roemer's account of "equality of access/opportunity," "A Pragmatic Theory of Responsibility for the Egalitarian Planner," *Philosophy and Public Affairs* 22 (1993): 146–66; John Roemer, *Theories of Distributive Justice* (Cambridge: Harvard University Press, 1996). All share the underlying intuition about eliminating unchosen inequalities, while providing space for inequalities due to choices for which individuals are responsible.

4. Richard Dagger, *Civic Virtues: Rights, Citizenship, and Republican Liberalism* (Oxford: Oxford University Press, 1997).

5. Private associations that originally had no intention of becoming politically active may find that they need to do so in order to ward off legislation that threatens their way of life. In so doing, they may help serve the broader cause of liberty and tolerance. Conversely, public associations that originally had no intention of providing social or economic benefits to their members may find that they need to do so in order to attract members.

6. Proponents of this Habermasian view are inclined to view associations with public aims as especially commendable and worthy of protection, whereas associations with only private or inward-looking goals are seen to be of less value, and perhaps even dismissed as forms of "civic privatism." For an example, see Iris Young, "State, Civil Society, and Social Justice," in *Democracy's Value*, ed. Ian

Shapiro and Casiano Hacker-Cordon (Cambridge: Cambridge University Press, 1999), 141–62. Young argues that "private" association (as distinct from "civic" or "political" association) "contributes little to the good of the wider society," can be "depoliticizing or brazenly self-regarding," and can contribute to a situation in which "whole communities or groups withdraw into associational privatism" (147).

7. See, for example, Loren Lomasky, "Classical Liberalism and Civil Society," in *Alternative Conceptions of Civil Society*, ed. Simone Chambers and Will Kymlicka (Princeton: Princeton University Press, forthcoming). People who endorse this libertarian view are inclined to view associations with private aims as especially commendable and worthy of protection, and to be skeptical about advocacy groups or "special interest groups" that seek advantages ("rent-seeking") from the state, and that encourage the state to go beyond its proper night-watchman role.

8. I am not claiming that any and all definitions of "civil society" should include these (and only these) three elements. We have different reasons for wanting to look at civil society, and for some of these purposes, it might make sense to exclude the economy and restrict it to nonprofit associations or, conversely, to expand it to include the family. How we define civil society will depend in part on the sorts of issues and questions we want to investigate. In my case, I am using the term *civil society* to highlight a set of issues about the way in which decisions about interaction with strangers affects the achievement of social justice. So I am defining civil society to include #2a, #2b, and #3 because all three involve the same link between freedom, civility, citizenship and social justice.

9. This is why my chapter deviates from the usual ordering of the sections, in which discussion of the needs and liabilities of civil society precedes the discussion of citizenship. For theories such as liberal egalitarianism, which have a robust and demanding conception of citizenship, there is no way to discuss the needs and liabilities of civil society except in reference to the requirements of citizenship.

10. Rawls, *Theory of Justice*, 3.

11. Rawls says that the "basic structure" of society is the primary subject of a theory of justice. *Political Liberalism* (New York: Columbia University Press, 1993), 257–89.

12. This may account for the recent interest in citizenship promotion among governments: e.g., Britain's Commission on Citizenship, *Encouraging Citizenship*, 1990; Senate of Australia, *Active Citizenship Revisited*, 1991; Senate of Canada, *Canadian Citizenship: Sharing the Responsibility*, 1993.

13. Kant quoted in William Galston, *Liberal Purposes: Goods, Virtues, and Duties in the Liberal State* (Cambridge: Cambridge University Press, 1991), 215.

14. Ibid., 220. Hence, recent theories of citizenship emphasize that citizenship requires a balance of rights and responsibilities. For a survey of recent work on citizenship theory, from which this section draws, see Will Kymlicka and Wayne Norman, "Return of the Citizen: A Survey of Recent Work on Citizenship Theory," *Ethics* 104, no. 2 (1994): 352–81. For a useful collection of recent articles, see Ronald Beiner, *Theorizing Citizenship* (Albany: State University of New York Press, 1995); Gershon Shafir, *The Citizenship Debates* (Minneapolis: University of

Minnesota Press, 1998). For a more historical survey of citizenship theory, see Michael Walzer, "Citizenship," in *Political Innovation and Conceptual Change*, ed. T. Ball and J. Farr (Cambridge: Cambridge University Press, 1989), 211–19; and the readings collected in Paul Barry Clarke, *Citizenship* (London: Pluto Press, 1994).

15. Alan Cairns and Cynthia Williams, *Constitutionalism, Citizenship, and Society in Canada* (Toronto: University of Toronto Press, 1985), 43.

16. Michael Walzer, "The Civil Society Argument," in *Dimensions of Radical Democracy: Pluralism, Citizenship, and Community*, ed. Chantal Mouffe (London: Routledge, 1992), 90. According to a recent survey, only 12 percent of American teenagers said voting was important to being a good citizen. Moreover, this apathy is not just a function of youth—comparisons with similar surveys from the previous fifty years suggest that "the current cohort knows less, cares less, votes less, and is less critical of its leaders and institutions than young people have been at any time over the past five decades." Mary Ann Glendon, *Rights Talk: The Impoverishment of Political Discourse* (New York: Free Press, 1991), 129. The evidence from Great Britain is similar. Derek Heater, *Citizenship: The Civic Ideal in World History, Politics, and Education* (London: Longman, 1990), 215.

17. For a helpful discussion and typology, see Galston, *Liberal Purposes*, 221–24.

18. Ibid., 227.

19. Stephen Macedo, *Liberal Virtues: Citizenship, Virtue, and Community* (Oxford: Oxford University Press, 1990). See also Robert Audi, "The Separation of Church and State and the Obligations of Citizenship," *Philosophy and Public Affairs* 18, no. 3 (1989): 259–96; Kenneth Strike, "On the Construction of Public Speech: Pluralism and Public Reason," *Educational Theory* 44, no. 1 (1994): 1–26.

20. This is why liberals cannot endorse a strong version of "civic republicanism." In one sense, civic republicanism refers to any view that highlights the importance of civic virtues, and the extent to which the functioning of a democracy requires certain virtues and identities among its citizens. In this sense, liberals must be republicans. But in another stronger sense, civic republicanism refers to the view that the best life—the most truly human life—is one that privileges political participation over other spheres of human endeavor. This view is inconsistent with liberalism's commitment to pluralism, and in any event is implausible as a general account of the good life for all persons. See Kymlicka and Norman, "Return of the Citizen," 361–62. For examples of this stronger sort of civic republicanism, see Ronald Beiner, "Citizenship," in *What's the Matter with Liberalism?* (Berkeley and Los Angeles: University of California Press, 1992); Adrian Oldfield, "Citizenship: An Unnatural Practice?" *Political Quarterly* 61 (1990): 177–87; Adrian Oldfield, *Citizenship and Community: Civic Republicanism and the Modern World* (London: Routledge, 1990); J. G. A. Pocock, "The Ideal of Citizenship since Classical Times," *Queen's Quarterly* 99, no. 1 (1992): 33–55; Quentin Skinner, "On Justice, the Common Good and the Priority of Liberty," in Mouffe, *Dimensions of Radical Democracy*, 211–24.

21. T. H. McLaughlin, "Citizenship, Diversity, and Education," *Journal of Moral Education* 21, no. 3 (1992): 235–50.

22. There are other possible reasons for encouraging political participation. Civic republicans, for example, will promote participation on the grounds that it

represents a uniquely valuable activity—perhaps even the highest form of human activity—and that a life without such participation is therefore substantially worse than a life of active political participation. See the references cited in n. 20. Communitarians might encourage participation as a means of strengthening feelings of communal identity and belonging, perhaps as a way of countering the threat of individual alienation and anomie in modern fragmented societies. However, liberal egalitarians are not likely to support these sorts of "perfectionist" reasons for encouraging participation, and will instead focus on the role of participation in ensuring justice. See my "Liberal Egalitarians and Civic Republicans: Friends or Foes?" chap. 18 in *Politics in the Vernacular: Nationalism, Multiculturalism, and Citizenship* (Oxford: Oxford University Press, 2001).

23. It is an interesting question what the state can or should do to encourage or even compel citizens to do their fair share in this regard. For example, would it be permissible to require people to vote (as in Australia)? Even if it is permissible, would it actually succeed in encouraging citizens to take a more active interest in fighting injustice?

24. See, for example, Richard Epstein, *Forbidden Grounds: The Case against Employment Discrimination Laws* (Cambridge: Harvard University Press, 1992). See also Lomasky, "Classical Liberalism and Civil Society."

25. See, for example, Chandran Kukathas, "Cultural Toleration," in *Ethnicity and Group Rights*, NOMOS *39*, ed. Ian Shapiro and Will Kymlicka (New York: New York University Press, 1997), 69–104.

26. Rawls, *Theory of Justice*, 96.

27. Quoted in John Murray Cuddihy, *No Offense: Civil Religion and Protestant Taste* (New York: Seabury Press, 1978), 6.

28. The claim that appropriate civility requires reciprocity is obviously a normative one, based on liberal egalitarian principles, not a claim about our everyday use of the term *civility*. In everyday usage, it would be quite normal to say that an oppressed person who smiles at his or her oppressor was being civil. A liberal-egalitarian account of civility, however, will insist that appropriate civility contain some element of reciprocity and moral equality.

29. My discussion here draws extensively on Jeff Spinner's account of civility. *The Boundaries of Citizenship: Race, Ethnicity, and Nationality in the Liberal State* (Baltimore: Johns Hopkins University Press, 1994), chap. 3. It also draws on Patricia White's account of civility, or what she calls "decency," although I disagree in part with her emphasis. "Decency and Education for Citizenship," *Journal of Moral Education* 21, no. 3 (1992): 207–16. She seems primarily concerned with improving the overall level of "decency" in society, rather than with eliminating glaring instances of incivility aimed at identifiable groups. For example, she compares the smiling and cooperative waiters in a Canadian café with the surly and uncooperative waiters in a Polish café (208), and argues that we should educate children to be friendly with strangers rather than surly. While I agree that it is a good thing for people to display this sort of decency, and that a minimal level of it is a precondition of a functioning democracy, I do not think this is the fundamental problem. From my point of view, waiters who are only minimally cheerful to all their customers are morally preferable to waiters who are generally very cheerful but who are surly to black customers. The latter may

display more decency overall, but their behavior toward an identifiable group threatens the most basic norms of liberal citizenship. However, I agree with White that it is important to be sensitive to the cultural variations in norms of civility (215).

30. Geoff Mulgan, "Citizens and Responsibilities," in *Citizenship*, ed. Geoff Andrews (London: Lawrence and Wishart, 1991), 39.

31. Oldfield, "Citizenship: An Unnatural Practice," 184.

32. Mulgan, "Citizens and Responsibilities," 40–41.

33. Katherine Fierlbeck, "Redefining Responsibilities: The Politics of Citizenship in the United Kingdom," *Canadian Journal of Political Science* 24 (1991): 592.

34. Sara Ruddick, "Remarks on the Sexual Politics of Reason," in *Women and Moral Theory*, ed. Eva Kittay and Diana Meyers (Totowa, N.J.: Rowman and Allanheld, 1987), 242.

35. Mary Dietz, "Citizenship with a Feminist Face: The Problem with Maternal Thinking," *Political Theory* 13, no. 1 (1985): 30; Lolle Nauta, "Changing Conceptions of Citizenship," *Praxis International* 12, no. 1 (1992): 31.

36. Mary Dietz, "Context Is All: Feminism and Theories of Citizenship," in Mouffe, *Dimensions of Radical Democracy*, 76.

37. Susan Okin, "Women, Equality and Citizenship," *Queen's Quarterly* 99, no. 1 (1992): 65.

38. Walzer, "Civil Society," 104.

39. Glendon, *Rights Talk*, 109.

40. Walzer, "Civil Society," 106.

41. Glendon, *Rights Talk*, 109.

42. See the debate surrounding Putnam's groundbreaking effort to establish the empirical link between government functioning and the number and vitality of civic associations. Robert Putnam, *Making Democracy Work: Civic Traditions in Modern Italy* (Princeton: Princeton University Press, 1993); Robert Putnam, "Bowling Alone: America's Declining Social Capital," *Journal of Democracy* 6, no. 1 (1995): 65–78. Putnam's claims are criticized in Sidney Tarrow, "Making Social Science Work Across Space and Time: A Critical Reflection on Putnam's *Making Democracy Work*," *American Political Science Review* 90, no. 2 (1996): 389–97; Margaret Levi, "Social and Unsocial Capital," *Politics and Society* 24, no. 1 (1996): 45–55.

43. For a more detailed discussion of the sorts of policies that might ensure fairer access to associational life, see Michael Walzer, "Equality and Civil Society," in *Alternative Conceptions of Civil Society*, ed. Simone Chambers and Will Kymlicka (Princeton: Princeton University Press, forthcoming). He mentions tax exemptions for nonprofit organizations, subsidies and subventions, matching grants and low-interest loans, and entitlements paid on behalf of individuals to privately run health and welfare services, and suggests that the assistance the state provides to associational life should be "directed first of all toward the weakest associations." However, he also notes that "it is much less difficult to describe a principle of egalitarian assistance—help the weakest groups first—than to imagine the process through which this principle might be realized."

44. Rosenblum, "Feminist Perspectives on Civil Society and Government," this volume.

45. This similarity is hardly surprising: feminists and liberal egalitarians are overlapping, not mutually exclusive, groups.

46. Walzer, "Civil Society," 106–7.

47. This membership rule was struck down by the American Supreme Court in *Roberts vs. Jaycees*, 468 U.S. 609 (1984).

48. Of course, there will be less hesitation to intervene in cases where people's basic human rights or bodily integrity are threatened by an association's practices (e.g., sexual abuse), or where members are denied a right of exit. For the centrality of a right of exit to any liberal-egalitarian theory of civil society, see Susan Okin, "Mistresses of Their Own Destiny? Group Rights, Gender, and Realistic Rights of Exit" (paper presented at the Annual Meeting of the American Political Science Association, 1998).

49. See Rosenblum, "Feminist Perspectives."

50. Nancy Rosenblum, *Membership and Morals: The Personal Uses of Pluralism in America* (Princeton: University Press, 1998), 173.

51. For a subtle and detailed discussion of these and other objections to the logic of congruence, see Rosenblum, *Membership and Morals*, esp. chaps. 1–3.

52. Amy Gutmann, *Democratic Education* (Princeton: Princeton University Press, 1987), 53.

53. Eamonn Callan, *Creating Citizens* (Oxford: Oxford University Press, 1997).

54. Gutmann, *Democratic Education*, 115–17.

55. This is an illustration of Rosenblum's point that we need to keep the whole range of civic virtues in mind when evaluating the impact of particular institutions on individuals.

56. T. H. McLaughlin, "The Ethics of Separate Schools," in *Ethics, Ethnicity, and Education*, ed. Mal Leicester and Monica Taylor (London: Kogan Page, 1992), 122.

57. For more detailed explorations of this theme, see Callan, *Creating Citizens*; McLaughlin, "Ethics of Separate Schools."

58. Spinner, *Boundaries of Citizenship*, 98.

59. Of course they may pose a threat to the interests of their own members, particularly their children.

60. I am disagreeing here with those who defend the exemption for the Amish by arguing that their separate schools provide adequate citizenship education. This was the view of the American Supreme Court, which said that the Amish education system prepared Amish children to be good citizens, since they became productive and peaceful members of the Amish community. *Wisconsin vs. Yoder* 406 US 205 (1972). This indeed is a common response by groups who are criticized for failing to abide by or to inculcate a particular civic virtue: How can anyone question our status as good citizens when we obey the law and pay our taxes? Adopting this minimalist conception of citizenship allows individuals to feel that they can be both good members of nonliberal groups and good members of the liberal state, without any conflict between the two. However, as I noted earlier, liberal-egalitarian citizenship requires more than being law-abiding and economically self-sufficient. A society of such minimal citizens has no chance of achieving justice, as liberal egalitarians conceive it. As Spinner argues, from a liberal-egalitarian point of view, the Amish are bad citizens, since they take no

interest in and accept no responsibility for remedying the inequalities in American society. *Boundaries of Citizenship*, chap. 5. For a critique of *Yoder*'s account of civic responsibilities, see Richard Arneson and Ian Shapiro, "Democracy and Religious Freedom: A Critique of *Wisconsin vs. Yoder*," in *NOMOS 38: Political Order* (New York: New York University Press, 1996).

61. As Spinner notes, there are unlikely to be many such groups, since the price of "partial citizenship" is to cut oneself off from the opportunities and resources of the mainstream society. *Boundaries of Citizenship*, chap. 5.

62. In the Canadian province of Ontario, for example, Catholic schools used to be publicly funded up to the end of elementary school, but Catholic high schools received no public funding.

63. A quite separate question concerns the status of national groups within a liberal-egalitarian theory of civil society—i.e., the status of groups who see themselves as "nations" within a larger state, and who seek political autonomy on a territorial basis, so as to maintain themselves as separate and self-governing peoples. Such territorial/national groups include Puerto Rico, Quebec, Catalonia, Flanders, and Scotland, as well as many indigenous peoples. Such groups do not wish to form associations within the dominant civil society, but rather want to form their own civil society on their own self-governing territory. They raise the question not of the status of groups within a liberal civil society, but rather of the boundaries of a particular civil society. We typically talk as if there is one civil society within each country. But in countries with such national minorities, it would be more accurate to say that there are two or more civil societies, divided along territorial lines, within the larger state. On this, see my *Politics in the Vernacular*, chaps. 10–15.

64. I have focused in this chapter on the role of civil society in nurturing certain habits and attitudes essential to liberal citizenship. To be sure, there are other things a liberal society needs from civil society. For example, groups in civil society often play a vital role in the democratic process in giving voice to particular interests that might otherwise be ignored, in developing mechanisms for representation and consultation, and in agenda formation. These are issues not so much of the virtues of individual citizens, but of social empowerment, and are particularly relevant for the category of public interest groups (#2a). A fuller discussion of civil society and liberal egalitarianism would need to explore what can or should be done to enhance the ability of civil society groups to provide voice and representation and to shape the public agenda.

65. Similarly, as I noted earlier, at the level of political theory, it is only in the last decade that liberal egalitarians have shifted attention away from a theory of just institutions to a theory of citizenship. So at the level of both theory and practice, these issues are comparatively new for liberal egalitarians.

66. See Rosenblum, *Membership and Morals*, 53–57.

67. For helpful comments, I'd like to thank William Galston, Nancy Rosenblum, Robert Post, Brian Barry, and Sue Donaldson.

Liberal Egalitarianism:
A Family of Theories, Not a Single View

William A. Galston

GENERAL COMMENTS

Will Kymlicka suggests, but does not stress, that "liberal egalitarianism" names a family of views rather than a single view. This raises the question of what one must believe to be a member in good standing of the family. I would offer the following list:

1. Liberty and equality are two ideas or principles of independent standing that cannot be reduced to a common measure of value.

2. Liberty and equality are reciprocally limiting, in that some collective acts to promote equality are restrained or ruled out altogether by the principle of liberty, and vice versa.

3. Liberty must be *equal* liberty, at least for all normal adults.

4. There is a distinction between moral equality and distributional equality. Moral equality is, roughly speaking, the idea that many of the empirical differences we observe among human beings are irrelevant to how they ought to be regarded and treated, while distributional equality involves the fair assignment of goods to individuals. Liberal egalitarians accept both moral equality and the validity of employing moral equality as a key premise in distributional arguments. For liberal egalitarians, no pattern of distribution is acceptable if its justification requires a premise that contradicts moral equality.

Liberal egalitarianism provides the theoretical basis for the center-left in the politics of contemporary Western nations. Against libertarianism, it holds that formal principles of economic and political liberty are necessary but not sufficient to define a morally adequate political outlook. Against what may be called collectivist egalitarianism (of which the Marxism of the defunct Soviet Union was a distorted and hypocritical instance), it holds that not all restraints on liberty are justified in the name of equalization, even when equalizing measures are endorsed by democratic majorities after informed deliberation.

The best-known contemporary theorist of liberal egalitarianism is undoubtedly John Rawls. The principles of liberty and equality figure at two key points in his theory. First, they are the defining features of the citizens whose agreement is required to constitute a stable, well-ordered society. Second, they are the subject matter of the two principles—the first dealing with liberty, the second with equality—that define Rawls's interpretation of social justice.

As this reference to Rawls suggests, liberal egalitarians disagree among themselves in at least two respects: first, how the conflicts between liberty and equality are to be understood and addressed; and second, how moral equality delimits legitimate distributional outcomes. Even within a political community whose members are unanimously and conscientiously devoted to liberal-egalitarian principles, there will be a zone of moral indeterminacy within which political contestation, deliberation, and choice hold sway.

Let me comment briefly on each of these definitional points.

(1) The relationship between liberty and equality is an example of what has come to be called value pluralism. How can we deal with the tensions that arise when plural values are brought to bear on practical questions? Three sorts of answers have been suggested:

(a) lexical priority—one value enjoys systematic priority over the others, such that its requirements must be fully satisfied before others begin to acquire moral weight;

(b) bare trade-offs—different individuals will offer one another (varying) conclusions about the balance to be struck among competing values, which conclusions are based on intuitions for which no further justification can be given;

(c) reason-based trade-offs—individuals exchange reasons for preferring one balance of competing values over others, which reasons may suffice to produce deliberative closure in particular choice-situations.

While Kymlicka acknowledges in passing that conjoining liberty and equality in "liberal egalitarianism" may prove problematic, he does not analyze these difficulties systematically. Brian Barry's account of the vicissitudes of Rawls's effort to establish the lexical priority of liberty over equality is an instructive complement to Kymlicka's discussion. We shall, he concludes, "have to accept the unavoidability of balancing. . . . [But] even if lexicographic priorities are not attainable, balancing might still be guided by general theoretical considerations."[1]

(2) At first glance, Kymlicka is offering an interpretation of liberal egalitarianism based on the lexical priority of equality over liberty. On this view, we first look to determine which inequalities are permissible from the standpoint of social justice and use collective action to remedy

those that are not. The principle of liberty then enters to protect individual choices concerning the use of morally acceptable holdings. Later on, however, he suggests a more complex picture: the principle of liberty functions as a moral constraint on collective action. There is no smooth inference from "Policy A promotes egalitarian social justice" to "We ought to do A." For example, even if civil associations such as hierarchical churches pull against beliefs and practices that promote egalitarian social justice, it would be a "mistake"—indeed, a "misuse of power"—for the state to intervene in an effort to reconstruct them.

(3) The principle of liberty in liberal egalitarianism is in itself egalitarian, in the sense that the guarantee is of equal liberty for all (normal adult) individuals. So it is a violation of liberal egalitarianism if (for example) women are systematically restricted in their ability to hold and dispose of property in ways that men are not. And this would remain true even if women as a group tended to use their holdings in ways that are likely over time to exacerbate inequality of holdings.

While the liberty principle is egalitarian, it is not nakedly so. Rather, it assumes certain background conditions of eligibility for the full enjoyment of equal liberty. For example:

(1) We may argue about precisely where the line between adults and nonadults should be drawn (and the location may differ depending on the specific issue and context), but few, if any, liberal egalitarians believe that there should be no such line.

(2) Certain acts are thought to warrant the suspension or removal of particular liberties. For example, conviction in the United States for serious felonies frequently results in the termination of the constitutionally guaranteed right to bear arms and even of the right to vote.

(3) Kymlicka defines egalitarianism in terms of the distribution of resources and opportunities. I will not contest the appropriateness of including this in the definition, but it is surprising that he stops there, because there is another, perhaps prior, sense of equality that focuses on the (moral) worth of individuals.

There are three ways of understanding this concept of moral equality: (1) as an ultimate ethical principle that cannot be further supported; (2) as a principle that ultimately rests on theological foundations (we are all God's children, we are equal in the sight of God, and so forth); and (3) as a principle resting on testable empirical and philosophical criteria—for example, that nearly all adults cross (or given appropriate upbringing, can cross) some threshold of rationality and moral responsibility. This may be an important example of what Rawls calls an overlapping consensus. I am inclined to believe that some version of (3) is at least part of the mix; it would not be hard to demonstrate that it is woven into the fabric of our political and legal system.

You cannot be an egalitarian if you deny moral equality. (Examples of nonegalitarians include Brahmins and slave owners who deny the full humanity of enslaved groups.) But the relation between moral equality and distributional equality is contested—more so than Kymlicka suggests. Consider the distributional inequalities that may result from inequalities of natural talents. I take it that members in good standing of the egalitarian club will reject the straightforward libertarian proposition that whatever the market metes out is acceptable. But egalitarians will be divided on the extent to which the public sector should intervene to correct or compensate. Some will argue for equalization up to a threshold, through minimum wage laws, wage supplements such as the Earned Income Tax Credit, and so forth. Rawlsians will want to maximize the well-being of the least advantaged groups. Some egalitarians believe so strongly in the superior moral quality of social relations among distributional equals that they will be willing to push for equalization even at the cost of sinking below Rawlsian maximin. So while it is plausible to declare, as Kymlicka does, that "a liberal-democratic state can secure justice only if citizens vote for political parties that will pursue just policies," in practice this is likely to leave a substantial zone for politics—even within the liberal-egalitarian camp.

CITIZENSHIP

Citizenship is the load-bearing beam in Kymlicka's liberal-egalitarian architecture. He is surely right to suggest that the citizens of liberal-democratic polities must be actively concerned with social justice, not only in their voting behavior, but also in their conduct within civil society. These concerns must flow from certain civic virtues, which not being innate must be cultivated (just where this happens is, as Kymlicka indicates, controversial and empirically murky). The liberal-egalitarian citizen stands somewhere between the libertarian citizen, whose only civic obligation is to respect the liberties of others, and the civic republican citizen, who is expected to give priority to public concerns and to systematically subordinate self-interest to the common good.

So far, so good. But here as elsewhere, Kymlicka tends to offer a single liberal-egalitarian account where I would stress a family of conceptions. Let me offer two examples of this difference of emphasis.

(1) Kymlicka briskly compresses the complex debate over "public reason" into the conclusion that certain kinds of considerations (faith-based

claims, for example) are ruled out as freestanding public justifications in liberal-democratic polities. My own view is that suitably articulated, the sorts of reasons Kymlicka wants to exclude are consistent with the respect we owe our fellow citizens. (It is a matter of some interest that Rawls, having begun by articulating what he calls an "exclusive view" of public reason along Kymlicka's lines, has now moved to a broader "inclusive view" closer to the position I recommend.)[2]

(2) As Kymlicka notes, the translation of the principle of nondiscrimination from government to civil society involves a "radical extension in the obligations of liberal citizenship." How radical an extension is a matter of debate. Consider the case of a hard-pressed widow who decides to supplement her meager income by renting out some rooms in her house. Staunchly traditional in her moral outlook, she disapproves of gays and cohabiting unmarried couples and does not want them as tenants. She has no desire to deprive them of the rights and liberties of citizens, but she regards their presence in her house as an outright violation of her personal moral convictions and an invasion of privacy. It appears to me that Kymlicka would want to extend the obligations of liberal-egalitarian citizenship to cover this case. I would be reluctant to do so, on the grounds that the "liberal" component of this conception denotes (among other things) a zone of privacy within which individuals can act in ways that would not be acceptable in the public sphere. For similar reasons, I would be reluctant to posit Kymlicka's interpretation of "civility" as an affirmative obligation of citizens: while I may not use force against those of whom I disapprove, it is by no means clear that I am debarred from expressing my disapproval, in public, in terms that they may well find insufficiently respectful.

BOUNDARIES

I agree with Kymlicka that the definition of "civil society" is somewhat arbitrary or—to put it differently—that the definition selected is likely to reflect broader theoretical commitments. Still, the discussion cannot even begin unless we reject the idea of the plenipotentiary state dominating every aspect of human life. The idea of civil society is an aspect of the broader idea of a zone of relations among persons substantially independent of state control. In the twentieth century, totalitarian regimes have directly assaulted this idea—for example, by turning labor unions, writers' organizations, and even churches into organs of state power. One widely held view is that our conception of civil society originated in the dissolution of the medieval synthesis of church and state and (after a period of debilitating conflict) the emergence of religious toleration. It transpired that a range of faiths could coexist within a single political community (how wide a range depended on local preferences and circumstances). Religious toleration may well have begun as a modus vivendi directed toward the abatement of pious cruelty, but it developed into a doctrine of principled limits to state power. If the laws of the state are backed by coercive force, then the law's writ runs no farther than the efficacy of coercion. In Locke's classic formulation, "True and saving religion consists in the inward persuasion of the Mind, without which nothing is acceptable to God. And such is the nature of the understanding, that it cannot be compelled to the belief of any thing by outward force."

This line of reasoning takes us only so far, however. Even if Locke is right about the understanding or conscience, clearly coercion can affect practices (including religious practices). The principal arguments in favor of an independent civil sector substantially insulated from state control are moral and practical—not conceptual or ontological.

Now (to reach the question posed), it does make a difference where the line is drawn between civil society and the state, but not as much of a difference as one might think. Wherever the line is located, state and civil society are not symmetrically situated. The reason is this: If X is deemed to be part of the state, then it is automatically subject to the norms binding all state institutions. But even if it is not considered to be part of the state, it may still be subject to many of these norms.

An example of the former: In 1944, the Supreme Court of the United States invalidated the Texas Democratic Party's refusal to admit black Texans to membership, thereby excluding them from participating in primary elections. The Court refused to accept the state's claim that the party's action was private or analogous to the membership decisions of a club. In managing the primaries, the Court found, parties performed a "state function" and were therefore required to conduct themselves in accordance with the Fifteenth Amendment.

An example of the latter: in 1984, the Supreme Court affirmed the constitutionality of a Minnesota civil rights law applied against the Jaycees, who had refused to accept women as full members. The argument was not that the Jaycees performed a state function, but that they were a "public accommodation" within the meaning of the act. The Court noted that many states and municipalities had adopted a "functional" and "expansive" definition of public accommodation with the aim of sweeping away barriers to economic advancement, social integration, and political power that had historically plagued disadvantaged groups. The Court came close to endorsing the view that a public accommodation is any organization whose activities significantly affect the distribution of opportunities in society and whose activities are not protected by First Amendment or privacy claims.

As Kymlicka rightly emphasizes, the extent to which nondiscrimination norms should be imposed on civil associations remains intensely controversial, within the liberal-egalitarian camp as well as across ideological lines. Kymlicka does not come down firmly on the side of the Supreme Court against the Jaycees, but in the main he associates himself with equality-based worries about the consequences of exclusionary policies. My own view is closer to the one articulated by Nancy Rosenblum: The "liberal" component of liberal egalitarianism denotes (among other things) a protected zone of voluntary association that may embody principles quite different from those of the polity as a whole. While there are indeed circumstances in which the state must act against exclusionary practices, exclusion from specific voluntary associations does not ipso facto breach norms of equal citizenship that the state should coercively defend.[3]

I do not believe that liberal-egalitarian political theory can avoid the challenge of weighing—in specific cases—the interests protected by civil society liberty claims against the egalitarian norms the state seeks to enforce. Virtually no one argues that laws against gender discrimination in employment should be enforced against the Catholic Church. But what about golf clubs that exclude blacks or Jews? It may well be that informal conversations at the fourteenth (or more likely, the nineteenth) hole will affect the distribution of economic and social opportunities. If that consideration is dispositive, then egalitarian claims of social justice will trump the liberty claims of the civil sector in the vast majority of cases, and an independent civil society becomes far more difficult to sustain.

NEEDS

Why should we care? This leads to the question of what (if anything) the state needs from civil society. My answer: quite a lot.

(1) To begin with, many have looked to civil associations as direct or indirect schools of citizenship. As Kymlicka emphasizes, this is an empirical question. Granting all the negative examples he adduces, I am a bit more optimistic about the evidence than he is. For example, many observers have noted the tendency of voluntary associations in the United States to organize themselves procedurally and constitutionally in ways that mirror the larger political order. It is difficult to believe that the experience of creating and then working within such organizations is not, on balance, citizenship enhancing. My own experiences in a wide range of associations, secular and religious, have fortified my view that these

association teach valuable civic lessons—especially about coping productively with intense disagreement.

(2) Rosenblum has raised the related question of moral development and of the moral psychology needed to sustain liberal-egalitarian polities. She conjectures that a free and diverse civil sphere, one that not only permits but actively encourages "shifting involvements," provides the experience of pluralism that helps us deal with difference and to distinguish among the forms of conduct appropriate to differences spheres of our lives.[4] This is particularly important if we believe that the circumstances of modern liberty are likely to foster both social diversity and social differentiation.

(3) Civil associations do real civic work—work that would otherwise have to be carried out by state institutions. This is important if you believe that the capacity of these institutions, while large, is not unlimited and that certain kinds of activities (those requiring a high degree of individualized discretionary judgment, for example) are not likely to be carried out well by centralized bureaucracies. From this perspective, a vigorous civil society enhances a political community's overall capacity for self-government. Conversely, excessive reliance on state institutions can prove enervating (this was the burden of Tocqueville's argument against French centralization).

(4) A classic liberal fear is that concentration of power without counterbalances opens the door to tyranny. To the extent that liberal egalitarianism remains liberal, it must continue to take this worry seriously. As I have seen close up, government officials sincerely dedicated to the principles of egalitarian social justice are tempted to apply these principles in ways that are counterproductive or inappropriate—just because (they believe) they have the power to do so. Of course there are huge differences between the United States in 1999 and (say) Poland in 1979, and corresponding differences in the social role of unions and the Catholic Church. But it would be reckless to assume that even stable liberal democracies can keep their balance indefinitely in the absence of countervailing power.

(5) Let us assume that a conception of social justice (whatever its content) will form only a portion of most individuals' conceptions of value. It follows that, beyond the common ground that an understanding of social justice may establish, most citizens will care intensely about a zone within which their broader sense of what gives meaning and purpose to life may be enacted-where appropriate, in the company of like-minded others. This is one of the core functions of civil society. We may conjecture (this is yet another empirical point) that state institutions that honor

this zone of expressive liberty are likely to enjoy a higher level of support, and to be regarded as more legitimate, than those that repress it. (Suppose the United States had not moved toward religious disestablishment during the early-nineteenth century. Wouldn't that have increased the probability that religious differences would be translated into civic disaffection? Conversely, can't we understand First Amendment religious liberty guarantees as sources of civic gratitude that helped turn non-Protestant immigrants into loyal citizens?)

Groups and Individuals

While it is true, as Kymlicka asserts, that liberal egalitarians are open-minded as to whether or when the government should deal directly with individuals or via groups, they are not indifferent. There is a rebuttable presumption in favor of direct relations between individuals and state institutions. After all, from a liberal-egalitarian perspective, every individual qua citizen (and for some purposes, qua person) enjoys equal and independent status in the eyes of the law. The complex case of Native Americans illustrates the proposition that direct relations between state institutions and communal organizations are somewhat anomalous, at least in the U.S. context. (Canada, Belgium, and the United Kingdom present somewhat different pictures, about which I know distressingly little but which it would be worthwhile to discuss.)

Having said this, some qualifications: First, U.S. history has created waves of what might be termed informal communalism, where public institutions deal with leaders of racial, ethnic, and religious groups (typically but not always recent immigrants) in effect as communal representatives, especially for distributive purposes. This is particularly likely when educational, linguistic, or economic barriers make it difficult for individuals to speak for themselves. Urban political machines offer one example of this.

Second, at least some conceptions of liberal-egalitarian social justice focus on outcomes for individuals as members of groups. I do not want to open up the endless debate over the compatibility between liberal-egalitarian principles and affirmative action. I note only that for many of its proponents, membership in certain groups means that individuals necessarily participate in, and are harmed by, communal disadvantages that cannot be reduced to the character or circumstances of specific persons.

Third, liberal egalitarianism (at least in its U.S. variant) does officially recognize some communal institutions. The examples I know best are religious. U.S. courts are very reluctant to intervene in disputes within religious communities, in part out of fear that state institutions will become entangled in ways that subvert constitutionally guaranteed religious liberties. Typically, no clear line can be drawn between—on the one hand—the right (as determined by religious charter) of particular individuals or factions to impose their will on the religious community and—on the other hand—the substance of doctrinal disputes. This is not to say that anything goes within religious communities. For example, if some members of a group allege that others are engaging in child abuse during religious ceremonies, state institutions must take cognizance and if necessary intervene. But a wide range of intrareligious disputes will not be governed by civil law. In these cases, public institutions must regard communal institutions and leaders as authoritative.

I would argue that the relationship between liberal-egalitarian state institutions and communal organizations should be guided by two over-arching principles. First, because communal organizations are understood as voluntary associations, the state must be vigilant in defense of exit rights for all individuals. Communal organizations must not be allowed to pursue policies that imprison individuals within them or impose undue burdens on those who wish to leave.

Second, while the state must respect communally based identities, it should refrain from acting in ways that freeze or codify them. An example of this error is offered by the U.S. Census, which for decades has employed a rigid system of racial and ethnic classification. This system has acted to create groups, and a sense of separate and distinct group identity, that did not previously exist. And as a consequence of soaring rates of intermarriage, the classificatory scheme is now experienced as procrustean by millions of U.S. citizens. (In a modest recognition of these difficulties, the 2000 Census allowed individual respondents the option of checking all the racial-ethnic boxes they believe apply.)

CONFLICTS

On the interpretation of liberal-egalitarian principles I find most plausible, the state is not seem as plenipotentiary. (The "liberal" component of this perspective stands in opposition to the republicanism of much Greek and Roman thought as well as to some postmedieval conceptions of absolute sovereignty.) Limits on legitimate state power arise from a variety of sources, including individual rights, family relations, and religious beliefs and practices. A crucial task of liberal-egalitarian theory and practice is to define the boundaries and when necessary adjudicate conflicts in ways sensitive both to general principles and to the facts of particular cases.

In this vein, the U.S. Supreme Court has held: that parents have rights to direct the education of their children that government cannot invade;

that no state can pass a law requiring all parents to send their children to public schools; that some faith communities can claim exemption from otherwise valid laws; and that some religious individuals may be granted exemption from compulsory military service based on their "conscientious objection."

One can believe, as I do, that these decisions were correct while affirming, as I do, the need for a common ground of citizenship based on shared commitments to liberal-egalitarian principles and the institutions needed to give them effect. To make these views mutually consistent, two things are necessary: first, we must define the requirements of citizenship in a suitably limited way; and second, we must be cautious and empirical about insisting that a particular set of arrangements, civil or educational, is essential for fostering citizenship, so understood. In her new book, Nancy Rosenblum has questioned what she calls the "logic of congruence"—the thesis that the survival and health of liberal-egalitarian polities means that civil associations must themselves be structured in accordance with liberal-egalitarian public principles. I share her skepticism.

Let me push my skepticism one step farther. In my view, the "liberal" component of liberal egalitarianism implies limits on legitimate state action. Within this perspective, citizenship is a very high value, but it does not trump everything else. The proposition that "Policy A would strengthen (or even is needed to strengthen) liberal-egalitarian citizenship" does not necessarily warrant the conclusion that "Policy A is the right thing to do," for there may be claims of liberty that restrict the power of the state to act—even in the name of bolstering core public institutions, practices, and beliefs.

We have come full circle, to my opening contention that liberty and equality are coequal values within liberal egalitarianism and that they sometimes stand in tension with one another. It is often possible to give good reasons why one should take priority in specific cases of conflict, but it is not possible to establish a generally valid lexical ordering between them. For this reason, among others, liberal-egalitarian theory does not abolish political controversy or obviate the need for political judgment. Rather, it defines the terms and limits of a form of public contestation that is at the core of modern politics.

Notes

1. Brian Barry, *Political Argument: A Reissue with a New Introduction* (Berkeley and Los Angeles: University of California Press, 1990), lxxi.

2. John Rawls, *Political Liberalism, with a New Introduction and the "Reply to Habermas"* (New York: Columbia University Press, 1996), 247–54.

3. Nancy Rosenblum, "Compelled Association: Public Standing, Self-Respect, and the Dynamic of Exclusion," in *Freedom of Association*, ed. Amy Gutmann, (Princeton: Princeton University Press, 1998), 75–108.

4. Nancy Rosenblum, *Membership and Morals: The Personal Uses of Pluralism in America* (Princeton: Princeton University Press, 1998).

A Critical Theory Perspective on Civil Society and the State

Kenneth Baynes

THIS ESSAY explores one perspective on the relation between civil society and government (or the state) largely indebted to Jürgen Habermas's critical social theory. Since my approach is clearly partisan, even within the broader tradition of critical theory, I will begin with a few words about this choice of perspective. Critical theory, as I understand it, refers to a tradition of social and political criticism that begins with the Institute for Social Research founded in Frankfurt, Germany, in 1931. The so-called Frankfurt School, of course, has deeper roots in the tradition of Western Marxism, and since its initial development under the influence of Max Horkheimer and Theodor Adorno, it has undergone significant internal change as well.[1] What the tradition of critical theory does share, apart from any other inner disagreements, is a commitment to extending the core ideas of liberalism, especially the idea of a free and rational society, to a critique of the institutions and practices of liberal society itself.[2] This strategy of "immanent critique" unites two otherwise quite divergent contemporary approaches within critical theory: Adorno's negative dialectics and Habermas's theory of communicative action. Negative dialectics is a general form of criticism that attempts to counter prevailing conceptions of reason, freedom, and the like by exposing the contradictory character that these ideals, it seems, inevitably assume within any particular set of social institutions and practices. By contrast, Habermas's theory of communicative action attempts to give a broader philosophical and sociological justification for the ideas of reason and freedom, given a (liberal) world in which these ideals are either cynically dismissed or, perhaps, given only a limited pragmatic or "ethnocentric" justification.[3] Although I think the task of a critical theory benefits from insights generated by both of these competing approaches, in the following I will limit myself to the more recent work of Jürgen Habermas. In the last analysis, I think his position offers the most promise for developing a normatively guided perspective on the relationship between civil society and the state.

The Ambiguous Legacy of Civil Society

Within the recent literature, civil society, whether it is considered as a normative ideal or as an empirical reality, appears as an extremely paradoxical, if not a simply contradictory (and hence impossible), phenomenon.[4] It is, to begin, situated rather precariously between the "private" and the "public": described as something private when contrasted to the state and as something public or quasi-public when contrasted to the family or sphere of personal intimacy.[5] It has, further, been characterized both as a "commercial society" that includes economic associations and as the domain of *non*-economic voluntary associations, but in either case as something that needs to be protected from market imperatives.[6] It has been identified, on the one hand, as an "amoral order" (Gellner) that relies primarily upon instrumental reason, and yet has also been described as a primary source for the civic virtues required to maintain a stable polity and move beyond the paucity of a merely "procedural liberalism." It is, according to some, primarily "individualistic" and based on what Gellner has call the "modularity of man," yet it is supposed to be able to resist the "atomism" that is often held to accompany such reasoning and behavior.[7] It is said to be a source of community and solidarity, yet not stifling or oppressive; a sphere of social homogeneity and identity; but also a sphere of plurality, diversity, and conflict.[8] For some, it is an inherently strong sphere, able to resist or even dominate the state; for others, it designates a fragile and weak set of voluntary institutions. Gellner has captured this tension particularly well: "Civil Society is that set of diverse non-governmental institutions which is strong enough to counterbalance the state and, while not preventing the state from fulfilling its role of keeper of the peace and arbitrator between major interests, can nevertheless prevent it from dominating and atomizing the rest of society."[9] Finally, like the concept of democracy it is (at least for some) intended to be an improvement upon, the concept of civil society often wavers between a normative and an empirical interpretation: It is described both as an already existing reality and as an ideal to be pursued. Given this wide-ranging characterization, it is perhaps not surprising that civil society has been invoked by advocates from both ends of the political spectrum, from conservative communitarians to radical democrats, as an alternative and/or corrective to the contemporary ills of liberal society.[10] It is reasonably clear as well that if the idea of civil society is to be of much service either analytically or empirically, a more circumscribed definition must be found.

In his *Elements of the Philosophy of Right* (1821) Hegel infamously located "civil society" (*buergerliche Gesellschaft*) as the second moment of "ethical life" (*Sittlichkeit*), between the family and the state. He thus broke with the earlier natural law tradition, which continued through Locke and Kant, that treated "civil society" and the state interchangeably, contrasting both to "natural society."[11] Hegel's distinction between civil society and the family was apparently based on his belief that the latter was "natural" and devoted to the satisfaction of more "particular" interests. Thus, if one wishes to continue to exclude the institution of the family within civil society, it will have to be for reasons other than these suspect assumptions.[12] There may be some reasons for distinguishing the domain of personal intimacy, love, and parenting from other forms of civil association, but clearly a critical theory needs to rethink the purposes and consequences of these differentiations. Similarly, following Habermas and others, when economic organizations cross a threshold of formal bureaucratization and systemic integration, there may be important sociological reasons for distinguishing them (together with the administrative state) from civil society. Jean Cohen and Andrew Arato, who have themselves been influenced by Habermas, consequently define civil society as "a sphere of social interaction between economy and state, composed above all of the intimate sphere (especially the family), the sphere of associations (especially voluntary associations), social movements, and forms of public communication."[13] Modifying their position slightly (e.g., by separating out the family), we have the following four-fold classification: family, civil society, economy, and state.[14]

In the following, I will first locate the place of civil society in Habermas's discourse theory of democracy. I will then consider some of the further implications and challenges posed by this account of the relation between civil society and the state.

Habermas's Two-Track Model of Democracy

In connection with his recent discourse theory of law and politics, Habermas has proposed a dual or "two-track" model of a deliberative democracy in which the idea of civil society is given a prominent role.[15] His general aim is to develop a model of democracy that will be both normatively attractive and empirically informative. In particular, at a normative level, he seeks to provide an alternative to both the traditional liberal contrast between constitutionalism and democracy and, in contrast to more classical (radical) democratic theory, to move beyond the conception of popular sovereignty as necessarily based upon a unitary or socially homogenous collectivity ("the people"). This aim is pursued in two ways: first, it regards liberal rights and popular sovereignty as two complementary and mutually supportive dimensions of "communicative freedom" (the capacity to accept or reject utterances on the basis of uncoerced, individual insight). In this way he hopes to reconcile the "liberty of the ancients" with the "liberty of the moderns" in a manner that gives an appropriate role to each. At the same time, the idea of a deliberative politics is an alternative to conceptions of democracy that locate legitimate power in the idea of a substantial or homogenous "will of the people." Although his favored target is Carl Schmitt's plebiscitary democracy and critique of parliamentarism, his criticism applies as well to some majoritarian and populist conceptions of democracy.[16]

Habermas introduces his model of deliberative democracy by way of a contrast between two highly stylized alternatives: liberal and republican (or communitarian). These have become familiar reference points in recent discussions. Cass Sunstein, for example, has recently summarized the liberal model well: "Self-interest, not virtue, is understood to be the usual motivating force of political behavior. Politics is typically, if not always, an effort to aggregate private interests. It is surrounded by checks, in the form of rights, protecting private liberty and private property from public intrusion."[17] By contrast, republicanism characteristically places more emphasis on the value of citizens' public virtues and active political participation. Politics is regarded more as a deliberative process in which citizens seek to reach agreement about the common good, and law is not seen as a means for protecting individual rights but as the expression of the common praxis of the political community.

Habermas's deliberative democracy attempts to incorporate the best features of both models while avoiding the shortcomings of each. In particular, with the republican model, it rejects the vision of the political process as primarily a process of competition and aggregation of private preferences. However, more in keeping with the liberal model, it regards the republican vision of a citizenry united and actively motivated by a shared conception of the good life as unrealistic and, at any rate, undesirable in modern, pluralist societies.[18] Since political discourses involve bargaining and negotiation as well as moral argumentation, the civic republican or communitarian notion of a shared ethical-political dialogue also seems too limited (*BFN*, 285). "Discourse theory has the success of deliberative politics depend not on a collectively acting citizenry but on the institutionalization of the corresponding procedures and conditions of communication, as well as on the interplay of institutionalized deliberative processes with informally constituted public opinions" (*BFN*, 298). What is central is not a shared ethos, but institutionalized discourses for the formation of rational political opinion.

The idea of a suitably interpreted "deliberative politics" thus lies at the core of Habermas's model of democracy. In a deliberative politics attention shifts away from the final act of voting and the problems of social choice that accompany it.[19] The model attempts to take seriously the fact that often enough preferences are not exogenous to the political system, but "are instead adaptive to a wide range of factors—including the context in which the preference is expressed, the existing legal rules, past consumption choices, and culture in general."[20] The aim of a deliberative politics is to provide a context for a transformation of preferences in response to the considered views of others and the "laundering" or filtering of irrational or morally repugnant preferences or both in ways that are not excessively paternalistic.[21] For example, by designing institutions of political will-formation so that they reflect the more complex preference structure of individuals rather than simply register the actual preferences individuals have at any given time, the conditions for a more rational politics (that is, a political process in which the outcomes are more informed, future oriented, and other regarding) can be improved.[22] One could even speak of an extension of democracy to preferences themselves, since the question is whether the reasons offered in support of them are ones that could meet the requirements of public justification.[23] What is important for this notion of deliberation, however, is less that everyone participates—or even that voting be made public—than that there is a warranted presumption that public opinion be formed on the basis of adequate information and relevant reasons and that those whose interests are involved have an equal and effective opportunity to make their own interests (and the reasons for them) known.

Two further features serve to distinguish Habermas's model of deliberative democracy from other recent versions.[24] First, this version of deliberative politics extends beyond the more formally organized political system to the vast and complex communication network that Habermas calls "the public sphere."

> [Deliberative politics] is bound to the demanding communicative presuppositions of political arenas that do not coincide with the institutionalized will-formation in parliamentary bodies but extend equally to the political public sphere and to its cultural context and social basis. A deliberative practice of self-determination can develop only in the interplay between, on the one hand, the parliamentary will-formation institutionalized in legal procedures and programmed to reach decisions and, on the other, political opinion-building in informal circles of political communication. (*BFN*, 275)

The model suggests a "two-track" process in which there is a division of labor between "weak publics"—the informally organized public sphere ranging from private associations to the mass media located within civil society—and "strong publics"—parliamentary bodies and other formally organized institutions of the political system.[25] In this division of labor, "weak publics" assume a central responsibility for identifying, interpreting, and addressing social problems: "For a good part of the normative expectations connected with deliberative politics now falls on the peripheral structures of opinion-formation. The expectations are directed at the capacity to perceive, interpret, and present encompassing social problems in a way both attention-catching and innovative" (*BFN*, 358). In particular, the task of interpreting social needs and problems, and shaping public opinion in response to them, must not be left to the formal political system.[26] However, political decision-making responsibility, as well as the further "filtering" of reasons via more formal parliamentary procedures, should remain the task of a strong public (e.g., the formally organized political system). As I will indicate below, however, this constraint need not rule out any room for democratic neocorporatist experiment.

Second, along with this division of labor between strong and weak publics and as a consequence of his increased acknowledgment of the "decentered" character of modern societies, Habermas argues that radical-democratic practice must assume a "self-limiting" form. Democratization is now focused not on society as a whole, but on the legal system broadly conceived (*BFN*, 304). In particular, he maintains, it must respect the boundaries of the political-administrative and economic subsystems that have become relatively freed from the integrative force of communicative action and are in this sense "autonomous." Failure to do so, he believes, at least partially explains the failure of state socialism.[27] The goal of radical democracy thus becomes not the democratic organization of these subsystems, but rather a type of indirect steering of them through the medium of law. In this connection, he also describes the goal of this model of democracy as one in which "public opinion" generated within civil society can make itself effective in the "strong public" of the formal political system without either supplanting its functions or itself becoming merely an arm or extension of the formal political system.

This raises a number of difficult questions about the scope and limits of democratization. Given the abstract and highly metaphorical language often employed in his discussion, it is not obvious what specific proposals for mediating between weak and strong publics follow from his model. Some have questioned, for example, whether he has not conceded too much to the critics of participatory democracy, and Nancy Fraser, in an instructive discussion of Habermas's conception of the public sphere, raises the question whether there might not be other possible "divisions of labor" between strong and weak publics.[28] I will return to this question in the discussion in the "Boundaries, Needs, and Liabilities" section.

However, a more general question that also arises in connection with this model of democracy is whether Habermas's confidence in the rationalizing effect of procedures alone is well founded. In view of his own description of "weak publics" as "wild," "anarchic," and "unrestricted" (*BFN*, 307–8), the suspicion can at least be raised whether discursive procedures will suffice to bring about a rational public opinion. To be sure, he states that a deliberative politics depends on a "rationalized life-world" (including a "liberal political culture") "that meets it halfway."[29] But without more attention to the particular "liberal virtues" that make up that political culture and give rise to some notion of shared purposes, it is difficult not to empathize with Sheldon Wolin's observation concerning the recent politics of difference. Describing the situation of someone who wants to have his claim to cultural exclusiveness recognized while at the same time resisting anything more than minimal inclusion in the political community, Wolin exposes a disturbing paradox within it:

> I want to be bound only by a weak and attenuated bond of inclusion, yet my demands presuppose a strong State, one capable of protecting me in an increasingly racist and violent society and assisting me amidst increasingly uncertain economic prospects. A society with a multitude of organized, vigorous, and self-conscious differences produces not a strong State but an erratic one that is capable of reckless military adventures abroad and partisan, arbitrary actions at home ... yet is reduced to impotence when attempting to remedy structural injustices or to engage in long-range planning in matters such as education, environmental protection, racial relations, and economic strategies.[30]

Habermas would no doubt share some of these same concerns about the conditions necessary for maintaining a liberal political culture, and his own focus on the mutual recognition as the basis of a legal community may make the requirements for inclusion less demanding than Wolin suggests. The question nevertheless remains whether Habermas's almost exclusive attention to questions of institutional design and discursive procedures provides an adequate basis for dealing with this paradox or whether he must not supplement his model with a more specific account of the "liberal virtues" or "ethical foundations" that must "meet these halfway."[31] I will pursue this topic in the "Citizenship" section below.

BOUNDARIES, NEEDS, AND LIABILITIES

Given his definition of the public sphere as a domain within civil society in which "private persons come together as a public," it is obvious that civil society and state will be dependent upon one another in a number of ways.[32] Many of the cognitive and motivational resources required by the state will be drawn from civil society while at the same time the maintenance and reproduction of the associations that comprise civil society will not be indifferent to the actions of the state and may, in various ways, even depend on state action. I will attempt to elaborate upon this claim in an order of descending abstraction.

(1) First, given Habermas's understanding of the concept, civil society clearly spans the more traditional liberal distinction between the "private" and the "public," since civil society refers to the set of social institutions and associations in which "private persons" first constitute a "public." For both conceptual and institutional reasons, "private" and "public" reciprocally define and constitute each other: a public comes about only when private persons (that is, those individuals who have been allowed sufficient private space or personal freedom in which to choose, pursue, and test alternative conceptions of the good) reason and deliberate about matters of common interest; yet the terms and limits of "privacy" and what determines the private sphere are (at least ideally) themselves a matter for public contestation, deliberation, and resolution. Though there may be long-standing and good reasons for demarcating a certain domain of choice and action as a (more or less) inviolable sphere of privacy, this is not a "natural" category that is discovered, but a socially constituted one that depends on the ongoing collective interpretations of the (political) community.[33] As Habermas has more recently expressed it, "private" and "public" autonomy—roughly, the liberty of the moderns and the liberty of the ancients—are "co-original" (*Gleichuersprunglich*), and neither can be specified or determined in the absence of the other.[34] Rather, for Habermas, these two dimensions of autonomy have their roots in a more general notion of communicative freedom: a basic moral capacity of individuals to be bound only by obligations generated through the exchange of mutually acceptable reasons.[35] This suggests an initial normative concept of freedom that is quite distinct from the liberal view of (negative) liberty as a realm of noninterference and law as necessarily a restriction upon such liberty.

(2) "Civil society," as a set of social institutions, is also "public" in the sense that it refers to the space of choice, action in which individuals, largely through membership in a variety of (more or less voluntary) associations, shape their individual and collective identities and, in turn, give expression to a "public opinion." However, as I suggested above, this "public" is distinct from the "strong public," or formal political system, however much the latter both shapes and is shaped by it. A "weak public" can properly emerge only when there exists a sufficient legal guarantee of the basic liberties of the person, expression, and association; yet the more specific scope and content given to these liberties by a political community requires (again in the ideal case) the continuing input of public opinion generated in the public sphere of civil society. It is against this general set of normative and institutional considerations, for example, that moral debates about the nature and scope of freedom of association can be interestingly posed.[36]

(3) This mutual dependence at both a conceptual and institutional level, of course, gives rise to a complex set of questions about the more specific forms of their interconnection:

(a) What are the available avenues and desirable mechanisms through which public opinion generated within a "weak public" might influence and constrain the deliberations of "strong public"?

(b) Does the state have a responsibility to ensure that voluntary associations of civil society are internally egalitarian and democratic? If so, what measures are available to it to achieve these aims?

(c) What responsibilities, if any, does the state have to support or promote voluntary associations within civil society, especially those whose continued existence might be threatened by changing market economies?

(d) What obligations and responsibilities does the state have to encourage or facilitate discussion among voluntary associations of civil society?

Two broad approaches to these questions seem unacceptable from the perspective of a critical theory aimed at fostering a deliberative politics. The first would be to leave the fate of associations of civil society completely to the whims of "consumer demand"—that is, to regard them just as idealized theories of the free market treat all entrepreneurial ventures: in accordance with the principles of "laissez-faire" and "caveat emptor." A second approach would amount to a blurring or even fusion of state and civil society by granting to the state the primary responsibility for ensuring the cognitive and motivational resources required for maintaining its own legitimacy. This is, I suppose, one way in which Rousseau's remarks on censorship and civil religion might be interpreted.[37] A third and more promising model, it seems to me, can be found in some of the recent discussions of "associative democracy" in which innovative approaches are sought to tap for democratic ends the many resources associations have to offer while at the same time taking steps to limit the effects of the "mischiefs of factions" that often accompany such associations.[38] As Joshua Cohen and Joel Rogers have expressed it, "[T]he core idea of associative democracy is to curb faction through a deliberate politics of association while netting such group contribution to egalitarian-democratic governance."[39] This third model points to the idea of a civil society, as a more or less spontaneous source of public opinion, that necessarily maintains a degree of independence from the state, even if it is not completely immune from state action and regulation. At the same time, though, the state is not viewed as a neutral arbiter or "night watchman" whose sole task consists in refereeing the competition of essentially "private" interests within civil society. Rather, the state possesses at least a limited responsibility for promoting and maintaining associations within civil society that themselves pursue democratic and egalitarian ends.[40]

Re (a): A number of more specific strategies suggest themselves here. To begin, a minimum requirement would seem to be the public financing of federal and state political campaigns in order to curb the extreme influence of money within our political system. Further, one might also explore ways in which the more familiar territorial forms of political representation might be modified and/or complemented by other modes of representation. These could range from attempts at "race-conscious gerrymandering" through proposals for cumulative voting, to proposals for group representation that would in certain instances supplement territorially based interest representation.[41] Finally, there is a need for critical assessment of the potential and limits of new communication media for strengthening the informal public sphere and shaping public opinion. This would involve, among other things, an honest assessment of the real potential for agenda setting from below opened up by the proliferation of cable networks and other computer and telecommunications technologies.[42] It would also require a more affirmative interpretation of First Amendment rights to secure more equitable access to communication resources and (somewhat paradoxically) increased public regulation of communication media.[43] In particular, constitutionally acceptable means need to be found to limit the commercialization of public media and to insulate the effects of corporate power if the mass media are to contribute to the deliberative ideal contained in Habermas's model of the public sphere.

Re (b): The state's responsibility for ensuring that the associations of civil society are internally democratic and egalitarian should depend on the role and power the particular association exercises within society as a whole.[44] However, given the vast array of associations and the multiple purposes they serve, any arguments for governmental intervention and regulation of the internal life of these associations must proceed with caution. In the model of "associative democracy" (in many respects a democratic appropriation of Hegel's "corporatism") the state delegates powers and responsibilities traditionally reserved to it if it can in turn be given certain assurances concerning the competency, accountability, and democratic governance of the association in question. Given such assurances, however, there may be good reasons for entering into such arrangements: As Hegel was also aware, associations (corporations) are often in a stronger position to be informed, to educate, to insure more equitable representation, and to manage problems than are the various institutions of the state. Of course, such experimentation must proceed with caution and with adequate opportunities for oversight and evaluation by all affected parties.

Re (c) and (d): Many associations of civil society cannot survive without the active support of the state.[45] At the same time, the state is not—and never has been—simply a "neutral arbiter," but frequently acts in ways that either facilitate or impede the life of associations of civil society. What, if anything, can justify such actions on the part of the state? I have argued elsewhere that the state violates a principle of liberal neutrality when it acts to promote a particular conception of the good life.[46] However, I have also argued there that the state has a responsibility to help maintain a liberal political culture and the social conditions necessary for its survival—and that means a diverse and robust civil society. In general, I think this means that the state must exercise caution not to enact policies or legislation that (intentionally) disadvantage associations that endorse the values of a liberal political culture. Further, in some cases, the state may even have positive responsibilities to insure the survival of associations against the "normalizing" effects of bureaucratization and consumerization of everyday life.[47] The rationale for such actions, however, must not be to promote a particular conception of the good or way of life, but rather the reasonable claim that its existence is threatened not by the voluntary choices of its members, but by the consequences or side effects of larger systemic forces in the society. There is, then, no right as such for associations to survive; rather, the state's responsibility is to help ensure that "exit" rights from associations of civil society are secured and that the free choices of individuals are not consistently undermined by larger societal forces.[48] Finally, it also seems plausible that for similar reasons the state should help to ensure that effective means of communication are made available to promote discussion and mutual understanding among the diverse associations of a liberal civil society.[49]

CITIZENSHIP AND CONFLICT

Habermas's two-track model of a deliberative democracy, along with the prominent role this accords to civil society, is also introduced as a way to move beyond the impasse between liberals and communitarians concerning their competing conceptions of citizenship and the virtues required for a robust democratic polity (or "civic republicanism" in Taylor's phrase). On the one hand, Habermas has from early on been critical of the "civic privatism" that has seemingly come to characterize much of contemporary liberal political life.[50] A model of the political process in which a thin, largely aggregative conception of citizenship is increasingly pressed between the role of citizen as "client" of the welfare state and "consumer" whose interests need to be met if politicians are to remain in office threatens both the public and private autonomy of citizens. On the other hand, Habermas is suspicious of calls for a renewed civic virtue in which the success of the democratic process is made to depend on strong patriotic identification and individual moral virtues. In an increasingly pluralistic society it is unlikely, according to Habermas, that calls for deep identification and patriotic sentiment will be successful. Habermas's own alternative can be sketched around two complementary features.

(1) Like Michael Walzer and his conception of the pluralist citizen and unlike communitarians such as Taylor and Sandel, Habermas does not locate the source of civic commitment and motivation in their strong identification or attachment to the larger political community, but rather in the variety of associations the state enables under its umbrella of protections. Briefly, it will be recalled that for Taylor the political liberties and virtues required for a robust democratic politics require a fairly high degree of individual self-discipline and commitment to "a shared immediate common good." In a nondespotic regime, the only acceptable source of this discipline is the citizen's own allegiance of "willing identification with the polis." It is this connection between political freedom (or self-rule) and patriotic identification that Taylor describes as the "republican thesis": It is an "essential condition" of a free regime that citizens have this kind of patriotic identification. According to Taylor, however, it is unlikely that the sort of patriotism required will be found within a liberal or "procedural republic," since this type of polity does not foster the appropriate political virtues and liberties and does not encourage the requisite "love of the particular" or "common allegiance to a particular historical community."[51]

According to Walzer, by contrast, "[the pluralist citizen] receives protection and shares in ruling and being ruled, not in spite of his plural memberships but because of them. Citizenship (as a moral choice rather than a legal status) is possible only if there are other groups than the state within the state, and it is fully accepted only by joining other groups along with the state."[52] Similarly, Habermas also locates the cognitive and motivational resources for deliberative politics primarily within civil society, where public opinion and communicative freedom are "generated." Further, Habermas's model also attempts to shift some of the burdens for securing democratic outcomes away from the individual virtues of an active citizenry onto the "anonymous network of communication" in civil society, together with a felicitous arrangement of institutions aimed at securing the influence of the informed and reflective deliberations of a "weak public" upon the formal political system.[53]

(2) At the same time, Habermas does not claim that a robust democratic polity can be achieved without any recourse to civic virtues. On the contrary, he has argued that the institutional infrastructure of civil society must be complemented by a "liberal political culture" and the "sup-

portive spirit of a consonant background of legally noncoercible motives and attitudes of a citizenry oriented toward the common good" (*BFN*, 499). In this context he has also endorsed Albrecht Wellmer's notion of a "democratic *Sittlichkeit*."[54] In contrast to the sort of "thick" patriotism advocated by Taylor and other communitarians, he describes his own proposal as a "constitutional patriotism" (*Verfassungspatriotismus*) in which a citizen's allegiance is primarily directed to the basic rights and principles expressed within the society's political constitution. This, in turn, requires that a relatively clear distinction can be drawn between the "political culture" of a nation-state and the wider culture of a society that might be quite pluralistic. A condition of citizenship or membership in the political community is that a citizen should endorse the basic rights and "constitutional essentials" of the polity, without necessarily assimilating him/herself to the wider culture of the dominant group(s) within the polity.

Objections can, of course, be raised against both of these features. Given that Habermas himself describes the associations of civil society as "wild" and "anarchic," is it really to be expected that they could produce the cognitive and motivational conditions even for Habermas's more restricted version of a constitutional patriotism? And how does the distinction between the political culture (which should be shared by all) and the larger societal culture(s) (which might be quite heterogenous) play itself out in the practice of citizenship and politics? Is it likely that, given such diversity, the "liberal political virtues" required for robust democratic polity can be successfully (and nondespotically) generated and sustained?

Although Habermas has not said very much about the more specific virtues that would be required even for his version of constitutional patriotism, some indication of them can be drawn from scattered remarks in his writings. Central among the political virtues required for "constitutional patriotism" will clearly be attitudes of civility, fairness, toleration, and reasonableness. I will limit my remarks here to the last two virtues.

(a) As many commentators have pointed out, toleration is an important yet elusive liberal virtue.[55] It asks that we live with what we might find deeply repugnant from a personal point of view. In this respect, it is an attitude that, despite its almost banal ring, is both extremely demanding and indispensable to a liberal political culture: On the one hand, we may personally (and justifiably) feel quite opposed to the practice or way of life we are asked to tolerate, yet, on the other hand, we are asked actively to affirm the right of others to engage in that practice or way of life (even though we need not have any regret should that practice or way of life cease to exist).[56] How is it possible to cultivate such an attitude, particularly in a pluralist society, where we are likely to frequently encounter attitudes and ways of life with which we disagree? And, secondly, what are the appropriate limits of such an attitude: Is it necessary to tolerate the intolerable? Is this paradoxical virtue simply one more symptom of an impoverished liberalism that finds itself obliged to defend practices it finds morally repugnant? These are not easy questions to answer, but several brief observations can be made. The distinction noted above between a political culture and the larger societal culture(s) is important here, since the former helps to set the basic frame and limits of the tolerable. In this respect it defines the minimal "core morality," the violation of which need not be tolerated, either from a legal or a moral point of view.[57] (I do not mean that, as a matter of policy, questions such as the legal regulation of hate speech or violent pornography are now immediately settled; but rather that this core morality provides the general framework within which a political community is properly bound to address those topics.) At the same time, however, matters that do not concern the "core morality" of the political culture are ones that all citizens have a moral obligation to tolerate. It may also be that, as part of an attitude of toleration, citizens also have an obligation to try to reach a greater mutual understanding of one another's perspective. The exercise of toleration thus may (*but need not*) develop into stronger forms of appreciation or "civic friendship."

(b) In the context of his exchange with Rawls, Habermas has defended a conception of public reason and corresponding conception of "reasonableness" as an important political virtue and one that is probably as demanding as the virtue of toleration. In connection with his version of "political liberalism" based on the idea of an "overlapping consensus" among divergent comprehensive moral or religious worldviews, Rawls has argued that, as a duty of civility, citizens have a moral obligation, when they consider how to cast their vote, to regard themselves as "ideal legislators" and ask whether the reasons in support of the proposed legislation or policy are ones that it is reasonable to think other citizens could also endorse. He introduces this idea of public reason in connection with an ideal of political legitimacy: "Our exercise of political power is proper only when we sincerely believe that the reasons we would offer for our political actions—were we to state them as government officials—are sufficient, and we also reasonably think that other citizens might also reasonably accept those reasons."[58] In response to criticism of his initial formulation, he now endorses what he calls an "inclusive" model of public reason, which allows citizens to act from reasons drawn from their comprehensive moral or religious convictions so long as they believe the positions they support could "in due course" also be supported on the basis of public reasons all affected could acknowledge on the basis of their shared conception of themselves as free and equal persons.[59] Rawls goes on to indicate that this "duty" applies only to political discussions within the "public political forum," and not to discussion within the larger "background culture" of civil society.[60] Thus, while it is permissible for a person to advocate laws, say, prohibiting same-sex marriages in various associations and forums of civil society, it would be inappropriate for that same person to make such an argument in a political forum where it is not reasonable for him or her to assume that the coparticipants (and cocitizens) could share the same grounds of the argument.[61] Nonetheless, it is clear that this still represents a quite demanding requirement for public reason.

In his own reflections Habermas is led to a similar conception of public reason and, if anything, gives it an even stronger interpretation.[62] "Anything valid should also be capable of a public justification. Valid statements deserve the acceptance of everyone *for the same reasons.*"[63] Thus, for Habermas, though it may indeed be possible for individuals to embed their shared political ideals within their own comprehensive moral or religious worldviews, this connection between private moralities and public reason does not provide a sufficiently stable basis for the legitimate exercise of coercive political authority. Rather, citizens must strive to find a basic political consensus (based on the idea of a "core morality" mentioned above) that all citizens can endorse as valid for the same (publicly available) reasons. The legitimate exercise of political power requires that the reasons that justify at least the basic principles of justice and "constitutional essentials" be ones that all citizens can endorse for the same reasons—that is, in view of their shared conception of themselves as free and equal. Moreover, the political virtue of reasonableness requires that citizens, in regarding themselves as "ideal legislators," seek to find for the policies and legislation they support reasons that they reasonably believe others could reasonably endorse.

Two important objections to this account of the civic virtues need to be addressed: Are they themselves exclusionary and/or sectarian in conception? And is it at all plausible to think that they can be effectively promoted and sustained within the two-track model of democracy sketched above?

(1) The first objection, which has been raised from some quite diverse perspectives, is that the virtues of toleration (and reasonableness) are not innocent, but rather function in ways that are both exclusionary and sectarian. Although this objection raises a number of extremely complex

issues, I want to claim in response that, when properly understood, these virtues do not have to have the exclusionary consequences its critics have claimed. While Kirstie McClure, for example, may be right that the practice of toleration asks, say, religious believers to regard the truth claims of their faith as matters of private belief, it does not follow that it constitutes an unjustifiable or unacceptable harm against them.[64] There is no guarantee that within a liberal polity matters of religious faith and practice or, for that matter, other individual or collective ways of life will remain unchanged. The question must be whether or not individuals have their equal rights and liberties denied them in their treatment by the state. It does not seem to constitute a harm or violation of a right to, say, freedom of speech if one is told that he or she is not morally entitled, in certain political forums, to press claims against others that others do not (and cannot reasonably be expected to) acknowledge. Similarly, the claim that citizens act unreasonably if they promote policies and legislation on the basis of nonpublic reasons does not per se imply that they themselves are the victims of exclusionary or sectarian politics. On the one hand, to claim that it is a violation of a moral duty to pursue positions on the basis of nonpublic reasons within the more narrowly circumscribed political public sphere does not mean that there are not many other forums available within civil society in which those views can be aired and discussed. Secondly, I have again not broached the difficult topic of when (or whether) it is permissible to respond to such moral infractions with legal remedies (for example, the legal regulation of hate speech).[65] Rather, my more general and limited point has been to claim that the civil duty of toleration does not necessarily imply an (unjustifiable) exclusion of others or their points of view.

(2) The second objection is equally challenging: Is it in fact reasonable to assume that in civil society characterized as "wild" and "anarchic" the social and cultural conditions will exist that would be required for the promotion and maintenance of the civic virtues of toleration and reasonableness? Habermas is himself quite aware of this challenge: "On account of its anarchic structure, the general public sphere is, on the one hand, more vulnerable to the repressive and exclusionary effects of unequally distributed social power, structural violence, and systematically distorted communication than are the institutionalized public spheres of parliamentary bodies" (*BFN*, 307–8). There can thus be, it seems, no guarantee that the associations arising within civil society will not be "tribalistic," inegalitarian, or ones that contribute to a culture of group bias and discrimination. Can a liberal political culture be fashioned and sustained under such conditions? It is unlikely that a definitive answer can be given to this question one way or the other. However, at least

until we have more evidence to the contrary, perhaps we should not be overly pessimistic about the possibilities for wider civility even in the face of a civil society that is deeply pluralistic and unruly. On the one hand, the form of civility that is required for a democratic polity may not need to be as "thick" as some communitarians and others have supposed. What is required, it would seem, is a liberal political culture that is based on, and incorporates in its own norms of civility, the "core morality" mentioned above. The bonds of civility may not have to reach so deeply into particular and often sectarian worldviews that it threatens their (at any rate always fluid) identities, and it may be possible to embrace the central elements of a core morality from the perspective of otherwise very different worldviews. (This, I take it, is an important insight of Rawls's idea of an overlapping consensus.)[66]

On the other hand, it is perhaps also the case that we have not sufficiently explored the ways in which government, through its regulatory policy, can help to promote the minimal bonds of civility. This indeed may be one of the major differences between the liberal egalitarianism of the welfare state and Habermas's "two-track" model of a deliberative politics.[67] The largely interventionist and regulatory practices of the liberal welfare state, some have argued, may be counterproductive to their own intended effects.[68] What is required—though it is by no means an easy task—is focus on the (limited) ways in which the state, in cooperation with institutions of civil society, can help to foster the virtues necessary for a liberal political culture.[69]

Conclusions

The preceding remarks have attempted to develop, at least in rough outline, one position on the relation between civil society and the state from the perspective of Habermas's critical social theory. In contrast to classical liberalism, which often blurs any distinction between civil society and a market economy, a critical theory will be much less sanguine about the attempts of voluntary associations of civil society to maintain and reproduce themselves by means of the "invisible hand" of the market alone. On the other hand, in contrast to the liberal egalitarianism of the contemporary welfare state, which often looks all too readily to the interventions of the regulatory state to compensate for the deficits of a market economy, a critical theory will also be suspicious of the state's attempts to provide for its own cognitive and motivational base. The "two-track" model of deliberative democracy proposed by Habermas thus assumes an important division of labor between the "weak publics" within civil society and the "strong public" of the state. At the same time, however, it acknowledges the variety of complex ways in which each is dependent on the other. At a normative level, as I have tried to suggest, this means a break with a theory of (natural) rights that treats the public and the private as clearly demarcated spheres of choice and action. At an institutional level, it means that a critical theory of society must remain open to new possibilities for institutional design and innovation that will work to foster and maintain a balance of strong and weak publics that together secure the public and private autonomy of citizens. These possibilities might include some of the suggestions outlined above, or still others that have not been considered. In any event, a critical theory will have to make its specific proposals for state intervention with caution, so as not to undermine civil society's own role in the production of civil bonds, but, at the same time, it cannot content itself with the thought that the status quo is the best we can do.[70] It is this dissatisfaction with the present state of affairs, together with the challenge to provide "the self-clarification of the struggles and wishes of the age" (Marx), that best expresses the aim of a critical social theory. A rethinking of the relation between civil society and the state must surely be an important part of such a critical project.

NOTES

1. For the history of the Frankfurt School, see especially Rolf Wiggershaus, *The Frankfurt School* (Cambridge: MIT Press, 1994).

2. See, for example, Herbert Marcuse, "Philosophy and Critical Theory," in *Negations: Essays in Critical Theory* (Boston: Beacon Press, 1968), 148.

3. On the latter see, for example, Richard Rorty, *Contingency, Irony and Solidarity* (New York: Cambridge University Press, 1989); and Habermas's critique of Rorty, "Richard Rorty's Pragmatic Turn" in *On the Pragmatics of Communication* (Cambridge: MIT Press, 1998).

4. See Jeffrey Alexander, "The Paradoxes of Civil Society," *International Sociology* 12 (1997): 115–33.

5. See especially Adam Seligman, "Between Public and Private: Toward a Sociology of Civil Society," in *Democratic Civility*, ed. Robert Hefner (New Brunswick, N.J.: Transaction, 1998); and for criticism based on this ambivalence, Carole Pateman, "Feminist Criticism of the Public/Private Dichotomy," in *Feminism and Equality*, ed. Z. Eisenstein (New York: New York University Press, 1989).

6. See Charles Taylor, "Invoking Civil Society" and "Liberal Politics and the Public Sphere," in *Philosophical Arguments* (Cambridge: Harvard University Press, 1995).

7. Ernest Gellner, *Conditions of Liberty: Civil Society and Its Enemies* (New York: Penguin, 1994).

8. A. O. Hirschman, "Social Conflicts as Pillars of Democratic Market Society," *Political Theory* 22 (1994): 203–18.

9. Gellner, *Conditions of Liberty*, 5.

10. For a quick overview, compare the various essays in *Community Works: The Revival of Civil Society in America*, ed. E. J. Dionne, Jr. (Washington, D.C.: Brookings Institution Press, 1998); and in *Toward a Global Civil Society*, ed. Michael Walzer (Providence, R.I.: Berghahn Books, 1995).

11. For a discussion of the significance of this shift, see Manfred Riedel, "'State' and 'Civil Society': Linguistic Context and Historical Origin" in *Between Tradition and Revolution: The Hegelian Transformation of Political Philosophy* (New York: Cambridge University Press, 1984).

12. From a legal perspective, it does not seem that it should be entitled to any more (or any less?) protection than other associations of civil society; see Richard Dien Winfield, *The Just Family* (Albany: State University of New York Press, 1998).

13. Jean Cohen and Andrew Arato, *Civil Society and Political Theory* (Cambridge: MIT Press, 1992), ix; see also Jürgen Habermas, *Between Facts and Norms: Contributions to a Discourse Theory of Law and Democracy*, trans. William Rehg (Cambridge: MIT Press, 1996), 367.

14. This classification also follows the one offered by Kymlicka in his contribution.

15. Habermas, *Between Facts and Norms* (hereafter cited as *BFN*); see also my "Democracy and the *Rechtsstaat*: Remarks on Habermas's *Between Facts and Norms*," in *The Cambridge Companion to Habermas*, ed. Stephen White (New York: Cambridge University Press, 1995).

16. See Jürgen Habermas, "The Horrors of Autonomy: Carl Schmitt in English," in *The New Conservatism* (Cambridge: MIT Press, 1990); for a related criticism of populist and majoritarian conceptions of democracy, see Joshua Cohen, "An Epistemic Conception of Democracy," *Ethics* 97 (1986): 26–38.

17. Cass Sunstein, "Preferences and Politics," *Philosophy and Public Affairs* 20 (1991): 4.

18. Habermas cites Frank Michelman's "Law's Republic" as an example of this sort of republicanism; he might also have referred to some of the writings of Charles Taylor. Habermas's own position seems closest, however, to the "Madisonian" republicanism of Cass Sunstein; see "Beyond the Republican Revival," *Yale Law Journal* 97 (1988): 1539–90.

19. See also B. Manin, "On Legitimacy and Political Deliberation," *Political Theory* 15 (1987): 338–68; and the interesting comparison offered by David Miller in "Deliberative Democracy and Social Choice," *Political Studies* 40 (special issue) (1992): 54–67.

20. Cass Sunstein, "Preferences and Politics," 5; see also Jon Elster, *Sour Grapes* (New York: Cambridge University Press, 1983).

21. See Robert Goodin, "Laundering Preferences," in *Foundations of Rational Choice Theory*, ed. Jon Elster, (New York: Cambridge University Press, 1985), 75–101.

22. Specific proposals for realizing the ideals of a deliberative politics could range from something like James Fishkin's idea of a "deliberative opinion poll" to alternative procedures of voting and modes of representation; see Fishkin, *Democracy and Deliberation* (New Haven: Yale University Press, 1990); Ian McLean, "Forms of Representation and Systems of Voting" in *Political Theory Today*, ed.

David Held, (Stanford, Calif.: Stanford University Press, 1991), 172–96; and Iris Young, "Polity and Group Difference," *Ethics* 99 (1989): 250–74 (which discusses the question of special or group representation).

23. Although I think Donald Moon overestimates the dangers of "unconstrained conversation," especially for individual privacy rights, he points to the difficult question concerning the kinds of institutional design that are appropriate to help ensure that the deliberations conducted in an "unconstrained conversation" influence the process of decision making. Should there, for example, be a system of public voting? See his "Constrained Discourse and Public Life," *Political Theory* 19 (1991): 202–29.

24. For further discussion of "deliberative democracy," see James Bohman and William Rehg, eds., *Deliberative Democracy* (Cambridge: MIT Press, 1998); and Jon Elster, ed., *Deliberative Democracy* (New York: Cambridge University Press, 1998).

25. Habermas takes these terms from Nancy Fraser, who used them to describe Habermas's two-track conception of the public. See "Rethinking the Public Sphere: A Contribution to the Critique of Actually Existing Democracy," in *Habermas and the Public Sphere*, ed. Craig Calhoun (Cambridge: MIT Press, 1989).

26. See *BFN*, 380; and Murray Edelman, *Constructing the Political Spectacle* (Chicago: University of Chicago Press, 1988).

27. See Jürgen Habermas, "What Does Socialism Mean Today?" *New Left Review* 183 (1990): 3–21.

28. Specific proposals for a shared "division of labor" can be found in recent discussions concerning "consociative" and "associative" democracy. See esp., Joshua Cohen and Joel Rogers, "Associative Democracy," *Politics and Society* (1992), and the discussion that follows.

29. *BFN*, 358; compare also Habermas's corresponding remark that a postconventional morality "is dependent upon a form of life that meets it halfway. . . . There must be a modicum of fit between morality and socio-political institutions." *Moral Consciousness and Communicative Action* (Cambridge: MIT Press), 207–8.

30. Sheldon Wolin, "Democracy, Difference, and Re-cognition," *Political Theory* 21 (1993): 480.

31. I have in mind, for example, something like Ronald Dworkin's recent remarks on the "ethical foundations" of liberalism in "The Foundations of Liberal Equality," *The Tanner Lectures*, vol. 11, (Salt Lake City: University of Utah Press, 1990); and Stephen Macedo's discussion in *Liberal Virtues* (Oxford: Clarendon, 1990). See also the related criticism of Habermas's "constitutional patriotism" from a Hegelian perspective, Andrew Buchwalter, "Hegel's Concept of Virtue," *Political Theory* 20 (1992): 576.

32. Habermas, *The Structural Transformation of the Public Sphere* (Cambridge: MIT Press, 1989), 27; and *BFN*, 366.

33. See also Seligman, "Between Public and Private." This has also been an important aspect of feminist criticisms of the traditional liberal distinction between the public and the private, see Pateman, "Feminist Critiques of the Public/Private Dichotomy."

34. *BFN*, chap. 3; see also my discussion in "Democracy and the *Rechtsstaat*."

35. For a discussion of communicative freedom, see Klaus Guenther, "Communicative Freedom, Communicative Power, and Jurisgenesis," in *Habermas on Law and Democracy*, ed. Michel Rosenfeld and Andrew Arato (Berkeley and Los Angeles: University of California Press, 1998).

36. See, for example, *Freedom of Association*, ed. Amy Gutmann (Princeton: Princeton University Press, 1998), in which the question figures prominently of whether the U.S. Supreme Court went too far in *Roberts vs. Jaycees* in requiring the Jaycees to grant full membership rights to women.

37. *On the Social Contract*, bk. 4, chaps. 7 and 8. I am not claiming that Rousseau must be read in this manner; I believe he can also be read in a way consistent with the position developed below.

38. See especially Joshua Cohen and Joel Rogers, "Secondary Associations and Democratic Governance," *Politics and Society* 20 (1992): 393–472; and the further discussion of their proposals in *Associations and Democracy*, ed. Joshua Cohen and Joel Rogers (New York: Verso Press, 1995).

39. Cohen and Rogers, "Secondary Associations," 425.

40. The sort of position I would like to stake out falls short of the "logic of congruence" criticized by Nancy Rosenblum in "Compelled Association," in Gutmann, *Freedom of Association*, and has, I think, affinities with Philip Pettit's notion of an "intangible hand" of regard-awards and sanctions. *Republicanism* (Oxford: Clarendon, 1997.) It would allow, on a case-by-case basis, for limited state intervention in the internal life of those associations whose effects on the lives of individuals are determined to be significant and for which there may not be any ready alternatives.

41. Cohen and Rogers, "Secondary Associations," 424; see also Lani Guinier, *The Tyranny of the Majority* (New York: Free Press, 1994), esp. chap. 5; and Iris Marion Young, *Justice and the Politics of Difference* (Princeton: Princeton University Press, 1990), chap. 6.

42. The extent to which such technologies can further democratic ideals is an open question, though much would seem to depend on questions of ownership and control. For an earlier cautious assessment, see Benjamin Barber, *Strong Democracy* (Berkeley and Los Angeles: University of California Press, 1984); see also J. Blumer, *The Crisis of Public Communication* (New York: Cambridge University Press, 1995).

43. See L. Bollinger, "The Rationale of Public Regulation of the Media," in *Democracy and the Mass Media*, ed. Judith Lichtenberg (New York: Cambridge University Press, 1990); and Cass Sunstein, *Democracy and the Problem of Free Speech* (New York: Free Press, 1993).

44. This seems to have been one of the guiding principles in the majority opinion of the U.S. Supreme Court in *Roberts vs. Jaycees*; see the discussion in Gutmann, *Freedom of Association*.

45. See Michael Walzer, "The Communitarian Critique of Liberalism," *Political Theory* 18 (1990): 17.

46. Kenneth Baynes, "Liberal Neutrality, Pluralism, and Deliberative Politics," *Praxis International* 12 (1992): 50–69.

47. See William Connolly, *Identity/Difference: Democratic Negotiations of Political Paradox* (Ithaca: Cornell University Press, 1991).

48. This position raises a number of extremely difficult questions about the

responsibility of the larger political community to maintain and support the life of minority cultures that I cannot take up within the limits of this chapter; see Will Kymlicka, *Multicultural Citizenship* (New York: Oxford University Press, 1995).

49. See the interesting proposal along this line by Samuel Fleischacker, "Insignificant Communities," in Gutmann, *Freedom of Association*.

50. Jürgen Habermas, *Legitimation Crisis* (Boston: Beacon Press, 1975), 75.

51. Charles Taylor, "Cross-Purposes: The Liberal/Communitarian Debate," in *Liberalism and the Moral Life*, ed. Nancy Rosenblum (Cambridge: Harvard University Press, 1989), 176.

52. Michael Walzer, *Obligations* (Cambridge: Harvard University Press, 1970), 227.

53. For an argument for limited "institutional design" along these lines, see Claus Offe, "Binding, Shackles, Brakes: On Self-Limitation Strategies," in *Cultural-Political Interventions in the Unfinished Project of Enlightenment*, ed. Axel Honneth et al. (Cambridge: MIT Press, 1992).

54. Albrecht Wellmer, "Conditions of a Democratic Culture," in *Endgames* (Cambridge: MIT Press, 1998).

55. See David Heyd, ed., *Toleration: An Elusive Virtue* (Princeton: Princeton University Press, 1996).

56. See T. M. Scanlon, "The Difficulty of Tolerance" in Heyd, *Toleration*.

57. I draw this idea of a shared "core morality" from Charles Larmore, *The Morals of Modernity* (New York: Cambridge Unversity Press, 1996), 12–13.

58. John Rawls, "The Idea of Public Reason Revisited," *University of Chicago Law Review* 64 (1997): 771.

59. Ibid., 776, 784.

60. Ibid., 768, and 775 n. 28.

61. Rawls, it seems to me, is in fact unclear as to whether this constraint applies to all citizens or only to legislators and candidates for public office (see "The Idea of Public Reason Revisited," 767–68, 769, where he suggests that all citizens are to think of themselves *as if* they were legislators).

62. Jürgen Habermas, " 'Reasonable' versus 'True,' or the Morality of Worldviews," in *The Inclusion of the Other* (Cambridge: MIT Press, 1998). I will not address the question here of whether Habermas has given the most sympathetic reading of Rawls; it is at least a reading that is widely shared; see also Joseph Raz, "Facing Diversity: The Case for Epistemic Abstinence," *Philosophy and Public Affairs* 19 (1990): 3–46.

63. Habermas, " 'Reasonable' versus 'True,' " 86.

64. Kirstie McClure, "Difference, Diversity, and the Limits of Toleration," *Political Theory* 18 (1990): 366.

65. See, however, the cautious defense of a regulation of hate speech by Joshua Cohen, "Freedom, Equality, and Pornography " in *Justice and Injustice in Law and Legal Theory*, ed. A. Sarat and T. Kearns (Ann Arbor: University of Michigan Press, 1996); and the very interesting critique of liberal arguments against the regulation of hate speech by Susan Brison, "The Autonomy Defense of Free Speech," *Ethics* 108 (1998): 312–39.

66. See John Rawls, *Political Liberalism* (New York: Columbia University Press,

1993) as well as the argument for mutual respect based on a principle of reciprocity despite deep moral disagreement, in Amy Gutmann and Dennis Thompson, *Democracy and Disagreement* (Cambridge: Harvard University Press, 1996).

67. See Habermas's discussion of a new legal paradigm, in contrast to both the classical liberal and the welfare state paradigms, in *BFN*, chap. 9.

68. See, among others, Avishai Margalit, *The Decent Society* (Cambridge: Harvard University Press, 1996).

69. See, again, the interesting proposal concerning the use of the "intangible hand" of the state for such a purpose in Pettit, *Republicanism*.

70. I take this to be one of the important insights in Nancy Rosenblum's arguments against the "logic of congruence" referred to in note 40 above.

Skeptics at the Celebration: Civil Society and the Early Frankfurt School

Stephen K. White

THE FRANKFURT SCHOOL of critical theory is often thought of as speaking with two voices. This distinction is chronological as well as substantive. On the one hand, there are the views of the early Frankfurt School thinkers, especially Theodor Adorno, Max Horkheimer, and Herbert Marcuse. On the other, there are the views of Jürgen Habermas and the large contingent that now associates itself with his thought to one degree or another. Habermas's work in the 1980s and 1990s can be brought to bear fairly directly on the topic of civil society, as Kenneth Baynes's essay illustrates. Civil society is that variegated space of institutions and practices that, for Habermas, reproduces itself primarily through "communicative action." It is distinguished from the state and economy, which constitute systemic patterns of interconnection, steering themselves through the media of administrative power and money.[1]

From a Habermasian perspective, contemporary democratic societies face an underlying persistent problem. The spheres of civil society experience a systematic threat that Habermas refers to as the "colonization of the lifeworld." In part, this means the invasion of the logic of commodity production and exchange into underlying processes of cultural reproduction. This notion is Habermas's variation on a long-standing critique of capitalism by the Frankfurt School. But the term "colonization" also applies to a threat from state power; and the highlighting of this threat of "juridification" marks a new wariness within critical theory toward ways in which the state can deplete the sources of "communicative rationality" and the possible flow of "communicative power" from within civil society to the state. These problems make the goal of invigorating civil society crucial. Democracy is healthy only when public spheres are continually confronting formal political institutions with the collective force of conviction generated from deliberative processes.[2]

So much for the Habermasian voice. If we ask, however, about the way the earlier voice of critical theory might engage the topic of civil society, things are less clear. Marcuse, Horkheimer, and Adorno were generally averse to any positive speculation about institutions. Early in their careers, this was at least partly due to that familiar Marxian reluctance to specify exactly what institutions are appropriate after the revolution. But later their reflections became disconnected from that anchor, because the very idea of revolution lost any systematic coherence. Then the aversion to institutional speculation appeared to become somehow tied to an idea of the responsibility of philosophical reflection itself.

Back in the 1950s, an American Protestant minister, Norman Vincent Peale, wrote a popular book entitled *The Power of Positive Thinking*.[3] Marcuse, by contrast, extolled what he called "the power of negative thinking."[4] Adorno would certainly have endorsed that commitment.[5] But what does this affirmation of negativity actually imply? Against what is critique directed and in the name of what is it launched?

As for targets of critique, at least in regard to the issue of civil society, I have no doubt that these critical theorists would direct their first fire at classical liberals. Accordingly, in a moment, I will try to engage some specific questions about civil society in the form of the sort of critique I think Marcuse and Adorno might offer to the answers presented by Scalet and Schmidtz's contribution to this volume. But before turning to that exercise, though, it is necessary to say something more generally about the basis from which such critique is launched.

As the image of revolution receded from these thinkers' views, both temporally and conceptually, the normative standpoint of critique became ever more amorphous. And yet it did not disappear. However uncertain, critique always retains a couple of footholds. It hovers in unspecific hopes of social reconciliation, and it erupts unexpectedly but continually out of the lived experience of injustice and suffering. In regard to the latter, Adorno writes: "[T]he physical moment tells our knowledge that suffering ought not to be." Suffering is "the unrest that makes knowledge move."[6] Such an emphasis is echoed in Marcuse's sense that there is a visceral or biological basis for political resistance. This minimalist appeal to an invariant ground for social critique continues to be joined, however, with a view that all other aspects of social reality are historically conditioned. Accordingly, these critical theorists always retained a concern to unmask efforts to reify aspects of capitalism, making them appear to have a life of their own outside of history. As Adorno puts it, "All reification is a forgetting."[7]

How might these resources be brought to bear on what could only be called the celebration of civil society over the last decade? As I said earlier, critical theory's main target here would be the classical liberal position. It earns this role for a couple of reasons. First, there is its basic assumption that the inclusion of economic organizations among the associations of civil society entails by definition a net increase in freedom.

Second, there is its fundamental reification of the boundary between state and civil society, as well as its reification of the liabilities the state poses for civil society.

Scalet and Schmidtz admirably set out the basic commitments of classical liberalism. The most foundational of these is that once the state secures the "basic rule of law," then civil society will allow human life to "flourish" to its highest degree. Civil society seems almost to take on a natural telos: there people tend toward the maximum of freedom, and there resides a "tendency to volunteerism." The slide toward reification is palpable. Accordingly, politics, bureaucrats, and the power over which they dispose can only constitute "an *alien intrusion*." With the state representing such a universal liability, people of good conscience have only one option: lend their shoulder power to pushing back the engine of the state.

Having established this bipolar social world as the invariant background, classical liberals can then take up what necessarily become leftover or residual issues. Now is when the question of economic power is raised to the level of discursive consciousness. But as soon as it is raised, we are told abruptly to be "realistic"; the threat or liability constituted by economic power is "surely . . . trivial in comparison to that posed by [the] state."[8]

The reified portrait of social life accordingly does its work. Economic power, when raised as a leftover issue, gets treated like leftovers from dinner: nudged back on the refrigerator shelf and forgotten. What are we to make of such a rhetorical strategy? When Milton Friedman used it in *Capitalism and Freedom*, first published in 1962, the social model of bipolarity could be placed against the background of Cold War bipolarity. Anxiety about the state at that time always involved talk of slippery slopes and a world potentially dominated by totalitarian states. No small threat indeed. But would it not be "realistic" to question whether, in the United States of today, this kind of worry does not begin to look a little obsessive? Would it not be "realistic" to think in terms of a more nuanced perception of what engenders suffering and thwarts human flourishing?

As I said earlier, Marcuse and Adorno do not really give us anything by way of an answer as to how to grapple systematically and institutionally with such questions. And classical liberals will no doubt worry that statist dreams lie in the background. At least in Marcuse's case, this suspicion may be warranted. Adorno, on the other hand, was, I suspect, utopian in such a way that he would want us to cry out against suffering whether it comes at the hands of civil society or the state.

But of course classical liberals have an advantage here. Suffering that comes from "visible" hands tends to be far more easily recognizable than suffering from "invisible" ones. The former usually seems to result more from coordinated, intentional action and thus blame can be more clearly assigned. From Adorno's perspective, however, this asymmetry would merely heighten the responsibility of philosophical thought to be attentive to the less obtrusive ways in which a civil society dominated by the logic of capital engenders suffering.

Contrast the city of Chicago with Frankfurt. I suspect many inner-city kids in the former experience outdoor life as a kind of low-grade imprisonment: little or no place to ride a bike safe from traffic; little or no place to simply lie down on a green expanse and look at the sky. A lot fewer kids in Frankfurt face this kind of low-grade suffering. In the post–World War II era, the state has clearly asserted sufficient power over zoning and land use to ensure what is an extraordinary system of parks within the city and easy access by public transportation to numerous state parks on the city's edge. Even more remarkable for an American to discover is the highly elaborate system of footpaths and bike paths that extend onto and across private land.

My point is not to idealize the German welfare state. It clearly has many problems and faces many tough choices about possibly reducing its range of activity. There is really not much that Adorno's legacy offers us in the way of enlightenment on most of these questions. Nevertheless, perhaps it can, first, make us a little more reluctant to frame such questions in terms of a reified picture of civil society and state, within which the liabilities reside overwhelmingly in only one sphere; and second, perhaps it can solicit from us a bit more sensitivity to the lived experience of suffering on the part of disadvantaged segments of the population. Beneath the din of the celebration of civil society—at least in its classical liberal guise—we should listen for the less obtrusive sounds.

None of what I have said should imply that the Habermasian voice of critical theory is wholly incapable of speaking to such a concern. As I noted earlier, and as Baynes's essay shows, Habermas is sensitive to ways in which the unfolding logic of market relations is blind to deformations of the lifeworld. Nevertheless, this notion of deformation or colonization is fairly abstract. It directs us to analyze a given social situation and ask: How are consensual processes tied to communicative action blocked, shunted aside, or left unexplored as the force of capital makes itself felt? This is, I would argue, a crucial heuristic question for a radical democratic imagination. However, by itself, it may focus us a bit too narrowly on explicit communicative processes and institutional procedures. A democratic imagination must also continually cultivate a sensitivity for the lived, but often unobtrusive, experience of suffering. Here is where we do well not to forget the earlier voice of critical theory.

Notes

1. Jürgen Habermas, *The Theory of Communicative Action*, vols. 1 and 2, trans. Thomas A. McCarthy (Boston: Beacon Press, 1984, 1987), vol. 2, pt. 6.

2. *The Theory of Communicative Action* 2:183–96, 283, 318–31, 356–73; and *Between Facts and Norms: Contribution to a Discourse Theory of Law and Democracy*, trans. William Rehg (Cambridge: MIT Press, 1996), 147–51, 366–71.

3. Norman Vincent Peale, *The Power of Positive Thinking* (Englewood Cliffs, N.J.: Prentice-Hall, 1952).

4. Herbert Marcuse, *Reason and Revolution* (Boston: Beacon Press, 1960), vii.

5. Max Horkheimer and Theodor Adorno, *Dialectic of Enlightenment*, trans. John Cummings (New York: Herder and Herder, 1972); and Theodor Adorno, *Negative Dialectics*, trans. E. B. Ashton (Continuum, 1973).

6. Adorno, *Negative Dialectics*, 203.

7. Theodor Adorno, *An Essay on Liberation* (Boston: Beacon Press, 1969), 4–6, 10–11, 30. Adorno is cited by Marcuse in *The Aesthetic Dimension* (Boston: Beacon Press, 1978), 73.

8. At least Scalet and Schmidtz admit that economic power is some kind of threat. Contrast Milton Friedman's move at this rhetorical point in his classical liberal analysis of power. After equating capitalism and freedom initially, Friedman then admits that there is such a thing as economic power; but he says not to worry, since it functions only in a benign fashion. Concentrations of capital are available to fund and encourage new, radical political ideas and movements. Without going into the historical adequacy of this claim about dissenting movements in American history, one could nevertheless note here that a mode of power that can only be used for good purposes is a strange phenomenon indeed on the social landscape. *Capitalism and Freedom* (Chicago: University of Chicago Press, 1962), chap. 1.

Feminist Perspectives on Civil Society and Government

Nancy L. Rosenblum

THERE ARE as many feminist perspectives as there are political theories, and then some. Contemporary feminists who subscribe to critical theory have a different perspective on civil society than do poststructuralists or "radical feminists," to say nothing of at least some conservative thinkers whose claim to feminism cannot be lightly dismissed. It is impossible to discuss the foundational differences that separate feminist theorists here. My approach is to survey feminist perspectives on our themes and to indicate significant areas of consensus and disagreement, without probing the theoretical roots of agreements and divisions. Fortunately, readers can refer to other essays in this volume for the foundations of feminist perspectives in liberalism, libertarianism, and critical theory. In addition, some feminist theory is rooted in religious traditions that women transform from within. Several of this volume's essays on religious perspectives address the status of women and the family, at least in passing.

Equally important for indicating the range of feminist perspectives on civil society and government, feminists writing from the vantage point of advanced industrial societies with established liberal democratic constitutions have orientations different from those concerned with democratization and development in other parts of the world. Feminism abroad is homegrown. At the same time it is often inspired by Western feminist theories, finds resources there, and adopts Western feminist objectives. Much of feminism is genuinely cosmopolitan.[1] Of course, feminism abroad grows out of experience with more damaging inequalities at law and in the basic needs of day-to-day life than feminists here now confront. Among them is the dependence of civil rights for women on ethnic and religious identity in matters of property, education, marriage, and divorce. Voluntarism does not characterize association in some places; membership affects the distribution of basic rights and benefits; and civil society is "segmented." The literature of feminism in relation to civil society as it has emerged within political and religious traditions around the world merits a report of its own.[2] I have regretfully restricted this discussion to Western, predominantly American, feminist theory that speaks directly to this volume's topical approach to civil society and government.

BOUNDARIES

Boundaries is a key term for feminist theorists. It is not much of an exaggeration to say that analyzing, deconstructing, and redrawing distinctions and "differences" is their main intellectual business. Male/female and public/private are the originals that spawned academic disciplines devoted to identifying the ideas and activities that threaten (or promise) to shift, subvert, erase, reverse, displace, or transcend the socially constructed boundaries feminists judge misplaced and harmful.[3]

In her essay for a companion Ethikon volume, Anne Phillips points out that civil society is not a significant organizing category in the feminist tradition.[4] By contrast, the public/private boundary is. Put simply, public/private designates the areas of social, economic, and political life collectively designated "public," from which many women have been excluded, and the domestic sphere, in which many but not all women have been sequestered. Feminist theorists have been intent on making two points: first, that political theory, particularly liberal theory, presents public/private as if it applies to all people, neglecting its historically gendered aspect; second, that where the gendered separation of spheres is acknowledged, patriarchal premises suggest that "separate spheres" is justified and that public life is the domain of men.[5] Feminist theory has labored to uncover and counter both propositions.

For feminist theorists, the public/private distinction and its critical corollary, "the personal is political," are shorthand for the idea that relations of domination and subordination along gender lines infuse social and domestic life. These are not spontaneous. Power relations and political decisions systematically structure so-called private spheres: from marriage laws and fiscal policies that affect family structure to the treatment of domestic violence in the criminal justice system. Women's public and private statuses are inextricably linked, even today, when women have formally equal civil and political rights and opportunities. This means that women's "private" needs and aspirations are not purely personal and individual but shared by the group, and that some forms of injustice are so long-standing and mundane as to be overlooked. These matters are proper subjects for political theory, political action, and public policy. Indeed, the most severe challenges to this divide depreciate the "personal" and "privacy" per se, collapsing public/private boundaries altogether; although a number of important efforts have been made to revalue privacy in feminist terms.[6]

Civil society/government does not correspond to this public/private boundary, and feminist theorists do not level the same wholesale critique at the civil society/government divide. On the one hand, respect for this boundary makes an appearance in feminist theory intent on protecting some dimension of independence for civil society as a relatively "free space" for women's activism and collective self-discovery free from state regulation and from government patronage, which often comes with strings that alter the directions of women's groups. This concern is shared by feminists interested in relatively formal and stable secondary associations that socialize women into mainstream "civic culture" and by feminists principally interested in "subaltern counterpublics," associations engaged in contestation and resistance, unorthodox political activities, and radical economic initiatives.[7] Of course, scope for freedom of association is also the concern of feminists who appreciate that it is not just instrumental but a good in itself, an essential element of freedom.

On the other hand, insofar as civil society/government suggests a strong barrier against government regulation and intervention on the model of the strict American separation of church and state, feminist theorists are willing to see the barrier lowered.[8] They accent the legal and political structures that shape the deeply gendered character of many associations and the coercive nature of private—that is, nongovernmental—power.[9] The corrective is to subject the associations of civil society to public norms of equality, enforced by the state.

Moreover, feminist theorists do not follow the usual course of political theory, which is to locate the family outside civil society as a natural and primary rather than "secondary association."[10] Because private choices with regard to sex, marriage, and reproduction as well as religious affiliation and certain other memberships are said to assume a degree of autonomy and consent women do not have or, alternatively, to be based on preferences distorted by inequality, feminist thinkers question the "private" and "voluntary" character of family and associational life. There is considerable variation among feminist philosophers, most notably between Habermasians and poststructuralists, on the ontological contours of women's agency and rationality, on the extent to which women can act outside the bounds within which they are socially constructed and regulated. But as I will observe again shortly, these disparities are not necessarily reflected in practical critiques of the family and secondary associations. We see a gap between ontology and political theory. In any case, given the connection between status within the family and in social and political spheres, feminist theorists are united in assigning the family a central place in civil society.[11]

Civil society/government does not correspond to the public/private boundary in another important respect. It is a corrective to gross claims that women are excluded from some singular "public sphere."[12] Civil society comprises plural, partial publics.[13] It is a reminder that "public" is not identical to formal political institutions but extends to cultural and social groups. In feminist theory, "civil society" and "public space" are imbued with progressive, normative significance—for good reason.

The history of women's organization and institution building takes place in civil society. The period from the 1870s to 1920s was the heyday of separatist associations in the United States, which included the opening of women's colleges, the establishment of professions like nursing and teaching, and voluntary associations like the women's club movement that claimed over one million members and linked local groups in nationwide networks and federations.[14]

Civil society draws attention to the political education and activism of seemingly immobilized women through associations that appear to be apolitical, reminding us that association and networks of associations are *the* source of collective action for those without formal political power, economic resources, or social prestige. That is true today in countries where women are effectively disenfranchised. Even after female suffrage in the United States, association has been more important for women's political influence than the vote. And women's associations have added to the "organizational repertoire" in politically significant ways.[15] The radical potential of voluntary association for mobilization and social reform is clear. I will say more about the transformation of groups into political actors below.

Today, the membership rolls of innumerable intermediate associations are dominated by women, and in some important groups women are predominant. The lesson of the "second wave" of the women's movement in Western democracies is that even progressive political groups like civil rights and antiwar groups in the 1960s and 1970s marginalized women members. The rapid integration of women into previously male-dominated mainstream associations is the dramatic story of contemporary civil society in the last several decades: from the National Democratic Party in the United States to representation on corporate and nonprofit boards. In a pair of moves, feminists have successfully integrated established associations and they have organized parallel business and professional associations and formed influential subgroups or caucuses within associations like the American Political Science Association. Women's studies programs in universities are another example of the mix of institutional integration and feminist innovation—affecting the policies, norms, discourse, and substantive purposes of institutions. Women members dissent from gendered structures and initiate reforms in churches, unions, and charitable groups. In workplaces women push for improvement in areas that are not susceptible to laws and litigation surrounding equal pay or sexual harrassment—from "glass ceilings" to flextime. Mary Fainsod Katzenstein calls this the "unobtrusive mobilization" of feminism.[16]

This picture is not complete without noting that many associations, particularly at the local level, have traditionally depended on the unpaid labor of women. The economic transformation of women and their movement away from volunteerism and the substitution of professionalism for volunteerism in innumerable organizations have had consequences for the structure and functions of civil society.[17] Feminist evaluations of these changes are mixed, for the sound reasons Susan Okin notes in her commentary.

Feminist theorists have a distinctive approach to locating and patrolling the civil society/government boundary, then. Freedom for association argues for independence from government intervention, but the need to enforce equal protection laws and the desirability of various forms of state support for groups argue for intervention. As with any boundary, protection is two-way, and feminist theorists also recognize reasons to protect government from the undue influence of particularist associations. A common feminist caution is that the "independence" of government, like "impartial government," is a ruse or impossibility and that government has typically reflected and reproduced inequality and oppression.[18] That is why "impartiality" vis à vis gender and civil rights is seen as disregard for the difference between formal and substantive equality at best, as an assimilationist ideal based on a male standard at worst. Rather, what is needed is public recognition of salient "differences" (radical feminists would say "domination") and compensatory differential rights and benefits.[19]

Nonetheless, skepticism of official impartiality does not signal rejection of government autonomy as an aspiration in areas relevant to feminism. Transformative public commitment to substantive equality clearly assumes the possibility that government does not simply mirror civil society, with its myriad groups that silence, exclude, or marginalize women. This attitude is captured in the title of a recent article, "Learning to Live with the State," and leads to a discussion of "needs."[20]

Needs

Civil society and government are mutually dependent. Feminist theory contains a catalog of benefits government provides or should provide to insure a flourishing civil society hospitable to women's needs and organization:[21]

• Legislation and judicial decisions beginning in the 1960s have given feminists an important armament in pressing their claims. Many feminist theorists advocate progressive constitutionalism designed to alter the social practices of secondary associations.[22] With exceptions (the rights of religious groups under the free exercise clause of the U.S. Constitution, for example), secondary associations must conform to statutory and constitutional requirements of due process and equal protection. Legal rulings have opened previously restricted membership groups to women. In the 1984 case *Roberts v. Jaycees* the U.S. Supreme Court required this quasi-social, quasi-business, quasi-civic association and a host of similar groups to admit women as full members.[23] These decisions incorporate feminist arguments that substantive equality requires that antidiscrimination law reach down into social groups as well as workplaces, schools, and "public accommodations." Because these groups are sources of social and economic opportunity, there is a compelling public interest in seeing that women are not excluded from the valuable goods and privileges membership provides.

• Antidiscrimination law applied to voluntary associations further reflects feminist arguments that state action is necessary to eliminate the moral harms and injuries to self-respect that accompany social exclusion. The idea is that discrimination is diffuse and woven from one sphere to another, and that government intervention is the principal means of unraveling this seamless web of second-class membership and second-class citizenship.[24] When government fails to intervene to sever the presumptive connection between certain capacities and sex, the argument continues, it morally legitimizes conventional gender roles and encourages inequality.

• The "welfare state" is a misnomer not only because it falls short of insuring welfare, but also because so much of its programming is provided by state/civil society partnerships. In the United States, government subsidies make up 50 percent or more of the budgets of secular and religious groups that provide social services, including innumerable groups run by and serving women, from battered women's shelters to child care programs. There has been "a blurring of boundaries between who is and is not a movement activist, between hierarchical and collective processes, and between movement and mainstream institutions."[25] Feminist theorists may resist this, and want to "decolonize" and "repoliticize" services to and by women, but they do not oppose public subsidies.[26] They also want government to insure that groups and subcommunities providing public goods are regulated, with safeguards for nondiscrimination both within the organization and in its distributions.

• Women and children make up the bulk of the poor, and women constitute a disproportionate number of the aged.[27] As principal beneficiaries of some forms of public support, women and children are the most disadvantaged by political attacks on federal and state programs. No degree of well-organized philanthropy and self-help can substitute for government in meeting basic needs and insuring fairness. Feminist theorists critique what Carole Pateman has called "the patriarchal welfare state" and the transformation of women from private dependents into clients dependent on a "patriarchal and androcentric state bureaucracy."[28] But when criticism of the welfare state shifts from the political left to the right or to libertarianism, and aims at retrenchment and privatization, feminist theorists defend state activism.[29]

• Inequalities between men and women are significant impediments to participation in associational life as they are to political participation. This has particular importance for those who see civil society as the seedbed of democratic participation. The worth of political rights and civil liberties depends on background conditions that give people the capability and opportunity to exercise them. The same holds for membership in associations. Except for religious groups, membership correlates with social and economic status—not surprisingly, since association is a matter of resources and skills. General social policies with regard to education and employment, particularly women's status in the workplace, provide a necessary floor for women's participation. Laws governing the workplace—hiring, promotion and pay, maternity leave with employment security, and child care policy—affect women's economic well-being and available leisure time. Association membership is in part a factor of free time (itself a complex matter involving conflict between the occupational life cycle and the life cycle of the family). Similarly, women's "vulnerability by marriage" is one of Susan Okin's powerful themes. It includes a domestic division of labor in which women's principal role in child care and household work amounts to a "double shift," the result in part of political decisions and at least partly remediable by legislation. These inequalities affect patterns of participation in civil society overall.

• The isolation some women suffer on account of family responsibilities, paralysis and fear produced by domestic violence or neighborhood violence, and disassociation resulting from depression or aggressiveness are all part of the larger problem of isolation. Anomie may be a graver problem for women today than is discriminatory exclusion. Government can facilitate these women's entry into associations indirectly by making child care and adult day care available, along with counseling and drug rehabilitation services. Government can also combat destructive isolation indirectly by making opportunities for work attractive and meaningful, since the workplace is the principal scene of recruitment into associations of all kinds.

- Government protection against violence toward women and the condition of fear and shame in which many women live deserves separate mention.[30] Feminist theorists indicate how laws, police conduct, and enforcement mechanisms are ineffective in protecting women against rape, sexual abuse including child abuse, and violence. Closely connected to this is the "silencing" of women. Proposed remedies include preventive measures, new tort crimes and criminal penalties, public policies of censorship, and public funding for programs to meet the large-scale needs of battered women and their children.

- In multicultural democracies where minority ethnic and religious groups claim self-government and legal recognition for personal law, government can and should vigorously enforce uniform civil and criminal laws that protect women from oppressive practices. Typically, the central focus of group rights claims is control over personal, sexual, and reproductive life via male control of women in matters ranging from property and education to child marriage, clitoridectomy, and "cultural defenses" against crimes like "marriage by capture" and infanticide.[31] Laws and judicial action are necessary to preserve the basic individual rights of women.

Reversing the question of needs, feminist theorists are also in accord about what government needs from civil society. The political legitimacy and stability of government and of particular policies are conditional on politically relevant groups having a reasonably effective political voice. Women must have resources of organization and leadership, access to public spaces for communication, and effective political representation. Formal civil and political equality does not suffice. That is why Carole Pateman asserts, "For feminists, democracy has never existed."[32]

The diverse justifications for insuring women's voice range from the injustice of exclusion per se so that inclusion has independent value, to the symbolic importance of women representatives for collective self-respect; from vigorous advocacy of women's interests and opinions, to the incorporation of "perspectives" said to be inseparable from personal experience and to require what Anne Phillips calls "the politics of presence."[33] I will say more about this below.

Many strands of feminist theory see the associations of civil society chiefly as preparatory arenas for political organizing and agenda building, political influence and representation. It is worth noting that feminists often place less emphasis on voting and electoral politics than on the development of a sense of political competence and the formation of a plurality of democratically organized associations outside of official political arenas. They look to civil society to generate not only elites who can represent women, but active citizens. Simplifying, feminists support two types of democratic theory that cast associations as seedbeds of democracy.

Democratic theorists from a variety of critical theory and liberal perspectives see participation in terms of deliberation. Here, the rationale for representation is that justice requires maximizing the perspectives that are brought to public discussion. The idea is that differences will be represented and preserved, but that the conditions imposed on deliberation are such that self-interest will be dislodged from its central place and the link between social inequality and political standing will be broken. The conditions of deliberation should allow for disinterested communication, the emergence of new interests and needs, and common understanding.[34] Some theorists of deliberative democracy argue for stringent "conversational constraints" and look for consensus and a universalizable conception of justice. The larger point, pressed home by feminist theorists, is that politics is "discursive"; that is, interpreting language and normative practices and altering understanding is a vital part of politics. The function of civil society is to give women (and men) experience not only in identifying needs and values but also in "taking the standpoint of the other," in discursive reasoning and grounds of public justification. Jean Cohen sees "an elective affinity between the discourse ethic and modern civil society as the terrain on which an institutionalized plurality of democracies can emerge."[35]

A second view sees democratic participation in terms of often irreducible conflict and inequality and argues that even if inequalities were evened out, few political outcomes are incontestably fair. This is not to say that adversary democracy is based on naked self-interest or that outcomes cannot rest on areas of agreement.[36] The point is that as "seedbed," civil society must provide women with more than education in deliberation. Women need multiple strategies and tools. They need to be able to sharpen areas of conflict, shape rhetoric, form organizations, weld effective alliances, raise money, and negotiate concessions, using political methods that often have little to do with deliberation.

Given these differences within democratic theory, there is broad agreement among feminists on the link between political voice and justified government policy, and on the fact that women's political voices are generated from below, from their unregulated self-organization in civil society. Since wherever there is freedom of association, pluralist groups of all kinds will flourish, including those dedicated to or unconsciously serving antifeminism, the question arises: What can be done to enhance feminist voices? What can make women full participants in deliberation or contestation?

Proposals to assign government a redistributive role begin with modest interventions like legal requirements altering the membership practices of restrictive groups (though differentially; on this view, all-female groups should be left alone as compensation for historical exclusion and to encourage women's leadership). Beyond that are proposals for government to counter inequalities of resources—leadership and organizational skills, funds, and so on—to help in repairing "associational disadvantage" by providing special benefits to weak groups (so long as they are the "right" groups). This entails providing public forums for meetings and avenues of communication such as free media airtime. Or it means offering special tax benefits and subsidies to associations that represent important social interests, and are internally democratic and other-regarding in their participation in policy making. The idea is to alter the "terms, conditions, and public status" of certain groups, including feminist groups, for democratic purposes.[37]

Alternatively, feminists argue that government should *restrict* the voices and activities of powerful groups judged to distort public discussion, drown out weaker voices, or have a corrosive or unfair influence on public life. These proposals magnify the difficulties that plague proposals to censor pornography (or only pornography portraying male domination of women): Who judges? Who identifies disadvantaged (or privileged) groups, against what baseline? The problem is particularly severe if we consider charges among women generally and feminists in particular that a particular "difference" is most salient, that a particular group that sees itself as progressive is really complicitous in the subordination of other women, and so on.

I have represented feminist perspectives on what government needs from civil society as grounded in larger democratic theories of political legitimacy, stability, and justice. Is there anything overarching that distinguishes a wide range of feminist perspectives on political socialization and organization? Several propositions have become virtual orthodoxies.

- Women bring distinctive substantive concerns to the public agenda. Women are future-looking, child-regarding, and value rather than despise dependency. Though the empirical evidence is not firm, there appear to be identifiable "gender gaps" on matters of war, capital punishment, and government spending overall.[38] Often the normative implication of this catalog is that women's interests are not selfish or particularist but disinterested and inclusive. Or that their "perspectives" can be distinguished from interests altogether because women do not conform to the rational calculator "economic man"; they reject "strategic paradigms" and distributive models.[39] They look beyond justice to reciprocity and care.
- Looking beyond substantive goals, women bring to political discussion distinctive experiences of subordination, exploitation, and

"otherness," and familiarity with the mechanisms through which they operate. They recognize power relations where men do not see them. They alert us to the sexual politics embedded in symbols and language, conventions of dress and comportment, forms of communication, and social roles that are implicitly organized around a presumptive "male subject." They justify reformed standards of merit, excellence, and success.

• Women's groups generally (or feminist groups specifically) exemplify particular modes of organization and communication. They tend to be horizontal rather than vertical and sometimes strictly egalitarian—downplaying leadership positions, minimizing division of labor, and aiming at decision making by consensus rather than through formal procedures. Aware of the conditions that silence women, they try to draw out members' voices. Their inner workings are designed to allow for the exhibition of empathy; they benefit from ways of thinking that took root in the family, in particular "attention" and an effort at identification with others. They incline to consultation and cooperation and are averse to conflict and direct exercises of authority.[40] They would replace "power over" by "power with."[41] They see compromise as aggressive deal making and favor consensus building. On some descriptions, women's groups are models of minidemocracy rightly understood. They actualize the norms of deliberative democracy, including respect, reciprocity, and so on.

There are feminist dissenters from all these claims. Theorists who follow Hannah Arendt and define politics and public life generally in terms of "agonistic" relations, resistance, and negativity object to this benign assessment of feminist groups. On this view, freedom appears only in struggle and resistance; in this spirit Julia Kristeva points up the large number of women in terrorist groups.[42] Also dissenting are theorists like Catherine MacKinnon, who caution that these presumably distinctive attributes are not really "ours" but patriarchal constructs that should not be uncritically affirmed.[43] On the institutional point, dissenting feminists argue that the organization and communication of small face-to-face women's groups cannot carry over into political arenas; size and purpose matter. They caution that the transmission belt model, which assumes that competence in decision making in secondary associations carries over into political decision making in official institutions, is unwarranted.

When it comes to feminist perspectives on the *values* civil society imparts to government, the answer is contingent and depends on the terrain of group life. Feminist theorists do not exhibit uncritical appreciation for civil society per se; clearly so if we think of religious associations. Some feminists see organized faiths (both established churches and new and imported religions) as irredeemably patriarchal, and are either militant secularists or radical reformers campaigning for doctrinal changes and reform of the internal government of religious life: the ordination of women priests, for example. Others are more sympathetic toward the complexity of women's spiritual needs, the variability of women's status within religious groups, the radicalism of faith-based social movements, and the fact that religious organizations have been unintended training grounds for women who apply these resources to feminist purposes.[44]

In any case, feminist theorists are more discriminating about the values civil society imparts than are contemporary left and right Tocquevillians, who attribute to it an exhaustive list of virtuous effects: countering atomistic individualism, downplaying rights for duties, cultivating habits of cooperation, generating social capital, and so on. Feminists are less likely to imagine that social capital is as fungible as capital or that "trust" developed in one arena is transferable to another. They recognize that interpersonal trust generated in face-to-face relations is contextual, does not extend automatically to impersonal settings, and is often unwarranted when it does.[45]

When it comes to their own groups, however, feminist theorists incline to the same sanguine assessment of the same wide range of beneficial effects as civil society enthusiasts generally. There is a propensity to portray feminist groups, in exhilarating moral terms, as "free public spaces." They are "liberated zones," "environments in which people are able to learn a new self-respect, a deeper and more assertive group identity, public skills." They represent feminist groups as the sociological correlate of their normative notions of public space.[46] The women's movement is "a *minimal utopia* of social life characterized by nurturant, caring, expressive and nonrepressive relations."[47]

When we reverse the question, it is less clear what *values* feminist theorists think government imparts to civil society. Those friendly to liberal civil and political rights regard legalism in the hands of independent courts and the fair administration of progressive policy as principal means of improving the condition of women. For the most part, however, feminists are rarely positive about legalism or bureaucratization, which Habermasians characterize as the colonization of the "lifeworld" and Foucauldians as disciplinary mechanisms that ought to be resisted. Other feminists simply see government agencies as depoliticizing. On this view, administrative centers remove decisions from democratic participation. More radically (and perversely), legal rulings and social policies, even when they serve equality, may be seen as narrowing rather than expanding the space of protest and resistance.[48] The antibureaucratic tradition within feminism is strong. It is one reason for enthusiasm for "insurgent" movements—oppositional associations geared to specific issues and aiming not at "seizing state power" but at pushing back the boundaries of bureaucratizing and commodifying influences.[49]

The principal positive thesis is that democratic government is a potentially progressive, tutelary force, inculcating and enforcing norms of gender equality (with consideration for salient differences) and mutual respect in many, if not all, arenas of civil society by coercive means and by using its powers of inducement and persuasion.

LIABILITIES

Civil society and government are potentially mutually constructive and reinforcing. In practice, however, forces within civil society and government are often inimical to feminism. Where there is freedom of association, civil society is hospitable to inegalitarian groups of all kinds: racist, sexist, hierarchic, militantly traditionalist, militaristic, and so on. So civil society poses a liability to the extent that groups effectively block or undermine the interests of women that democratic government is formally committed to advancing. Courts and legislatures must strain to create new protections (affirmative action, say), which are difficult to enforce and provoke backlash against government activism to which women are particularly vulnerable.

Civil society also poses a liability to the state insofar as celebration of voluntariness and mistrust of government encourage the devolution of public responsibilities to local agencies and social groups that reinforce parochialism, conservatism, and inequality. On the other side, hyperpluralism can balkanize social and political life and "overload" government, underscoring the view that government is incapable of solving problems and reinforcing arguments for limiting public responsibilities.

Feminist theorists are also sensitive to the fragmentation and multiplication of conflicting women's groups. From the start women's rights movements have been opposed by organizations of women—mobilized, radical, and antifeminist.[50] Divisions are apparent among feminist groups too. Consider the divide between the most visible feminist groups that focused resources on reproductive rights and the ERA on the one side and groups committed first of all to family-oriented public policies like child care on the other side.[51] Feminist groups are not all "mainstream" or civic-minded, either. Consider groups organized for direct action—anarcha-feminism, eco-feminism, feminist spiritual groups with their pagan and witchcraft rituals, self-dramatizing groups like the Guerrilla Girls. All engage in expressive public action and level political demands. If women's groups are sufficiently radical and transformative, particularly if they are antiliberal, they challenge government institutions and purposes directly and dramatically. The point is, pluralism can unsettle policy makers without pointing in constructive directions. It can raise the level of overt political conflict and inhibit alliances, particularly when feminist groups are uncompromising or bent on purely symbolic goals.

For its part, government poses a liability for civil society when it recognizes and supports groups resistant to equality. Government as patron sets conditions on public funding that disadvantage women: imposing a gag rule on doctors that prevents them from providing medical information about abortion, for example. Government poses a liability when it uses resources as inducements to divert groups from their original purposes and ideology.[52] The only way to contain the mutual liabilities of civil society and government I have described is increased participation in feminist groups and other associations that advance equality.

Groups and Individuals

Clearly, some functions of government require direct dealing with individuals: the criminal law, for example. Need-based entitlement programs evaluate applications from individuals or heads of families. Civil rights and antidiscrimination claims are typically brought by individuals (often at enormous personal cost), though their cases may be precedent-setting and the outcomes important for women "similarly situated."

When it comes to the distribution of public goods and benefits, feminists do not appear to have a single position about group-conscious preferences and directing public support to associations run by or for women. For example, women's health cooperatives, along with other providers, have been beneficiaries of government funding, but is this policy more desirable than health insurance individuals can carry to all sorts of providers? What is preferable: income supplements or tax benefits to individuals and families to purchase child care (or public "wages" to women and men who care for their children and others at home) or public subsidies to child care organizations generally ("neutrally"), some of which are bound to be traditionalist?

On the larger matter of individual versus group rights, feminists agree with advocates of minority rights or identity group rights more generally. At least as a corrective to injustice, measures to equalize liberty and opportunity to groups disadvantaged by long-standing social and political practices are justifiable. Anything less signals disregard for equal rights. That said, it is not always a simple matter to characterize a policy in terms of individual/group rights. Affirmative action is based on ascriptive characteristics of the group and recognition of a collective history of discrimination and disadvantage, but the benefits redound to women personally and individually; the principal effect is the development of their personal capabilities and opportunities. This explains feminists' concern that affirmative action, while justified, is assimilative—a way for beneficiaries to integrate into social worlds governed by male standards. It does little to sustain self-identification for women as feminists first of all or solidarity in these everyday contexts, and threatens to erase valued differences. The hope that simply by their presence in business or education women will serve as caring role models for other women or challenge traditionalist structures is not baseless, but affirmative action per se is no assurance.[53]

One thing is plain: the range of group claims made on behalf of women is limited. Unlike religious groups, women have rarely claimed exemption from general laws and obligations—their struggle has been for inclusion. And unlike multicultural groups, "women" do not qualify for and have not asserted group rights to self-government; none of the grounds used to advocate for group autonomy or separatism apply. But in civil society, voluntary separatist associations and insulated subcommunities of women are possible. A rich array of groups preserve (or invent) women's "culture": poetry and music, art, spirituality, computer networks, and so on. These mirror the cultural associations of ethnic groups. There are also religious, racial, and ethnic associations proper that sustain multicultural practices valued by women, some of which are unobjectionable to feminist theorists. Precisely to the extent that these are "partial publics" and not closed enclaves, their separatism is a matter of degree, usually quite limited. In short, the question of government interaction with women as a group is necessarily a question of integrating women into every area of social and political life (with or without "assimilation"), not group autonomy.

The larger issue behind the question of government action via individuals or groups is political representation and whether and where women should be given preferences or guaranteed decision-making authority.

Note first that representation in associations and in official political arenas are not interchangeable. Jean Cohen explains: "[T]he conceptual analysis of representative constitutional democracies implies a distinction between civil and political publics. The former are 'weak' yet relatively unconstrained publics in which deliberation and expression predominate over the chance or pressure to 'decide.' Civil publics exercise influence and symbolic power. The latter are 'strong' publics: involving not only deliberation but also decisions backed up by state sanctions."[54] This may go too far, since participation in decision making within associations significantly structures social life. Nonetheless, the point that official political institutions are distinct holds.

Feminist theorists advocating guaranteed political representation sometimes focus on women's participation in agenda setting and deliberation by policy makers on the model of corporatist structures. Iris Marion Young prescribes "group analysis and group generation of policy proposals in institutionalized contexts where decisionmakers are obliged to show that their deliberations have taken group perspectives into consideration."[55]

More often political representation means women's official presence as authoritative decision makers—reserved seats in political party delegations or party lists, legislatures, local government, and administrative agencies. In no democracy has formal political equality been translated into proportionate representation by women in electoral or nonelectoral offices. As Anne Phillips points out, "We all know there are more men than women in politics, but the details still come as a shock."[56]

On the most severe view, what is just for a group and required for its stable and secure identity must be acknowledged as authoritative. What is required is not just representation but effective control over outcomes. Iris Marion Young proposes group veto power regarding specific policies that affect women directly, citing reproductive rights policies as an example.[57]

Further divisions arise once we ask where "women," rather than specific subgroups of women based on race, class, or some other commonality, merit representation. As Judith Butler puts it, "The minute that the category of women is invoked as *describing* the constituency for which feminism speaks, an internal debate invariably begins over what the descriptive content of that term will be."[58] The point is captured in the title of Elizabeth Spelman's essay "Just Who Does She Think 'We' Is?"[59]

This critique of "reification" is carried over, amplified, into political theory and the question of *political* representation. The potential for disaggregation is infinite. It leads to ever more refined notions of salient differences among women. It is allied to feminist critiques of the notion of an integral, autonomous self, as well. Interestingly, some of the most vigorous critics of essentialism—poststructural analysts of the infinitely situated, fragmented "self," who represent "woman" as "an undesignatable field of differences," who want to "relieve the category of its foundationalist weight in order to render it as a site of permanent political contest"[60] (Julia Kristeva's "only strangeness is universal")[61]—concede the strategic importance of some standard "woman" and the necessity of speaking as and for women for political purposes. And on the other side, feminist theorists indifferent to philosophical questions about "the self" and identity are finely attuned to differences when it comes to politically salient interests and policies. We are reminded that ontological questions and political preferences are separable.

Of course, the fact that we cannot attribute unity to women as a group and that not all women have the same interests does not mean that they do not also have important interests in common that are not shared by men. This does not go very far in addressing the issue of representation, though. It does not tell us whether it makes sense to think that affirmative action in education and employment has a useful counterpart in preferences for political office. Nor does it guide us in thinking about who can claim to represent some designated group of women and how they can be held accountable to their wider public.

One useful way of considering group representation is to distinguish between theorists principally concerned with the advancement of feminist agendas—with specific interests and opinions—from those principally concerned with "the politics of presence." This distinction tracks the conceptual distinction between the idea that identity arises from interests and the idea that interests arise from identity: that is, those who argue that "for historical personal reasons of the particularity of our experience, our interests are causally associated with the group's interest" and between those who begin with "identification" and argue that "we value our group and therefore we have an interest in its success."[62]

Put starkly, the former argue for representation by women because they are thought to be better agenda setters and more influential advocates for feminist concerns. These advocates of representation acknowledge that this is a contingent question; women appointed or elected may be "unrepresentative" in terms of their education, income, and the like. They also allow that given the proliferation of antifeminist political groups, including women's groups ("will class trump gender?")[63] commitment to feminist goals outweighs commitment to women representatives per se. Chantal Mouffe has argued that radical democratic citizenship requires the construction of a common political identity, and that political participation aimed at equality for women is a struggle on many fronts, which may not be exclusively for or by women. In short, sexual difference should become effectively nonpertinent.[64]

Put starkly, advocates of the "politics of presence" argue that representation by women is necessary to correct for historic exclusion and to authentically reflect women's "perspectives," which are rigorously distinguished from objective interests and opinions. The issue is shared experience and authenticity, faithfulness to discursive feminist agendas. The underlying idea is familiar from multiculturalist theory and identity politics generally: no one else can speak for members of the group whose experiences or "ways of life" are inaccessible to outsiders, and the group's self-conception, estimate of disadvantage and needs, and so on, must be taken as authoritative. Here, effective attainment of feminist goals and accountability are secondary; after all, affirmations of "presence," "recognition," and "empowerment" are compatible with political impotence.

The limitations of feminist identity politics emerge clearly when the subject is political representation. Organization and rhetoric aimed at self-respect and solidarity are inadequate vehicles for representation. (So is radical disaggregation of the political category *woman*.) To be meaningful, it is necessary to look beyond ascriptive or virtual membership in the demographic category *woman* to "card-carrying" membership in associations. I have called this imperative "filling in the empty politics of recognition."[65] Women's *movements* need not be formalized. Their power lies precisely in their ability to influence outsiders; many women could go along and benefit without affiliation. When it comes to political representation, however, agendas and accountability require representatives, male or female, to be *responsible to* and well as *for* specific, organized constituencies in civil society. Both responsivenss and accountability are elusive when the link between politics of interest and identity is broken, and when there are few bridges between national spokespersons and prominent advocates and actual local groups—the concrete institutions of civil society.

CITIZENSHIP

Civic prerogatives and duties have risen to the top of the agenda of political theorists today. It is a triumph of feminism in Western democracies that women have formal equality and are obligated to perform the minimalist list of formal civic duties—paying taxes, performing military service (with the familiar caveats) when called, and serving on juries. Moral and political theorists now propose a radical expansion of that list: moving beyond elections to encompass civic aspects of everyday life. Proposed catalogs of civic duties now comprise every conceivably valuable action and virtue, from neighborliness to industriousness. And for many political theorists today, the associations of civil society are (or should be) not just gentle "seedbeds of civic virtue" but "boot camps of citizenship."

Feminist theorists are rightly of two minds about these developments. On the one hand, they take a skeptical view of the moralization of citizenship with its expansive ideals of civic duties and social work. Familiar with obligations that are assigned rather than taken on—nonvoluntary obligations that are frequently gender-coded and that prize selflessness— they are understandably wary. It is one thing to oppose a contract model of social life and another to disavow voluntarism altogether.[66] It has seldom worked to women's advantage. The expansion of duties like neighborliness and other exhibitions of caring have historically fallen to women; "rocking the cradle of state" alludes to women's moral superiority as citizens, but also to women's work.

Feminist theorists are also understandably skeptical of the priority assigned citizenship and of invocations of civic community, with its over-lay of masculinist/militarist/republicanism or its overlay of homogeneity and tradition-based values. Common vocabulary, "shared values," and civic virtue all have antifeminist histories, particularly when community is "communitarian"; that is, when it prizes the situatedness of embedded selves and stable, constitutive social roles. Public morality typically in-vokes religious and secular norms hostile to feminism and lesbianism especially as regards sexuality, bodily integrity, and family forms.

On the other hand, the remoralization of citizenship, at least as an aspiration, is recognizably aligned to feminist goals. A civic ideal that deemphasizes self-reliance and acknowledges inevitable dependency, mutual care, and responsibility for others could mean revaluation of the innumerable services women regularly perform under guises other than citizenship. If they were recognized as public goods, they would be pub-licly valued and rewarded, made universal and taken on by men. Some feminist theorists go a step further to argue that strong civic ideals har-ness women's supportiveness and enable "more cooperative and commu-nal ways of pursuing common interest."[67] Specifically, "the feminist model of community, based on the experience of motherhood, is an ad-mitted ideal," where "the members of the group, in acknowledged non-voluntary relations of obligation with one another, take as one of their primary responsibilities the growth into individuality of each member."[68]

To my mind, the most important contribution of women's history and feminist political theory lies in exploring what I will call "indirect citizen-ship." Feminists have brought home the fact that what counts as a matter of public interest is changing and contested; there is no authoritative catalog of politically cognizable interests and needs and no authoritative boundary to the political domain. The corollary when it comes to civil society is that voluntary associations are only sometimes formed for pur-poses of political advocacy and influence.[69] Initially at least, they are not political voices, or even public voices, except within the partial public of members. Most often, members of groups formed for nonpolitical pur-poses engage in political expression as a result of the unanticipated inter-nal dynamic of group life or some external impetus. They publicly advance opinions or support the political activities of other groups as an adjunct to their principal purposes—often sporadically. In short, associa-tion typically *precedes* political expression, and association voices emerge as an indirect result of groups' interests and membership practices. The alternative assumption, that voice precedes association, supposes that independent individuals intend the same communication and that asso-ciation simply aggregates and amplifies their voices.

Women's groups epitomize the unpredictable transition from associa-tions unconcerned with politics and public interest to advocacy groups.

The original purpose of association may have been as inward oriented as consciousness raising aimed mainly at overcoming members' passivity and self-abnegation, or charitable work, or religious fellowship. All have branched out, in every possible combination, forming wide networks. Sarah Evans and Harry Boyt describe how women use organizational skills learned in nonpolitical associations to form groups geared to advocacy and, at the same time, how nonpolitical groups find a political voice.[70] This stands in contrast to every narrow accounting of what constitutes significant participation and bona fide feminist politics—an accounting based on a group's formal organization and declared purpose and presumptive goals. On this severe view, specific groups are designated "boot camps" for citizenship, and "citizenship is not just one identity among others," but primary.[71] My point is the need to recognize the dynamic interaction between membership and voice, and freedom of association as a condition for meaningful citizenship. There is no assurance that associations and political messages will be feminist or democratic, of course. Simply, this is the dynamic by which feminist and democratic voices are created.

This picture of indirect citizenship resembles postmodernism in its appreciation of radical pluralism, but the resemblance conceals an important difference. Civic-oriented feminism is preoccupied with concrete associations engaged in purposive organization and decision making with articulated normative goals. Postmodernism is preoccupied with weakening "scripts," "sites of radical resignification," disciplined selves constituted by power rising up to defy situatedness and shatter contexts. In this version of feminist theory, not only civic associations but institutional relations among feminists and others, including associations and reform movements and organized resistance, fall from view. So do articulated goals and accountability. They are eclipsed by personal liberation from identity via philosophical or linguistic "resignification," by "agentic possibilities."[72] They are not readily amenable to moral or political evaluation, in contrast to the pluralist groups that comprise indirect citizenship.

Conflict

The question How is conflict handled? requires us to ask, Handled by whom? For feminists personally, one way of handling conflicting demands is to disregard citizenship and wider publics and to focus instead on separatist associations and subcommunities in which they feel at home. Culture creation that resists hegemonic forms is bottom-up, the argument goes, and women should concentrate on associations where they are not bound to mimic male attributes, where they can find safe havens and solidarity, and experiment with woman-oriented lifestyles.

For some active feminists preoccupied with self-protection or hostile toward nonfeminists (or all men), the ideal is to live in an environment that requires them to look "outside" as little as possible. They spurn multiple and overlapping memberships. As citizens, they drop out.

The opposite way of handling conflict is impossible since no one is *only* a citizen. Women whose lives are devoted to advocacy or public office also belong to religious groups, say, and have families. And in these political arenas, they are subject to cross-pressures. Like any political advocate or public official, they must negotiate the variable demands of groups whose interests they have at heart. Compromise is the stuff of active citizenship, though it does not come easily to principled feminists, as Jane Mansbridge illustrates in *Why We Lost the ERA*.

For the most part, feminists simply endure all sorts of contradictory roles and demands just as other people do in a heterogeneous society where we have a plurality of attachments. We negotiate pushes and pulls by meting out time and energy sporadically; we are sometimes active members, sometimes passive, as Albert O. Hirschman explained: the salience of one or another association for us is unstable.[73] When conflicting demands become too pressing, we choose among our loyalties and leave, though exit is not irreversible. Generally speaking, the conflicts we face arise *among* our roles in civil society rather than between the demands of membership and the obligations of citizenship. Feminists have written the book on conflicts between family responsibilities and work, and between these and social and political activism—on the ideal of "balance." Or, we labor to redefine obligations in various arenas, to reassign roles in the division of labor. (Sometimes, too, we engage in mundane "resistance": gossip, sabotage, absenteeism, insubordination, feigned ignorance, humor.)[74]

Feminists may handle deeper conflicts by not attending to them. We segment our affiliations and elements of identity. We are rarely asked to reconcile belonging to an Orthodox Jewish congregation and exhibiting a strong feminist orientation at work. Just as we tolerate groups whose purposes we oppose, we tolerate opposing purposes in our own lives. We segment our experiences, and assign limits to philosophies that, if we were perfectly consistent, would be overarching and comprehensive, covering all our values and virtues.

Poststructuralist feminists have given fragmentation considerable thought, arguing that though we are socially constructed, the elements of disciplined selfhood are not fixed. We are "potentiality," and can reinvent identities as we navigate spheres. They elevate this not uncommon phenomenological experience into an ideal. The arena of freedom is opposition—to gender conventions in particular. Integrity does not depend on being anything, presumably including feminist or citizen, "all the way down." Of course, radical self-making implicitly assumes a background of relatively stable cultural roles and affiliations—where else do the materials of self-fashioning come from? In any case, the idea is not to overcome but to exploit "disciplinary productions," to parody the fixed identifications presumed to exist.

None of this speaks to the more profound conflicts between membership and citizenship confronted by women in traditionalist ethnic subcommunities or faiths for whom it is not obvious that the solution is simply to shed these attachments in favor of a life of feminist egalitarianism.

I have spoken of how feminists handle these conflicts. If the question is whether conflicts should be handled by government intervention to transform incongruent groups and associations, feminist theorists are once again divided. Those who advocate strong civil liberties resist the "logic of congruence," which says that civil society should be forced to reflect liberal democratic values and practices "all the way down" in every social sphere. In contrast, many feminists qualify this commitment and argue that civil liberties, including freedom of association, should be restricted to advance egalitarian goals and enhance women's voices. They favor government censorship of pornography. They argue that government should require partners to share domestic chores and income, and that churches should be required to ordain women priests as a condition of tax status as a charitable organization. They prescribe differential laws requiring men's business groups to admit women members but permitting women's groups to exclude men. They want gender segregation in public education on the theory that girls' competence and self-esteem are fostered in all-girl classrooms. Though insofar as they recognize purposes for maintaining the civil society/government boundary, for all the reasons I have discussed, feminist theorists propose certain limits to government's authority to pattern social life.

This is not the only or best way of categorizing feminist prescriptions for handling conflict. I want to end by pointing to a more profound division among contesting feminisms, which arises from a mix of social analysis and temperament.

In general, growing interest in civil society theory among Western political theorists today is a response to crises of the welfare state and perceptions of moral and civic decline in established democracies. Feminist theorists from different political orientations contribute to this discussion.

Contrast this with the motivating concerns of social scientists after World War II, who saw the erosion of civil society as a factor in the rise of totalitarianism, and the reemergence of associational life as a vital buffer between atomistic individuals and a Leviathan state. They were moved by more intense anxiety and assigned a more purely political role to civil society. Some contemporary feminist theorists resurrect this anti-totalitarian orientation—except that they do not see civil society as a relatively autonomous public space for voluntary association. They see "commodification," "massification," and sometimes violence "all the way down." Their hope is to create tiny cells in the interstices of overarching systems of power for "resistance," often purely individual, rejecting reformist groups in favor of endless small struggles.[75] Their aim is to demonstrate that the "juridical model of power as oppression and regulation is no longer hegemonic."[76] These feminists have no truck with the innumerable mundane associations—religious and charitable, home owners' associations and advocacy groups—in which women satisfy personal and collective wants, benefit from and create social goods, and institutionalize values.

Between these two social analyses and tempers there is little common ground, except for one patch: In speculating about associations of women—whether dedicated to ordinary pursuits, social restructuring, democratization, or spontaneous resistance—feminist theorists are utopian. Indeed, feminist theorists are almost alone in preserving a particle of utopianism. As motivation, aspiration, or critical standpoint, utopianism is an essential element of political theory. In feminist works utopianism is the dominant temper. Adrienne Rich warned against "the urge to leap across feminism to 'human liberation,'" but her caution has not doused this urge.[77] For feminists whose perspective is critical theory, "[n]ot only rights but needs, not only justice but possible modes of the good life, are moved into an anticipatory-utopian perspective."[78] For liberal feminists, "[t]he notion of the standpoint of women . . . suggests that a fully human moral or political theory can be developed only with the full participation of both sexes."[79] Even avowedly antiutopian poststructuralists allow that playing with fixity of gender identification "may well serve the goals of the feminist project to establish a transhistorical commonality between us."[80] I said earlier that feminist thinkers are more discerning than other advocates of civil society. They resist the urge to see it as the "indeterminate normative spring of all good things."[81] They assign government a potentially transforming role. Still, within their varying accounts, when feminist theorists come down to earth from the higher reaches of language and philosophy, they locate utopianism in civil society.

Notes

1. Arguments by antiliberal feminists in the West, protesting rights talk as dictatorial or colonialist, are rebutted by feminists here and abroad who appreciate the enduring emancipatory power of rights and the cross-cultural aspects of

inequality. See the exchanges in Susan Okin, *Is Multiculturalism Bad for Women?* (Princeton: Princeton University Press, 1999).

2. See for example essays by Martha Nussbaum, Yael Tamir, and Carole Weisbrod in *Obligations of Citizenship and Demands of Faith: Religious Accommodation in Pluralist Democracies*, ed. Nancy L. Rosenblum (Princeton: Princeton University Press, forthcoming).

3. See generally Joan W. Scott, "Deconstructing Equality-versus-Difference, or, The Uses of Poststructuralist Theory for Feminism" in *Applications of Feminist Legal Theory for Women's Lives*, ed. D. Kelly Weisberg (Philadelphia: Temple University Press, 1996), 611–23. For a postmodernist critique of male/female see Judith Butler, "Gender Trouble, Feminist Theory, and Psychoanalytic Discourse" in *Feminism/Postmodernism*, ed. Linda J. Nicholson (New York: Routledge, 1990), 324–40.

4. Anne Phillips, "Does Feminism Need a Conception of Civil Society?" in *Alternative Conceptions of Civil Society*, ed. Simone Chambers and Will Kymlicka (forthcoming, Princeton University Press, 2002) 1; Jodi Dean, "Including Women: The Consequences and Side Effects of Feminist Critiques of Civil Society," *Philosophy and Social Criticism* 18, nos. 3–4 (1992): 379–406.

5. For a terse statement see Carole Pateman, "Feminist Critiques of the Public/Private Dichotomy," in *The Disorder of Women: Democracy, Feminism, and Political Theory* (Stanford, Calif.: Stanford University Press, 1989).

6. Anita L. Allen, *Uneasy Access: Privacy for Women in a Free Society* (1988); Linda C. McClain, "Reconstructive Tasks for a Liberal Feminist Conception of Privacy," *William and Mary Law Review* 40, no. 3 (March 1999): 759–94.

7. The phrase "subaltern counterpublics" is Nancy Fraser's in *Justice Interruptus* (New York: Routledge, 1997), 81.

8. The most important "cut" at this is by Habermasian theorists discarding public/private and utilizing the notion of system (administrative/judicial and economic) and lifeworlds; family and civil society comprise the latter. See Seyla Benhabib and Drucilla Cornell, introduction to *Feminism as Critique* (Minneapolis: University of Minnesota Press, 1987), 5ff. For incisive criticism of these redrawn boundaries see Nancy Fraser, "What's Critical about Critical Theory," in Benhabib and Cornell, *Feminism as Critique*, 31–56.

9. Much of this literature derives, explicitly or implicitly, from Marxist critiques of civil society and "bourgeois rights."

10. Unlike most theorists of civil society, feminists typically include the family. They are divided when it comes to business enterprises and market relations. Feminist theorists are likely to exclude them if they build goods and values like "solidarity, meaning, and consensual coordination of interaction" into their definition of civil society from the start; they are likely to include them if they see workplaces as principal sites of political education.

11. This observation is shared by antifeminist social critics who point to the connection between the decline of the nuclear family and general moral decline.

12. Nancy Fraser criticizing Habermas's singular public sphere in *Justice Interruptus*, 76.

13. I distinguish membership groups from "identity groups"—really populations to which we ascribe shared characteristics, objective or subjective, for some

particular purpose. Ascriptive identity groups must take some organized shape— at least have self-appointed spokespersons—before they become active elements of civil society. Iris Young objects that both "aggregate model" and "association model" groups conceive of individuals as "prior to collectives"; "identity groups" are those whose meanings "partially constitute people's identities." Her identity groups cut across unorganized social groups and organized associations. Iris Marion Young, *Justice and the Politics of Difference* (Princeton: Princeton University Press, 1990), 44.

14. Estelle Freedman, "Separatism as Strategy," in *Feminism and Community*, ed. Penny A. Weiss and Marilyn Friedman (Philadelphia: Temple University Press, 1995), 85–104; Theda Skocpol, "Advocates without Members: The Recent Transformation of American Civic Life" in *Civic Engagement in American Democracy*, ed. Theda Skocpol and Morris P. Fiorina (Washington, D.C.: Brookings Institution Press; New York: Russell Sage Foundation, 1999), 461–510.

15. Elisabeth S. Clemens, "Organizational Repertoires and Institutional Change: Women's Groups and the Transformation of American Politics, 1890– 1920" in Skocpol and Fiorina, *Civic Engagement in American Democracy*, 81–110.

16. Mary Fainsod Katzenstein, *Faithful and Fearless: Moving Feminist Protest inside the Church and Military* (Princeton: Princeton University Press, 1998).

17. William Galston made this salient point at the Ethikon Conference.

18. See for example Iris Marion Young, "Impartiality and the Civic Public," in Benhabib and Cornell, *Feminism as Critique*. This parallels the argument in moral philosophy that moral reasoning cannot transcend particularist perspectives. Cf. Seyla Benhabib's revision of Jürgen Habermas in "The Generalized and the Concrete Other," in *Situating the Self* (New York: Routledge, 1992).

19. Drucilla L. Cornell, "Gender, Sex, and Equivalent Rights" in *Feminists Theorize the Political*, ed. Judith Butler and Joan Scott (New York: Routledge, 1992), 280–96. Catherine MacKinnon, "Difference and Dominance: On Sex Discrimination," in *Feminism Unmodified* (Cambridge: Harvard University Press, 1987), 32–45.

20. Drude Dahlerup, "Learning to Live with the State," *Women's Studies International Forum* 17, no. 2–3 (1994): 117–27.

21. There is one notable gap in the literature. Despite Foucault's instruction to conceive power as productive, feminist theorists, including poststructuralist legal scholars, pay surprisingly little attention to corporate law, tax law, and constitutional law, which provide the framework within which associations define their purposes and carry out their activities.

22. The phrase is Robin West's, *Progressive Constitutionalism* (Durham, N.C.: Duke University Press, 1994).

23. 468 U.S. 609 (1984).

24. "Men who are uncomfortable associating with women in such social settings are unlikely to become less so if discomfort remains a valid justification for exclusivity. And such discomfort is not readily confined. Those who have trouble treating women as equals at clubhouse lunches will not readily escape such difficulties in corporate suites or smoke-filled rooms." Deborah Rhode, "Association and Assimilation," *Northwestern University Law Review* 106 (1986): 109.

25. Claire Reinelt, cited in Mary Katzenstein, *Faithful and Fearless*, 39.

26. On the impact of state funding on women's organizations see Claire Rei-nelt, "Fostering Empowerment, Building Community: The Challenge for State-Funded Feminist Organizations," *Human Relations* 47, no. 6 (1994): 685–705.

27. James T. Patterson, *America's Struggle against Poverty, 1990–1994* (Cambridge: Harvard University Press, 1994), 218ff.

28. Carole Pateman, "The Patriarchal Welfare State," in *The Disorder of Women*.

29. Fraser, "What's Critical about Critical Theory?" 47, 50.

30. See for example Robin West, *Caring for Justice* (New York: New York University Press, 1997).

31. Susan Moller Okin, "Is Multiculturalism Bad for Women?" *Boston Review* (October/November 1997): 25–28.

32. Carole Pateman, "Feminism and Democracy," in *The Patriarchal Welfare State* (Cambridge: Harvard University Press, 1987), 210.

33. Anne Phillips, *The Politics of Presence* (Oxford: Oxford University Press, 1995).

34. Variations of deliberative theory impose more or less severe conditions on deliberation—preserving particular standpoints or moving toward generalized standpoints; the extent to which they anticipate that reasoned arguments will produce consensus or just outcomes is variable as well. This is the main thrust of Habermasian feminist theory, which emphasizes a nongovernmental "space" where individuals communicate through argumentation and criticism on matters of general concern.

35. Cited in Seyla Benhabib, "Models of Public Space," in *Situating the Self : Gender, Community and Postmodernism in Contemporary Ethics* (New York: Routledge, 1992), 105.

36. The principal feminist writer on adversary democracy is Jane Mansbridge in numerous works including "Using Power/Fighting Power: The Polity" in *Democracy and Difference: Contesting the Boundaries of the Political*, ed. Seyla Benhabib (Princeton: Princeton University Press, 1996), 46–66.

37. Joshua Cohen and Joel Rogers, "Secondary Associations and Democratic Governance," *Politics and Society* 20 (1992): 393–472.

38. See for example David O. Sears and Carolyn L. Funk, "Self-Interest in Americans' Political Opinions," in *Beyond Self-Interest*, ed. Jane Mansbridge (Chicago: University of Chicago Press, 1990), 147–70. What is firmly documented is the diffuse nature of feminist self-consciousness even among women who are not self-identified as such. Cf. Mary Fainsod Katzenstein, "Feminism within American Institutions: Unobtrusive Mobilization in the 1980s," *Signs* 16, no. 11 (1990).

39. See Jane J. Mansbridge, "The Rise and Fall of Self-Interest in the Explanation of Political Life," in *Beyond Self-Interest*, 3–22.

40. In practice, women's groups take all sorts of forms—hierarchic, mass-membership groups that are really staff-run "mailing-list" organizations, aggressive adversary groups, and so on.

41. See Jane Mansbridge's foreword to Mary Parker Follett, *The New State* (University Park: Pennsylvania State University Press, 1998).

42. Julia Kristeva, "Women's Time," in *Feminist Theory: A Critique of Ideology*, ed. Nannerl O. Keohane, Michelle Z. Rosaldo, and Barbara C. Gelpi (Chicago: University of Chicago Press, 1982), 31.

43. MacKinnon, "Difference or Dominance," 39.

44. See the essays by Martha Nussbaum and Carole Weisbrod in Rosenblum, *Obligations of Citizenship and Demands of Faith*.

45. Though the feminist variation on this transmission-belt theme has it that discrimination against women in one sphere is contagious.

46. Benhabib, "Models of Public Space," 103.

47. Benhabib and Cornell, *Feminism as Critique*, 4.

48. See for example Wendy Brown, *States of Injury* (Princeton: Princeton University Press, 1995).

49. Andrew Arato and Jean Cohen, cited in Young, *Justice and the Politics of Difference*, 82.

50. On the "other" women's movements from anti–abortion rights to anti-busing see the essays in *No Middle Ground: Women and Radical Protest*, ed. Kathleen M. Blee (New York: New York University Press, 1998)

51. Carole Joffe, "Why the United States Has No Child-Care Policy," in *Families, Politics, and Public Policy*, ed. Irene Diamond (New York: Longman, 1983), 168–82. See also Rita J. Simon and Gloria Danziger, *Women's Movements in America* (New York: Praeger, 1991).

52. See the balanced account of battered women's collectives in Claire Reinelt, "Fostering Empowerment."

53. Carole Pateman levels a similar caution about workplace participation in *"The Civic Culture*: A Philosophic Critique," in *The Disorder of Women*, 166–67.

54. Jean Cohen, "American Civil Society Talk," manuscript, 32.

55. Iris Marion Young, p. 184. She argues for legally required group based representation in restructured democratic municipalities (252); "justice might require a fundamental reorganization of state and national government" *Justice and the Politics of Difference*, (253).

56. The key work is Anne Phillips, *Engendering Democracy* (University Park: Pennsylvania State University Press, 1991), 61.

57. Young, *Justice and the Politics of Difference*.

58. Judith Butler, "Contingent Foundations: Feminism and the Question of 'Postmodernism,'" in Butler and Scott, *Feminists Theorize the Political*, 15.

59. Elizabeth V. Spelman, "Simone de Beauvoir and Women: Just Who Does She Think We Is?" in *Feminist Interpretations and Political Theory*, ed. Mary L. Shanley and Carole Pateman (Philadelphia: Pennsylvania State University Press, 1977), 199–216.

60. Judith Butler, "Contingent Foundations" in *Feminist Contentions*, ed. Seyla Benhabib, Judith Butler, Drucilla Cornell, and Nancy Fraser (New York: Routledge, 1995), 41.

61. Julia Kristeva, *Nations without Nationalism* (New York: Columbia University Press, 1992), 21. For extensive discussion see Benhabib et al., *Feminist Contentions*.

62. Russell Hardin, cited in Nancy L. Rosenblum, *Membership and Morals* (Princeton: Princeton University Press, 1998), 337. It provides some insight into why women generally have not supported women's issues more than men have, and why some segments of women have.

63. Wendy Kaminer, "Will Class Trump Gender?" *American Prospect* 29 (1996): 49–52.

64. Chantal Mouffe, "Feminism, Citizenship, and Radical Politics," in Butler and Scott, *Feminists Theorize the Political*, 368–84.

65. Rosenblum, "Identity Groups and Voluntary Association: Filling in the Empty Politics of Recognition," chap. 9 in *Membership and Morals*.

66. Virginia Held, "Mothering versus Contract," in Mansbridge, *Beyond Self-Interest*, 287–304.

67. Carol Gould, *Rethinking Democracy* (Cambridge: Cambridge University Press, 1989), 293–94.

68. Mansbridge, "Feminism and Democratic Community," Russell Sage Foundation, working paper no. 25 27. "The starting condition is an enveloping tie, and the problem is individuating oneself." Held, "Mothering versus Contact," 289, 300.

69. Rosenblum, "Membership and Voice," chap. 6, in *Membership and Morals*.

70. Sara M. Evans and Harry C. Boyt, *Free Spaces* (New York: Harper and Row, 1992).

71. Mouffe, "Feminism, Citizenship, and Radical Politics," p. 378.

72. Butler, "For a Careful Reading," in Benhabib et al., *Feminist Contentions*, 138.

73. Albert O. Hirschman, *Shifting Involvements* (Princeton: Princeton University Press, 1982).

74. This list is James Scott's, cited in Katzenstein, "Feminism within American Institutions: Unobtrusive Mobilizations in the 1980s," *Signs* 16, no. 11 (1990): 33.

75. Jana Sawicki, "Foucault and Feminism: Towards a Politics of Difference," in *Feminist Interpretations and Political Theory*, ed. Lyndon Shanley and Carole Pateman (Cambridge: Blackwell, 1991), 225.

76. Judith Butler, "Variations on Sex and Gender," in Benhabib and Cornell, *Feminism as Critique*, 138.

77. Cited in Sawicki, "Foucault and Feminism," 226.

78. Benhabib, "The Generalized and the Concrete Other," 93.

79. Susan Moller Okin, *Justice, Gender, and the Family* (New York: Basic Books, 1989), 107.

80. Though the "us" is understood to be a construction without foundation, based on the denial of identity. Butler, *Feminist Contentions*, 339.

81. Stephen White articulated the "chicken soup" of civil society this way at the Ethikon conference.

Comment on Nancy Rosenblum's "Feminist Perspectives on Civil Society and Government"

Susan Moller Okin

NANCY ROSENBLUM'S essay places valuable and much needed emphasis on the diversity of feminisms as they bear on questions of civil society and government. Feminism includes differences in perspective, modes of argument, areas of primary focus, and positions on the political spectrum. Nevertheless, as Rosenblum points out, questioning the traditional boundaries of politics has been a major task of the work of many feminists.[1] So has showing how boundaries need to be redrawn when we refuse to tolerate in political theory the simultaneous neglect and assumption of the work that women have traditionally done and still do most of—that is, the work of the domestic sphere. This suggests that we critically assess some of the questions that the authors of this volume have been asked to attend to, with gender in the forefront of our minds.

Why is this necessary? Because the questions focus on civil society and the state, without paying attention to the third side of the Hegelian triangle—the family. To do this is to beg many of the most important questions that feminists have asked and worked on for the last two centuries, but especially the last thirty years. It is to assume that society is not gender structured, and to ignore the inequalities of the sexes in all spheres, as well as their connections from sphere to sphere. As I address the suggested topics, the problems that this neglect causes for any feminist—by which I mean anyone for whom equality between the sexes is an important value—should become apparent.

BOUNDARIES AND NEEDS

The boundary between "public" and "private" has been of considerable significance for feminist theories. They have pointed out that for several centuries of political theorizing, it has frequently been unclear whether "public" includes the state and civil society, with families alone inhabiting the "private" sphere, or whether "public" refers only the state, and both civil society and the family are to be understood as "private." This important ambiguity could not have continued for so long unnoticed without the unexplored assumption—often implicit—of women's unpaid work within that most private part of the private sphere, the family, where reproduction takes place and where basic and crucial human needs, both physical and psychological, are met. Natural law theories from Aristotle to Aquinas and in some cases down to the present have added to the influence of these prejudices, with their views that women are naturally inferior to men and that reproduction and household labor are their natural roles.

The public/private ambiguity and its underlying assumption that political theory need not concern itself with women's unpaid domestic labor are not the whole problem. There is also the fiction, which Rosenblum points out, that families are nonpolitical and not subject to criteria such as justice. There is yet that other fiction, that men and women can fairly be judged "the same" in regard to their performance in the workplace, civil society, and politics, even though women's current roles within virtually all families are far more complex and demanding. As Rosenblum makes clear, feminists—for all their diversity—have challenged these ambiguities and unveiled these fictions. They insist not only that families be included and addressed, rather than being assumed but left invisible, when what is "nongovernmental" is discussed, but also that both the inevitable effects of state policy on families and the internal political aspects of families be fully kept in mind. Thus feminism has seriously disrupted some previously assumed boundaries, and many feminists have argued that the state, in order to promote equality for women, should play a larger role both in regulating civil society and the family and in ensuring that women are represented more fairly in politics.

Probably because of women's age-old role as the primary fulfillers of basic daily human needs, women's associations in civil society have often focused on providing for such needs. It is a little known fact that women's quilting societies in the United States—while unlikely to occur to many as a significant example of civil society—provided enormous assistance to the soldiers fighting the Civil War. Initially producing quilts to meet the basic daily needs of the soldiers, they evolved from Ladies' Aid Societies to Soldiers' Aid Societies, and went from the direct provision of quilts to the men at the front to the large-scale sale of quilts to raise money for the war effort. In total they raised, in the course of the Civil War, as much value in quilts and money for the war effort, $4.5 million, as an entire year's federal budget for that war. They were very soon so influential for the abolitionist/Union cause that Lincoln responded in June of 1861 by establishing a federal agency, the U.S. Sanitary Commission, to coordinate their activities.[2] Theda Skocpol has recently elaborated on another case in which women's civil associations had a major impact on politics concerning basic needs—this time during peacetime. Early in the twentieth century, women's groups at the local, state, and national levels, especially those coordinated nationally in the General Federation of Women's Clubs and the National Congress of Mothers, exerted crucial influence that enabled policy changes helpful to poor women and children living without male support. Indeed, the Mothers' Pensions that were enacted by the vast majority (forty in all) of the states between 1911 and 1920 resulted largely from the lobbying and public relations efforts and cross-class support of these women's organizations. In both of these late-nineteenth- and early-twentieth-century examples, of course, the powerful influence of the women's civil associations occurred before their members were enfranchised![3]

Some have argued that the great changes in women's roles over the last thirty years have had a major impact on the voluntarism that is so central to much of civil society. I think there is little doubt that this is so, though how one evaluates it is another matter. Many upper-middle- and upper-class women in previous generations used their leisure (for many hired household help as well as not working for pay) to provide much of the unpaid labor that went into many volunteer organizations, from the most highly political to those focused entirely on charitable giving. Many such women are now full-time career women with professional aspirations much like men's. Unfortunately from the point of view of those relying on women's voluntary work, many women not only have full-time careers but are the primary or coequal parents of young children. Sometimes they still manage to participate in civil society, but often they have used up their time and energy in meeting the needs of their paid work and families. In some parts of the United States, affluence allows the old system to work still to some extent. Women who are married to high-earning men and are sufficiently traditionalist in outlook to prefer not to have paid jobs do continue to provide some of the free labor that helps, for example, tax-deprived public school systems to remain tolerably good ones and homelessness from becoming a way of life in their communities. But all this is very much class based, of course. There are precious few communities today where large numbers of women, as well as some men, are both financially able and willing to provide the free labor that keeps these parts of civil society alive. Moreover, the places that most need this kind of help are usually those where it is least available, which will remain the case unless people with time and goodwill begin to think less locally about the meaning of "community" than many tend to these days.

LIABILITIES, AND GROUPS/INDIVIDUALS

As Rosenblum's chapter suggests, a feminist perspective complicates these sets of questions, too. Another role of women in civil society in the United States has been as dissenters within male-dominated and male-privileging institutions. Mary Katzenstein's *Faithful and Fearless: Moving Feminist Protest inside the Church and the Military*, shows this clearly.[4] The book depicts vividly the very different roles feminists have played within two large institutions. It also demonstrates the impact on these roles of the extent to which the state and its laws and norms are able to affect the internal organization and power structure of the various institutions of civil society. Katzenstein shows how feminists in the military since the 1960s have been able to enlist the power of antidiscrimination law, such as Title VII of the Civil Rights Act and the Equal Pay Act, to advance their causes—from equity in dependents' benefits to admission to branches of the armed forces formerly closed to women—in a gradualist manner. They were able to advance women's equality within the framework of liberal feminism, and without challenging the main presuppositions or conventions of the military. In the Catholic Church, by contrast, the constitutional separation of church and state has halted the reach of the arm of antidiscrimination law. There, feminist aspirations among both nuns and laywomen—with the option of significant legal reform unavailable to them—took a far more radical turn. Ultimately, they challenged not only the whole patriarchal nature of the Catholic hierarchy, but also much of Catholic theology, including the idea of God as male.

What is a liability—not being allowed to discriminate—for some *groups* in civil society often means liberation or inclusion for some *individuals*. Should the Jaycees in the early 1980s have been allowed to remain an exclusively male organization? Should women be allowed to protect some all-female spaces, such as girls' schools or women's colleges? I, along with many feminists, do not see these cases as symmetrical. Requiring the Jaycees to admit women (or rather, in the particular case, forcing the National Jaycees to revoke their denial of affiliation to local Jaycee branches that admitted women) was perceived as a liability by many male Jaycees. But including women in social circles important for their work was a significant antidiscrimination decision for many female professionals and businesswomen. In the case of all-female institutions that want to remain such, admitting males brings with it the likely liability of the women's losing positions of leadership—as has happened at many previously female educational and other institutions. But the reverse hardly ever happens. All in all, the harms suffered by men from being excluded by, say, Smith or Wells College, could hardly be compared with the injury to women of being shut out of the Jaycees, or even being excluded from colleges such as Dartmouth or Haverford. As Rosenblum notes, many feminists claim—in this respect similarly to those arguing the issue of race-based exclusion—that the state's recognition of differences and of the right to preserve an exclusionary association should depend on the relevant history, in particular whether the difference at issue has historically involved domination or not. I think this way of thinking about whether institutions of civil society should be required to abide by antidiscrimination law makes a lot of sense. Since many institutions of civil society have a long history of hostility to women's equality, this way of thinking justifies more male than female institutions being forced to integrate, just as it does all-white ones more than African American ones.

Whether the institutions of civil society prove liabilities or opportunities for women or for feminist causes depends, of course, on which institutions one is talking about and, as I just mentioned, whether governmental constraints such as antidiscrimination law apply, or should apply, to them. In most otherwise liberal parts of the world, as in the United States, some religious institutions are currently immune to a large extent from such law, though in some fairly recent cases, the courts in the United States have moved away from allowing churches and other religious groups to practice internal sex discrimination, just as they had earlier clamped down on racially discriminatory practices. This still remains a contentious issue, however, which several other contributors to this volume address. Within Catholicism and much of Christian fundamentalism, within Orthodox Judaism, and within most of Islam, women are excluded from the most important religious roles, and thus from the most important seats of power and decision making within the respective religions. Women are also, in some religious contexts, required to be segregated during or to refrain from some parts of worship, to dress in extremely restrictive ways, to shave off or cover their hair, and to accept considerable inequality within marriage. Through all of these practices, the message is conveyed to young girls from a very early age that they are very different from boys, that it is right and proper for women to be controlled by men, and for the rules of their religion to be interpreted, revised, and executed by men only.

One important relevant question here is: Should any such institution of civil society either be publicly subsidized or have tax-exempt status? I think the answer is clearly no in any state that claims to be liberal. A good test to apply is to ask whether an institution that treated persons of different *races* in such ways is given such public recognition and privilege. This question has by now been decisively answered negatively in most liberal states, yet public privileges are still accorded to religious institutions that discriminate severely and in many ways against women. A second important question is: Should such groups be permitted to discriminate internally in such ways at all? Here I think the most liberal answer is yes, but only in certain cases, and only so long as the members of such groups are able to choose to join or not to join them freely as adults, in full awareness of what they are entering into. By "in certain cases," I mean that each such religious group should have to demonstrate that its sex-discriminatory practices are an essential part of its system of beliefs. Thus those who join it know full well what they are committing themselves to. The "full awareness" means that the children of current members should not be exposed to anything discriminatory in their parents' religious practices while they are young, lest those of the subordinated sex absorb a sense of inferiority. This would present a major challenge to educators within some religions. It would also require that the young people, preferably during adolescence, when they have acquired some powers of critical thinking, learn about a variety of religious, as well as secular, beliefs. In the company of several other authors in this book, I think it is one thing for an informed, mature young woman, well aware of other options, to *join* freely a religious organization that confines her in various ways, denies her equality with men in marriage and divorce and in religious rites, or otherwise restricts her opportunities for participation and leadership. It is entirely another, and a very illiberal, matter to raise children—especially girls—in such an environment, without exposing them to alternative ways of life. I believe the latter is a serious violation of their civil rights.[5]

Rosenblum covers well many other questions about groups and individuals, and I have no major disagreements with what she says. I am more convinced by those feminists who, like Anne Phillips, think that women need to be actively represented or "present" in politics than with those like Chantal Mouffe, who think that "sexual difference should become effectively nonpertinent" in politics. As I have argued in *Justice, Gender, and the Family,* I wish sexual difference *would* become "effectively nonpertinent" in social life in general, but until it does, I do not think that the representation of both sexes will become less pertinent in political decision-making bodies.[6]

CITIZENSHIP AND CONFLICT

One aspect of women's participation in civil society that Rosenblum does not stress as much as others is the important role, mentioned earlier, that it played during the long era before women were enfranchised in 1920. Then, various associations of civil society were often the only way women had of gaining power and sometimes even becoming very

effective actors in politics understood in the conventional sense. Aboli-
tionism, the Civil War effort, the temperance movement, the women's
suffrage movement itself, and many of the reformist organizations of the
Jacksonian and later the Progressive eras—including those aimed at
urban reform, aid to new immigrants, and the provision of birth control—would have been far weaker and less effective without the efforts
of women. This includes both the few women who gained fame from
them—from Elizabeth Cady Stanton, Harriet Tubman, and Sojourner
Truth to Frances Willard, Jane Addams, and Margaret Sanger—as well
as the thousands whose names no one remembers. Before women attained the vote or the right to serve on juries, participation in civil society was the only way in which they *could* be citizens. In many of these
examples, as is well known, the organizations were quite successful in
attaining their goals. Looking at a previously unrecognized case in some
detail, Massahos shows that in at least one state, Iowa, the Soldiers' Aid
Societies were sufficiently powerful to affect the state government's
behavior. Disliking the ways that male officials treated them and their
contributions to the war effort, they not only refused to cooperate, withholding their quilts and money; they also lobbied the legislature to
change its regulations and succeeded in getting one of their leaders—a
woman—appointed to a salaried state office. As Massahos writes, this
"association of persons without the constitutional right to vote was able
to extend the boundaries of political constraints by utilizing the constitutional right to associate to achieve its political goals."[7]

Thus, from a feminist point of view, it has not infrequently been a
good thing that civil society has been able to influence the state in the
case of quite conflictual issues, since only through some of its civil organizations was the disenfranchised half of the population able to achieve
and to use political influence. Since women have become enfranchised,
this avenue of influence is somewhat less crucial to them in the United
States. But in many less-developed countries in recent decades, a vast
new "civil society" that ranges from very local groups to international
nongovernmental organizations has developed to fight against many
forms of oppression of women and for a wide variety of women's rights
and women's modes of empowerment. It has been largely through the
work of this network of feminist civil society that women's human rights
have come to the world's attention as much as they have during the
1980s and especially the 1990s.[8] Thus, some of the most oppressive practices women suffer from are beginning to be challenged in countries
where they had existed for centuries and in which women, whether formally enfranchised or not, are still very far from being equal citizens with
men.

NOTES

1. See for example Susan Moller Okin, *Justice, Gender, and the Family* (New York: Basic Books, 1989), esp. 124–33; Frances Olsen, "The Myth of State Intervention in the Family," *University of Michigan Journal of Law Reform* 18, no. 4 (1985): 835–64; Carole Pateman, "Feminist Critiques of the Public/Private Dichotomy," in *The Disorder of Women: Democracy, Feminism, and Political Theory* (Stanford, Calif.: Stanford University Press, 1989); and Anne Phillips, "Does Feminism Need a Conception of Civil Society?" in *Alternative Conceptions of Civil Society*, ed. Simone Chambers and Will Kymlicka (forthcoming, Princeton: Princeton University Press, 2002).

2. Debera Massahos, "Patchwork, Power, and Politics: Quilt Groups of the Civil War Era Become Effective Political Associations" (senior honors thesis, Department of Political Science, Stanford University, 1995), 93–94.

3. Theda Skocpol, *Protecting Soldiers and Mothers: The Political Origins of Social Policy in the United States* (Cambridge: Harvard University Press, 1992), esp. chap. 8.

4. Mary Fainsod Katzenstein, *Faithful and Fearless: Moving Feminist Protest inside the Church and the Military* (Princeton: Princeton University Press, 1998).

5. See Cass Sunstein, "Should Sex Equality Law Apply to Religious Institutions?" and Okin, "Reply," in *Is Multiculturalism Bad for Women?* ed. Susan Moller Okin (Princeton: Princeton University Press, 1999).

6. See n.1 above.

7. Massahos, "Patchwork, Power, and Politics," 6.

8. See Martha Alter Chen, "Engendering World Conferences: The International Women's Movement and the UN," in *NGOs, the UN and Global Governance*, ed. Thomas G. Weiss and Leon Gordenker (Boulder, Colo.: Lynne Rienner, 1996).

Natural Law, Civil Society, and Government

Fred D. Miller, Jr.

THE ANCIENT Greek philosopher Heraclitus (ca. 500 B.C.) declared that "all the laws of human beings are nourished by the one divine [law]; for it holds sway as far as it wishes and is sufficient for all and remains over and above." He evidently identified this divine law (νόμος) with the first principle of nature (called the λόγος, or "account"), which was objective and universal: "therefore it is necessary to follow the common; but although the account is common, the many live as if they had private understanding."[1] These metaphorical remarks contain the seeds of the natural law perspective: the view that, apart from the plethora of human laws, there is a "higher" law, which is universal and independent of opinion or agreement, which is discoverable by reason, and which provides human laws with an ultimate sanction or justification. The central claim is that human laws are not *merely* the product of conventions or power relations; for laws are correct or justified only if they conform with nature.

The Greeks applied the term νόμος not only to written laws (for example, those ratified by a political assembly and recorded publicly) but also to unwritten laws (customs, traditions, and other norms transmitted orally and preserved only in memory). Therefore, when Heraclitus says that the divine principle suffices for all, he implies that it is a foundation for communal existence in the broad sense, encompassing both politics and other forms of social cooperation. But the ancients did not distinguish between government and civil society in the way that moderns do. This raises the questions: Can traditional theories of natural law accommodate this distinction? And, if so, what light does this perspective shed on the relationship between government and civil society?

NATURAL LAW: A BIPOLAR PERSPECTIVE

The idea of natural law has, remarkably, endured for two and a half millenniums, evolving and adapting to changing historical, religious, and philosophical circumstances.[2] The natural law perspective is not at all monolithic, but has included a wide spectrum of viewpoints. Two of these are still influential: a traditional, more conservative view and a modern, more liberal approach.

The traditional view originated with classical thinkers such as Plato (427–347 B.C.), Aristotle (384–332 B.C.), and Cicero (106–43 B.C.), as well as Christian theologians such as Saint Paul (d. A.D. 65). The most influential traditional theorist was Saint Thomas Aquinas (ca. 1224–74).[3] He defines law (*lex*) generally as "an ordinance of reason for the common good made by the authority who has care of the community and promulgated,"[4] and distinguishes four types of law:[5] (1) Because the whole universe is governed by God acting according to reason, the universe is subject to eternal law (*lex aeterna*). (2) Natural law (*lex naturalis*) is the "sharing in the eternal law by intelligent creatures." Although all creatures are subject to God's law, rational beings partake in it more perfectly, because they can share in eternal reason, through which they have a natural aptitude to their proper acts and ends. (3) Human or positive law (*lex positiva*) is derived by reason from natural law. This does not mean any established ordinance whatsoever, but only those consistent with natural law: "if on any head it is at variance with natural law, it will not be law, but spoilt law."[6] (4) Divine law (*lex divina*) is laid down by God; but, unlike eternal law, it is revealed through faith rather than by reason.

According to Aquinas, natural law can be apprehended by human reason independently of religious revelation. Just as a demonstrative science like geometry proceeds from self-evident first principles, practical reason starts from self-evident precepts of natural law. We grasp these legal precepts by means of a kind of moral intuition (*synderesis*), which is a natural habit or disposition. "The first principle for the practical reason is based on the meaning of good, namely, that it is what all things seek after. And so this is the first command of law, 'that good is to be sought and done, evil to be avoided'; all other commands of natural law are based on this."[7] To apply this principle, reason must apprehend good and evil, and it does this by ascertaining the objects to which human beings are inclined by nature.

Here Aquinas follows Aristotle's teleological theory that human beings have certain natural ends or objective goods. For example, human beings, like all other entities, naturally seek to preserve their own existence. Natural law is thus concerned to preserve and defend human life. Also, human beings strive to reproduce themselves, so that natural law is concerned with sexual relations, the care of children, and so forth. Finally, human beings uniquely strive for ends involving rationality. Natural law is thus concerned with such matters as knowing the truth about God and avoiding incivility in the social sphere. This describes the general program of natural law: by discerning human goods we may derive specific precepts of natural law. These precepts serve, in turn, as criteria for justifying or criticizing human conventions, institutions, and actions.

The application of natural law to individual cases is extremely difficult. Later Scholastics developed the method of casuistry to formulate and apply general rules to particular issues (*casus*). Unfortunately, "casuistry" acquired a sinister connotation from those who abused it by drawing fine legal distinctions to rationalize unethical conduct. But such a method is indispensable for resolving complex moral problems through abstract principles.

Modern philosophers continued to speculate about natural law, but their theorizing took new directions following the Protestant Reformation and the scientific revolution.[8] They included Hugo Grotius (1583–1645), Samuel Pufendorf (1632–94), and many others, but John Locke (1632–1704) was the most influential. Locke eschewed Aristotelian metaphysics, which was under withering fire from scientists and philosophers of the seventeenth century.[9] He speaks of natural law as applying initially to the "State all Men are naturally in."[10] He argues, "The State of Nature has a Law of Nature to govern it, which obliges every one: And Reason, which is that Law, teaches all Mankind, who will but consult it, that being all equal and independent, no one ought to harm another in his Life, Health, Liberty, or Possessions."[11] Locke identifies the law of nature with the law of reason. "It is certain that there is such a Law, and that too, as intelligible and plain to a rational Creature, and Studier of that Law, as the positive law of Commonwealths, nay possibly plainer."[12] Like Aquinas, however, Locke affirms that the law of nature ultimately derives from God: "For all Men being all the Workmanship of one Omnipotent, and infinitely wise Maker; All the Servants of one Sovereign Master, sent into the World by his order and about his business, they are his Property, whose Workmanship they are, made to last during his, not anothers Pleasure." According to the law of nature, "Every one as he is bound to preserve himself, and not to quit his Station wilfully; so by the like reason when his own Preservation comes not in competition, ought he, as much as he can, to preserve the rest of Mankind, and may not unless it be to do Justice on an Offender, take away, or impair the life, or what tends to the Preservation of the Life, Liberty, Health or Goods of another."[13] Accordingly, natural law implies that individuals have moral obligations to God and to one another. This includes not only negative obligations not to infringe on others' rights, but, as another passage indicates, duties of charity:

> As *Justice* gives every Man a Title to the product of his honest Industry, and the fair Acquisitions of his Ancestors descended to him; so *Charity* gives every Man a Title to so much out of another's Plenty, as will keep him from extream want, where he has no means to subsist otherwise.[14]

For Locke, then, natural law implies both individual rights and interpersonal duties.[15]

Modern natural law theories view human beings as by nature free and equal. Locke's state of nature is a state of perfect equality and liberty, in which human beings live together "according to reason, without a common Superior on Earth, with Authority to judge between them."[16] It is "a condition, which however free, is full of fears and continual dangers," so that individuals join in a society with others and put themselves under government for the sake of "mutual preservation of their Lives, Liberties, and Estates."[17] In political society, positive, written laws "are only so far right as they are founded on the Law of Nature, by which they are to be regulated and interpreted."[18]

Proponents of natural law—traditional and modern—generally agree that natural law takes precedence over human positive laws; and that human reason can grasp the existence and content of this higher law without reliance on religious faith. But moderns dissent from traditional law theorists on some crucial issues. Locke holds that "all men are by Nature equal,"[19] and that they all have equal rights to life, liberty, and estate. The latter includes the right to self-ownership and the right to acquire private property. Many recent neo-Thomist natural law theorists, however, recognize equal human rights. Jacques Maritain concedes that "in ancient and mediaeval times attention was paid, in natural law, to the *obligations* of man more than to his *rights*," and that a great achievement of the eighteenth century was "to bring out in full light the *rights* of man as also required by natural law." But Maritain also complains of a modern overemphasis on rights. "A genuine and comprehensive view would pay attention *both* to the obligations and the rights involved in the requirements of natural law."[20]

Locke also prizes the right of freedom as "the Foundation of all the rest."[21] "Liberty is to be free from restraint and violence from others."[22] In contrast, Pope John Paul II upholds the traditional view that "freedom consists not in doing what we like, but in having the right to do what we ought."[23] The two approaches collide when it is debated whether people should have "the right to do wrong" in specific cases, for example, to commit immoral sexual acts.

In summary, two variants of the natural law perspective currently influence social philosophy and public policy: the traditional view espoused by Aquinas and the modern view associated with Locke. The former is often reflected in official pronouncements of the Roman Catholic Church, but its adherents include moral realists and various analytic philosophers.[24] The ideas of Locke influenced the American Founders. "The Laws of Nature and of Nature's God" were invoked in the American Declaration of Independence,[25] and Locke's views still resurface in recent political philosophy and legal theory, especially in the United States.[26] The traditional, conservative pole is more concerned with moral virtue as a social goal, while the modern, liberal view emphasizes personal autonomy. The antinomy between virtue and freedom is vexing, because a credible natural law perspective must find a way to accommodate *both* liberty and perfection as constituents of the human good. As they try to meet this challenge, natural law theorists fill a spectrum of positions between the traditional and modern poles.

GOVERNMENT AND CIVIL SOCIETY

The derivation of human laws from natural law is based on Aristotle's principle that man is by nature a political or social animal. Stoic philosophers, including the Roman emperor Marcus Aurelius (A.D. 121–80), also invoke the natural law of community. The doctrine is echoed in Aquinas and in Grotius, who ascribes to man "an impelling desire for society, that is, for the social life," and in Locke, who agrees with "the judicious [Richard] Hooker" (1554–1600) that "we are naturally induced to seek communion and Fellowship with others."[27]

The principle that man is a political animal is difficult to interpret, because Aristotle's expression πολιτικὸν ζῷον, "political animal," is vague. Strictly, the term πολιτικὸν, "political," derives from πόλις, "city-state."[28] But Aristotle also uses "political" in a broader sense to include social animals such as wasps, ants, and cranes.[29] Recognizing this double meaning, Aquinas translates πολιτικὸν ζῷον into Latin as *animal sociale et politicum*.[30]

Aristotle argues that the city-state is the most inclusive and sovereign community.[31] It is "complete" and attains "the goal of self-sufficiency," so as to "exist for the sake of the good life."[32] The city-state provides the citizens not only with material resources but also, more importantly, the moral education and cultural opportunities requisite for the virtuous and happy life. Aristotle concludes that the city-state should have moral authority over its individual citizens.

Aristotle's argument for the primacy of the city-state has been criticized for confusing two different notions under the rubric of "city-state": government and society. *Government* in the modern sense possesses a monopoly over the legitimized use of coercive force within a definite geographical area. It discharges narrowly political functions (executive, legislative, judicial) and provides certain public goods (for example, maintaining the peace and defending against external enemies). In contrast, *society* in the inclusive sense encompasses the wide array of associations that people need to meet their basic needs and flourish: households, local communities, personal friendships, fraternal clubs, religious groups, schools, business organizations, and so forth. Society in this all-inclusive sense contains an intricate web of human relationships, voluntary as well as coercive, private as well as public, through which individuals can find sustenance, companionship, and happiness.

The modern term "state" is used in different senses, referring, for example, either to government or to a society with a government. These two notions are, however, "fused" in Aristotle's conception of a city-state. He maintains that the city-state exists "not only for the sake of life, but, more so, of the good life."[33] He accordingly rejects the "night watchman" view of the city-state—that is, "a community of persons in a territory with the aim of not doing mutual injustice to themselves and of promoting exchange."[34] He objects that "the city-state ought to care about virtue in so far as it is truly called a city-state, and not one in name only." This is the concern of good legislation—for "the city-state is the community in living well of households and families, for the sake of a complete and self-sufficient life."[35]

This would have seemed plausible to Aristotle's contemporaries who shared his "fused" conception of the city-state and did not distinguish the political realm from other spheres of life such as religion, family, marriage, education, production, and trade. For example, in Athens the public assembly regulated the religious calendar, including all sacrifices and festivals. This degree of political control was feasible because the Greek city-states were small, homogeneous, tightly knit communities.

The attempt to transpose Aristotle's ideal to the modern state, however, encounters difficulty; the state qua society contains many different types of association with diverse ends, and government is only one of these. Even if it were true that the state qua entire society had as its end the virtuous and happy life, it would not follow that the state qua government had as *its* proper function the use of coercive force to make the citizens virtuous and happy.

Modern social philosophers developed the notion of *civil society* in part to clarify and delimit the proper role of government.[36] The notion was popularized by Scottish Enlightenment theorists such as Adam Ferguson (1723–1816) in *An Essay on the History of Civil Society* (1767). G.W.F. Hegel (1770–1831), in the *Elements of the Philosophy of Right*, distinguished civil society (*bürgerliche Gesellschaft*) as a form of association mediating between the family and government. Civil society in this sense includes various forms of association transcending family units, which are voluntary, spontaneous, or customary, and not necessarily the result of legislation or governmental edicts. Society as a whole encompasses all forms of association, including the family household, civil society, and government.

The natural law perspective must take into account the distinction between civil society and government. Therefore, civil associations as well as government are subject to nature-based norms. Each form of association should promote the common good of its members, serving their relevant human needs and enabling them to develop and exercise their relevant capacities and virtues. For example, professional associations should be organized in such a way that its members develop their natural talents and practice them so that they lead productive lives and achieve a sense of self-worth. Such associations should also operate in such a way that they do not impede the self-realization of nonmembers.

BOUNDARIES BETWEEN CIVIL SOCIETY AND GOVERNMENT

Traditional natural law theorists often liken the community to a living organism. For example, Aristotle argues that the city-state arose naturally out of more primitive natural associations such as family households and villages. The city-state thus exists by nature. It came into existence for the sake of life or survival, and it exists for the sake of the good life, that is, to promote the highest human ends.[37]

The city-state is a "community of families and villages in a complete and self-sufficient life."[38] It is naturally prior to its constituent communities. Just as the ultimate end of an organism takes precedence over the functions of its parts, the ultimate end of the city-state (namely, the good life of the citizens) supersedes the aims of its subsidiary communities. If part and whole come into conflict, the part must acquiesce. This *principle of community authority* typifies the traditional natural law perspective. It implies, for example, that the government should uphold common standards of decency and moral conduct upon the entire society. Hence, positive law must embody morality.

This would raise the specter of moral totalitarianism, were it not offset by the *principle of subsidiarity*, which is implicit in Aristotle's own critique of Plato's proposal that children, women, and property should belong to the citizens in common.[39] Aristotle argues that a system of private families and private ownership is superior to communism on a number of grounds: The former system is less likely to breed conflict; it inclines the citizens to take better care of their children and property; and its existence facilitates virtues such as friendship, generosity, and moderation.[40] These arguments can be extrapolated to modern business corporations, labor unions, religious denominations, benevolent societies, and other associations comprising civil society. This principle of subsidiarity was defended by Pope Pius XI (1922–39):

> Just as it is wrong to withdraw from the individual and commit to the community at large what private enterprise and industry can accomplish, so too it is an injustice, a grave evil, and a disturbance of right order for a larger and higher organization to arrogate to itself functions which can be performed by smaller

and lower bodies.... Of its very nature, the true aim of all social activity should be to help individual members of the social body, but never to destroy or absorb them.[41]

The traditional natural law perspective therefore leaves room for civil society. As John Finnis observes, the term "subsidiarity" "signifies not secondariness or subordination but assistance; the Latin for help or assistance is *subsidium*."[42] It assigns to government "the function of assisting individuals and groups to co-ordinate their activities for the objectives and commitments they have chosen, and to do so in ways consistent with the other aspects of the common good of the political community."[43] Civil associations are not to be swallowed up. They have distinctive functions, which they should be able to carry out autonomously without interference, provided that they do not subvert the end of the whole. It is the role of government to ensure that this overarching end is realized.

Modern theorists like Locke, however, deny that the state is naturally prior to the individual. Instead, government is a purely human creation. Locke argues that human beings exit the state of nature and "joyn in Society with others . . . for the Preservation of their Lives, Liberties and Estates, which I call by the general name, Property. The great and *chief* end, therefore, of Mens uniting into Commonwealths, and putting themselves under Government, is the Preservation of their Property."[44] The chief instrument for achieving this end is the system of positive laws: "the first and fundamental positive Law of all Commonwealths is the establishing of the Legislative Power; as the first and fundamental natural Law, which is to govern even the Legislative it self, is the preservation of the Society, and (as far as will consist with the publick good) of every person in it." The legislative power is inherently limited: it "can never have a right to destroy, enslave, or designedly to impoverish the Subjects."[45] Whenever government exceeds its proper bounds, that is, "whenever the Legislators endeavor to take away and destroy the Property of the People, or to reduce them to Slavery under Arbitrary Power, they put themselves into a state of war with the People, who are thereupon absolved from any further Obedience, and are left to the common Refuge, which God hath provided for all Men, against Force and Violence." The people have a right to revolution, "a Right to resume their original Liberty" and to establish a new legislature to "provide for their own Safety and Security, which is the end for which they are in Society."[46]

On the Lockean view, government is confined by natural law to protecting the life, liberty, and property of its subjects. Hence, society as a whole does not resemble the classical city-state, that is, a hierarchical community ordered by government to some higher good. By enforcing the rule of law and the institutions of private property and contract, government maintains a constitutional framework necessary for civil society, which consists of a host of semiautonomous associations, which differ widely in purpose, structure, longevity, and conditions of entry and exit.

MUTUAL NEEDS

A government or state has a monopoly over the legitimate use of coercive force in a specific geographical region. It consists of deliberative bodies, courts, police, armies, and bureaucracies. Civil society consists of a wide variety of association: voluntary, customary, or spontaneous, with economic, cultural, religious, political, scientific, educational, eleemosynary, or other goals. In order for civil society to exist and thrive, certain preconditions must be met. First, there must be toleration of a diversity of views: religious, cultural, scientific, aesthetic, and so forth. Second, there must be protection of private property and contracts to enable individuals to cooperate in a variety of different associations and to coexist peacefully as they pursue their respective goals. Third, and most importantly, there must be the rule of law, so that governmental officials as well as private individuals are restrained by objectively defined laws that prevent them from doing whatever they please.

Hence, civil society cannot exist without a government. In an anarchy where individuals and associations could be suppressed by roving gangs, civil society could not survive. By the same token, civil society cannot endure in a totalitarian or authoritarian state, disdainful of individual rights and the rule of law. Yet civil society can subsist in a variety of social systems, including democratic capitalism, democratic socialism, and constitutional monarchy. Proponents of natural law would no doubt disagree over the proper scope of government. The modern, liberal pole tends to favor a more limited role for government. At the libertarian extreme it would be restricted to the protection of individual negative freedom, private property, and contracts, and to the provision of a small set of public goods such as defense against foreign invasion. Others would recommend a publicly financed "safety net" for genuinely needy persons and certain universally available services such as education and social insurance. The traditional, conservative pole would assign to government the duty to uphold morality and decency and perhaps also religious values. But all contemporary natural law theorists recognize the need for a substantial and vigorous civil society.

After the collapse of Communism in Eastern Europe and the Soviet Union, many new countries faced the problem that they lacked an effective government, a functioning economy, and a viable civil society. It is not feasible to address any one of these problems in isolation. Civil society cannot arise without a protective constitutional framework of human rights and the rule of law, while the attempt to impose such a constitution upon an unready population can be self-defeating or even disastrous. In traditional terms, they need "civic virtue" to rely on one another to discharge their offices responsibly. In modern parlance, they require "social capital": traits such as reciprocity, moral obligation, duty toward community, and trust. They must understand and appreciate their political institutions, must keep themselves informed about the issues, and must be willing to participate when and where it is appropriate. They must be committed to the above-mentioned principles necessary for civil society: toleration, respect for rights, and the rule of law. Social scientists have argued that high-trust societies are better equipped to maintain the institutions of democratic capitalism.[47]

Moreover, there must be amity and trust among the population. A society can be in a natural condition only if the citizens bond together in friendship and shared values (a condition of *concordia*, or ὁμόνοια). Virtuous individuals are willing even to lay down their lives for their fellow citizen and country. But, as Aristotle recognized, civic friendship is inherently limited because it encompasses the entire citizenry. A universal friendship becomes watery, "just as a little wine mixed in a lot of water makes the mixture imperceptible."[48] More particular forms of association are needed to draw people together and establish solidarity, including clubs, religious congregations, and convivial associations.[49] The citizens are bonded by a multiplicity of personal friendships that reinforce one another like pieces of straw woven together into a basket capable of bearing a heavy load.[50]

Civil society is a sphere in which citizens can learn to trust and rely upon one another. Finally, they must be willing to support and defend their government when it is needed. These civic virtues should be instilled in families and fostered in civil society. The lesson is clear: Government and civil society are deeply interdependent, and they must develop in tandem.

MUTUAL LIABILITIES

Civil society and government may also pose threats to each other. The very attributes by which they lend support to each other can become liabilities. Diverse groups may feel indignant when their values and interests are opposed. Plato described the tribalistic conception of justice as "doing good to one's friends and bad to one's enemies."[51] He warned that disagreements between groups within city-states often led to faction (στάσις) or civil war,[52] which Aristotle also viewed as a disease of the city-state arising from ethnic and economic differences.[53]

A similar problem troubled the American Founders, including James Madison (1751–1836):

> Liberty is to faction what air is to fire, an aliment without which it instantly expires. But it could not be a less folly to abolish liberty, which is essential to political life, because it nourishes faction than it would be to wish the annihilation of air, which is essential to animal life, because it imparts to fire its destructive agency.[54]

Madison realizes that it is impractical to try to avoid faction by imposing the same beliefs, passions, and interests on everyone. Individuals will arrive at different opinions as long as they are free to exercise their reason, and "the diversity in the faculties of men, from which the rights of property originate, is not less an insuperable obstacle to a uniformity of interests. The protection of these faculties is the first object of government." Yet the resulting economic inequalities inevitably lead to "a division of the society into different interests and parties." Madison concludes that "the latent causes of faction are . . . sown in the nature of man" and that the danger of faction is the unavoidable price of liberty. Madison's proposed remedy, a republican form of representative government with checks and balances, makes it very difficult for any group to exploit the others. But such a solution presupposes that the citizens are committed to republican institutions, which may be undermined by internecine conflict.

Conversely, as history amply testifies, government can be a menace to civil society. A state like Hitler's Germany, Stalin's Soviet Union, or Ayatollah Khomeini's Iran nullifies the prerequisites of civil society: toleration, respect for individual rights, and the rule of law. But these are fragile even in democracies, as the American Founders warned, pointing to the excesses of ancient democracies.

Friction between government and civil society results when government tries to enforce moral ordinances. During the Middle Ages there were laws against usury, based on arguments deriving from Aristotle, Aquinas, and others that charging interest on loans was an unnatural use of money.[55] Such laws impeded the development of financial and commercial associations, and encouraged prejudice toward religious minorities who were permitted to collect higher interest.[56] Today the most conspicuous debates over natural law and public policy involve issues of sexual morality, reproduction, censorship, and life and death. For example, many traditional theorists argue that abortion violates natural law because it is the killing of an innocent unborn human being.[57] Regardless of the soundness of this reasoning, it is exceedingly difficult to enforce in a pluralistic society. Conflict erupts whenever public officials try to prevent individuals and families from carrying out decisions to terminate pregnancies and to prohibit medical practitioners and associations from carrying out these decisions. Similarly, many traditional theorists condemn artificial birth-control devices and sexual practices such as homosexuality and sodomy, but attempts to prohibit them have also been highly divisive in pluralistic societies.

Government may pose subtle dangers for civil society even when it has good intentions. Alexis de Tocqueville (1805–59) warned that the rise of social democracies could lead to a "type of oppression . . . different from anything there has ever been in the world." Individuals could become increasingly detached from one another as they become more dependent upon the government, "an immense, protective power which is alone responsible for securing their enjoyment and watching over their fate. That power is absolute, thoughtful of detail, orderly, provident, and gentle." Like an overprotective parent, "it provides for their security, foresees and supplies their necessities, facilitates their pleasures, manages their principal concerns." By creating a culture of dependence, government stifles individual enterprise:

> Having thus taken each citizen in turn in its powerful grasp and shaped him to its will, government then extends its embrace to include the whole of society. It covers the whole of social life with a network of petty, complicated rules that are both minute and uniform. . . . [I]t does not break men's will, but softens, bends, and guides it; it seldom enjoins, but often inhibits, action; it does not destroy anything, but prevents much being born; it is not at all tyrannical, but it hinders, restrains, enervates, stifles, and stultifies so much that in the end each nation is no more than a flock of timid and hardworking animals with the government as its shepherd.[58]

By undertaking to solve every problem for its citizens, government crowds out civil society by rendering private associations and local communities redundant or devitalized. There is evidence that Tocqueville's worries were prophetic. During the nineteenth and early-twentieth centuries in the United States, numerous fraternal societies such as the Elks and Moose provided insurance and mutual aid for members and charitable assistance to the needy. Examples included Mooseheart, an orphanage maintained by the Loyal Order of Moose, and a hospital in the Mississippi delta by poor rural blacks through the Knights and Daughters of Tabor. These cooperative associations suffered serious declines with the rise of the welfare state.[59]

GROUPS AND INDIVIDUALS

A society is a complex whole composed of parts in different senses. Individual persons are in a sense the ultimate parts or members of society. They belong to local communities (neighborhoods and towns) and various associations with diverse purposes, which are, in another sense, parts of society. A society composed of overlapping heterogeneous associations is even more complex than an organism composed of distinct cooperating organs. A government is a peculiar form of association that exercises authority over the entire society, including not only individuals but also subsidiary associations. But many of these associations have governing bodies of their own that exercise authority over their membership. This raises the question of when government should interact directly with individuals and when it should operate indirectly through communal associations.

The traditional natural law perspective relies on two principles: the principle of rulership and the aforementioned principle of subsidiarity. According to *the principle of rulership*, society requires government as a supreme authority, as argued by Aquinas:

> If, then, it is natural for man to live in the society of many, it is necessary that there exist among men some means by which the group may be governed. For where there are many men together and each is looking after his own interest, the multitude would be broken up and scattered unless there were also an agency to take care of what appertains to the common weal. In like manner, the body of a man or any animal would disintegrate unless there were a general ruling force within the body which watches over the common good of all members. With this in mind, Solomon says: "Where there is no governor, the people fail."[60]

If individuals or groups have opposing aims, it is proper for government to try to resolve these conflicts, for example, by establishing appropriate legal institutions involving property and contracts. If a group or individual seeks to use force to advance its own aims at the expense of other groups or individuals, or if two parties fall into conflict, it is necessary for government to intervene directly and restrain their actions. Social order is in the common interest, and this can obtain only if there is a sovereign agency to maintain order. Moreover, if some individuals or groups are treated unjustly, government must take appropriate palliative measures. What this implies in detail is subject to different interpretations: from a narrower libertarian view to a more expansive welfarist view. The natural law perspective would, however, be opposed to utilitarian schemes that undertake to promote the interests of the majority at the expense of the minority; for the natural law perspective has traditionally understood the "common good" as what is good, so far as it is practicable, for each and every member of the community.[61] Where conflicts exist among different individuals or social classes, the common good should be promoted so far as it is practicable.

In addition to these coordinating and corrective roles, government is also needed to provide certain public goods. In general terms, a public good, such as national defense or an unpolluted environment, is equally available to everyone, and it is impossible to exclude noncontributors from the consumption of it. The "problem of public goods" is that if individuals realize that they can benefit from a public good without contributing to its provision, many will fail to contribute, even though it would be good for everyone if it were produced. Hence, the natural law perspective implies that the government should provide it.

However, *the principle of subsidiarity* is also necessary to protect communal associations from excessive governmental control and intrusiveness. To the extent that individuals and subsidiary social units can realize their natural ends on their own, the government should not usurp their prerogatives but should instead serve as a facilitator. The perfection of the individual members of society requires that they develop their capacities by doing things for themselves rather than having things being done for them. They will better accomplish this if they are active in lower-level civil associations. Hence, government should defer to such associations wherever possible.[62] For example, government should encourage and protect private eleemosynary associations, to enable individuals to cultivate and practice the virtues of benevolence.

Tensions between the principles of subsidiarity and rulership are evident in the sphere of religion. Jesus Christ advised, "Render to Caesar the things that are Caesar's, and to God the things that are God's," but Christian political thinkers have not agreed about what exactly this implies. During the Middle Ages, the Roman papacy clashed frequently with the Holy Roman Empire and other European principalities. The Catholic Church envisaged itself as an autonomous association governed by its own canon law and answerable to God rather than to worldly monarchs. With its numerous clergy and vast property, the church became virtually a state within a state, challenging mundane regimes for ultimate authority. With the Protestant Reformation, there was a movement toward "established" churches, which were sanctioned and supported by government. Many modern natural law theorists question whether religious organizations can fulfill their functions when they are wards of government. This problem is compounded if the moral teachings of the church conflict with the policies and practices of the government that is subsidizing it. An alternative solution was adopted in the First Amendment to the U.S. Constitution, where the right of free religious exercise was acknowledged but Congress was prohibited from establishment of religion. This approach reflected the modern natural law view that the primary responsibility of government was to protect *freedom* of religion but not to promote any particular creed. This was not meant to imply that religion was unimportant or illusory. Rather, the role of government is to secure the freedom necessary for religious practice. But the precise implications of the First Amendment remain in dispute.

The scope of government must also depend on empirical issues regarding the nature and sources of order, for example, in the economic sphere. Traditional natural law theorists have tended to be suspicious of capitalism. For example, Heinrich Rommen remarks, "The property system of private capitalism with its unrestrained freedom of ownership, with its mobilization of all real property, with its tendency toward giant corporations and trusts, and with its division of each people into a relatively few 'haves' and a great many 'have-nots'" has for a long time failed to perform its "natural-law social function."[63] These theorists favor extensive governmental control over the economy, because they assume, with Aquinas, that "there must exist something which impels toward the common good of the many, over and above that which impels towards the particular good of each individual."

This assumption was challenged by modern economists like Adam Smith (1723–90), who argued that when individuals produce and exchange goods for their own self-interest, they also thereby increase the wealth of the entire society.

> He generally, indeed, neither intends to promote the publick interest, nor knows how much he is promoting it. By preferring the support of domestick to that of foreign industry, he intends only his own security; and by directing that industry in such a manner as its produce may be the greatest value, he intends only his own gain, and he is in this, as in many other cases, led by an invisible hand to promote an end which was no part of his intention.[64]

F. A. Hayek describes the phenomenon alluded to by Smith as "spontaneous order." Hayek remarks, "One of the achievements of economic theory has been to explain how such a mutual adjustment of the spontaneous activities is brought about by the market."[65] Many economists have commented on the coordinating role of the market; for example, "The normal economic system works itself. For its current operation it is under no central control, it needs no central survey. Over the whole range of human activity and human need, supply is adjusted to demand, and production to consumption, by a process that is automatic, elastic and responsive."[66] The extent to which the market can be relied upon to produce economic order continues, of course, to be debated. But to the extent that it can, a natural law perspective will tend to support an economic system of capitalism with private businesses, trade associations, labor unions, and consumer organizations. In a system of democratic capitalism the government will not arrogate to itself the proper functions of these subsidiary groups, but will uphold the rule of law and try to ensure that none gains unfair advantage.

Those who distrust the free market will advocate regulation and centralized planning by governmental agencies. But even these must, by the principle of subsidiarity, concede a legitimate role for appropriate subsidiary associations, such as labor unions. This issue arose in the 1980s when the Polish Communist government tried unsuccessfully to suppress the union Solidarity. The proper level of government interaction with unions continues to be an issue in Europe today. How far government should defer to and support such associations is a question for casuistry: the application of an abstract precept to complicating and difficult circumstances.

Citizenship

The word *citizen* derives from the Latin term *civis* (Greek, πολίτης) which meant "member of the city" (*civitas* or πόλις). The locus classicus for this concept is again in Aristotle, who argued that a citizen is not a mere resident or cohabitant of the city, but a possessor of political rights such as the right to hold deliberative or judicial office.[67] Although most inhabitants (including women and slaves) were excluded from full citizenship even in the most extreme Greek democracies, the ideal of citizenship as possession of political rights was revived with the rise of modern democracies.

Aristotle also implies that citizens have certain moral rights (that is, just claims against other members of the community). Justice, in the Aristotelian tradition, aims at the common advantage, and this means the mutual advantage, that is, the interest of *each and every* citizen. This is clear from his description of the best or fully just constitution. He states that "a city-state is excellent due to the fact that the citizens who partake in the constitution are excellent; but in our case all the citizens partake in the constitution." He adds that in the most choiceworthy constitution, each of the citizens is excellent. He also maintains that "a city-state should be called happy not by viewing a part of it but by viewing all the citizens."[68] Hence, every citizen has the right to participate in the flourishing life of the city-state.

Locke understands the common good along similar lines: Government is "for the Preservation of every Mans Right and property, by preserving him from the violence or Injury of others." Hence, the magistrate should use "Terror to inforce Men to observe the positive Laws of the Society, made conformable to the Laws of Nature, for the public good, i.e. the good of every particular Member of that Society, as far as by common Rules, it can be provided for."[69] To be sure, Locke construes the common good more narrowly than does Aristotle, as consisting in the protection of individual rights. But he agrees with Aristotle in taking the common good to involve, as far as possible, the good of every member of society. The natural law perspective thus generally understands justice in terms of mutual advantage: a society is just only if its constitution protects the well-being of each and every citizen.

According to the natural law perspective in general, the rights of citizens ultimately derive from their natural rights as human beings. Natural law theorists disagree, however, as to the status of citizen rights. Those who accept Aristotle's political naturalism will be inclined to view citizenship as a core right. That is, the right to private property and other civil rights would derive from more basic political rights. But other theorists who agree with Locke that human beings possess their basic natural rights such as property rights even in a state of nature will view citizenship as a derivative and instrumental right. That is, individuals acquire political rights when they enter into political society, and these rights are valuable to the extent that they are necessary for the mutual preservation of their natural rights to their lives, liberties, and estates. The latter approach takes a more individualistic and liberal view of citizenship, whereas the former is more inclined to civic republicanism and other communitarian views.

The natural law perspective is not, as such, committed to any particular constitutional principles, including the democratic ideals of egalitarianism and popular sovereignty. Aristotle and other traditional theorists tend to think that rule by a morally impeccable monarch is the ideal, but in practice a "mixed constitution" is best, which combines the strong points of democracy, oligarchy, and aristocracy.[70] Aquinas reasons along these lines:

> The best form of government is in a political community or kingdom wherein one is given the power to preside over all according to his virtue, while under him are others having governing powers according to their virtue, and yet a government of this kind is shared by all, both because all are eligible to govern, and because the rulers are chosen by all. For this is the best form of polity, being partly kingdom since there is one at the head of all, partly aristocracy insofar as a number of persons are sent in authority, partly democracy, i.e. government by the people, insofar as the rulers can be chosen from the people, and the people have the right to choose their rulers.[71]

Locke also permits a variety of constitutional forms. When the commonwealth is formed, the majority will establish the sort of regime that meets their approval: democracy, oligarchy, hereditary or elective monarchy.[72] Hence, natural law theorists have been monarchists as well as democrats, although they have in practice favored a mixed constitution, or what Locke calls "compounded and mixed forms of Government."[73]

As noted earlier, the natural law perspective tends to emphasize responsibilities together with rights. According to the traditional approach, the lawgiver should strive to make the citizens morally virtuous.[74] For Locke, as noted earlier, individuals have obligations to themselves and others, including duties of charity. Hence, Locke and, to a greater extent, the traditional natural law theorists differ from classical liberal theorists, who recognize unconditional interpersonal obligations of only a negative sort, for example, not to initiate force or fraud. The emphasis on virtue and obligation also sets these theorists apart from egalitarian or welfare liberals, who regard rights as unconditional entitlements and hold that mere need rather than desert is a proper basis for just claims against the community. This suggests that a nonproductive surfer has the same right to sustenance as a diligent gardener. Such a viewpoint could lead to a proliferation of entitlements and discourage a sense of personal responsibility.[75]

The natural law perspective holds that citizens have the responsibility to support the political community whose fruits they enjoy. First, they are obligated to obey the laws. This duty is subject, however, to an important qualification, because human positive laws may be either just or unjust. According to Aquinas, if human laws are just, they are binding in conscience, because they are derived from the eternal law. Aquinas sets out three necessary conditions for justice: the aim must be the common good, the lawgiver must not exceed his authority, and burdens must be fairly imposed on the subjects. An unjust law fails to satisfy one or more of these conditions. However, Aquinas argues that one should comply with the laws, even if they are unjust, in order to avoid scandal or disorder. But a law may also be unjust because it violates divine law: "such are the laws of tyrants which promote idolatry or whatsoever is against divine law. To observe them is in no wise permissible, for as is said in the *Acts* [5:29], 'We must obey God rather than men.'"[76]

One also has a moral obligation to carry out one's civic responsibilities. If one is fortunate enough to live under a just constitution, one must of course carry out one's duties: for example, voting, sitting on juries, holding office, and serving in the armed forces. But what if there is a tyrannical ruler? Traditional theorists like Aquinas have generally argued that one should obey a tyrant in order to avoid even greater evils—subject to the exception noted above, that one must not violate divine laws.[77]

The citizens must be morally educated if they are to exercise their rights in a responsible manner, and here civil society has an indispensable role. The process begins in the family household, where children should be brought up to understand the difference between right and wrong and acquire habits of virtuous conduct. The process should be reinforced in other organizations, including religious and fraternal associations. Some natural law theorists like Aristotle argue for a public system of education for all the citizens: "one should not consider any citizen as belonging to himself alone, but as all belonging to the city-state, since each is a part of the city-state."[78] The education of all the citizens should have the same aim, which is a life of moral virtue and philosophy. Further, moral habituation requires the government and laws, because the laws have compulsory force and people will not respond to anything else.[79] Indeed, this is the highest aim of politics: The true statesman "wishes to make his fellow citizens good and obedient to the laws."[80] This remains a goal of the traditional natural law perspective.[81]

Since the Reformation modern natural law theorists have tended to regard moral and religious education as an individual responsibility. Some favor private education generally. Locke maintains that "the Nourishment and Education of their Children, is a Charge so incumbent on Parents for their Childrens good, that nothing can absolve them from taking care of it."[82] Along with the duty to rear and educate their children, parents have authority over them. Locke optimistically adds, "yet God hath woven into the Principles of Human Nature such a tenderness for their Off-spring that there is little fear that Parents should use their power with too much rigour; the excess is seldom on the severe side, the strong bypass of Nature drawing the other way." Locke does allow that parents may alienate the business of education by putting the tuition of their children in others' hands.[83] Government might intervene if parents fail to meet their obligations to their children, who are not the mere property of their parents but possess from God and Nature the right to be nourished and educated.[84]

Most natural law theorists would in any event resist a proposal for universal moral education on the grounds that compulsory moral education would compromise the government's primary duty to safeguard the citizens' freedom. Aristotle, however, anticipated this objection with the observation that "one ought to think that living for the constitution is not slavery but salvation."[85] But this reply seems problematic if one accepts the pluralistic view that the human good can take a variety of incommensurable forms For example, special-interest groups might try to influence or capture educational institutions in an attempt to valorize their peculiar moral codes.

The traditional theorist might rejoin that without public moral education, there is no assurance that the citizens would possess the common values and shared vision required for them to rely upon each other in a naturally ordered society.[86] Liberal democracy faces the problem that if the citizens are devoted solely to their personal pursuits and neglect their political duties, the constitution cannot endure.

CONFLICTING OBLIGATIONS

Membership in overlapping groups gives rise to conflicting loyalties. In *Antigone*, the Greek tragedy by Sophocles (ca. 496–406 B.C.), the heroine defies a ruler and carries out her familial duty to bury her brother. She tells the ruler that his edict is in violation of a higher law:

> Nor did I think your orders were so strong
> That you, a mortal man, could over-run
> The gods' unwritten and unfailing laws.
> Not now, nor yesterday's, they always live,
> And no one knows their origin in time.[87]

In Plato's *Crito* Socrates seems to approach this dilemma differently. After Socrates has been condemned to death by an Athenian jury, his comrade Crito arranges for his escape, and argues that Socrates owes it to his children and his friends to take his leave. Socrates replies that his duty to the laws of Athens take precedence. "One must not give way or retreat or leave one's post, but both in war and in courts and everywhere else, one must obey the commands of one's city and country, or persuade it as to the nature of justice."[88] In contrast, the English novelist E. M. Forster, one of the "Cambridge Apostles," said, "If I had to choose between betraying my country and betraying my friend, I hope I should have the guts to betray my country." He also makes a (perhaps ironic) religious appeal: "Dante places Brutus and Cassius in the lowest circle of Hell because they had chosen to betray their friend Julius Caesar rather than their country Rome."[89] But a government could not endure if citizens routinely gave precedence to personal loyalties. How, then, are these competing demands to be adjudicated?

For Aristotle, in a good society the citizens will naturally regard each other as friends and hence treat each other justly, because "all justice is in relation to a friend";[90] "in every community there is thought to be some form of justice, and friendship, too."[91] Therefore, citizens must treat each other justly and keep their obligations as citizens.

This solution seems open to the objection that there are different forms and degrees of friendship. Aristotle himself distinguishes the "perfect" friendship based on virtue from lesser forms, where one loves others only in so far as they are pleasing or useful. In a friendship of virtue one loves others because they are good persons and thus values them for their own sakes. But this requires intimate contact: "There is nothing so characteristic of friends as living together."[92] Thus the friend becomes "another self."[93] Living together for humans involves "sharing in discussion and thought . . . and not, as in the case of cattle, feeding in the same place."[94] In contrast, political friendship is based on utility.[95] "One cannot have with many people the friendship based on virtue," since one cannot be intimate and familiar with a multitude of citizens.[96] This presents a conundrum for Aristotle's solution to the problem of conflicting obligations, because he also holds that one's just obligations are correlated with friendship. If one commits an unjust act,

> the injustice increases by being exhibited towards those who are friends in a fuller sense: e.g. it is a more terrible thing to defraud a comrade than a fellow citizen, more terrible not to help a brother than a stranger, and more terrible to wound a father than any one else. And the demands of justice also naturally increase with the friendship, which implies that friendship and justice exist between the same persons and have an equal extension.[97]

This suggests that Aristotle would have to agree with E. M. Forster that if one were forced to choose between betraying a true friend and betraying one's fellow citizens, the duty to one's friend should take precedence.

Aristotle points a way out of this difficulty, however, if one views non-governmental associations as parts of a greater whole:

> Now all forms of community are like parts of the political community; for men journey together with a view to some particular advantage, and to provide something that they need for the purposes of life; and it is for the sake of advantage that the political community too seems both to have come together originally and to endure, for this is what legislators aim at, and they call just that which is to the common advantage. Now the other communities aim at some particular advantage, e.g. sailors at what is advantageous on a voyage with a view to making money or something of the kind, fellow-soldiers at what is advantageous in war, whether it is wealth or victory or the taking of a city that they seek, and members of tribes and demes. Some communities seem to arise for the sake of pleasure, viz. religious guilds and social clubs; for these exist respectively for the sake of sacrifice and of companionship. But all these seem to fall under the political community; for it aims not at present advantage but at what is advantageous for life as a whole.[98]

Aristotle's argument, then, is that the city-state has as its aim the good life as a whole, whereas subsidiary forms of association have merely subordinate aims. For example, they may aim at the provision of material necessities or physical security. They may also aim at pleasurable activities that enhance the quality of life. But because they have subordinate aims, these nongovernmental communities are subordinate to the whole, and the implication is that the duties of citizenship take precedence over the obligations of particular membership.

This assumes that society is like an organism, in which subsidiary associations have functions that serve the overarching aim of the whole system. And, even granting this as a regulative ideal, most, if not all, actual societies fail to realize it. Rather than having moral virtue as their paramount aim, they may aspire to the accumulation of wealth, military power, sybaritic self-indulgence, or—what is most common—an array of conflicting values. Considerations such as these led later philosophers such as the Cynics and Epicureans to conclude that "living according to nature" requires opting out of political life in favor of isolated communes or total solitude. Were they mistaken to draw this conclusion? If nongovernmental associations were to promote the ends of its citizens more effectively than society as a whole, the natural law perspective might have anarchist implications.

Liberal natural law theorists generally reject the ideal of the social organism. Rather, the primary function of the government is the protection of the equal rights of individuals to life, liberty, and property. Within this framework individuals may pursue happiness in a variety of nongovernmental associations. It might be argued that the political obligations of citizens have lexical priority over obligations to nongovernmental associations, because effective political institutions are a prerequisite for civil society. But the obligations are relatively minimal and unlikely to interfere with other duties, except in emergency circumstances such as war (when one might face a dilemma like Jean-Paul Sartre's of whether to defend one's government or care for a relative). Moreover, to the extent that existing polities deviate from the ideal—for example, by failing to protect or even violating individual rights—the duties of citizenship have diminished force.

Conclusion

The natural law perspective generally assumes that human beings are naturally disposed to join in communities in the pursuit of certain natural ends or objective goods. Communal existence is complex, involving families, governments, and many sorts of associations, all of which are important for human nature. But any community can be evaluated as better or worse depending on how effectively it promotes human nature. Social existence by rational beings requires rules, customs, and laws, which ought to promote human nature.

The natural law perspective has often had a religious dimension, but Christian natural law theorists from Saint Paul to John Locke have also maintained that natural law was accessible to the reason even of nonbelievers. Hence, despite considerable historical overlap, the natural law perspective is distinct from the Christian.[99]

The natural law perspective has conservative and liberal poles. The traditional pole is more conservative and especially concerned with issues of morality, decency, and social justice. But it agrees that government should respect and protect the functioning of subsidiary nongovernmental associations, provided they do not subvert the higher end. The modern pole is more liberal, limiting the role of government to protecting individual rights and providing a framework of freedom and security within which nongovernmental associations may carry out their diverse functions. Actual proponents of natural law today tend to fall somewhere between these two poles.

Where one finds oneself on this spectrum depends on one's considered view of human nature—for example, on how central and important one thinks personal liberty or self-directedness is in the actualization of our human nature. But this points to a deeper epistemological problem. Natural law theory assumes that human beings have certain natural capacities, faculties, and tendencies that it is good for them to exercise. These include life itself, health, physical growth, sexual reproduction, sociality, intellectual development, spontaneity, spirituality, and so forth. According to natural law theory, it is possible to determine the relative importance of these natural human capacities and to prescribe rules of conduct safeguarding them. Skeptical critics of natural law retort that there is no objective basis for distinguishing "natural" from "unnatural" conduct, so that the invocation of these labels is merely religious, rhetorical, or ideological, rather than scientific. Further, it is unclear how one could achieve a political consensus over such matters in practice. Critics of natural law protest that it is Panglossian to expect that different sides could ever come to agree that abortion or homosexual unions are unnatural. In contrast, the issue of global warming—is the world's average temperature increasing as a result of emissions from human technology?—is still disputed but will probably be resolved soon by means of scientific evidence. In order to be credible, the natural law perspective needs a decision procedure for distinguishing between "natural" or "unnatural" practices without begging the question. This methodology would rely on the findings of evolutionary biology, psychology, anthropology, economics, and other sciences.[100]

Critics of natural law also point to its "dark side." Theorists like Aristotle have countenanced social conditions as "natural" because they occur "always or for the most part," for example, the dominion of human beings over the rest of nature, the subordination of women to men, and even slavery. Feminist, egalitarian, and environmentalist critics condemn such acquiescence to dominance relationships that are actually based on coercion and habituation as exposing the untenability of natural law. But the natural law perspective has endured for over two thousand years because it has repeatedly adapted itself to new discoveries about human nature, and about government and civil society. For example, Francisco de Vitoria (ca. 1486–1546) and Bartolomé de Las Casas (1474–1566) condemned the enslavement of native Americans by the Conquistadors as in violation of natural law.[101] Judging from the past, the natural law perspective can endure as long as it remains open to the insights of scientists, philosophers, theologians, and its own critics.

NOTES

1. Heraclitus, "On Nature," in *Die Fragmente der Vorsokratiker*, 6th ed., ed. H. Diels, rev. W. Kranz (Berlin: Weidmann, 1952), 22B114 and 2.

2. General histories include Heinrich A. Rommen, *The Natural Law: A Study in Legal and Social History and Philosophy*, trans. Thomas R. Hanley (1936 (German); Indianapolis: Liberty Fund, 1998); Michael Bertram Crow, *The Changing Profile of the Natural Law* (The Hague: Martinus Nijhoff, 1977); A. P. d'Entrèves, *Natural Law*, 2nd ed. (1972; reprint, New Brunswick, N.J.: Transaction, 1994). For discussion of natural law in the wider context of legal thought see J. M. Kelley, *A Short History of Western Legal Theory* (Oxford: Clarendon, 1992). James V. Schall, "The Natural Law Bibliography," *American Journal of Jurisprudence* 40 (1995): 157–98, is an overview of recent secondary literature.

3. Aquinas discussed natural law as part of a general treatment of law in the *Summa Theologiae* I-II, QQ. 90–97. Translations are from vol. 28 of the Blackfriars edition by Thomas Gilby, O.P. (New York: McGraw-Hill, 1963). This discussion of Aquinas owes much to Anthony J. Lisska, *Aquinas's Theory of Natural Law: An Analytic Reconstruction* (Oxford: Clarendon Press, 1996).

4. Aquinas, *Summa Theologiae* I-II, Q. 90 a. 4.

5. Ibid. Q. 91.

6. Ibid. Q. 95 a. 2. Here Aquinas follows Saint Augustine (354–430), who declares, "There never seems to have been a law that was not just" (*De libero arbitrio* I.5)

7. Aquinas, *Summa Theologiae* I-II, Q. 94 a. 2; cf. I, Q. 79 a. 12.

8. See Leo Strauss, *Natural Right and History* (Chicago: University of Chicago Press, 1953) on the contrast between classical and modern theories of natural right. Recent overviews include Richard Tuck, *Natural Rights Theories: Their Origin and Development* (Cambridge: Cambridge University Press, 1979); Stephen Buckle, *Natural Law and the Theory of Property: Grotius to Hume* (Oxford: Clarendon Press, 1991); and Knud Haakonssen, *Natural Law and Moral Philosophy from Grotius to the Scottish Enlightenment* (Cambridge: Cambridge University Press, 1996).

9. Locke in fact drew on Aristotle in his earlier untitled lectures in Latin on natural law, but these remained unpublished in his lifetime, and were only recently rediscovered. They are available in two editions with translations: *Essays on the Law of Nature*, ed. Wolfgang von Leyden (Oxford: Clarendon Press, 1954);

and *Questions Concerning the Law of Nature*, ed. Robert Horwitz, Diskin Clay, and Jenny Strauss (Ithaca: Cornell University Press, 1990).

10. Locke, *Second Treatise of Government* II.4. All quotations from the two treatises are from the revised edition of Peter Laslett of Locke's *Two Treatises of Government* (Cambridge: Cambridge University Press, 1963), except that Locke's frequent italics are have been suppressed where they might be misleading or confusing to the reader.

11. Ibid. II.6.

12. Ibid. II.12; but cf. IX.124 for a more cautious note.

13. Ibid. II.6.

14. *First Treatise of Government* IV.42.

15. See John Simmons, *The Lockean Theory of Rights* (Princeton: Princeton University Press, 1992), esp. 95–102.

16. Locke, *Second Treatise of Government*, III.19.

17. Ibid. IX.123.

18. Ibid. II.12.

19. Ibid. IV.54.

20. Jacques Maritain, *Man and State* (Chicago: University of Chicago Press, 1951; reprint, Washington, D.C.: Catholic University of America Press, 1998), 94.

21. See Locke, *Second Treatise of Government* III.17.

22. Ibid. VI.57.

23. Homily delivered October 8, 1995, in Oriole Park at Camden yards in Baltimore. Text printed in the *New York Times*, October 9, 1995, B15.

24. This account is oversimplified, because there are two contending schools of "traditional" natural law theory today, which disagree over the need for strong metaphysical foundations such as an Aristotelian teleological theory of human nature. They are disagree over whether there is a hierarchical ordering of objective goods (with moral virtue and ultimately spirituality at the apex) or whether there is an incommensurable plurality of such goods. One school (represented by Henry B. Veatch, Ralph McInerny, Russell Hittinger, Anthony Lisska, Pauline Westerman, et al.) holds that teleology is crucial and that there is a hierarchy of human goods with spirituality and moral virtue at the apex. The other school (represented by Germain Grisez, John Finnis, Joseph Boyle, Robert P. George, et al.) rejects Aristotle's "metaphysical biology" and also countenances an incommensurable plurality of intrinsic goods. The latter position is defended by John Finnis, *Natural Law and Natural Rights*, corrected ed. (Oxford: Clarendon Press, 1988) and Robert P. George, *In Defense of Natural Law* (Oxford: Oxford University Press, 1999). It is criticized by Russell Hittinger, *A Critique of the New Natural Law Theory* (Notre Dame, Ind.: University of Notre Dame Press, 1987); and Pauline C. Westerman, *The Disintegration of Natural Law Theory: Aquinas to Finnis* (Leiden: Brill, 1998). The two sides also disagree over the interpretation of Aquinas. In spite of these theoretical and exegetical differences, however, the two camps frequently agree on practical issues of public policy, such as abortion, contraception, and sexual morality. Since they seem to be in general agreement on the practical issues discussed here, I shall not discuss this controversy further. For essays representing diverse approaches to natural law and its critics see

Robert P. George, *Natural Law Theory* (Oxford: Clarendon Press, 1992); and Robert P. George, *Natural Law, Liberalism, and Morality* (Oxford: Clarendon Press, 1996).

25. See Scott D. Gerber, *To Secure These Rights: The Declaration of Independence and Constitutional Interpretation* (New York: New York University Press, 1995), chap. 1. See˙ also Andrew J. Reck, "Natural Law in American Revolutionary Thought," *Review of Metaphysics* 30 (1977): 686–714, who notes that the American patriots were called "the disciples of Mr. Locke." On Locke's influence on the American founding see Jerome Huyler, *Locke in America: The Moral Philosophy of the Founding Era* (Lawrence: University of Kansas Press, 1995); and Michael P. Zuckert, *The Natural Rights Republic: Studies in the Foundation of the American Political Tradition* (Notre Dame, Ind.: University of Notre Dame Press, 1996).

26. For influence of natural law theory on the Supreme Court today, see Scott D. Gerber, *First Principles: The Jurisprudence of Clarence Thomas* (New York: New York University Press, 1999), chap. 2. In the field of political philosophy, Robert Nozick argues that the Lockean view implies a libertarian theory of rights with a strong commitment to individual freedom, private property, and limited government. *Anarchy, State, and Utopia* (New York: Basic, 1974).

27. Aristotle, *Politics* I.2.1253a1–3; Marcus Aurelius, *Meditations* III.4, 11; Aquinas, *Summa Theologiae* I–II, Q. 95 a. 4; Grotius, *De Iure Belli et Pacis*, Prolegomena, 6; Locke, *Second Treatise* II.15, quoting from Hooker's *Laws of Ecclesiastical Polity* I.10. A noteworthy exception is Thomas Hobbes, who rejects Aristotle's thesis that human beings are by nature social animals: e.g., "We do not therefore by nature seek society for its own sake, but that we may receive some honour or profit from it; these we desire primarily, that secondarily." *De Cive* I.I.2.

28. Aristotle, *Politics* I.2.1253a1–39.

29. Aristotle, *History of Animals* I.1.488a7–10.

30. Aquinas, *Summa Theologiae* I–II, Q. 95 a. 4.

31. Aristotle, *Politics* I.1.1252a1–7.

32. Ibid. I.2.1252b27–30.

33. Ibid. III.9.1280a31–32.

34. Ibid. 1280b29–31.

35. Ibid. 1280b33–35.

36. See A. B. Seligman, *The Idea of Civil Society* (New York: Free Press, 1992).

37. Aristotle, *Politics* I.2.1252b30–32.

38. Ibid. III.9.1280b40–1281a1.

39. Ibid. II.1.1261a2–9, criticizing Socrates' proposal in Plato, *Republic* 423c–424a and 449a–466c.

40. Aristotle, *Politics* II.5.1263a8–b14.

41. Pius XI, *Quadragesimo Anno* (Encyclical of 1931), cited by Heinrich A. Rommen, *The Natural Law*, 194 n. 5.

42. John Finnis, *Natural Law and Natural Rights*, 146.

43. Finnis, "Natural Law and Limited Government," in George, *Natural Law, Liberalism, and Morality*, 6.

44. Locke, *Second Treatise* IX.123–24.

45. Ibid. 134–35.

46. Ibid. XIX.222.

47. See Francis Fukuyama, *Trust: The Social Virtues and the Creation of Prosperity* (New York: Free Press, 1995), who draws on the research of Robert D. Putnam, *Making Democracy Work: Civic Traditions in Modern Italy* (Princeton: Princeton University Press, 1993); and of Edward C. Banfield, *The Moral Basis of a Backward Society* (Glencoe, Ill.: Free Press, 1958). The concept of "social capital" was introduced by James S. Coleman.

48. Aristotle, *Politics* II.4.1262b15–24.

49. Ibid. III.9.1280b35–39.

50. Nicholas F. Jones argues that the remarkable stability of the ancient Athenian democracy was to a significant degree due to an intricate web of associations including the demes, phylai (tribes), phratries (clans or brotherhoods), social clubs, schools, religious cults, and so forth, in *The Associations of Classical Athens: The Response to Democracy* (Oxford: Oxford University Press, 1999).

51. See Plato *Republic* I.332d5–6.

52. Ibid. V.470c5–d2; and Plato, *Laws* I.628b1–2.

53. Aristotle, *Politics* V is devoted to the causes and cures of this problem.

54. Madison, *The Federalist*, no. 10.

55. Aristotle, *Politics* I.10.1258b2–7; Aquinas, *Summa Theologiae* II-II, Q. 78.

56. See Joseph A. Schumpeter, *History of Economic Analysis* (New York: Oxford University Press, 1954), 103–4. Murray Rothbard, *Economic Thought before Adam Smith* (Hants, UK: Elgar, 1995), 103–8, discusses how the later Scholastics at Salamanca steadily rehabilitated the practice of charging interest.

57. See, e.g., Finnis, *Natural Law and Natural Rights*, 117, 124.

58. Alexis de Tocqueville, *Democracy in America*, trans. George Lawrence (New York: HarperCollins, 1988), 691–92.

59. For a detailed history see David T. Beito, *From Mutual Aid to the Welfare State: Fraternal Societies and Social Services, 1890–1967* (Chapel Hill: University of North Carolina Press, 2000).

60. Aquinas, *De Regimine Principum* I.1.8–9, in *On Kingship, to the King of Cyprus*, trans. G. B. Phelan (Toronto: Pontifical Institute of Mediaeval Studies, 1949). Compare *Summa Theologiae* I, Q. 96 a4.

61. "The *common good* means not only the good of all in general, or as a whole, but the good of every class and, so far as practicable, the good of every individual." John A. Ryan and Francis J. Boland, C.S.C, *Catholic Principles of Politics*, cited in Rommen, *Natural Law*, 214 n. 46. In *Nature, Justice, and Rights in Aristotle's "Politics"* (Oxford: Clarendon Press, 1995), chap. 6, I argue that this is the original meaning of "the common advantage" for Aristotle.

62. See Christopher Wolfe, "Being Worthy of Trust: A Response to Joseph Raz," in George, *Natural Law, Liberalism, and Morality* 134.

63. Rommen, *Natural Law*, 228–29.

64. Adam Smith, *An Inquiry into the Nature and Causes of the Wealth of Nations*, ed. R. H. Campbell, A. S. Skinner, and W. B. Todd (Oxford: Clarendon Press, 1976), IV.II.9.

65. F. A. Hayek, "The Principles of a Liberal Order," in *Studies in Philosophy, Politics, and Economics* (Chicago: University of Chicago Press, 1967), 167.

66. J. A. Salter, *Allied Shipping Control* (Oxford: Oxford University Press, 1921), 16–17.

67. Aristotle, *Politics* III.1–5; see my *Nature, Justice, and Rights in Aristotle's "Politics"*, chap. 5.

68. Aristotle, *Politics* VII.13.1332a32–38, 9.1329a23–24.

69. Locke, *First Treatise of Government* IX.92.

70. Aristotle, *Politics* III.6–17; IV.8–9 and 13.

71. Aquinas, *Summa Theologiae* I-II, Q. 105 a. 1.

72. Locke, *Second Treatise of Government* X.132.

73. Ibid.

74. Aquinas treats virtue theory and legal theory as complimentary elements in a complete moral philosophy. Virtue ethics is discussed in *Summa Theologiae* I-II QQ 49–89, which precedes his discussion of law.

75. The conflict between desert and entitlement is a theme of Lloyd L. Weinreb, *Natural Law and Justice* (Cambridge: Harvard University Press, 1987).

76. Aquinas, *Summa Theologiae* I-II, Q. 96 a. 4. Martin Luther King followed Aquinas here: "A just law is a man-made code that squares with the moral law or the law of God. An unjust law is a code that is out of harmony with the moral law. To put it in the terms of Saint Thomas Aquinas, an unjust law is a human law that is not rooted in eternal and natural laws. Any law that uplifts human personality is just. Any law that degrades human personality is unjust. All segregation statutes are unjust because segregation distorts the soul and damages the personality." M. L. King, "Letter from Birmingham Jail," *A Testament of Hope: The Essential Writings of Martin Luther King, Jr.*, ed. James Melvin Washington (San Francisco: Harper and Row, 1986).

77. Aquinas, *De Regimine Pricipum* I.6.

78. Aristotle, *Politics* VIII.1.1337a27–29.

79. Aristotle, *Nicomachean Ethics* X.9.1180a18–30.

80. Ibid. I.13.1102a9.

81. See for example, Robert George, *Making Men Moral: Civil Liberties and Public Morality* (Oxford: Clarendon Press, 1993).

82. Locke, *Second Treatise of Government* II.67.

83. Ibid. II.69.

84. Locke, *First Treatise of Government* IX.90.

85. Aristotle, *Politics* V.9.1310a34–36.

86. Alasdair MacIntyre, *After Virtue*, 2nd ed. (Notre Dame, Ind.: University of Notre Dame Press, 1984), and Michael Sandel, *Liberalism and the Limits of Justice* (Cambridge: Cambridge University Press, 1982), criticize liberal individualism along these lines.

87. Sophocles, *Antigone*, trans. Elizabeth Wyckoff, in *The Complete Greek Tragedies*, ed. David Grene and Richmond Lattimore (New York: Modern Library, 1954), lines 452–56.

88. Plato, *Crito* 51b7–c1. In Plato's *Apology* 29d2–4, however, Socrates says that he must obey the god Apollo rather than the Athenian jurors if they disagree. In this respect he seems to agree with Antigone.

89. E. M. Forster, *What I Believe* (London: Hogarth, 1939), 8.

90. Aristotle, *Eudemian Ethics* VII.10.1242a20.

91. Aristotle, *Nicomachean Ethics* VIII.9.1159b28.

92. Ibid. 5.1157b19.

93. Ibid. IX.9.1170b7.

94. Ibid. 1170b11–12.

95. Aristotle, *Eudemian Ethics* VII.10.1242b21.

96. Aristotle, *Nicomachean Ethics* IX.10.1171a19.

97. Ibid. VIII.9.1160a3–8.

98. Ibid. 1160a9–24.

99. The Christian perspective will be examined more fully in another chapter.

100. For example, Larry Arnhart argues that natural law political theory can be given a modern scientific foundation, in *Darwinian Natural Right: The Biological Ethics of Human Nature* (Albany: State University of New York Press, 1998). For other recent deployments of natural law theory in social philosophy and policy see *Natural Law and Modern Moral Philosophy*, ed. Ellen Frankel Paul, Fred D. Miller, Jr., and Jeffrey Paul (Cambridge: Cambridge University Press, 2001).

101. See Brian Tierney, *The Idea of Natural Rights: Studies on Natural Rights, Natural Law, and Church Law* (Atlanta: Scholars Press, 1997), chap. 11.

Natural Law: A Response

William M. Sullivan

IN THE ILLUMINATING contrast he draws between the ancient and medieval tradition of natural law and modern natural right, Fred D. Miller characterizes natural law thinking as having functioned as a regulative ideal. One of the salient characteristics of that regulative ideal has surely been natural law's claim to universal truth and validity. This claim has a certain poignancy today. On the one hand, modern thinkers are rightly skeptical about claims to universal validity, given what we understand about the importance of "local knowledge" and the historical conditioning of concepts. At the same time, the exigencies of living in and trying to make sense of an increasingly interconnected planetary civilization have placed the issues of cosmopolitanism and universal rights and standards high on the practical agenda.

This cosmopolitan side of natural law thinking, which was developed after Aristotle but before the coming of Christianity, belongs to Stoicism. However, this aspect of the tradition does not play an explicit role in Miller's account. In what follows I would like to call attention to this important strand of the tradition by noting the ways in which several of the core issues and tensions of Stoic natural law continue to resonate, in amplified form, in contemporary discussions of civil society, the state, and a cosmopolitan world context. At the same time, these considerations can help to situate Miller's contrast between medieval and modern natural law.

The great issue that motivated the Stoic development of natural law thinking concerned the terms of human cooperation, considered on the largest scale. Many of today's urgent problems, including the containment of violent conflict within and between states, the rights of refugees and the obligations of nations, the socially destabilizing effects of global economic changes, and environmental protection, raise again the issue of how common standards can be developed and made efficacious amid evident diversity of polity, law, religion, and tradition. These developments have once again placed two questions central to Stoic natural law thinking on the historical agenda, and with some urgency. The first is whether reasonable, convincing justification can be given for some set of universal principles of human cooperation, and how specific these norms can actually be. The Stoic tradition formulated the question as whether some account of the terms of cooperation can be established along the lines of what nature, especially human nature, requires for its fulfillment. The second, related question, concerns the institutionalization of these principles, how such general norms can be made effective in the actual practice of diverse national societies.

The necessary historical condition for posing such questions was the development of universal empires, first the Persian and then Alexander's conquests. The Hellenistic successor states to Alexander's empire and the rise of Rome's dominion made the question of common or universal standards of justice a practical, not just theoretical, question. Thus, the Roman jurists distinguished *ius naturale*, which aimed to be universal and rationally defensible, and applicable to all persons even in the face of the bewildering variety of beliefs and practices obtaining among different societies, from the *ius gentium*. This "law of nations" referred to the divergent customs and laws in use in the variety of actual societies.

At the heart of this question was a sociological issue that defined a key tension within natural law thinking and foreshadowed the modern concern about civil society and state. The independent Greek cities and the Roman Republic had been "communal states," in which citizenship meant the freedom of individuals to participate in the life of the state. Yet, even in democracies, citizenship was a jealously guarded privilege that excluded in principle women, foreigners, and slaves. By contrast, the Persian system set a different pattern, creating a gap between a cosmopolitan ruling class who took part in running the polity, on the one hand, and all other subjects, who could have only private interests. This demarcation tended to relativize distinctions among the vast unenfranchised majority so that ideas of universal humanity became somewhat more plausible in principle. Over time, despite the high cultural prestige of the ideals of the old communal state, the Roman world-polity came to resemble the Persian, so that Roman law recognized both the distinctiveness of particular legal traditions among subject nations and elements of something akin to the modern, individualistic notion of private or negative freedom, especially in civil, or property, law.[1]

This development fell short of institutionalizing a full-fledged civil society. However, the Roman system did create and protect a sphere of normative order within which individual subjects, who eventually became "citizens" at law, could conduct private affairs ideally free from arbitrary state interference. In the theoretical realm, the social conditions of the Hellenistic and Roman eras encouraged Stoic thinkers to break with the earlier Greek precedent of identifying full humanity with citizenship in a specific polis. Instead, the Stoics developed a more "cosmopolitan" understanding of both humanity and citizenship that, while holding to much of the moral spirit of the citizen ideal, attempted also to recognize the universality inherent in the idea of a humanity possessed of "reason," as they termed free self-direction. This idea, in turn, further suggested the legitimacy of activity outside the moral community of the classical city.

Fred D. Miller has admirably summarized some of the key tensions and conflicts within the natural law tradition by presenting several of its articulations in the work of Aristotle, Thomas Aquinas, and John Locke. This enables Professor Miller to contrast the "organicist" understanding of the relation between individual and society in medieval natural law thinking with the individualism of modern natural rights theory, and then to draw out some of the implications. Something of the same ground is also opened up in John Coleman's comparison between Protestant and Roman Catholic approaches to society and politics. The link between these two positions was in fact the Stoic effort to construct a frame of moral reference able to unite the individual, "civil" dimension with a "political" or communal ethos of concern with the common good. In modern political philosophy, this tension reappears in the contrast between theorists such as John Locke, David Hume, and Adam Smith, for whom the state became largely instrumental to the "civil" realm of individuals and voluntary association, on the one hand, and those advocates of a civil society embedded within a complex but participatory state such as that described by Montesquieu, Hegel, and Tocqueville.

Professor Miller traces the natural law tradition to Aristotle, who followed Plato in rejecting Sophistic relativism, finding the full expression of human flourishing in the realized life of the "communal state" of the autonomous Greek city. We might characterize Aristotle's understanding as something like fully embedded natural law, since on his account it was inconceivable that the values and norms of civic life, through which the fulfillment of human nature was mediated, could exist apart from this institutional embodiment. One of the major implications of this position, of course, was the necessary restriction of flourishing, and thus full humanity, to the community of citizens as well as, somewhat more arguably, to Hellenes alone.

By contrast, it was of the essence of the subsequent "cosmopolitan" movement of philosophy known as Stoicism to assert that human flourishing was possible for all. Stoics held humans to be "by nature" equal in worth regardless of sex, ethnicity, or status. The basis of this claim was the Stoic idea that all humans participated in a larger "city," as they described the cosmos: the community of gods and humans linked by participation in the common and universal logos. This was expressed in the famous Stoic idea of "cosmopolis." The notion of a cosmic logos pervading and directing all, which rational beings could consciously understand and follow, allowed Stoics to speak metaphorically of "right reason" as a kind of natural "law" immanent within human understanding. Through participation in this reason individuals might transcend the domination of instinctive desires to realize transcendent value in practice, thus fulfilling their humanity.

This was a complex "regulative idea." Its core was the idea of the logos or reason that gods and humans share, albeit unequally, as not simply calculative but practically prescriptive in a very specific sense. Right reason, as was implied by the idea of the world as city, was concerned above all with social relationships, with the proper treatment of other rational beings as members of a potential community of justice and fellowship.[2] The Stoic ideal of life pointed toward a community of persons free from instinctive or social controls, living in harmony with the universe through their common participation in cosmic reason.

The Stoics carried over unmistakably Aristotelian moral elements in their notion of human flourishing. But Stoic virtue was no longer necessarily tied to an actual "communal state"—and therefore it was no longer necessarily restricted to a particular ethnicity, social status, or gender. Instead, by emphasizing human participation in transcendental value within the "community of gods and men" available through "right reason," the Stoics effectively disembedded the sacred from the particular civic cults. This meant that moral virtue itself, rather than a political order, became the locus of the sacred. As a result, individuals could be conceived as emancipated from the communal constraints of the institutions of household and polis.

This shift relativized all institutional embodiments in principle, but its practical basis was the intense associational life of the philosophical community. By locating value in a "private," voluntary community outside and beyond the communal state, the Stoics did what the other philosophical schools were doing: they created a kind of dual or "virtual" citizenship. Ideally, the true city was realizable wherever human beings associated in relationships of moral equality, justice, and friendship with each other.

By placing the locus of the sacred not in particular institutional arrangements or persons but in a "regulative ideal" that could be shared in by all, the Stoics provided a new source of moral energy. At the same time, they introduced a severe tension into social life. It became unclear how and to what extent philosophically awakened persons owed loyalty to the polity in which they had citizenship. By stressing the importance of the voluntary, cosmopolitan community of like-minded persons—citizens and noncitizens, free and slave—philosophy was creating a model of association that was in tension with the social and legal structures in which ancient civilization remained rooted. This helps explain the periodic persecution of philosophical sects, especially Cynics and Stoics, in the early Empire. Christianity would come to repeat a similar pattern on a much wider, more popular basis.

While its ideals never defined the political project of more than small, though sometimes influential, minorities, Stoic notions of the natural law did have significant influence in the Greco-Roman world. Stoic ideas were widely diffused, especially through Roman law, the medium through which the Roman world-polity organized itself. Natural law was explicitly invoked in Roman jurisprudence as a kind of "regulative ideal" that defined the "natural" structure of human relationships in reference to which actual social institutions were to be understood. There was frequent tension between this Stoic notion of "natural" relationships and common usage among extant societies, the *ius gentium*. Natural law therefore generated a permanent tension between practice and ideal. Thus arose legal definitions from the second and third centuries A.D. found in Justinian's *Code* on slavery: "Slavery is an institution of law common to all peoples [*ius gentium*] by which, in violation of the law of nature, a person is subjected to the mastery of another. . . . [S]o far as natural law is concerned, all men are equal."[3]

The tension between the civic ideals of the Roman polity and its practical despotism, like the tension between the classical notion of citizenship and the life of the private association, was never fully mediated, even for the ruling classes. Remarkably, the threatened moral cohesion and weakening élan of the Roman state was sublated in the state-church system erected by Constantine and his successors. Especially in the West, the Catholic Church found itself heir to both these tensions and the administrative model of the Roman state. Christendom took up and extended the important legacies of jurisprudence and philosophical natural law, including the same tension between the universal but largely ideal norms of equality and individuality and their concrete embodiment in a society of orders and status.

In its Christian reformulation, as theorized at the height of its development by Thomas Aquinas, the individualistic, private, even anarchistic aspects of Stoic natural law philosophy were both recognized and at the same time anchored by a doctrine of strong authoritative institutions. Aided by the medieval recovery of Aristotle's texts, this tendency to reembed the sacred was consistent with the "pastoral" tendency of the Church to accommodate to the world while seeking to "leaven" it. So, secular institutions, including secular political powers, could be considered corporate entities, given "charters" of relative autonomy on the natural law basis of their presumed contributions to the common good. For the natural law tradition, this represented a significant advance in clarifying the normative basis for the associations of what would later become civil society. For Christianity, as for Stoicism, the ultimate locus of value remained not in the institutional order itself but in a transcendent purpose. This meant that individuals and private groups as such acquired a moral value in principle. Voluntary organization apart from state control became a moral, if not always a legal, option.

The historical watersheds of the Reformation and Enlightenment that attended the emergence of modern ideas of natural right and civil society greatly strengthened the legitimacy of individual conscience and action. Not surprisingly, with these historical developments came a revival of interest in Stoic ideas of natural law, now taken directly from the ancient texts rather than filtered through medieval theology. The neo-Stoic revival of the early modern period was part of that larger "disciplinary revolution" that transformed the cultural order of European societies. The neo-Stoic movement of the sixteenth and early-seventeenth centuries sought to replace the fissured institutional order of a now-divided Christendom with a normative order that could cross confessional frontiers at a time of intense religious warfare. Thinkers such as Justus Lipsius appealed to both Catholics and Protestants with his notion of a cosmopolitan moral order within which national states and their affairs could be conceived according to principles analogous to law.[4] More so than either ancient Stoicism or medieval Thomism, neo-Stoicism was an activist project to leverage change in worldly conditions.

In the new climate of opinion that followed the Reformation, natural law theories lay the groundwork for the modern self-understanding of the polity and constitution as a regime of rights. The new understanding of natural law legitimated individuals as the moral basis of all institutions. But at the same time it intensified the moral demands made on individuals. More than ever before, persons and institutions were expected to embody transcendent ends of virtue and justice, as in the intense ethic of vocation and civic responsibility espoused especially by Protestantism and continued, in secularized forms, in contemporary Western societies. These developments gave new urgency to the search for structures of order that could both protect individual and group liberties and yet secure justice and social stability.

Since the eighteenth century this search has taken two main theoretical forms. In both of these the legacy of natural law thinking remains evident. The Locke-Hume version of liberalism has conceived of political institutions as neutral instruments arising out of the individual search for security and prosperity. In this tradition, freedom is understood as primarily private or "negative," restricting state intrusion into the activities of civil society. By contrast, the Montesquieu-Hegel tradition has seen the state as more churchlike, as a moral agency charged with fostering justice and civic spirit in a more "positive" sense of freedom as social participation, as well as with protecting civil rights. This contrast reappears on the level of national polities as well, with the "Lockean" United States more focused on economic liberties and private rights, as against the European emphasis upon social citizenship and group inclusion in the polity.

It is surely noteworthy, as John Coleman has shown, that the European corporatist polities owe a great deal to the updated natural law theories espoused by the religious successors of Christendom. This inclines them toward a more "Catholic" type of polity, in which the voluntary principle embodied in the idea of civil society is given free play but placed within a strong institutional matrix designed to uphold and promote a civic ethic of mutual support and inclusion. The American polity is, by contrast, distinctly more "Protestant" in spirit, suspicious of authoritative social integration. But these differences are not only "confessional." As we have seen, these differences also correspond to the historic polarity within the natural law tradition itself, the tension between individual, private freedom, and civic participation.

In addressing the challenge of discerning or inventing an institutional order capable of sustaining the partly conflicting goals of the modern project, we are continuing to use the heritage of natural law. Moreover, all contemporary polities and the international order itself find themselves struggling to harmonize or at least balance the needs for state functions and the activities of civil society. This is particularly so under the impact of increasingly global communications and economic activity. For these historical reasons, the classic Stoic insistence that human welfare requires the search for fundamental principles of human cooperation that reach beyond claims of particular polities has reappeared in our time. It would not be an exaggeration to say that this theme, in its practical as well as theoretical import, has emerged as the inescapable horizon of contemporary discussions of ethics and politics.

NOTES

1. See Michael Mann, *The Sources of Social Power*, vol. 1, *A History from the Beginning to* A.D. 1750 (Cambridge: Cambridge University Press, 1986), 246–47.

2. See Malcolm Schofield, *The Stoic Idea of the City* (Cambridge: Cambridge University Press, 1991), 57–92.

3. Quoted in Michael Grant, *The World of Rome* (New York: New American Library, 1960), 140.

4. See Gerhard Oestreich, *Neostoicism and the Early Modern State*, trans. David McLintock (Cambridge: Cambridge University Press, 1982).

A Limited State and a Vibrant Society: Christianity and Civil Society

John A. Coleman, S.J.

IT WOULD BE foolhardy, indeed, and risk a superficial mere "skimming view" to attempt, in the small compass of one essay, any comprehensive or encyclopedic overview on the topic of Christianity's position on the state and civil society. The competing *Staatslehren* (where there even is one!) of different Christian theological "families," such as Catholics, Calvinists, Lutherans, Anabaptists, and the Orthodox, do not fully agree or even always converge on their doctrines of the state and society.[1] To avoid this trap of even trying to achieve a fully rounded summary of the varying positions, I will focus primarily on the tradition I know best: the social teaching of Catholicism.

Yet I will also raise up the Reformed tradition's theory about the "spheres of creation" as a useful conversation partner and, at times, perhaps a corrective to the Catholic theory of subsidiarity and the common good. These two seem, on balance, the two major traditions in contention among most Christian authors who engage in social theology about state and society. Some authors, such as Don Browning, see a certain complementarity and convergence between these two traditions.[2] Recent Catholic social thought explicitly evokes the "covenantal" aspect which lies behind the theory of spheres of creation.[3] Others, such as Max Stackhouse, suggest deeper abiding tensions between the two.[4]

Before we move to look more closely at social Catholicism and a comparison with the Calvinist tradition of spheres of creation, however, we need to avert several special difficulties in treating a long spiritual/theological/historical/cultural tradition such as Christianity in a book that compares it with several of the more recent (and less culturally pluralistic) traditions. Christianity shares with other world-religious traditions, such as Hinduism, Confucianism and Judaism, an existence of thousand of years and an embodiment in quite diverse epochs and cultures. Some of these normative texts clearly are anchored in premodern understandings. In places, the Christians have been in ascendancy; in other places, in a minority. In still other places, they have suffered persecution and oppression. Naturally, Christianity's attitude toward the state has varied depending on whether it has been in or out of power. It is very difficult to capture the religious traditions in any simple ahistorical ideal type.

Moreover, we need to attend to three other aspects when treating Christianity's conceptions of civil society and the state. (1) Christianity complicates the comparative project by introducing, inevitably, a third term to the equation: *the church*, civil society, and the state. As we will see, the church does not usually think of itself as just one other free association within civil society, totally equivalent to the other free associations. (2) Christianity has been in a—often centuries long—contact and dialogue with many of the other traditions treated in this book: natural law, liberalism, and, more recently, feminism. (3) Christianity in recent decades has absorbed new and important experiences about the relevance of civil society that reshape its classic doctrines.

CHURCH, STATE, AND CIVIL SOCIETY

One obvious place to look for a sense of the Christian range on positions on state government and civil society is to inspect the varying doctrines concerning church-state relations.[5] Although the church in no way exhausts civil society, it tends to belong in that realm rather than the state.[6] Even those Christians who held (or those few who continue to hold) some variant of a position supporting a state-sponsored church would still generally appeal also to a version of a doctrine of the "freedom" of the church from too much governmental control or entanglement.

The freedoms of civil society (the freedoms of speech, association, etc.), as they arose in the West at least, derive ultimately from a Christian provenance, rooted in an assertion of the liberty of the church (*libertas ecclesiae*). Ernst Troeltsch argued as much when he contended that the early church, in demanding to be conceived of as a separate sphere whose authority was derivative from God and conscience before God and not from the state, made its main contribution to social theory to anchor a *novum* in history: "free spaces" in society that did not derive their legitimacy directly from the state.[7]

The Christian churches have often claimed this "free space" not just for the church but for families as well. Both classic Catholicism and Protestantism saw the family as an "autonomous sphere of creation" whose authority derived directly from God and not through the mediation of the state, civil society, or even the church. Hence, the family is also, while within civil society, not on an even par with other associations of civil society. Its derivative theological authority is stronger than the authority of the other associations. Frequently, a theological position on the "freedom of the church" will closely mirror a larger position on civil society, as in arguments which contend that the church itself flourishes best and most freely in societies which, more generally, allow free markets and freedom of speech, assembly, petition, and mobility.[8] But if the church is conceived of as *in* and, perhaps, as an essential anchor of civil society, most Christian theorists—at least with anything approaching a somewhat robust ecclesiology (i.e., the doctrine of the church)—see the church as also somehow a species apart from the other free associations of civil society. Its authority derives from God and not from the state or the associational nexus of civil society. The church is *in* but not really fully *of* civil society. Few Christian theologians or churches want to assimilate the church entirely under the rubric of broader secular accounts for civil society, even if the church is seen as appropriately located in civil society and, thus, free from direct state governance or ordering.

CHRISTIANITY AND THE OTHER TRADITIONS

Throughout its history, Christianity has almost never existed (in fact or in its own theory) as a hermetically sealed-off religious enclave, untouched by or unrelated to other religious voices or more "secular" social movements.[9] Early Christian thinkers engaged in a dialogue with and selective absorption of elements from Stoicism and the civic republican tradition of Rome, especially as found in Cicero. Both the notion of a common good and an appeal to a natural law, found in a number of Christian doctrinal families (but especially strongly within Catholicism), derive originally from these pre-Christian traditions. Saint Ambrose wrote his own Christian analogue to Cicero's Stoic *De Officiis*.[10] Augustine appropriated his central notions about the justice that could be found in a this-worldly republic from Cicero's *De Re Publica* (arguing, of course, that, because it lacked real justice, there never really was a Roman republic).[11]

In Augustine and, later, Aquinas and in some seventeenth century Reformed thinkers, such as Justus Lipsius and Samuel Pufendorf, we find a strong convergence with elements of the natural law and virtue traditions of the Roman Stoics.[12] David Burrell has argued that there was even a vigorous interreligious conversation (often focused on questions of state and society)—at least among the intellectuals in the three traditions—among Judaism, Islam, and Christianity in the Middle Ages.[13] Aquinas, in the *Summa Contra Gentiles* at any event, shows a strong acquaintance with the thought of Maimonides and of the Islamic Aristotelians.

In a similar way, Protestantism (relatively early) and Catholicism (strongly in the twentieth century but already incipiently in the nineteenth in representative figures such as Lamennais and de Montelbert in France and Bishop von Ketteler in Germany) have long wrestled with the challenges and experience of liberalism and, later, socialism.[14] From John Locke onward, Christianity has been in partial contestation, argument, and—once again—selective appropriation and transformation of elements from the liberal and the liberal-egalitarian traditions. Since World War II, social Catholicism has both incorporated and transmuted elements from the rights and democracy language of liberalism and addressed critical theory.[15] Moreover, both the Protestant and Catholic traditions have, more recently, engaged in dialogue with (including selective retrieval, appropriation, transformation and/or rejection) feminist theory.[16] Contemporary Catholic natural law arguments, to cite another example, seem as akin, in places, to more modern variants of natural law than to medieval accounts, based on a now-rejected teleology.[17]

It would be a serious mistake, then, to take the classic periods of medieval or counter-Reformation Catholicism and Reformation Protestantism and reify them as if they have not continued as living and growing traditions. In that sense, Christianity has long since been in dialogue with modernity and with some of the other traditions represented in this volume. As a result, some of what now seems typically Protestant or Catholic (at least in their more liberal variants) stems from that engaged argument and appropriation.

CHRISTIANITY, CIVIL SOCIETY, AND RECENT SOCIETAL UPHEAVALS

In 1989, Pope John Paul II (long before the theme became recherché) sponsored a high-level symposium at the Vatican on the topic of civil society. Luminaries such as Leszek Kolokowski, Adam Michnik, and Jürgen Habermas had the pope's attentive ear for three days of dialogue on that topic. At the time William Safire, the *New York Times* columnist, stated that this symposium was little noted in the press yet might be one of the most important events of the year. Clearly, in his social encyclical issued in 1991, *Centissimus Annus*, the pope echoed many of the themes of a market and civil society, what the pope praises as "a society of free work, of enterprise and of participation."[18] In a similar way, the World Council of Churches has been conducting, for many years now and at different locales, regular sophisticated colloquiums on civil society. The term *civil society*, usually traced to Hegel, may postdate medieval or counter-Reformation Catholicism and reformation Protestantism but both of these two traditions claim to find traces for it in their own traditions.

Moreover, the churches have struggled firsthand with the reality of civil society (or its foreclosure) in the post–World War II periods and again in the late 1960s through 1989. The churches were faced with the dilemmas of being situated in authoritarian dictatorships or totalitarian regimes that restricted not only the liberty of the churches but more fundamental human liberties. Often, in places such as Chile, Poland, and Brazil and in Hungary and East Germany, the churches (predominantly Protestant in East Germany and Catholic in Chile, Poland, and Brazil) served as the only institutional carriers of (or protective umbrella for) any oppositional civil society. A rich comparative sociological literature exists that documents the Christian churches' role as midwives to a reborn (or firstborn in some cases) civil society in the transition from dictatorships.[19] Solidarity in Poland and the transitions to democracy from dictatorship in Spain, the Philippines, Chile, and Brazil all attest to the church's role in these laboratories in the construction of civil society. To be sure, a more cynical reading of a recent Catholic championing of civil society might wonder how deep are the roots of this newfound turn to civil society in a church which, even into the 1950s, could support a fusion of church and state in Salazar's Portugal and Franco's Spain. Others suspect a more Machiavellian motive in the Catholic support of civil society movements as a covert and merely tactical support for the interests of the church. Postcommunist Poland might be an instructive case here, where some factions of the church hierarchy seem to have reverted to elements of a confessional state. Still, these elements in Poland are deeply contested by intellectual Catholics and, precisely, on a Catholic theoretical basis, grounded in the teaching of Vatican II. Adam Michnik, the dissident Polish former communist, at least gives some credibility to the perduring sincerity of the Catholic turn toward civil society.

In the nature of the case, this essay, much like other essays in this volume, is mainly theoretical, engaging in a comparative analysis of alternative visions and traditions of conceiving civil society and the state. But it would be a serious mistake to think for one moment that Christian thinking on civil society and the state has been spun only from some theoretical or doctrinal weave of classic texts. Fifty years of intense experience of dissent from totalitarian regimes and of ongoing coalitions with more secular dissidents in various societies have engraved on Christianity's recent memory the wisdom of guaranteeing a separately institutionalized, quasi-autonomous realm of civil society as a "free public space." It would take another and differing essay, of course, to detail the cases that have fed into this experience of the churches in helping to forge civil society, but the reader is warned not to see the theory sketched as coming only from revelation, the Bible, or dogma.

But this is not to say that theology has not had an independent role to play in mediating the varying Christian positions on church, state, and civil society. It will help to sketch at least some of the fundamental theological questions that will determine the differing Christian positions on these three concepts.

Theological Background Questions Shaping Christian Theories of Church, State, and Society

A number of theological questions lurk behind divergent Protestant and Catholic views on church, state, and civil society. Any easy correlation between and among these competing Christian positions is difficult. I rehearse several of these key theological topics here less to argue for any substantive position on any one question than to indicate the extreme difficulty in forging any unitary Christian or even Protestant position on state and civil society. Presumably, both Catholics and Protestants will have to parse carefully through these questions to reach any fully argued position on church, society, and state. Among these theological issues are:

(1) What is the nature of the church or the religious people? Is it a merely voluntary association of persons (among, perhaps, many such associations, even if united for religious purposes)? Does the church therefore see itself as subject to the self-same limits and rules as any other voluntary association in society? Or does the church, rather, represent a juridical and ordered institution ordained by God? If the latter, its claimed authority will always be potentially in conflict with the authorities of the state or civil society. The query Whether to obey the laws of God or of the state? haunts Christian history. The church will rarely see itself as *merely* another unit within civil society. Behind this question of ecclesiology lies a second: Who speaks for the church on public issues in society and with what intrinsic religious warrant?[20]

(2) What is the nature of the state? To what degree is it primarily the result of sin? To what degree ordained by God even from the beginning? The Reformers, steeped in a reading of Augustine, generally followed him in seeing the state as a result of sin rather than an originary intention of God for creation. Sociality for Augustine was prelapsarian. The state was not. Yet even in a postlapsarian epoch, this postulated priority of sociality over the state need not necessarily lead to any special privileging of civil society over the state. Sin may require instead a powerful constraining state. Thomas Aquinas (and his followers, even among Protestants) tended more broadly to accept the need for an indispensable coordinating authority of the state among plural actors, even had Adam never fallen.[21]

Are there permanent or accidental aspects of the state (war making, coercion, office holding, oath taking) inconsistent with Christian discipleship? How does the church handle such religious conflict? (E.g., by demanding from its members conscientious objection against serving in armies or police forces? By refusing to allow them to take oaths in law trials?) To what extent (if at all) can the state be perfected to serve more closely the purposes of the kingdom of God?[22]

(3) These last sets of questions relate to the underlying Christian doctrines of creation, sin, and redemption/sanctification. Those Protestant Christians (e.g., Wesleyans) and Catholics who have a stronger teaching on the actual transformative power of sanctification might foresee more positive possibilities ingredient in the state than those who think that sin perdures strongly (perhaps even *just* as strongly, even if not "imputed" to the believer because of "justification" through the merits of Christ) even after redemption. And when might this process of redemption/sanctification (extending even to the social order) begin? Postmillennialists (such as, for example, those who espoused the social gospel tradition in America) may be more likely to see the possibility of a gradual social perfection accruing in and through state and society (a "social salvation" to counteract social sin) than premillennialists, who expect a catastrophic declension in societal morals and order before the second coming of Christ.[23]

Whatever their position on the relation between sin and redemption, most Protestants nurture a relatively strong sense of sin, such that they foster limited expectations of what a state or society can achieve.[24] Following Augustine, they see even the "best case scenario" as a kind of "rough justice," in sharp tension with Christian normative ideals of community, virtue, and neighbor love. Moreover, their sense of sin tempers any inflated enthusiasm for governmental or societal exercises of power. Neither the state nor civil society is *privileged* as a locale somehow less sinless. As Reinhold Niebuhr, a major modern retriever of political Augustinianism, argued, we need a check-and-balancing of powers in society in order to hold any power center in check against its *expected* sinful aggrandizements.[25]

(4) To what degree must the church or the people of God be independent of the state? Is there a gradation in forms of church-state relationship, some more in accord with Christian concerns than others? Does the independence of the church and state deny all relationship between the two? Is God sovereign over the state also? If so, in what forms does this sovereignty of God over the state manifest itself? Traditionally, the Anabaptist view, for example, expects little convergence between church and state or church and "secular" civil society. It calls for a counter-cultural witnessing more than for direct efforts to sustain, nurture, or transform the commonly social.[26]

Catholicism and Calvinism, however, are more open to a true transformative power of Christian input on the state and society. Calvinism, because of Calvin's more positive "third use of the law" (to direct people toward righteousness, as opposed to Luther's two, solely negative, uses of the law: to convict the sinner and coerce wrongdoers), has a broader sense than Lutheranism or the Anabaptist tradition of openness to a sense of a kind of natural-law structuring of the social and what Calvin called natural "equity."[27] The Calvinist doctrine of spheres of creation and the cognate, but distinct, Calvinist federal tradition in theology and politics come closer to that "world transforming" impetus in Christianity similar to that found in some strands of post–Vatican II social Catholicism.[28]

(5) What obligations toward the state have the church and Christians as citizens with dual loyalties? To what extent should the church support the aims of government? Is patriotism a Christian virtue? If so, on what grounds and with what limits?[29]

(6) To what extent is state sovereignty (if there is legitimately any such thing) limited by a broader global sense of what Catholics, as members of a worldwide communion of Christians, would call an "international or global" common good, which would relativize somewhat any state or national civil society?[30]

(7) With what means and under what conditions may Christians oppose a tyrannical or unjust government? Theological traditions among Protestants differ on the question of the legitimacy of revolution or organized protest against unjust laws. Luther was intransigent in demanding continuing submission to unjust rulers as a kind of worthy punishment of the subjects' general sinfulness. The Reformed tradition (and Catholicism) is clearer about the legitimacy of resistance to tyrannical government as a corrective to unjust law and in pointing to an *orderly* resistance to unjust government through recourse to the rank of the magistrates in the civil service of government.[31]

(8) How virtuous can a government be? How does Christianity enhance this virtue? If little in the way of virtue is to be expected in governments, is civil society a more privileged locale for the exercise and nurturance of a virtuous citizenry? What are the roles of order, peace, justice, welfare, and the care for societal freedom as part of God's intentions for creation (or for redemption)?[32]

Thomas Sanders, from whom this list of theological topoi is mainly derived, contends that very few of these questions have attracted the sustained attention of Protestant-wide bodies, with the exception of religious liberty, the nature of the church, and the *religious* base for social and political responsibility.[33] John C. Bennett has claimed that "there is no one Protestant doctrine concerning church-state relations."[34]

The Catholic Theory of Church-State

Nor (given the range of theological questions we saw above) should we expect that there would be only *one* Catholic position on church-state questions. Writing at the time of the Vatican Council II debates on the Declaration on Religious Liberty (*Dignitatis Humanae*), John Courtney Murray could distinguish five different positions in the Council debates in the *aula*.[35] One was the older Catholic view that "error" had no rights, that only the one who is in the truth, therefore only the Catholic, has an intrinsic and natural right to religious freedom. Moreover, this reactionary stance claimed for the Catholic Church a preeminent juridical position *within* the state apparatus as something demanded by faith and reason. As the nearly unanimous vote in favor of the Declaration on Religious Freedom at the Council showed, this position was held by a decidedly minuscule minority. Those rearguard Catholics who may continue to hold it lack articulate spokesmen or suasive argument and would seem to be ruled out by the authoritative character of the conciliar document. Yet, clearly, variants of the older Catholic integralism (i.e., the claim for a church hegemony over the morality of state and society when Catholics are a majority) continue to exist among extreme traditionalist Catholics.[36]

Among those who did support a declaration on religious freedom at the Council, some pleaded for a merely practical document, a declaration of pastoral policy rather than a statement of theological principle. They were countered by the argument that this might seem to be the work of opportunists, a dubious—you will excuse my embarrassment at the consecrated term—jesuitical act of mental reservation.

Still others wanted to ground the declaration upon the indubitable Catholic principles of the freedom of the act of faith and the freedom of conscience (and a concomitant duty to follow a sincere, even if erroneous, conscience). To say "error" has no rights is a category mistake. Only persons have rights. Their human dignity demands respect for their deepest self-definition as religious and the integrity of their conscience. Atheists, too, have this same religious liberty. But proponents of the final declaration contended that this tack alone would not eventuate in a rationally justified stance in favor of religious expression *in the public order*. The subjective rights of conscience could still be countered in public by the claimed objective claims for truth.

Significantly, Murray's case for religious freedom of both persons and ecclesial groups is very closely linked to and dependent upon a corollary Catholic argument for civil society and its mediating structures. At crucial points, Murray's argument for religious liberty subsumes a case for subsidiarity and the common good as crucial middle terms in his argument. The Catholic case for religious freedom, Murray contended, is tied to the Catholic understanding of a limited government and the proper sway (and autonomy) of the free spaces in civil society. To this I will return shortly.

After the Council, the final two, seriously competing, Catholic theological positions on religious liberty remained Murray's and a second position, largely that of French theologians who want to root religious freedom *entirely* in theological grounds (e.g., the freedom of the act of faith; the rights of personal and collective conscience). Murray countered by arguing that the ultimate case for religious liberty must rest on a complex, religio-political-moral-juridical structure of argument that appeals simultaneously to the exigencies of human nature and the learning experiences (including experiences of constitutional structures) of history. As Yale theologian George Linbeck has remarked about similar Protestant moves to substantiate religious liberty purely on particularist Christian theological premises: "There is no way one can show, on these grounds alone, why responsible persons who are not Christian should grant religious liberty to all. Moreover, a purely theological argument for religious liberty does not lend itself to civil discussion in a broader secular context."[37]

Murray wanted the Vatican II document to include a clear statement about the *juridical* need to enshrine religious liberty as a *civil* right in a constitutional government of limited powers. The Declaration on Religious Liberty did, in fact, follow Murray on this point.[38] Murray—and the documents of the Vatican Council—was clear, however, that the Council was not, in their declaration of religious liberty, arguing for some "privatization" of religion or separation of church from *society*. This represents a not trivial point.

For Murray saw *Dignitatis Humanae* as a forerunner for the final document of the Council, *Gaudium et Spes* (the Church in the Modern World). By setting the church free to pursue, vigorously, its social ministry *in civil society*, the Declaration on Religious Liberty set a tone for that final document. As Murray notes, "*Gaudium et Spes* is clear that the church's ministry is religious, not political in nature; yet the animating religious vision of the Gospel has substantial political potential." (39) The general thrust of the postconciliar Catholic social thought has been to fight vigorously against narrow "church" conceptions of the religious task and the pervasive privatization of religion. It champions what Jose Casanova calls a new form of "public religion in the modern world," in a civil society that is not seen as some neutral private sphere, but rather as one in alignment with the state.[40]

The key issue here, it seems to me, is the extent to which an understanding of separation of church and state promotes or restricts the church's role as a mediating structure *in civil society*. What scope, beyond worship and catechesis within the sacristy, is allowed to the church for action in education, welfare, health, the media, and the world of work and economics? The strategy and style for church influence upon the tenor of culture and societal life has changed dramatically in the post–Vatican II era, with the church's adoption of a new posture of dialogue and pluralist participation in society. But there is no evidence that its ambitions toward having some legitimate access and voice and influence upon the quality and morality of public life have in any way diminished. Social Catholicism contests a view that would set up some putatively neutral "technical rationality" in the economy and technology as absolutely free from any deeper moral assessments. In this point, post–Vatican II social Catholicism is actually closer to critical theory in places than to classic liberalism.

The Link between Catholicism's Sense of Its Own Mission and Its Theory of State and Society

To understand the church's shift to an admittedly new position on religious liberty, it is essential to turn to a classic Catholic distinction between state and civil society. I want to develop this distinction because it bears out my contention that the Catholic structure for the argument for religious liberty is simultaneously a strong case for civil society and its mediating institutions.

The state's true care for religion, Murray argued, is restricted to its care for the freedom of religion. Its care consists in the state's recognition of the church's claim, under the rubric of *libertas ecclesiae*, for immunity in the juridical order in matters touching religion (free exercise and no establishment). Murray and the Vatican document on religious liberty shifted the burden of a *public* role for religion from the state—which in Murray's view, in any event, is simply incompetent to make *any* judgments about religious truth whatsoever—to the wider society, the people acting through their voluntary mediating structures and corporate groups. No one should be coerced into religious behavior, since "[t]he truth cannot impose itself except by virtue of its own truth, as it makes its entrance into the mind at once quietly and with power."[41] But neither should others be restrained from a public expression of religion in civil society or in the context of the national life.

The freedom asserted in *Dignitatis Humanae* as a limit on state power, however, is much more than the freedom of the church or of individual religious consciences. The document signals as well the rightful freedom of mediating corporate groups. Indeed, it envisions as normative neither the confessional state nor the laicist secular state, but the limited constitutional state. There is a juridical as well as moral and theological premise to *Dignitatis Humanae*: "The demand is also made that constitutional limits should be set to the powers of government in order that there may be no encroachment on the rightful freedom of the person *and of associations.*"[42]

State Versus Society

In its classic distinction between state and civil society, Catholic social thought contains a strong animus against the view that the public sphere is synonymous with the government or the formal polity of the society.[43] It does not want, however, to relegate civil society to the purely *private* sphere. Here, I would argue, social Catholicism, like feminism and critical theory in their own contexts, *contests* elements of modernity, but now within an acceptance of a differentiation that is not a premodern organicism. Some would restrict the church's public role to a mere undergirding for reciprocity, duty, and responsibility generally and would eschew, as inappropriate, any religious advocacy on specific policy issues.

Jose Casanova, drawing mainly on modern Catholic case studies, has argued, to the contrary, that there *is* a proper role for public religion in modernity. Casanova notes that from the normative perspective of modernity, religion may enter the public sphere and assume a public form only if it accepts the sanctity of the principle of freedom of conscience. It can also do so only if it *does* accept some legitimate differentiation of spheres in modern society (but differentiation need not mean total autonomy).

But once that sanctity of conscience and the rightful quasi autonomy of secular spheres are acknowledged, Casanova argues, modernity's often unthinking privatization of religion can be legitimately contested in at least three instances:

(a) "When religion enters the public sphere to protect not only its own freedom of religion but all modern freedoms and rights and the very right of a democratic civil society to exist against an absolutist, authoritarian state." The very active role of the Catholic Church in the processes of democratization in Spain, Poland, and Brazil and the role of the Lutheran and Reformed Churches in East Germany in similar processes serve as illustrations of this first case.[44] In these test cases, almost only the religious historic carriers of freedom alone continued capable of sustaining and protecting the modern freedoms and rights in authoritarian regimes.

(b) "When religion enters the public sphere to question and contest the absolutized lawful autonomy of the secular spheres and their claims to be organized in accordance with principles of functional differentiation *without regard to extraneous ethical or moral considerations*" (emphasis mine). The Pastoral Letters of the American Catholic Bishops questioning the "morality" of the state's nuclear policies and of the lack of "justice" in the inhuman consequences ingredient in certain elements of a capitalist economic system which tends to absolutize rights to private property and claims to be totally self-regulating by unchecked market forces, are examples of this second—note modern, not premodern—contestation in public by religion. As the American bishops state forcefully in their letter on the American economy, their desire is to open a wider public deliberation, not to impose their own solutions.[45]

(c) "When religion enters the public sphere to protect the traditional life-world from administrative or juridical state penetration, and in the process opens up issues of norm and will formation to the public and collective self-reflection of modern discursive ethics." This represents Casanova's third case of a justified public resort by religion in the modern world.[46] Casanova mentions here the societal debates about abortion by religious groups, but other examples might include public debates about capital punishment, euthanasia, genetic engineering, and the like. What is key here is that religion only challenges in civil society and public deliberation and does not impose by recourse to state power.

Just as feminists and some critical theorists are calling for a reopening of what seemed a settled set of boundaries about public-private, so a public version of Christian religion *within civil society* contests views of the privatization of religion that make religion irrelevant or assume that it is somehow "in bad taste" to expose one's religiosity publicly.[47]

Seyla Benhabib takes on the liberal model of "public dialogue" with its "neutrality" rule about any public discussion of "human goods," as opposed to procedures. This rule imposes, according to Benhabib, "conversational restraints" that function as "gag rules." Entire ranges of matters get excluded from public deliberation—from the private economy to the realm of norm formation. As Benhabib notes: "The model of a public dialogue based on conversational restraint is not neutral, in that it presupposes a moral and political epistemology; this in turn justifies an implicit separation between the public and private of such a kind as leads to the silencing of the concerns of excluded groups." It also glosses over and ignores the extent to which the political order inevitably involves contestation and struggle. "All struggles against oppression in the modern world begin by redefining what had previously been considered 'private,' non-public and non-political issues as matters of public concern, as issues of justice, as sites of power which need discursive legitimation."[48]

Casanova captures well the contestation quality of the new forms of *modern*—not premodern—public religion (of which social Catholicism is one prominent case) that have emerged since the 1980s around the world:

> What is at issue is the need to recognize that the boundaries themselves are and need to be open to contestation, redefinition, renegotiation, and discursive legitimation. According to Benhabib, "If the agenda of the conversation is radically open, if participants can bring any and all matters under critical scrutiny and reflexive questioning, then there is no way to *predefine* the nature of the issues discussed as being ones of justice or the good life itself prior to the conversation. This should include all boundaries: private and public; moral and legal, justice and the good life, religious and secular." ... What I call the 'deprivatization' of modern religion is the process whereby religion abandons its assigned place in the private sphere and enters the undifferentiated sphere of civil society to take part in the ongoing process of contestation, discursive legitimation and redrawing of the boundaries.[49]

This is not to say that all forms of public religion—or all forms of public Catholicism, for that matter—are good either in themselves or for the body politic. It is to say that social Catholics will and do contest liberal theories which claim that the state must be neutral in respect to all definitions of the human good. It is to say that social Catholicism (and other forms of public religion in the modern world) give rise to protest movements against claims about the "inevitability and benign invisible hand" of the globalization process, against the arms race, against ecological destruction, against the despoilment of native peoples, against social engineering schemes affecting families. This is much more than some simple generic undergirding by religion of societal norms of reciprocity, duty, and responsibility.

To be sure, world Catholic social movements are not of a piece. Neoconservative Catholics such as Michael Novak and Richard Neuhaus contest parts of the thrust ingredient in the post–Vatican II social Catholicism.[50] In places, some Catholic movements remain integralist. Yet a pattern has emerged worldwide, ranging from the defense of Indian rights by the Canadian Catholic Church; the land commissions in Brazil and elsewhere in Latin America to protect the people from the expropriation of their lands by economic forces claiming to represent "modernization"; the American bishops' yearly support for economic development in inner cities; the human rights commissions in many countries mainly staffed by church people.[51] At least in its official documents and in its proposed church-world strategy—if not always in its empirical behavior—the general thrust of postconciliar Catholic thought has been to oppose narrow "churchy" conceptions of the religious task and the pervasive privatization of religion.

The justification for this deprivatization of religion in Catholicism can appeal to two signal warrants (among many!). In 1971, the Synod of World Bishops claimed that "[a]ction on behalf of justice and participation in the transformation of the world fully appear to us as *a constitutive dimension of the preaching of the gospel*, or, in other words, of the church's mission for the redemption of the human race and its liberation from every oppressive situation."[52] The very document on religious liberty that accepts the modern differentiation of church and state is unyielding about the *public* scope for religion *within civil society*: "It comes within the meaning of religious freedom that religious bodies should not be prohibited from freely undertaking to show the special value of their doctrine in what concerns the organization of society and the inspiration *of the whole of human activity*. Finally, the social nature of the human and the very nature of religion afford the foundation of the human right to hold meetings and to establish educational, cultural, charitable and social organizations, under the impulse of their own religious sense."[53]

Clearly, this is not John Rawls's or Bruce Ackerman's program for neutrality about public goods.[54] If classic liberals and even some modern liberal egalitarians might feel uncomfortable with this new form of modern public religion, they might take some comfort in the Catholic insistence on a variant of a limited state. Catholic social thought does not assume that everything public must ipso facto be governmental. In distinguishing between state and society it also distinguishes between the public order entrusted to the state—an order of unity, coercion, and necessity, an order that includes essential elements of the common good through the state's coordinating and regulative activities, crucial for distributive justice, which cannot be guaranteed only by the free market or free rational choice mechanisms—and the elements of the common good that are entrusted to the whole society, a zone of comparative freedom and pluralism.

Catholic social thought is pluralistic in its insistence on the limited service character of the state. The state exists as an instrument to promote justice and liberty. The ends of the public order entrusted primarily or essentially to the state's nurturance of the common good are fourfold: public peace, public morality (based on civil practices and truths), welfare and justice, and the freedom of the people. As Murray puts it, "[T]he democratic state serves both the ends of the human person (in itself and its natural forms of social life) and also the ends of justice. As the servant of those ends, it has only relative value."[55] If the state is both subject to and the servant of the common good, it "is not the sole judge of what is or is not the common good." Moreover, "in consequence of the distinction between society and state, not every element of the common good is instantly committed to the state." On the contrary, "government submits itself to judgment by the truth of society; it is not itself a judge of the truth of society."[56]

Perhaps the clearest and most developed statement of this Catholic distinction between state and society is found in Jacques Maritain's now-classic book *Man and the State*. Maritain ascribes to the state an instrumental, service character that is a part—the topmost part and agency, to be sure—of the whole society which he calls "the body politic." The state is the part that specializes in the interest of the whole! Its authority is derivative. It exists not by its own right and for its own sake, but only in virtue and to the extent of the requirements of the common good.

At least two corporate units in society, the family and the church, have rights and freedoms fully anterior to the state. Other corporate units—voluntary associations such as universities, labor unions, agencies in the public interest—stake out a zone of free sociality in society. The right to voluntary association is based on the social nature of the human person whose sociality is not exhausted by citizenship in the state. Maritain asserts that "the state is inferior to the body politic as a whole and is at the service of the body politic as a whole."[57] He denies that the state, as such, is a subject of rights or is the head of the body politic. It serves a purely instrumental role in the service of the people, the proper subject of rights. Note how in this view, civil society—what Maritain calls "the body politic"—is not merely a residual category or some sphere of privacy. The Catholic limited state contains more communitarian impulses and assumes that the state does have a proper, if limited, role in ensuring the common good. Its overlap with the liberal constitutional state is real but imperfect. Catholic notions of the common good make some liberals nervous. The common good assumes the possibility of some substantive set of public goods not totally subordinated to the purely procedural notion of the right. In Catholic theory, a societal common good must be achieved by the processes of deliberative democracy, never imposed by the church.[58]

Subsidiarity

Maritain argues that mediating structures should be as autonomous as possible because family, economic, cultural, educational, and religious life matter as much as does political life to the very existence and prosperity of the body politic. Normally, the principle of subsidiarity should govern the relation between state and mediating structures "since in political society authority comes from below through the people. It is normal that the whole dynamism of authority in the body politic should be made up of particular and partial authorities rising in tiers above one another to the top authority of the state."[59]

Subsidiarity began life as an esoteric Catholic term, first coined in 1931 by Pius XI in his encyclical *Quadragesimo Anno*, although the principle to which it points has long existed in democratic social theory and is found in social Catholicism at least from the time of Charles Montelembert in the first half of the nineteenth century.[60] It also presently serves, along with the common good—largely because of the intervention of the Catholic socialist Jacques Delors, who served as European Commission president in the early 1990s—as one of the two major policy aims of the European Economic Community.

Subsidiarity is a derivative rule of the state-society distinction. Its purpose is to delineate both the moral right and the moral limitations of state interventions in cultural, social, and economic affairs. Its formulation reads: "It is a fundamental principle *of social philosophy* . . . that one should not withdraw from individuals and commit to the community what they can accomplish by their own enterprise and industry. So, too, it is an injustice and at the same time a grave evil and disturbance of right order to transfer to the larger and higher collectivity functions which can be performed and provided by the lesser and subordinate bodies. Inasmuch as every social activity should, by its very nature, prove a help to members of the body social, it should never destroy or absorb them."[61]

Subsidiarity rests entirely on secular warrant. It is in no sense a religious maxim nor does it find direct warrant in the Bible. It grew out of reflection on social experience, not revelation. Catholic social thought looks to it as a congealment of historic wisdom about the arrangement of social orders. It is a presumptive rule about where real vitality exists in society. Clearly, as *Quadragesimo Anno* realized and *Mater et Magistra* made very clear, the state can and must intervene for public welfare when intermediate associations are deficient. As *Quadragesimo Anno* puts it, the state legitimately acts to "encourage, stimulate, regulate, supplement and complement" the action of intermediate groups.[62] But the presumption is that such intervention, while justified in the name of the common good, should never "destroy or absorb" the lesser or intermediate bodies. In point of fact, the principle of subsidiarity is simply a Catholic version of the theory of democratic pluralism to be found, in more secular guise, in Tocqueville, Durkheim, and, more recently, Michael Walzer.[63]

The "secular" warrants for subsidiarity are many. Thus, E. F. Schumacher, in invoking it, explicitly contends that the principle is a rule for efficiency, the best way to increase both productivity and participant satisfaction.[64] H. A. Rommen insists on intermediate structures as a fountain of creativity and experiment: "The state is not creative but individual persons in their free associations and their group life are creative."[65]

Maritain's argument for subsidiarity is redolent of Emile Durkheim's communication theory of government in *Professional Morals and Civic Ethics*, where Durkheim pleads for intermediate associations because the state is too abstract and distant. As Maritain puts it, "To become a boss or a manager in business or industry or a patron of art or a leading spirit in the affairs of culture, science and philosophy is against the nature of such an impersonal topmost agency, abstract so to speak and separated from the moving particularities, mutual tensions, risks and dynamism of concrete social existence."[66]

The principle of subsidiarity is not writ large on the fabric of the universe because it is a distilled wisdom, an empirical generalization from experience and a maxim for ordering a sane society rather than an ontological principle or a phenomenological description of how states always or actually operate. It would take another essay to discuss efforts to enforce subsidiarity *within* the church, where the legitimacy of the principle has been acknowledged at the highest levels but, in practice, frequently discounted.[67] Clearly, tension remains between Catholic ecclesiology, which continues to see the church in hierarchical-organicist terms, and the Catholic theory of the good "secular" society, which is no longer seen as organicist and where egalitarian and not hierarchical norms prevail—just as it would take another essay to assess contestations by Catholic feminists of continuing patriarchal elements *within* the church.

The principle of subsidiarity is of renewed interest today precisely because of some new threats to the voluntary society. The first is the extensive growth of the regulatory state, which will not be easily dismantled for romantic visions of some simpler society. The second stems from the fact that increased government regulation and intervention is coupled with the growth of "professional monopolies." Detailed regulations, certification, and preconditions imposed upon the service sector of society, coupled with an expansion of market metaphors, lead to fears they are pricing voluntary agencies out of the market in health and, increasingly, in welfare.[68] Alternately, they may be turning the nonprofit voluntary sector into a mirror of the logic of the market and the logic of the state.[69]

Catholic social thought links subsidiarity to two other principles: solidarity and the common good. "No bigger than necessary" has a corollary—as big as necessary, however, to achieve the common good. Especially when faced with the behemoth of economic concentration and power, Catholic social thought allows and expects the state to retain certain regulatory powers for the protection of the common good. It has never held that government is best which governs least. The state does have some indispensable roles to play in furthering the common good.

Subsidiarity may sound like a mere bromide, but it has some bite in actual policy debates. Take, for example, welfare reform, with which Catholic voices (e.g., Catholic Charities U.S.A., the United States Catholic Conference) have strongly engaged. Catholics opposed schemes such as Texas's complete privatization of the administration of welfare by total outsourcing and turning its administration over to the for-profit Lockheed Martin. This move denies a legitimate and necessary role for the state in overseeing care for the common good. On the other hand, Catholics have also supported some outsourcing and rejected government monopoly over deliverance of welfare services by appealing to subsidiarity. The government, in this view, must provide a *fair* framework, but agencies of civil society should be engaged in the actual deliverance of welfare. Cynics may simply dismiss this as a species of protection for Catholic institutional interests, but it is remarkable just how consistent Catholic social policy on welfare has been on these points since the mid-1930s.[70]

The Economy and the Common Good

Social Catholicism tends to fear the totalitarianism of the market as much as that of the overregulatory state. Catholic human rights theory includes *social* as well as *civil* rights.[71] Social Catholicism assumes a priority to meeting basic needs in determining the direction of the economy. It justifies even some cases of nationalization of property, if necessary to counteract monopoly, and champions worker codetermination schemes in industry.[72] The tradition is best described as social democratic in its thrust. It accepts a market economy without buying into a myth of a totally self-regulating market. The market may be part of civil society but it is an unequal and hegemonic part. Left to its own devices, it undermines the very mutuality, loyalty, and commitments that make for good civil society. So Catholic social thought demands that the economy must recognize needs and be participatory and ecologically sustainable as well as productive. The economy is for being and not just having. There must be fair sharing.[73]

Again, one of the major Catholic complaints about the 1996 Welfare Reform package was that it scouted any independent claim to justice based on human need. Catholics applauded the work rules inasmuch as access to work is seen as a deeply central element in what the American bishops have called justice as participation in the economy.[74] But work rules alone—a merit based source for justice in distribution—do not sufficiently acknowledge the claims of need.

The connection between the Catholic case for religious liberty and its wider theory of state and society should by now be clear. The freedom of the church that the church calls for must be such as not to penalize or impede its freedom to pursue its religious mission, as it understands it, in society. But the church's self-understanding in terms of its mission to society rests on particularist theological warrant. We cannot expect that self-understanding to become public property enshrined in law. The church can garner public support for the freedom it demands for itself in fidelity to gospel warrant only if it states its case *simultaneously* on secular warrant. Social Catholicism is notoriously bilingual. It appeals both to gospel images and to what John Rawls has called "public reason."[75]

The secular warrant for the argument for the kind of relation to society the church seeks is the argument for mediating structures as a key element in public policy. As John Courtney Murray clearly saw, the freedom of the church is inextricably linked to other civil freedoms: "The personal and corporate free exercise of religion as a human and civil right is evidently cognate with other more general human and civil rights—with the freedom of corporate bodies and institutions within society, based on the principle of subsidiary functions; with the general freedom for peaceful purposes, based on the social nature of man; with the general freedom of speech and of the press based on the nature of political society."[76]

The Subsidiarity and the "Spheres of Creation" Tradition

It may be useful to compare this Catholic variant to other theological families. Anabaptists accept the zone of civil life as the sphere of spontaneity and creativity but limit the state severely. As one statement from an Anabaptist position puts it, "[T]he real dynamic of society does not lie in the state; state action is obviated when subordinate groups, like the church, effectively deal with education, health, relief and social security. Christians should not rely too much on the state and thus become completely obligated to it."[77] Clearly in this tradition, there is no sense of the state's role in furthering the common good.

One Calvinist variant of "spheres of creation" was very instrumental in carving out the kind of subsidiarity state in the Netherlands. The *Gereformeeden* conclude to something akin to subsidiarity in their slogan, Sovereignty in our own circle. *Gereformeeden* control over their own mediating structures serves as a crucial check on idolatrous claims of state sovereignty, even when the state provides subsidy.[78] But the permeability of the boundaries between state and the other spheres, while not ruled out in exceptional cases, is less clear than in Catholicism. There is a weaker sense that the state, as such, has any legitimate roles to play in securing the common good.[79] At times, the "sovereign spheres" are given such an autonomy that it is unclear (1) what to do if they fail to achieve the goods that are entrusted to their scope; and (2) how to adjudicate conflicts between the spheres that constitute civil society among themselves or with the state.[80] Moreover, authors differ strongly on how many spheres of creation there are. The answers range from three (e.g., the state, family, church) to as many as seven or more.[81] The more the range of such orders and spheres, the broader and more sophisticated the possibilities for a rounded and interesting notion of civil society. Much of the Christian Right in America, by restricting themselves exclusively to church and family, make it impossible to really conceive of a civil society. Finally, absent some sense of a "natural law" or "public reason" to ground outreach beyond revelation to fellow citizens, this account of "spheres of creation" is often not very bilingual. It relies entirely on biblical warrants alone.

Closest to the Catholic vision of the common good, solidarity and subsidiarity, it seems to me, is the Calvinist federal tradition of covenantal theology. As one treatise puts it, society is built up from the bottommost units of the family and associational life into towns, cities, and provinces and, finally, a federal commonwealth. "In each case, a covenant creates the more comprehensive level of political order. But the more inclusive entity does not negate the significance, participation, and consent of the covenanted groups that comprise it. Each level retains its importance and its integrity as an operative community with appropriate governmental functions."[82] Federal theology seems to envision something akin not only to subsidiarity, but to a needed role of the most inclusive unit (presumably the state) to act for the commonweal. But here, unlike Maritain's notion of civil society as an encompassing concept, the body politic, the concept of civil society seems to be atomized into leveled and compartmentalized units. Their relation is mainly to the topmost unit or the next encompassing level. No full-blown theory of solidarity and the common good unites the levels to each other.

BOUNDARIES, NEEDS AND LIABILITIES

In the Catholic theory of civil society and the state, subsidiarity (freedom, spontaneity, creativity, grass-roots consensus, the anchoring of a sense of belonging) sets *presumptive* boundaries to the limited state. But the boundaries can be permeable because subsidiarity is juxtaposed to solidarity and the common good. Against views that would judge civil society always good and the state presumptively bad and suspect, or the state as expendable and civil society sufficient, or, finally, views of an omnicompetent state, social Catholicism sees the state as structurally and permanently necessary to secure the common good. It knows, as a recent document, *A Call to Civil Society*, puts it, that there can be a bad civil society![83]

It is more difficult for me to find a similar presumptive rule to adjudicate the permeability of boundaries between the state and the other spheres in the "spheres of creation" doctrine. How do these spheres interact among themselves (church, family, economy, universities, private associations, lower levels of civic life, etc.), and in what sense do they serve "public" functions that enjoin some version of state regulation, supplementation, complementarity, and nourishment? The "sovereignty" or "autonomy" of the spheres is clearly stated. Their interdependence and cohesion is not well explicated.

In any event, as David Martin argues, "Christianity creates counter-cultures *above* and below the unity of the natural society."[84] The state itself, whatever the empirical vigor and counterbalance of civil society, is held to a higher law: justice, respect for human dignity and the common good. It is also limited by legitimate loyalties not just to the "little platoons" of civil society, but to an interdependent "objective" common good in global society.

In the tradition I have been expounding, civil society needs the state for those public goods the state alone can provide or guarantee: the coordination of order, a structure of civility and peace among pluralist visions of the good, the regulation of welfare and justice, the forging of a "common civic faith and purpose" that cross-cuts any one particularist tradition.[85] Notoriously, the mechanisms of civil society (remaining voluntary, dispersed, conflictual, and following a kind of free-choice market mechanism) cannot, of themselves, guarantee the fulfillment of fundamental human needs (the "social" rights) or fair distributive justice.

In turn, as the subsidiarity literature insists, civil society offers a zone of freedom, spontaneity, creativity, a grass-roots anchoring of "belonging." It remains the primary locale for the anchoring of virtue. In point of fact, moral traditions are strongly rooted in the religious institutions and the neutral state cannot easily promulgate a unitary theory of virtue.[86] The face-to-face seedbed where mutuality, trust (what Jacques Maritain once referred to as "civic friendship") is inculcated primarily in civil society.[87] Yet the necessary morality of both the economy (keep contracts, pay fair wages, etc.) and the state (pay taxes, vote, be responsible and informed as a citizen) depend on this prior vivid experience of reciprocity, duty, responsibility, and solidarity.[88]

The major liabilities the state poses to civil society occur when it sacrifices subsidiarity to centralizing efficiency or turns the "common good" into a mere interest balancing. The state that knows it is partially entrusted with the common good can also forget that it does not have a monopoly on its definition. It can also substitute the morality aimed at abstract others (e.g., law and market) for any attention to the need for a more richly textured experiential seedbed for mutuality, reciprocity, and social trust.

In turn, civil society may become enthralled to one sector of it: the economy. This in turn can dictate what counts as state action for the public good. As *A Call to Civil Society* well puts it: "Business, labor and economic institutions do not exist apart from the rest of civil society. That the economy is part of civil society demonstrates that it is part of our moral order as well—not some extrinsic force and certainly not an end in itself but rather a major reflection of our judgments about the conditions for human flourishing and the larger meanings of our common life."[89] Civil society can try to substitute its often chaotic voluntarism and its ideals of freedom for the need for coordinating and regulating activities by the state. It can substitute particular interest for the common good. Not in my neighborhood, after all, is a kind of call from the zone of civil society! There seems no one magic abstract rule to control these liabilities. Vigilance and citizen participation to monitor not only the state but the economy and the other institutions of civil society seem necessary.

CITIZENSHIP

Christians see the authority of the state as God derived. Hence, they tend to see the duties of citizenship as incumbent on them. In point of fact, at least in America, those who are church members do tend to vote more often, be engaged more in voluntarism in civil society, and give more money to charity and philanthropy.[90] Indeed, more than other forms of voluntary civil associations (again in America), churches seem to add to elements of the democratic potential to society.[91]

Christian theorists have sometimes complained of the leveling character of citizenship ideals, their being tied too closely to purely procedural norms and their introduction of relativistic notions of morality or truth into the common life (perhaps, even, their claim to permit, for the sake of common life or peaceful consensus, behavior the disciple judges repugnant and seriously sinful). The rules of the game of citizenship substitute a realm of public opinion for an arena of substantive truth. Some disciples see and decry this citizen arena as purely a "naked public square."[92]

Theorists of citizenship, for their part, have not lacked legitimate complaints about the deleterious intrusion of an ideal of Christian discipleship into the commonwealth of citizens. The brutal and passionate wars of religion, to be sure, spawned the Enlightenment ideals of secular reason and religious tolerance.

The litany of complaints against the intrusion of discipleship into citizenship reaches back to Roman times. A typical rebuke—voiced strongly by Rousseau—is that the Christian ideal of a universal solidarity undercuts urgent commitment to *this* particular nationally defined sovereignty and general will.

Other complaints of citizens to the disciples have noted the other-worldliness of the Christian ideal, its lack of seriousness about the historically contingent. The Marxists, for their part, talk of the ideological misuses of religion to compensate for the suffering of the poor or to legitimate the wealth of the dominant. A final rebuke notes the way Romans 13:1–7 has often been interpreted to legitimate a mere dutiful citizenship, a mere passive obedience, rather than that more active, critical engagement of citizen-politicians so eloquently espoused by Michael Walzer. As Walzer contends, "[T]he citizen/voter is crucial to the survival of democratic politics; but the citizen/politician is crucial to its liveliness and integrity."[93] The empirical evidence cited at the beginning of this section does not seem to bear out claims that Christians are less active citizens than others; *e contrario*.

Many disciples conflate their ideals of discipleship and citizenship. At times this can inject a hypermoralism into citizenship life. Citizens are not called to be saints. As Michael Walzer once noted about citizenship, "[T]he standards are not all that high; we are required to be brethren and citizens, not saints and heroes." At least one strand in Christian thinking, however—that of the Thomists—will not allow a conflation of law and morality as if they were, at all points, the same. Thomas insisted that not all acts of vice are to be forbidden by human law, nor are all acts of virtue to be enjoined by it, but only what, given the moral development and customs of a particular society, is reasonably possible in order to promote the common good.[94]

The law that regulates citizenship duties must be moral, but it does not enshrine all of the moral. The morality of citizenship in this Thomistic sense would seem to agree with Walzer that the citizenship ideal does not have to look to saints and heroes. In an intriguing throwaway line in his book of essays, *Citizenship Today*, D. W. Brogan claims that "a Christian citizen has more duties than and different from those that the state defines and demands."[95] Brogan feels Christians are always minimally called to the duties and demands the state legitimately defines. But they must go beyond that humane minimum to try to inject some wider ideal of neighbor-love into the social fabric. Christian ideals might add to the wider repertoire of citizenship such notions as a countercultural vision of a more ideal community and of forgiveness. Christians may feel called to add a note of self-sacrificing agape to the justice ideals of citizenship. But this is supererogation, not the content of the citizenship ideal itself. By its nature, modern citizenship must be an *equal* citizenship, held commonly by believers and nonbelievers.

GROUPS AND INDIVIDUALS

Social Catholicism champions the right to association as rooted in the radical sociality of humans. It does not have any firm rules about when government should interact with individuals mainly through communal associations. Rhetorically, the tradition, in its official statements, strongly endorses a right to one's culture (especially for ethnic or enclave people in a wider pluralist society) and to one's language. But beyond this rhetorical evocation of the right (which would seem to demand communal associations to keep the language and culture alive in a situation when a people is a minority), no firm rules about how to deal with the situations where communal rights are denied have been proposed.[96]

CONFLICT

Christians have shown a certain allergy toward the idea of social conflict. Social Catholicism, in earlier periods, held to an overly organicist and unitary vision of social life. This has been more recently displaced by a greater openness to struggle and some forms of social conflict. Donal Dorr, for example, has traced the calls for the poor "to struggle" and to join other societal groups in the "struggle for justice" in recent documents of social Catholicism.[97] One virtue of the Reformed tradition's view of society is that it has a less organicist heritage. Social Catholicism can learn from that, although, as Dorr notes, it has already in liberation and political theology and in recent documents shed that earlier organicist bias. And Protestant thought—as Robert Bellah has recently argued—lacking a stronger communitarian bias when voluntarism blots out older and richer notions of the covenant—does tend to undercut any sense of a "possibly" common good.[98]

Clearly, with its sense of a higher law to civil law (even if the authority of those who propagate civil law comes ultimately also from God), Christianity knows and has embodied civil disobedience. As the Book of Acts puts it, the apostles said to the authorities, "We must obey God and not the laws of men" (Acts 4:19). Christian theories of a justified revolution tend to follow the rules for a just war. It must be a last resort. There must be a reasonable chance of success in achieving a just new society. The means used must be proportionate and protect innocent life. The end must be the restoration of civil peace. Presumption always lies against any resort to violence. The more mild conflictual forms of social protest, struggle or civil disobedience, exact a less heavy calculus. They can more easily be countenanced or even mandated, especially if non-violent. Here again, however, the rule seems to read that the act of conflict or disobedience will not undermine respect for law and rightful governmental authority. Ultimately, such acts envision a return to a civil conversation about the goods to be pursued in common.[99]

In the end, however, as Paul Ricoeur has argued, there is a kind of *aporia* in the relationship of citizenship and discipleship:

> It is not responsible (and is even impossible) to deduce a politics from a theology. This is so because every political involvement grows out of a truly secular set of information, a situational arena which proffers a limited field of possible actions and available means, and a more or less risk-taking option, a gamble, among these possibilities.[100]

Politics remains more art than science, an art, moreover, exercised in a world not yet fully redeemed and transformed by grace, in that paradoxical arena that mingles coercion with rationality and justice. The disciple neither knows better than the unbeliever nor necessarily loves more that truly political common good which might be both genuinely possible and enhance justice and the common life.

NOTES

1. Many American evangelicals simply lack anything like a coherent *staatslehre*. But see two more thoughtful recent attempts at one in Charles Colson, *Kingdoms in Conflict* (New York: William Murrow, 1987); and Michael Cromartie, ed., *Disciples and Democracy* (Grand Rapids, Mich.: William Eeerdmans, 1994).

2. Don Browning et al., *From Culture Wars to Common Ground* (Louisville, Ky.: Westminster/John Knox, 1997), 243–44.

3. For an appeal to covenant language to root Catholic social teaching, see "Economic Justice for All" (the U.S. Bishops on the Economy), in *Catholic Social Thought: The Documentary Heritage*, ed. David O'Brien and Thomas Shannon (Maryknoll, N.Y.: Orbis, 1992), 586–88.

4. Max Stackhouse, "Theology and the Global Powers: Revising Our Vision of Civil Society" (paper presented at a conference on Religion, Social Capital, and Democracy, Calvin College, October 16–17, 1998), 11–12.

5. Thomas Sanders, *Protestant Concepts of Church and State* (New York: Holt, Rinehart and Winston, 1964); and John Bennett, *Christians and the State* (New York: Charles Scribner's Sons, 1958).

6. See Jose Casanova, *Public Religions in the Modern World* (Chicago: University of Chicago Press, 1994), 40–66.

7. Ernst Troeltsch, *The Social Teachings of the Christian Churches*, vol. 1, trans. Olive Wyon (New York: Harper and Row, 1960).

8. One argument for this is found in Michael Novak, *The Spirit of Democratic Capitalism*, 2nd ed. (Lanham, Md.: Madison Books, 1991).

9. Beware, however, of calling anything truly "secular" before the eighteenth century. Plato, Aristotle, the Stoics, and John Locke are not secular.

10. Roy Defarri, ed., *Saint Ambrose: Theological and Dogmatic Works* (Washington, D.C.: Catholic University Press, 1963); Marcus Tullius Cicero, *On Duties*, ed. M. T. Griffin and E. M. Atkins (New York: Cambridge University Press, 1991).

11. Augustine, *The City of God*, ed. D. B. Zema and Gerald Walsh (New York: Fathers of the Church, 1950), XIX.21.

12. Samuel Pufendorf, *De Jure Naturae* (London: Oxford University Press, 1934); Justus Lipsius, *Justi Lipsii de Cruce Libri Tres* (Amsterdam: Andreae Frisii, 1670).

13. David Burrell, *Freedom and Creation in Three Traditions* (Notre Dame, Ind.: University of Notre Dame Press, 1993); *Knowing the Unknowable God: Ibn-Sina, Maimonides, Aquinas* (Notre Dame, Ind.: University of Notre Dame Press, 1986).

14. Thomas Bokenkotter, *Church and Revolution: Catholics in the Struggle for Democracy and Social Justice* (New York: Doubleday Image, 1998), 39–173. For an overview of Christianity and socialism, Denis Janz, *World Christianity and Marxism* (New York: Oxford University Press, 1998).

15. For Catholic rights theory, David Hollenbach, *Claims in Conflict: Retrieving and Renewing the Catholic Human Rights Tradition* (New York: Paulist Press, 1979); R. Bruce Douglas and David Hollenbach, eds., *Catholicism and Liberalism* (New York: Cambridge University Press, 1994); for contemporary Catholic dialogue with critical theory see J. B. Metz and Jean Pierre Jossua, eds., *Christianity and Socialism* (New York: Seabury Press, 1977); and J. B. Metz, *Faith in History and Society* (New York: Seabury Press, 1980).

16. For Catholic feminist theoretical voices see Elizabeth Schussler-Fiorenza, *Bread, Not Stone* (Boston: Beacon Press, 1985); *Discipleship of Equals: A Critical Feminist Ekklesia-logy of Liberation* (New York: Crossroad, 1993); Rosemary R. Reuther, *Sexism and God Talk: Toward a Feminist Theology* (Boston: Beacon Press, 1983); for a representative Protestant view of feminism, cf. Letty Russel and J. Shannon Clarkson, eds., *Dictonary of Feminist Theologies* (Louisville, Ky.: Westminster/John Knox Press, 1996).

17. Robert George, ed., *Natural Law Theory* (New York: Oxford University Press, 1992); John Finnis, *Natural Law and Natural Rights* (New York: Oxford University Press, 1980). But see the more theological account of natural law in Jean Porter, *Natural and Divine Law* (Grand Rapids, Mich.: William Eeerdmans Co., 1999).

18. *Centessimus Annus*, in David O'Brien and Thomas Shannon, eds., *Catholic Social Thought: The Documentary Heritage* (Maryknoll, N.Y.: Orbis Press, 1992), 465.

19. Michael Fleet and Brian Smith, *The Catholic Church and Democracy in Chile and Peru* (Notre Dame, Ind.: University of Notre Dame Press, 1997); Scott Mainwaring, *The Catholic Church and Politics in Brazil* (Stanford, Calif.: Stanford University Press, 1986); Jeffrey Klaiber, *The Church, Dictatorships, and Democracy in Latin America* (Maryknoll, N.Y.: Orbis, 1998); for a Protestant perspective, Guillermo Cook, *The Expectation of the Poor* (Maryknoll, N.Y.: Orbis Press, 1986). See also the many entries on East German churches in the English-based periodical *Religion in Communist Lands*.

20. The Who speaks for the church? question is raised on the Protestant side by Paul Ramsey, *Who Speaks for the Church?* (Nashville, Tenn.: Abingdon, 1967); a Catholic position is found in J. Bryan Hehir, "The Right and Competence of the Church" in *One Hundred Years of Catholic Social Thought*, ed. John Coleman (Maryknoll, N.Y.: Orbis, 1991), 55–71.

21. The classic case for governmental authority, absent sin, is Yves Simon, *A General Theory of Authority* (Notre Dame, Ind.: University of Notre Dame Press, 1962).

22. For a more optimistic view of the state and society's relation to the kingdom of God, Jon Sobrino, *Christology at the Crossroads* (Maryknoll, N.Y.: Orbis Press, 1978).

23. Walter Rauschenbush, *A Theology of the Social Gospel* (New York: Abingdon, 1945). Rauschenbush spoke of "social salvation." For premillennial views, Michael Lienesh, *Redeeming America: Piety and Politics in the New Christian Right* (Chapel Hill: University of North Carolina Press, 1993).

24. For a profound sensibility to sin by a Catholic writer, Bertrand de Jouvenal, *On Power* (Boston: Beacon Press, 1968).

25. Reinhold Niebuhr, *Moral Man and Immoral Society* (New York: Charles Scribner's Sons, 1960); Reinhold Niebuhr, *Christianity and Power Politics* (Hamden, Conn: Archon Books, 1969).

26. For another Anabaptist view, Stanley Hauerwas and William Willison, *Resident Aliens: Life in the Christian Colony* (Nashville, Tenn.: Abingdon, 1989).

27. Allen Verhey, "Natural Law in Aquinas and Calvin," in *God and the Good*, ed. Clifton Orlebeke and Lewis Smedes (Grand Rapids, Mich.: William Eeerdmans, 1975), 80–92.

28. For an argument that post–Vatican II Catholicism has its own world-transforming analogue to the Protestant ethic, see Ivan Vallier, *Catholicism, Social Control, and Modernization* (Englewood Cliffs, N.J.: Prentice-Hall, 1970), 148–61. This world-transforming strand in social Catholicism can be seen in recent Catholic social encyclicals and the rise of liberation theology.

29. I treat many of these issues in John Coleman, "The Two Pedagogies: Discipleship and Citizenship," in *Education for Discipleship and Citizenship*, ed. Mary Boys (New York: Pilgrim Press, 1989), 35–75.

30. Jacques Maritain, *Man and the State* (Chicago: University of Chicago Press, 1951), 53, denies sovereignty to the state.

31. Philippe Duplessis Morney's *Vinciciae Contra Tyranos*, published in 1579, treats of a just revolution. Charles McCoy and J. Wayne Baker, *Fountainhead of Federalism: Heinrich Bullinger and the Covenantal Tradition* (Louisville: Westminster/John Knox, 1991), 47–50; for Aquinas on the right to oppose tyranny, *Summa Theologiae* II-II, 42, 2 ad 3.

32. This list of the ends of government is found in John Courtney Murray, *We Hold These Truths* (New York: Sheed and Ward, 1960).

33. Sanders, *Protestant Concepts of Church and State*, 279.

34. Bennett, *Christians and the State*, 205.

35. John Courtney Murray, "Religious Freedom," in *Freedom and Man*, ed. John C. Murray (New York: P. J. Kenedy and Sons, 1965).

36. John Coleman, "Catholic Integralism as a Fundamentalism," in *Fundamen-*

talism in Comparative Perspective, ed. Lawrence Kaplan (Amherst: University of Massachusetts Press, 1992), 74–95.

37. George Lindbeck, "Critical Reflections," in *Religious Freedom*, ed. Walter Burghardt (New York: Paulist Press, 1977), 54.

38. The call for a juridical guarantee for religious freedom as a civil right in *The Declaration of Religious Liberty*, no. 6. The text is found in David O'Brien and Thomas Shannon, eds., *Renewing the Face of the Earth: Catholic Documents on Peace, Justice, and Liberation* (Garden City, N.Y.: Doubleday, 1972), 291–306.

39. John Courtney Murray, "The Issue of Church and State at Vatican Council II," *Theological Studies* 27 (March 1966): 599–600.

40. Casanova, *Public Religions in the Modern World*.

41. *Declaration on Religious Liberty*, no. 1.

42. *Declaration on Religious Liberty*, no. 6.

43. See Jean Bethke Elshtain, "Relationship of Public to Private," in *The New Dictionary of Catholic Social Thought*, ed. Judith Dwyer (Collegeville, Minn.: Liturgical Press, 1994), 796.

44. Casanova, *Public Religions*, 57–58, for these three conditions for a modern, public religion.

45. U.S. Catholic Bishops, "Economic Justice for All," in O'Brien and Shannon, *Catholic Social Thought*, 604, for a call for a "common deliberation" about economic policies.

46. Casanova, *Public Religions*, 58.

47. For any public expression of religion as a form of bad taste, see Richard Rorty, "Religion as Conversation Stopper," *Common Knowledge* 3, no. 1 (1994): 1–2.

48. Seyla Benhabib, "Models of Public Space: Hannah Arendt, the Liberal Tradition, and Jürgen Habermas," in *Habermas and the Public Sphere*, ed. Craig Calhoun (Cambridge: MIT Press, 1991), 82.

49. Casanova, *Public Religions*, 65.

50. Cf. Richard Neuhaus's monthly comments in his journal, *First Things*. Michael Novak authored his own lay commission's neoconservative counterargument to the 1985 Bishops' Pastoral on Economic Justice.

51. For the Canadian Bishops on Indian Rights, cf. "Northern Development: At What Cost?" in *Do Justice: The Social Teaching of the Canadian Catholic Bishops*, ed. E. F. Sheridan (Sherbrooke, Quebec: Editions Paulines, 1987), 275–86. For human rights commissions in Chile, see Brian Smith, *The Church and Politics in Chile* (Princeton: Princeton University Press, 1982), 318–27.

52. "Justice in the World," in O'Brien and Shannon, *Catholic Social Thought*, 289.

53. *The Declaration on Religious Liberty*, in O'Brien and Shannon, *Renewing the Face of the Earth*.

54. John Rawls, *Political Liberalism* (New York City: Columbia University Press, 1993); Bruce Ackerman, *Social Justice in the Liberal State* (New Haven: Yale University Press, 1980). Rawls and Ackerman see a problem of basing human or basic citizenship rights on a religious foundation that is not shared. In their view, human rights are too important to be held hostage to foundational arguments.

55. Murray, *We Hold These Truths*, 308.

56. Murray, *The Problem of Religious Freedom*, 42.

57. Maritain, *Man and the State*, 13.

58. Not all liberals privilege the right always over the good. William Galston, for example, allows a place for some nonprocedural goods in *Liberal Purposes: Goods, Virtues and Diversity in the Liberal State* (New York: Cambridge University Press, 1991). Nor do all Catholics agree that the state has a role in defining and enacting the common good. Alisdair MacIntyre argues that the common good must be entirely defined in civil society, not by the state, in his chapter "The Political and Social Structures of the Common Good," in *Dependent Rational Animals* (Chicago: Open Court, 1999), 129–54.

59. Maritain, *Man and the State*, 11

60. For Montelembert's championing of subsidiarity in the 1840s see Bokenkotter, *Church and Revolution*, 52–55.

61. In O'Brien and Shannon, *Renewing the Face of the Earth*, 62.

62. Ibid.

63. Cf. Michael Walzer, "The Problem of Citizenship," in *Obligations: Essays in Disobedience, War, and Citizenship* (Cambridge: Harvard University Press, 1970), 203–28.

64. E. F. Schumacher, *Small Is Beautiful* (New York: Harper and Row, 1973). Schumacher, as a Catholic, was familiar with subsidiarity.

65. H. A. Rommen, *The State in Catholic Thought* (St. Louis: B. Herder and Co., 1945), 253.

66. Maritain, *Man and the State*, 21; Emile Durkheim, *Professional Ethics and Civic Morals* (London: Routledge and Kegan Paul, 1957), 73ff.

67. Cf. John Coleman, "Not Democracy but Democratization," in *A Democratic Catholic Church*, ed. Eugene Bianchi and Rosemary Reuther (New York: Crossroad, 1992), 226–47.

68. Catholic Charities U.S.A. agencies must now compete with for-profit companies such as Lockheed-Martin for welfare caseload outsourcing in welfare-to-work programs. William Ryan, "The New Landscape for Non-profits," *Harvard Business Journal* (January–February, 1999), 127–36, contends that the competitive entrance of for-profits into welfare deliverance will erode commitments to community development initiatives among nonprofits.

69. The merger of nonprofit hospital systems has made of them giant bureaucracies driven by the bottom lines of the requirements of the law and the market.

70. For Catholic policy voices in the welfare reform debate appealing to subsidiarity and the common good, Thomas Massaro, *Catholic Social Teaching and U.S. Welfare Reform* (Collegeville, Minn.: Liturgical Press, 1998); U.S. Catholic Conference Administrative Board, "Moral Principles and Policy Priorities on Welfare Reform," *Origins* 24, no. 41 (March 30, 1995): 674–78. For a consistent double appeal to subsidiarity yet a legitimate governmental role for the common good in Catholic welfare policy, see Dorothy Brown and Elizabeth McKeown, *The Poor Belong to Us: Catholic Charities and American Welfare* (Cambridge: Harvard University Press, 1997); John A. Coleman, "American Religion and Policy Advocacy: Catholic Charities U.S.A. and Welfare Reform," *Journal of Policy History* 13, no. 1 (January 2001): 73–108.

71. Hollenbach, *Claims in Conflict*.

72. For an argument to nationalize property if necessary to bring about true competition against monopoly, see *Quadragesimo Anno*, no. 42 in O'Brien and Shannon, *Catholic Social Thought*, 67.

73. Philip Land, "The Earth is the Lord's: Thoughts on the Economic Order," in *Above Every Name: The Lordship of Christ and Social Systems*, ed. Thomas Clarke (New York: Paulist Press, 1980).

74. For justice as participation in the economy, David Hollenbach, *Justice, Peace, and Human Rights* (New York: Crossroad, 1988), 71–83.

75. Rawls, *Political Liberalism*, 11–15; Don Browning, *From Culture Wars to Common Ground*, 243, attributes this Catholic bilingualism (rooted, in part, in natural law) to the Catholic ease in addressing public issues in society and rooting their case (for their own church public) in the Bible *and* in secular warrant (for the broader public). He contrasts this to the difficulty of elements of the New Christian Right to disentangle their "civil" from "sacred biblical" discourse.

76. Murray, *The Problem of Religious Freedom*, 26–27.

77. Cited in Sanders, *Protestant Concepts of Church and State*, 107.

78. For subsidy politics in the Netherlands: Arend Lijhart, *The Politics of Accommodation* (Berkeley and Los Angeles: University of California Press, 1968); John A. Coleman, *The Evolution of Dutch Catholicism* (Berkeley and Los Angeles: University of California Press, 1978), 58–87.

79. Abraham Kuyper, *Calvinism* (New York: Fleming and Revell Co., 1890) seems to allow some governmental intrusion on the separate spheres in strong emergency situations. But it is quite abnormal.

80. Browning, *From Culture Wars to Common Ground*, 77, seems to argue that the assumption is that the divine will wants the diverse spheres of creation to be unified. But the mechanism for doing so—short of God's will and action—is left hanging.

81. Stackhouse, "Theology and Global Powers" lists four orders of creation. Evangelicals who are part of James Dobson's Focus on the Family network mention only three: state, church, and family. Kuyper, *Calvinism*, seems to have envisioned seven.

82. McCoy and Baker, *Fountainhead of Federalism*, 58.

83. The Council on Civil Society, *A Call to Civil Society* (New York: Institute for American Values, 1998), 14. The Council is a joint effort of Catholic, mainline Protestant, Evangelical, Jewish, and secular voices.

84. David Martin, *Dilemmas of Contemporary Religion* (Oxford: Basil Blackwell, 1978), 37.

85. For the need for a nontheologically based "public philosophy," see Council on Civil Society, *A Call to Civil Society*, 12.

86. Ibid., 8.

87. Jacques Maritain, *Christianity and Democracy* (New York: Charles Scribner's Sons, 1944), 50–51.

88. For this argument that the "abstract moralities" of law and economy need face-to-face anchoring of mutuality and trust in civil society, Allan Wolfe, *Whose Keeper?* (Berkeley and Los Angeles: University of California Press, 1989).

89. Council on Civil Society, *A Call to Civil Society*, 11.

90. For the involvement of church members in civic participation: John Wil-

son and Thomas Jonaoski, "A Contribution of Religion to Volunteer Work," *Sociology of Religion* 56, no. 2 (Summer 1995): 325–38; Robert Wuthnow, Virginia Hodkinson, et al., *Faith and Philanthropy in America* (San Francisco: Jossey Bass, 1990).

91. Sydney Verba, Kay Schlozman, and Henry Brady, *Voice and Equality* (Cambridge: Harvard University Press, 1995) gives the evidence of the democratic potential in church membership.

92. Richard Neuhaus, *The Naked Public Square* (Grand Rapids, Mich.: William Eeerdmans, 1984).

93. Michael Walzer, *Spheres of Justice* (New York: Basic Books, 1983), 308.

94. *Summa Theologiae* I-II, 96 a.2, 3.

95. D. W. Brogan, *Citizenship Today* (New York: Macmillan, 1963), 103.

96. The Canadian Catholic philosopher Charles Taylor takes up this Catholic theme of linguistic and cultural rights and applies it to policy in his essay "The Politics of Recognition," in *Multiculturalism*, ed. Charles Taylor (Princeton: Princeton University Press, 1994).

97. Donal Dorr, *Option for the Poor: A Hundred Years of Catholic Social Teaching* (Maryknoll, N.Y.: Orbis, 1992), 288–316.

98. Robert Bellah, "Flaws in the Protestant Cultural Code: Some Religious Sources of America's Problems," *America* (July 21–August 6, 1999), 9–14.

99. For the metaphor of civic conversation as a ground for civility, see the chapters "Creeds at War Intelligibly" and "The Origins and Authority of Public Consensus," in Murray, *We Hold These Truths*, 102–39.

100. Paul Ricoeur, *Politiek en Gelof: Essays van Paul Ricoeur*, ed. Ad Peperzak (Utrecht: Ambo, 1968), 87. I do not have French originals that appeared in *Esprit* available to me. I argue that "the moral concept of citizenship in a religiously pluralistic world will have to be based on a wider notion than discipleship— probably, at root, in a non-theological understanding of the rights and duties of membership in the commonwealth or the tradition of civic republican virtue." "The Two Pedagogies," 37.

Christianity, Civil Society, and the State: A Protestant Response

Max L. Stackhouse

I AM DELIGHTED to have a chance to respond formally to John Coleman, for I have done so often in my mind and too seldom in person. He is one of the most important Christian thinkers in the area of social thought. Obviously a deeply committed Roman Catholic, he is also one who has taken some pains to study major strands of Protestant thought, just as many Protestants who are committed still to motifs from the Reformation have tried to sympathetically reengage the Roman Catholic tradition since Vatican II. However, I engage his chapter as one who is convinced that the view he takes as his counterfoil, the "Reformed tradition's theory about the 'spheres of creation,'" offers an even more convincing account of the nature of civil society and politics, and what they demand of us, than does even his most agreeable kind of Roman Catholicism. I say this with full awareness that with the election of Popes John XXIII and John Paul II, some major reconvergences of the whole tradition are apparent. It is all the more important, thus, that we all discuss how we both may become more catholic and more reformed, and how we can marshal the deeper unities and common resources of our faith to benefit civil society, political life, and humanity generally. After all, the destiny of the West—both internally and in its external impact—will be substantially shaped by the practical consequences of the interaction of religion and society, for many of the core structures of the West are founded on theological presuppositions, even if these assumptions are overlaid by non-, post-, or even antireligious constructs. If we do not understand this, we will not understand civilization or be able to shape its structures and dynamics at the deeper levels.

Coleman and I agree that there are many strands in the Christian reading of social/political matters that offer persistent minority reports, but that two main streams of the tradition generated the most articulate frameworks to deal with the analysis and guidance of the complex social systems in which we live. This is so because these two streams have already deeply stamped our institutional forms and our habits of mind, and because these two streams see it as part of the duty of the faithful ever and again to influence and repeatedly reform the recalcitrant aspects both of the human soul and of the social and political environments of the common life for the well-being of all. These traditions have thus developed distinctive models of society as a part of their "public theology." One of these may be called the "hierarchical-subsidiarity" view, most fully articulated by the Roman Catholic tradition, but held by others as well,[1] and the other the "federal-covenantal" view, most fully articulated by the Reformed tradition, but also held by others.[2]

These two positions share more than they dispute, at many levels. Both oppose those secular understandings of human existence wherein legitimate social life consists only of voluntary agreements constructed by autonomous individuals on the basis of rationally calculated marginal utility. They also oppose those pagan views that see persons as little more than a manifestation of some collective spirit or interest. The one view denies the ethical sociality of humans; the other obscures the moral dignity of the human person, including the capacity to transcend collective consciousness. The rejection of these two ideologies entails also suspicion of the "two agent" theory of some social contract theory—the view that the private individual (who may or may not have religious preferences, familial connections, and cultural or commercial interests—all of which are voluntary and private matters) and the public state are the only two decisive forces in human affairs, and that each must support and sustain the other.[3]

Still, significant differences remain, and it may help clarify matters to identify the points of divergence as they bear on our questions. The fundamental differences, I think, were artfully stated by F. W. Dillistone almost a half century ago. He recognized, as did Ernst Troeltsch before him, an intimate relationship between theology, ecclesiology, and social philosophy. In *The Structure of the Divine Society* he compared two models. The hierarchical-subsidiary model presumes a naturally differentiated, complex "body" ordered by means of a dual internal hierarchical structure, one spiritual and internal, one material and external, that aids the many parts or "organs" of the whole fulfill their innate tendency to actualize virtue and the common good. In contrast, the federal-covenantal view is a "pluralist" model in which religious and other institutions in society—familial, cultural, economic, educational, medical, and the like, including political ones—are conceived as a matrix of potentially networked associations, each held together by bonds of a set of pledged agreements that while each would pursue the purposes to which it is distinctively called, all would be governed by commonly debated but also commonly accepted principles of right and wrong.[4] Both of these views avoid the perils of libertine individualism and political totalitarianism and both support the view that between the person and the collective are the decisive "organs" or institutions of the civil society. The difference is this: one view sees these as comprehended by a natural moral solidarity made effective by compassionate but magisterial leadership that seeks to guide the whole to fulfill innate good ends. The other view sees various spheres of life, each populated by associative "artifacts," each constructed on the basis of a common discernment of need and a calling to fulfill that need, a recognition of a pluralism of institutions with possibly conflicting ends, and an ongoing critical analysis of our interpretations of transcendent principles of right that may be used to assess the presumption of innate tendencies to virtue, magisterial leadership, and any singular view of the common good.

The reason that we need to debate, and not simply ignore, such remaining divergences is that many believers share something of what might be called a cybernetic theory of society.[5] That is, while we acknowledge the tremendous power of multiple material forces, from evolutionary psychology to material interests, in shaping who we are and how we live in complex relationships, we hold that religious and social convictions, as relatively low-energy systems, are able both to interpret with remarkable accuracy the nature of those systems *and* to substantially guide their functioning—at least when there is an appropriate linkage between the ideas and the social systems of life.[6] However much we are formed by the high-energy systems of our chemistry and our instincts, our social and historical contexts, or the ways in which we find ourselves embedded in communities or traditions, we are not simply nature's effect, society's puppets, or an ensemble of our communities of origin. We have some capacity to exercise freedom precisely as we resist, affirm, interpret, or creatively reconstruct the decisive, if lower-energy, possibilities these provide. This is especially important for societies shaped by Christian (and, to a degree, Muslim or Buddhist) frames of reference, for these are "converting" religious traditions that have had enormous influences in changing cultures.[7]

The higher-energy systems to which I refer are, at the first level, family, politics, culture, and economy. I say "at the first level" for these are the social "spheres" or "sectors" found in every viable society—an observation that gave rise to the view that they were part of "nature" or "creation." They are present (in various forms) in all societies because the inevitable energies of Eros, Mars, the Muses, and Mammon must be structured in order to aid and not harm social life.

Thus every society will have a family structure, an institution for controlling violence, a cultural system, and an economic order.[8] They, and various other "spheres" of civil society, such as those of the professions—for example, education, law, medicine, and technology (engineering, architecture, and the like)—are found in complex form only in quite developed societies. These spheres, together with religion and the primary spheres, constitute civil society in contemporary civilizations, and may well be implicit in the practices of all societies. The relationships between what I here call "spheres," each of which pursues its own virtues and ends, are ordered both by the more general functional requirements of society at large and by a conviction that all are governed by a moral order that transcends the society—indeed, that has divine roots.[9] I take this to be a matter on which Professor Coleman and I agree, although we are both aware that some dispute it. If this is so, it implies that the kind of religion linked into these systems is fateful for the form of civil society, and thus also for the state as the political instrument, and is not the author or master of either the civil society or of the religious loyalties and commitments at its core. A politically or nationally or class or gender or aesthetically focused religion, for example, will bend the whole social system in particular directions, as would, say, a wisdom or healing or law or technique oriented one. Thus, getting religion as right as we can, establishing its own integrity, and getting it properly linked into these other social realities is both extremely subtle and quite decisive.

It does seem that some objections can be raised about the hierarchical-subsidiarity view. It may indeed be based on three debatable assumptions that shape both how reality is perceived and a sense of what we ought to do about it. These three beliefs are: that society has, or should become a kind of "solidarity" marked by a kind of political sovereignty, that this whole has or should have a cohesive or unified inner disposition, and that both its exterior unity and its interior orientation should be sustained by an inevitable and necessary hierarchy that both represents the whole and serves it. Thus, all parts of the society should seek the "common good," and the virtuous person will act sacrificially for the well-being of this whole.[10] Coleman appears to agree with many other contributors to the current debates on civil society, that it is essentially about a "community" that has both civil and political aspects, and that the former, if vital, best serves the latter. However, his accent on the doctrine of subsidiarity, like the accent on "democratic participation" in less overtly theological views, puts the priority on "lower-level" forms of community and association, and demands a kind of "servant leadership" for their sake of those who have higher authority.

The questions that can be raised about this view is whether it is, and whether it should be, the case that "solidarity," demanding a hierarchy of leadership that comprehends particular social political units, should be the case, and whether that whole involves the coincidence of civil society, moral order, and political sovereignty. Even if we recognize that we live in a universe, and thus in something of a wholistic system, the way of thinking about the whole may be conceived in a quite alternative manner—one fateful for our views of civil society and political life. It seems plausible, for instance, that society is constituted by a series of pluralistic sectors, spheres, and specific institutional relations, some "natural" in the sense that they are functionally prerequisite for a society to exist at all, some "historical" in the sense that they are constructed at specific times and places to fulfill useful roles in civilization for a time, and some "religious" in that they point to metaphysical and moral forces that are both transnatural and transhistorical. At none of these levels is it at all clear that they do or must coincide with political boundaries.

On the contrary, it is quite likely that several of these spill over national, social, and religious borders in ways that no political or national spiritual authority can, or should be able to, control—a fact that, if true, would make solidarity quite dubious as a value. People from these various areas of the common life may form overtly political associations, called factions, advocacy groups, community organizations, coalitions, lobbying networks, or even parties, with links to people in other places and with various religious convictions, to construct or deconstruct political regimes, to bend or block political policies toward what they care about in civil society and around the world. Wherever these are vibrant, we can be assured that civil society is well developed. Their vitality, however, may also indicate that civil society is being experienced as under threat and that leaders are mobilizing resources from sources near and far to provide the means to meet the threat. Civil society may also be alive and well when people feel no need to participate in these because they are involved in other cooperative activities, both at home and with links around the world, that seem more fateful for personal or social well-being. In short, the more active people are in civil society, the less interested they may be in politics. Many do not think that politics is, or should be, all that important for what is really going on in life. When this happens, politics is, in one sense, simply restored to its place as one among several spheres of civil society, no more determinative for the whole than economics and education, art and technology, family life, culture, law, and religion.[11]

The very multiplicity of the areas of human action suggests not a common, organic whole, but a pluralism of spheres and sectors in which humans live. Let us consider, for example, the significance of how daily newspapers and weekly magazines are organized—national politics and international affairs, economics and business, science, health and technology, sports, arts and entertainment, education, religion, hobbies and human interest, and so forth. Or consider the various course listings in any one of the social science departments in the university. psychology, which deals with intra- and interpersonal relationships; economics, which deals with commercial and financial relationships; political science, which deals with power and policy relationships; anthropology, which deals with cultural and customary relationships; sociology, which deals with the interaction of systems and the attitudes toward them. Or the main divisions of law: constitutional law, business law, criminal law, family law, international law, patents, tax law, and the like. I mention these to suggest that society is not a solidary unit coincidental with a religious culture and a polity; rather, civil societies are a complex set of spheres and sectors, populated by a host of "principalities and powers, authorities and dominions," to use New Testament images, constantly changing and variously arranged according to shifting historical developments and dynamic spiritual and moral influences.

Contemporary society, particularly, is a clustered network of institutions, each having its own pyramid of inner organization with its own moral and spiritual purpose, each negotiating its way through a welter of interactions. This has become more and more dramatic in our increasingly global society, where most of the spheres, sectors, areas of interest and engagement, or religions, and most of the institutions within them, have become voluntary and have escaped the control of any singular unified political or priestly control.

In brief, a massive pluralism of goods and a welter of rights in complex interaction, not solidaristic unity or hierarchic order, is the shape of society. In this context, the more complex the society becomes and the more global it is in reach, politics becomes but one subordinate cluster of institutions necessarily accountable to a much larger whole, and every hierarchy will be downsized in its functional utility and impact.

It is doubtful that nation-states will cease to be; but it is likely that they will become parts of larger federations of various kinds, frequently serving nonpolitical ends. In that context, the principle of "subsidiarity" becomes (as Coleman argues) even more important, especially as a reminder that higher levels of authority in each area must not only define and repeatedly refine the coordinating principles, purposes, and values of that area of life, but must help its members negotiate the complex relationships with other spheres, sectors, and areas. Neither they nor any single religion, however, will comprehend the whole, although it is the special task of religion to point to what does. That keeps society open. If we forget this, civilization and civility shrivel.[12]

In such a context, the definition of what constitutes the common good is and must be highly provisional, for what we hold to be "common" is often much too tied to the nationalistic definition of the whole, and thus our view of what is "good" may prematurely close off options that are better kept open. It is better to suggest that each area of human life is to be covenantally ordered internally, and related by federal agreements to other areas under a common discernment of the universal moral order that governs the world. What often passes for the "common good," in this view, is neither common enough nor good enough to meet that test. This suggests that our discernment of what is common and good is basically to be guided by the awareness of what is universally right. Thus, characteristically, in the Reformed (as well as the Jewish) traditions the Ten Commandments are taken as a revealed witness to what is right and wrong, and ideas such as "self-evident truths" (as in Locke), "the categorical imperative" (as in Kant), and, "universal human rights" (the United Nations Declaration) are taken as "the law written on the heart" (to echo Paul).[13] These are the foundations of a free, morally ordered society, definitive for what we can accept as common and good because they are equally true everywhere and practically useful to all people in all circumstances of life with their many aims and ends.[14]

Obviously, this view questions the virtue of solidarity, especially as it has developed in modern social Catholicism. If solidarity means obeying the command to love the neighbor, to overcome enmity or need, and to form bonds of both faith and service by constructing new organizations in civil society that manifest the right, then the term may be embraced. But if it means a demanded loyalty to prescribed beliefs, a required obedience to culturally and socially (or even biologically) preprogrammed ends, or an expected moral identification with our class or race or nation or religious community of origin, it will have to be seen, as Augustine saw the virtue of the Stoics, as "splendid vice." That is because it too often prevents us from being converted to a higher vision—especially to what some of us call "the Kingdom of God" or "the New Jerusalem," that cosmopolitan community of grace and compassion beyond every social group and historical achievement in church or society. Under the plumb line of this standard, we see ourselves in multiple alliances to fulfill our several vocations in the various spheres, sectors, and areas of life, the comprehensive integration of which is not realized in a church or a state. This would entail a fresh view of responsible citizenship in a global civil society, a new, indirect relationship of person and state, and a wider vision of the catholicity of the churches and the ecumenicity of the great world faiths.

This would, at best, take the form of federal-covenantal renewal in the midst of nature and history, guided by a public theology that points toward that universal righteousness that is likely to be realized only in another life. In this view, civil society, with all its associations, is to serve an end other than its own, or the state's, fulfillment, and we make a tragic error if we reverse these priorities.

Notes

1. The concept of "subsidiarity" was apparently first used in church polity in opposition to the proposed declaration on papal infallibility by Bishop Dupan-

loup of France in the debates of Vatican I. He and others argued that higher authorities (in the church) were to be auxiliary to, furnishing aid and support for, local and regional bodies, not ruling over them as a secular power might. As is well known, the opposition failed and infallibility was affirmed, accepted also by this bishop. However, the concept of "servant leadership" expressed something integral to the whole tradition, and the term "subsidiarity" gradually became accepted as a way of stating that the higher authorities must serve the lower, and local, needs when the latter are incapable of solving a particular problem. This idea was applied, eventually as a statement of a social-ethical ideal in both church doctrine and political life, in a way that both affirmed and qualified notions of local and regional integrity in church and society. It is of considerable importance that it has become a dominant category of the European Union as a way of relating transnational to national authority.

2. This point is made, if somewhat polemically, by James Hastings Nichols, *Democracy and the Churches* (Philadelphia: Westminster Press, 1951); more recently by William J. Everett, *God's Federal Republic* (New York: Paulist Press, 1988); and most masterfully by Daniel Elazar, *The Covenant Tradition in Politics*, 4 vols. (Piscataway, N.J.: Transaction Publishers, 1995–98).

3. This I take to be the Bentham/Mill tendency on one side, the Hobbes/Rousseau tendency on the other. I have traced the devastating impact of these utilitarian and contractual views, as they became established in public policy, on religion, family life, and civil society in *Covenant and Commitments* (Louisville, Ky.: Westminster Press, 1997), esp. chap. 4.

4. F. W. Dillistone, *The Structure of the Divine Society* (London: Lutherworth Press; Philadelphia: Westminster Press, 1951). Similar points were made by Ernst Troeltsch, whom Coleman cites, in *The Social Teaching of the Christian Churches* (1911, German; New York: Harper and Bros., 1931).

5. I take this insight to be a continuing contribution by Talcott Parsons to social theory. See, e.g., *Societies* (Englewood Cliffs, N.J.: Prentice-Hall, 1966), esp. chap. 2.

6. I am convinced that the modern concept of civil society derives from the awareness of freedom from nature's dictates, from the conventions of society, and from the demands of political rulers, given with a notion of a relationship to God—which also required covenantal participation in "nonnatural consociations." This idea was articulated for modernity in a fresh way by Johannes Athusius, *Politics*, abridged and translated by F. S. Carney, with a preface by C. J. Friedrich (Boston: Beacon Press, 1964). The relationship of "grace" and "natural law" in these relations, however, has a deeper root, as recently argued in Michael Cromartie, ed., *A Preserving Grace: Protestants, Catholics, and Natural Law* (Grand Rapids, Mich.: Eerdmans Publishers, 1987). For an influential view that acknowledges the historic role of religion but doubts the ongoing capability of faith or church to generate a viable civil society, see Adam Seligman, *The Idea of Civil Society* (New York: Free Press, 1992).

7. This is a major theme of the volume edited by John Witte and R. C. Martin, *Sharing the Book: Religious Perspectives on the Rights and Wrongs of Proselytism* (Maryknoll, N.Y.: Orbis Books, 1999), which includes my article, written with Deirdre Hainsworth, "Deciding for God: The Right to Convert in Protestant Perspectives," 201–30.

8. These are the four I treat in my address, "Theology and the Global Powers: Revising Our Vision of Civil Society," to which Coleman refers in his chapter (e.g., n. 4). It is my contention that the medieval concept of the three natural "estates," which are reflected in Lutheran (and, in some texts, Calvinist) ideas of the "Orders of Creation" (family, religion, and regime), omit the economy (previously seen as a natural function of the household, with it governed by the regime) as an independent arena of human action. Thus, I spoke of the construction of the corporation as a new institutional matrix for economic life—a major force in civil society, not fully acknowledged as such by many contemporary observers. The term "sphere" is drawn from an influential post-Enlightenment Calvinist perspective, made famous by Abraham Kuyper's *Calvinism* (New York: Revell, 1899), reprinted often as *Lectures on Calvinism* by Eerdmans Publishers. This term corresponds to the "department of life," frequently used by his friends Ernst Troeltsch and Max Weber, and to what later theologians such as Karl Barth and Dietrich Bonhoeffer call "Orders of Preservation" or "Mandates." The latter terms, as I have tried to show in several places, involve both "natural communities" and socially constructed institutions such as universities, hospitals, advocacy organizations, and television stations. These vary in their number and relationship (to each other and to the "primary orders") according to material conditions, historical developments, and spiritual-moral influences.

9. This is one of the main insights of Emil Brunner in his Gifford Lectures after World War II. See his *Christianity and Civilization* (New York: Charles Scribner's Sons, 1948); and it is a central point of my *Creeds, Society, and Human Rights: A Study in Three Cultures* (Grand Rapids, Mich.: Eerdmans Publishers, 1985), as we faced both the Soviet system and the decolonialized countries in a new way. "Civil society" will be differently arranged not only modestly in a Reformed as compared to a Catholic setting; but more dramatically in a Hindu, Muslim, Marxist, or Confucian one. Each will assign a different role to politics and have a distinct view of the duties and rights of citizens. But an absence, repression, or marginalization of a theological view is devastating.

10. The predominant form of this pattern is very old, and is stated in a famous letter of Pope Gelasius in 494. It is claimed that there are two powers in society, the spiritual and the temporal, the latter to be subsidiary to the former. Much non-Roman teaching has a similar pattern, conceiving "society" as a single body and having twin authority structures, one spiritual and one political. This is true not only in Lutheran lands, where the contrast of Law and Gospel emphasized the distinction between outer and inner, but also in all those countries influenced by the Caesaro-Papist traditions of Eastern Orthodoxy, by Erastian doctrines as in Anglicanism, and by the several continental lands effected by the Peace of Westphalia. In the latter cases, temporal authority is held to be the guardian of the spiritual, with the spiritual responsible for the moral texture of society. These all have coincidental boundaries that comprehend religious and political authorities, and see civil society as subject to both. The rise of the secular nation-state has often been seen to be the more radical subordination and privatization of religion, as political authority took responsibility for civil society. This latter view is now increasingly under question, a fact that accounts for the renewed interest in both the models under discussion here. See, e.g., José Casanova, *Public Religions in the Modern World* (Chicago: University of Chicago Press, 1994).

11. It is surely the case that human societies need governments and hierarchies of various kinds for particular purposes; but only in some periods do they become the comprehending institutions many claim them to be. We have known for centuries that the form they take can be, and is, shaped by complex social dynamics, by human decisions, and by perceptions of what is ultimately the holy, righteous, and virtuous life—at least since Samuel debated with God the issue of whether to anoint kings in ancient Israel, since Plato and Aristotle debated the ideal forms of governance, since the *Arthashastra* presented a model of "good" (as opposed to evil or bad) rule by a maharaja, and since Confucias instructed his students on the virtuous form of society and polity.

12. This is a critical insight of both David Landes's massive *The Wealth and Poverty of Nations* (New York: Norton, 1998); and of Daniel Elazar's summary volume of his four-volume study *Covenant and Civil Society*. It is also a significant theme in Francis Fukuyama's twin volumes, *The End of History and the Last Man* (New York: Free Press, 1992) and *Trust: The Social Virtues and the Creation of Prosperity* (New York: Free Press, 1995). These authors suggest, from rather different standpoints, that economic and moral issues are more comprehensible than political ones and that when political or familial orders attempt to comprehend the whole, they tend to limit the vitality of civil society.

13. The firm support of human rights by Catholic and Protestant leaders, especially since World War II, is a key points of convergence.

14. An artful perspective on this vision can be found in Wilhelm Roepke, *The Moral Foundations of Civil Society* (New Brunswick, N.J.: Transaction Press, 1996); or in the older J.F.A. Taylor, *The Masks of Society: An Inquiry into the Covenants of Civilization* (New York: Appleton-Crofts, 1966).

Civil Society and Government:
Seeking Judaic Insights

Noam J. Zohar

Does the Jewish tradition have anything to say about civil society? The answer depends as much upon how *civil society* is defined as upon any investigation into Judaic sources. According to one rather strict conception, the entire notion of civil society—and the ideals, problems, and solutions attributed to it—is situated within the framework of modern ideologies of individualism and liberty. Insofar as traditional Judaism does not adopt this democratic stance, with its emphasis on individualism and liberty, it must regard the project and problematics of "civil society" as inherently alien.[1]

Now in fact I believe that the distance between traditional Judaism and democratic thought is smaller than is often suggested; the notion of individual rights, for example, finds expression in classical halakhic discussions, as will be illustrated below. But my exposition in this chapter will not be built upon this contested ground. Rather than searching (in vain) for direct statements about the questions before us, I will seek to apply Judaic sources and insights to the issues of civil society, arguing by extension and analogy. And the scope of the questions themselves will be widened as I adopt a broad notion of "civil society," covering the entire set of institutions and associations that stand between the individual and the overarching state.

In discussing these matters from the perspective of the Jewish tradition, it is essential to distinguish between three main periods. First, there is the biblical period, when Israel existed as a sovereign kingdom (or rather, mostly, two parallel kingdoms). Then, there is the long period of exile, when disparate Jewish communities lived within gentile states or empires, often exercising some degree of autonomy. And finally, there is the modern state of Israel, proclaiming itself a "Jewish and democratic state."

This division into periods is meant as no more than a rough sketch. For in the biblical narrative Israel begins its history, as it were, in a state of exile, from the Patriarchs' residence in Canaan to the Israelites' sojourn in Egypt. Then too, during the last centuries of the period of the Hebrew Bible, most of the people lived again in exile, with only a small segment returning to found the Second Commonwealth.[2] And even though the Jewish population in the Land of Israel later grew larger, most of the time they were not a sovereign kingdom. It seems best, then, to speak of three *phases* of Jewish historical existence: *monarchy, exile,* and *statehood.* My remarks will therefore refer specifically to the context of these distinct phases as appropriate.

It was the phase of exile that prevailed throughout most of Jewish history. In the exilic situation, the affairs of state and society were addressed predominantly from the perspective of a Jewish group living within an alien state. When we consider the idea of a "civil society" distinct from the state, an analogy may be drawn to the Jewish exilic paradigm of an autonomous community within the gentile state.

From another perspective, however, the Jewish community might itself be likened to a state, particularly in those times and places in which it enjoyed greater autonomy and extensive powers over its members. Issues akin to those that interest us here may thus be raised with regard to the intracommunal arrangements: What proportion of the group's affairs was conducted centrally, and how much was left for smaller associations and organizations?

Working with these different perspectives, the application of the state/civil society distinction becomes relative. The exilic phase is marked by the fact that political society is nested: group within group. Some of our questions can best be illuminated, from the Jewish tradition, by thinking of the entire Jewish community as a component of civil society within the larger state; others, by thinking of smaller units within Jewish society in their relations to the self-governing community.

Boundaries: Torah versus State Law

"The Law of the Kingdom is Law"

How did Jews in exile perceive the proper division of power between their community and the host state? It might be thought that there would be no principled acceptance of *any* division of power, since in principle the Torah—God's teaching—is supposed to govern all aspects of life, private and public. The state might thus be regarded merely as an alien force, which must be accommodated even while we try to maximize the extent of communal self-government. The crucial question can be put in terms of *law*: Can a community committed to God's revealed law recognize as valid the laws of a human state?

In fact, *halakhah* (the Jewish tradition of normative discourse) adopted the dictum, first formulated in the third century, that "The law of the kingdom is law" (BT Bava Kama 113a-b). This meant that "the kingdom," as distinct from just anyone wielding brute force, can issue edicts that get recognized as "law" and thus *ought* to be obeyed. Now the crucial question was, what is the legitimate realm of state legislation—and what realm should be preserved, as far as possible, to be governed by the Jewish community under its internal halakhic norms?

A characteristic statement can be found in a medieval commentary on a talmudic ruling concerning the validity of legal documents, signed by gentile witnesses and issued under the auspices of state courts. Such deeds effecting various transactions are generally valid, "except for writs of divorce" (BT Gittin 9b). The distinction is explained in terms of the difference between the universal norms of justice, which (rabbinic tradition teaches) are binding upon all "Noahides" (i.e., all of humankind),[3] on the one hand, and particular Jewish norms, such as those defining matrimonial law, on the other hand. Rashi (eleventh century, France) in his classical commentary writes that non-Jews "are not [deemed effective agents for] severing [a halakhic marriage] since they are not party to [halakhic] matrimonial law. Noahides were, however, commanded to institute justice—[therefore all other legal transactions are valid]."

Universal norms are properly administered by the common state. The Jewish community—and by the same token, other communities as well—should autonomously administer its particular norms, such as those pertaining to marriage. This division assumes that individuals belong to, and marry within, distinct ethnic/religious communities.

Torah Law and Religious Communities in the Modern State

In modern times, such communal autonomy has been greatly curtailed by the state's assertion of jurisdiction in all areas. It is not surprising, perhaps, that the state of Israel has retained a system of special jurisdictions in "personal law," under which each person belongs to a particular religious group and is subject to its religious courts. But even in liberal democracies that refuse to authorize such jurisdiction, religio-cultural groups have shown significant capacity for surviving via voluntary adherence. A crucial question here is whether group autonomy is in fact consistent with the universal demands of justice, considering especially the vulnerable members of the group, whose adherence may in fact be far from truly voluntary.[4] In Israel, moreover, individuals have no real option but to belong to a group and be (with regard to "personal law") its legal subjects.

The injustices inherent in the Israeli system invite the conclusion that the boundary between state and ethnic/religious groups should be pushed firmly to the point of excluding such groups from wielding any legal power over their members. Against this, it is plausible to evoke, from within the biblical tradition, opposition to having the power to make and enforce the law reside fully and exclusively in the state.

Unlike other monarchs in the ancient Near East, the Israelite king was not a promulgator of laws; these were given in God's Torah.[5] Popular loyalty to a law above any royal decree is an important element in resistance to injustice propagated by the state. In the history of the Israelite monarchy, this is exemplified in the story of Naboth's vineyard (1 Kings 21:1–20). Naboth at first successfully resisted the king's pressure to yield or sell his vineyard, clearly relying on an accepted notion of his legal rights. Finally, the king had to resort to fabricated charges and a false trial in order to overcome this resistance and have Naboth killed; the fierce critique, led by the prophet Elijah, eventually led to a popular revolt.

This aspect of the biblical tradition is continued in the notion, prevalent among traditional Jews, that the supreme law is Torah law; a state law that fundamentally conflicts with it is thus invalid. In this sense, religious society can be seen as an important source of resistance to state-sponsored evil. "The *law* of the kingdom is law"—but some decrees are not "law" at all, and should be opposed.

Torah Study and Educational Institutions

The centrality of adherence to Torah is expressed in the fact that its study is the most highly valued practice in Jewish traditional society. Education in the Torah is seen as the personal duty of every parent (traditionally, primarily every *father*), though its exercise is commonly achieved through the services of a professional teacher, engaged jointly by the parents—or, in the traditional community, by the communal officers.

Hence, care should be taken with regard to the claim that Judaism has an ancient ideal of public education. This is true in the sense that Torah education was offered to all (male) children; but it was not an education for future *citizens* offered by the state, but rather education of the next generation of the *covenant*, overseen by the covenantal community.

Accordingly, in the wake of emancipation, Jewish communities were concerned over the state's intervention in education even more, perhaps, than over its intervention in marriage or divorce. And in contemporary Israel, the educational system is one of state-sponsored parochial schools. At full parental discretion, children are educated in any of a great variety of schools, so that each kind of religious (or secular) community can replicate itself. There is little appreciation—particularly in traditional circles—for any suggestion that the state has a crucial stake in the content of education. The boundary between the concerns of the state and those of the spiritual community is delineated with Torah—and education—outside the purview of the state.

LIABILITIES (AND NEEDS)

The State as Liability: Religious Anarchism

There is a strand in the biblical tradition that views the very existence of the state—specifically, in those days, the monarchy—as a major liability. The book of Judges portrays what might be termed a "civil society" *without* a state, governed by local elders. When Gideon leads the Israelites to military victory, we are told that

> the men of Israel said to Gideon, "Rule over us—you, your son, and your grandson as well; for you have saved us from the Midianites." But Gideon replied, "I will not rule over you myself, nor shall my son rule over you; the Lord alone shall rule over you." (Judg. 8:22–23)[6]

It might be argued that the regime upheld by the pious Gideon—clearly endorsed by the author—amounts not to anarchy but to theocracy: there is a king, albeit not human but divine. But since no human institution is legitimized as God's agent, the actual picture is best defined, I think, in terms of (religious) anarchism.

Here there is a sharp contrast between the message of these chapters in the book of Judges (6–9) and the message of the book as a whole, and especially its concluding chapters with their plaintive refrain: "In those days there was no king in Israel; everyone did as he pleased" (Judg. 21:25, and cf. 18:1, 19:1). The centralized state mechanism of the monarchy is established in the wake of the failure of stateless civil society. The monarchy, though endorsed by God, is promoted over against the prophetic protest that, in demanding a king, the people were rejecting their divine king (1 Sam. 8–12).

Arguably, then, it was only the Davidic dynasty, directly elected by God, that could wield legitimate power in His name. A strand of religious opposition to any other human claim of state power has persisted throughout Jewish history. The fundamental critique of state power extended with even greater force to the great empires, as in the prophet Habakkuk's classical litany about the looting Chaldeans (Hab. 1; although even on this there was a rival prophetic vision—cf. Jer. 27).

The other side of this same coin is, of course, that a community with such a tradition will be seen as posing a liability to the state. During the last decades of the Second Commonwealth, the so-called Zealots led the rebellion against Rome, and in their efforts to subdue the repeated revolts the Romans sought to repress the Jewish religion.

In the exilic phase, Jewish teaching had come to accept the rule of the alien state (cf. above, the section "Boundaries"), yet the state was seen as a constant threat to the community's integrity. Jews were generally expected to resolve any conflicts or complaints internally; those who turned to gentile courts or rulers were deemed traitors and—where circumstances allowed—treated quite harshly.

The Community and Voluntary Associations

As indicated above in the introductory section, an alternative analogy might be drawn: the Jewish community as a whole might be compared to a state, containing elements of civil society in the form of certain functional subgroups within it. In the medieval Jewish community, we find a "burial society" (called *hevra kaddisha*—literally, "the holy association"), a sick-care society, and so forth. The members' time is volunteered, and necessary funding supplied mainly by votive contributions. The community certainly needs these societies, not only in the sense that its members rely on their services, but also in the sense that the societies are seen as discharging collective obligations.

These voluntary associations, in turn, tacitly rely on the community. The burial society takes care of the dead, but it is the community that provides the cemetery. The sick-care society undertakes visiting the sick, which also involved ministering to them; but payment for feeding and care of the destitute is provided by the basic welfare system of Tzedaka, funded by communal taxation.

GROUPS AND INDIVIDUALS

Taxation in a Corporate Society

For the community in exile, it was deemed very important that individual members not deal directly with the state. This may be easily explained in terms of the community's vital interest in maintaining its authority over members. In the context of medieval corporate society, this authority rested first and foremost on the premise that the state authorities deal only with the corporate community.

Nevertheless, kings and princes often considered it advantageous to deal directly with individuals. This was a thorny issue, especially when it involved taxes. The standard procedure was for the prince to demand a certain sum from the community as a whole; its officers then proceeded to assess each member according to his wealth. The community sometimes stood to lose much if a separate arrangement was allowed for a wealthy member. What is interesting for us is not communal opposition to such an arrangement in itself, but rather the arguments offered in disallowing it.

Most often it could be assumed that the prince's profit from the separate taxation lay in the fact that the individual's direct payment was not deducted—at least, not in its entirety—from the collective levy. This was criticized in terms of fairness: whatever total sum was due to the prince, it was the community who knew best how to justly divide the burden among its members. The individual making his separate arrangement was in fact unfairly transferring some of his due burden to his fellows.

What places the community, rather than the prince (or state), in a better position to determine a fair distribution among its members? The answer is far from self-evident, for after all, the community officers are often themselves powerful and wealthy individuals who have a personal stake in the distribution of the tax burden. Indeed, several medieval discussions record concern over the officers' possible partiality, and require a sacred oath of good faith. Still, the traditional view is that insiders have both more information and a better sense of the communally accepted values and notions of fairness.

In contemporary states, the powers of taxation reside in the government and not in associations constituting civil society. Yet perhaps a similar rationale can apply to other activities that require special knowledge and an intimate sense of specific values and norms. I have in mind practices like self-regulation by members of a profession. For this to be effective, of course, there must exist at least as much trust in the integrity of the profession's officers (e.g., its ethics committee) as that engendered in the past through a sacred oath.

Families and Individuals in the Bible

Overall, the Hebrew Bible does not speak univocally on the relative importance of individuals versus groups; and scholars offer rival reconstructions of the history of ideas concerning these matters in biblical Israel. I cannot hope to offer here any compelling summary. Instead, let us look briefly at two examples pertaining to the standing of individuals in relation to their families—immediate and extended.

Paraphrasing Aristotle, it might be said that the smallest unit of civil society is the family. A basic tenet of biblical criminal law is that "Parents shall not be put to death for children, nor children be put to death for parents: a person shall be put to death only for his own crime" (Deut. 24:16)—a rule clearly seeking to contest prevalent norms of collective punishment: each member of the family must be judged alone.[7] Yet this principle, promulgated in the context of retributive justice, does not extend as clearly to the context of distributive justice, the setting of our second example.

The primary distribution in biblical Israel was that of the land—apportioned to all males of mature age. A distribution to these males, evidently as heads of households, leaves all others—primarily all females—as dependents. Presumably, the land's yield is subject to secondary distribution within the family. It is worth noting that the primary distribution is conducted by lottery, with a concomitant emphasis on quantitative equality (see Num. 26:52–56). But no procedural mechanisms of fairness are established for intrafamilial distribution.

Against this background, it is striking that the daughters of Zelophehad were able to gain recognition of their claim to a stake in the land in lieu of their deceased father, who had no sons. In these (atypical) circumstances, each of the five women was granted the status of individual landowner. Yet even as individuals, they remained also part of their tribe, and were not freed from the tribesmen's control of individual landholdings. As females, their land might be lost to the tribe when they married and their holdings eventually passed on to their sons (whose tribal affiliation would be determined paternally). An effort to strike a balance between individual and tribal rights is evident in the compromise ruling, delivered by Moses:

> This is what the LORD has commanded concerning the daughters of Zelophehad: They may marry anyone they wish, provided they marry into a clan of their father's tribe. No inheritance of the Israelites may pass over from one tribe to another, but the Israelites must remain bound each to the ancestral portion of his tribe. Every daughter among the Israelite tribes who inherits a share must marry someone from a clan of her father's tribe. (Num. 34:5–9)

Here, as in numerous other contexts in biblical law and practice, great importance is granted to family and tribe. Against this background, what stands out is the emphasis—evidently rather revolutionary—on the individual standing of each person in any administration of justice, whether human or divine.[8]

CITIZENSHIP?

Townsmen as Neighbors and Partners

If it is far from clear what, in the Jewish tradition, should be called "state" and what "civil society," it is even less clear what in this tradition is the corollary of "citizen." The word *ezrah*, used in modern Hebrew for "citizen," is adapted from biblical usage, where it means "native," as distinct from a resident (alien)—as in the command, "The stranger that sojourneth with you shall be unto you as the home-born [*ezrah*] among you" (Lev. 19:34).[9] In the Mishnah, the core document of Rabbinic Judaism,[10] the statement that touches most closely upon this issue is found in a rule about compelling an unwilling resident to share in certain expenditures for security:

> They compel him [to share] in [the cost of] building a wall and gates for the town, and a bolt for the gates. R. Shimon ben Gamaliel says: Not every town requires a wall. How long shall one reside in town to be considered a townsman? Twelve months. If, however, one acquires a residence there, one is considered a townsman immediately. (Bava Batra 1:5)

Even here, I have taken some liberty in translation with the phrase "to be considered a townsman," for the Hebrew lacks such a term. Literally, the sentence reads: "How long shall one reside in town *so as to be like the men of the town?*" Indeed it might be said that in the posing and answering of this question, we witness the *birth* of a (rudimentary) notion of citizenship. The context is instructive: this chapter of the Mishnah begins with rules about the wall between two neighbors (called "partners" because they share a courtyard), and the fifth clause (cited above) opens with a rule about relations between several house owners who share a courtyard—

> They compel him [to share] in [the cost of] building an antechamber and door for the courtyard. R. Shimon ben Gamaliel says: Not every courtyard requires an antechamber.

—and moves on from this directly to the rule about a town. The town is conceived, it seems, simply as a supercourtyard, requiring more elaborate defenses. And the thinking appears very libertarian: the majority cannot compel a minority to contribute to any project, but only to these specific measures, recognized as "requisite." Now, since the wall and gates take long to build and are expected to endure for many years, there is a need to determine who is a "man of the town" (this can be contrasted with the Rabbinic discussion elsewhere about how much each traveler in a caravan must contribute for emergency rescue).[11]

To be precise, it seems the issue here is one of determining *residence* (for tax purposes) rather than *citizenship*. Even in the alternative account of the Tosefta,[12] which presents a richer view of the townsmen's mutual obligations (e.g., building an aqueduct, buying a Torah scroll for the synagogue, and more), belonging to a town consists simply in sharing in the provision of public goods. Of "citizenship" in a moral sense, as the function or condition of special virtue, there is scarce evidence in any of the Rabbinic texts.

"The Community of Israel"

Having said all the above, it is worth emphasizing that the Judaic tradition is by no means radically individualistic. Great value is placed upon belonging to a collective; Jewish identity lies in belonging to the People Israel (*am yisra'el*), who constitute the covenantal community. The core of the covenant is a commitment to live according to God's commandments, and it has a dual character; every Israelite is obligated individually and is also responsible for the collective obligation. The Rabbis express the idea of mutual responsibility by saying that each Israelite became a "guarantor" for each and every of his fellows.[13]

Thus great moral /spiritual significance is attached to membership in the covenantal community. But is this membership akin to citizenship? The answer hinges upon the function and focus of this community; and, since the Torah's commandments are numerous and pertain to many things, upon that which is identified as their central concern.

On one view—which I shall call "priestly"—the central issue in fulfilling the covenant is maintaining the temple ritual. This is the least "political" conception of the People Israel: they are primarily a community of worship, and whatever earthly affairs they may conduct are significant mainly in the support they provide for the temple cult. This is how the Second Commonwealth was conceived at its inception (see Ezra 1:1–6, 7:11–28).

A second view, which I shall call "prophetic," holds the opposite, pronouncing the temple ritual as decisively secondary in relation to interpersonal morality and social justice. Now, if the crucial challenge of the covenant is in protecting the vulnerable and "redeeming Zion in Justice" (cf. Isa. 1:27), it might be argued, perhaps, that membership in the covenantal community amounts to membership in a political community. But this seems something of an overstatement; for the focus is on relations between persons—or even between social classes—rather than on political roles and institutions or on the governance of the city or state. An important exception here is the explicit concern with the honesty of the judiciary. According to the prophets, the entire society is held to account for suffering the perversion of justice. So in this specific sense, every Israelite has a citizen-like stake in the polity's judicial institutions.

Another perspective on covenant and citizenship grows out of the third view, pervasive in many biblical books but most clearly associated with the message of Deuteronomy. On this view, the most crucial aspect of the covenant is the prohibition of idolatry. According to many interpreters, the underlying idea has a political character: God is Israel's (divine) sovereign, and idolatry constitutes high treason. Being an Israelite thus means being a member of a religious collective dedicated to the eradication of idolatry. For Maimonides, who (many years later) came to explain a large part of the Torah's commandments in terms of the battle against idolatry, being Jewish is defined as being a citizen of a monotheistic polity.[14]

It is important to note that this community, the People Israel, is not necessarily coextensive with any actual political community. This is true especially in the exilic phase, when Jews belong politically to a *local* Jewish community or to the host non-Jewish state or to both.[15] But it is true also in contemporary Israel, which as a political community has many citizens who are non-Jewish (as well as many who see their Jewish identity in ethnic, rather than religious, terms)—and whose Jewish population in any case includes only a minority of the covenantal People Israel.

It is true that the medieval *kahal* (Jewish community) was conceived and experienced as a concrete instantiation of the greater whole, *kneset Yisrael* ("congregation of Israel"). Thus for example, the *kahal*'s ultimate sanction was the ban (*herem*), under which a person would be completely shunned by all members of the community. This was perceived as being separated from "all of Israel," and indeed Jews of other localities were required to abide by the ban pronounced by the culprit's own community.[16]

Membership was attributed, as it were, from the top downward: one was a Jew, a member of the People Israel—and then, by virtue of this Jewish identity, one was (derivatively) also a member, together with other local Jews, of the *kahal* of a particular town.[17] In the terms of our present discussion, the morally significant membership was in the "civil society" of the (dispersed) People Israel. This affiliation then determined the scope of the local, more mundane political community, and the parameters for its operation.

In the modern state of Israel, the political community encompasses numerous non-Jews. Israeli citizenship, then—unlike belonging to a medieval *kahal*—is not dependent upon membership in the Jewish people. Nevertheless, the two are connected through the "Law of Return," under which Israeli citizenship is granted to any Jewish immigrant. Moreover, Israeli law, in a system taken over from the Ottoman Empire, places individuals under the jurisdiction of religious courts for purposes of "personal law" (chiefly, marriage and divorce), and each person's affiliation must therefore be determined. Hence state officials (and, in disputed cases, state courts) have been called upon to decide whether particular individuals are Jews. There has been a string of controversies, whose theme is often labeled the Who is a Jew? question.

If Israeli law turns to the Jewish tradition, it is not for defining the notion of "citizenship"—which does not fit easily into the traditional discourse—but for defining the notion of "Jew." Due to the major changes in Jewish history and society in modern times, this definition is a matter of deep ideological struggle—particularly between those adhering to a religious conception of Jewishness and those opting instead for a national or ethnic conception.[18] Moreover, opting for a religious conception opens the door to further controversies, as each of the various religious movements within Judaism has its own standards and procedures for conversion, whereby a non-Jew may become a Jew. If these movements are seen as components of civil society, then the state finds itself curiously—and perhaps unhappily—depending on them for defining a crucial element in its constitutive institution of citizenship.

Conflict

According to the tradition, a Jew's primary commitment is to the Torah. No local *kahal* may act contrary to Torah, and it should not be obeyed if it does so act.[19] Likewise in the Jewish monarchy (according to the retroactive pronouncements of halakhic discourse),[20] if the king issues commands countervening Torah law, they must be disobeyed. And in the streets of Jerusalem (less often in Tel Aviv) one can see bumper stickers proclaiming, The laws of Torah have priority over the laws of the state!

How far must one carry this commitment? In general, whenever disobeying state law might entail danger, the requirements of Torah law are set aside. This does not apply, however, to three issues. If anyone—including the state—requires a Jew to transgress the prohibition of bloodshed, incest, or idolatry, he must "be killed rather than transgress" (BT Sanhedrin 74a). Significantly, the duty of martyrdom is extended to cover the commandments in conditions of state persecution against the Jewish religion. In any direct test of allegiance, the covenantal commitment must reign supreme.

In many traditional circles today, a similar attitude finds expression in less dramatic, everyday circumstances. As indicated above, the realm of Torah study is seen as belonging to the religious community rather than to the state. But Torah study is much more than the stuff of children's education. The traditional ideal is that everyone should engage in the study of Torah for as much of his time as possible. Jewish communities have supported a class of Torah scholars who devote their lives to study and teaching. Moreover, even individuals who end up pursuing other careers often spend their formative years as adolescents and young adults as students at a *yeshivah* (talmudic academy).

All this produces what we might call a "Torah society," a formally voluntary network of religious culture, learning, and practice. The normative claims of this network are felt to have clear priority over those of the larger society or of the state, which are seen as wholly external. Allegiance to this "civil society" is potentially detrimental to the development of a civic spirit with respect to the state or to fellow citizens. Of course, this need not be so; in certain traditional circles, a duty of loyalty to the state has been posited and promoted in the internal terms of traditional halakhic discourse. But unless this is expressly worked out, the state will tend to be regarded with indifference, at best, and with a cynical, exploitative attitude, at worst.

Such an attitude, where prevalent, can produce sharp conflicts. In contemporary Israel, advocates of nascent notions of citizenship find themselves in bitter confrontation with many adherents of Torah society. The main contested issues are, first, massive state support for those engaged in Torah study and, second, a perception of double loyalty. Members of the "Torah society" are perceived—often rightly—as being more loyal to the claims of that society than to those of the state as a whole.

Moreover, the question of loyalty arises poignantly in the context of the Israeli educational system. Israel's system of public education is in principle pluralistic: the Ministry of Education operates several so-called streams. In addition to the "general" stream, these include, for example, the Arabic school system and a religious-Zionist system.[21] The latter is distinguished from the schools of the non-Zionist ultra-Orthodox. The ultra-Orthodox educational arrangements are themselves quite varied, ranging from complete separatists who refuse all state funding and are completely free from any state supervision, to so-called "recognized" schools, which the state partly funds, requiring in return that certain subjects (such as arithmetic) be taught in addition to Torah study. In recent years, the Ministry of Education has also listed an officially sanctioned class of "nonrecognized" schools, which get state funding with virtually no supervision.

The sources of conflict lie not only in what the non-Zionist schools do not teach—for example, history or civics courses—but in what they do teach: a fundamental allegiance to Torah and to rabbinic leaders rather than to the state or its laws. Admittedly, allegiance to Torah is also taught in the religious-Zionist schools; but in the past, this was perceived as nonproblematic, as their ideology has always held the state and its authority in positive regard. In the 1980s and 1990s, however, religious Zionist ideology commonly took a radical bent, strongly opposing any withdrawal from the territories conquered in 1967. In the context of political negotiations over prospective withdrawals, students and graduates of this stream often experience an intense internal struggle between the two commitments that they internalized without realizing their potential for coming into conflict. Their revered rabbis might pronounce a particular government policy illegitimate—without denying that, in principle, the halakhah itself requires also obedience to state authority.

For the non-Zionist groups, there is much less of an internal conflict: subject to considerations of prudence, their ideology clearly places rabbinic authority above whatever authority (if any) is accorded to the state's laws or officers. The conflict for them, then, is external; and for the state, the question is, arguably, not only whether to continue to fund schools fostering such ideology, but whether to tolerate them altogether.

I began this chapter by noting the three distinct phases of Jewish history. It seems fair to say that the condition of exile has not only been the longest, but has also had a formative effect with regard to the state/civil society dichotomy. In a crucial sense, Jewish experience is that of a society striving (often with difficulty and tension) to maintain its integrity as distinct from the surrounding political domain. Hence the essential challenge to this tradition in the modern setting is this: To what extent can a Jewish perspective embrace the vision of a full-blown state, transcending the particular interests of a defined religious community?

NOTES

1. Suzanne Stone's essay, in an earlier volume in this series, tends to adopt this stance.

2. Since these Jews chose not come to live in the land of Israel, it may be more appropriate to describe them as "diaspora" rather than "exile"—echoing the preferred self-description of many contemporary Jews.

3. Talmudic discussions define a set of norms binding upon all humankind, akin to natural Law and called the Noahide Code. For an extensive discussion, see David Novak, *The Image of the Non-Jew in Judaism: A Historical and Constructive Study of the Noahide Laws* (New York: Edwin Mellen Press, 1983).

4. I have in mind here primarily issues of gender hierarchy, as discussed cogently by Susan Moller Okin in "Feminism and Multiculturalism: Some Tensions," *Ethics* 108 (1998): 685–701.

5. See M. Noth, *The Laws in the Pentateuch* (London: SCM Press, 1984), 14.

6. The translation here, and in most biblical citations below, is from the New JPS version, *Tanakh, The Holy Scriptures* (Philadelphia and Jerusalem: Jewish Publication Society, 1985).

7. In 2 Kings 14:6 we are told, with some admiration, of a king who actually lived up to this rule, and did not put to death the sons of those who had slain his father.

8. For an extended polemic in this spirit, see Ezek. 18:1–20.

9. This is the Jewish Publication Society (JPS) old translation (Philadelphia, 1917). Similarly, the King James version reads "one born among you"; the New JPS offers, anachronistically, I think, "The stranger who resides with you shall be to you as one of your citizens."

10. Compiled in the Galilee by Rabbi Judah the Prince around c.e. 200. An English translation by H. Danby was published by Clarendon Press, Oxford, 1933, but the text here is in my own translation.

11. Such a scenario is discussed in the Talmud, BT Bava Kama 116b.

12. A complementary compilation, redacted soon after the Mishnah in the third century. The reference here is to Tosefta Bava Metzia 11:17, 23.

13. See BT Sotah 37a-b, where this is computed to produce a staggering number of covenants.

14. See Maimonides, *The Book of Knowledge* ("MT") "Laws Concerning Idolatry," chap. 1, and *The Guide of the Perplexed*, trans. S. Pines (Chicago: University of Chicago Press, 1963), pt. 3, chapters 29ff., and particularly in explaining circumcision, 3:49 (pp. 609–10).

15. Spinoza therefore argued that after the fall of the ancient Israelite kingdom, Torah law—the law of the Jewish polity—had become obsolete. There were no more people to whom it could apply, for the Jews had, in exile, become citizens of other states. B. Spinoza, *Tractatus Theologico-Politicus*, trans. Samuel Shirley (Leiden: E. J. Brill, 1991), chap. 5.

16. The theoretical and spiritual links between the local *herem* and the powers inherent in the people as a whole are set forth in the classical medieval treatment of these matters, Nahmanides's "Mishpat ha-Herem."

17. A similar hierarchy of membership obtains in the United States. One is primarily a citizen of the United States, and by virtue of that has the right to reside in—and thus become a citizen—of any particular state.

18. A famous instance of this struggle was the 1968 Shalit case, decided in the Israeli Supreme Court; see *Select Judgments of the Supreme Court of Israel*, special vol., ed. Asher Felix Landau and Peter Elman (Jerusalem: Ministry of Justice 1971), 48–191.

19. It was recognized, however, that political necessity—"the needs of the hour"—might require temporary deviation from Torah law. Moreover, according to certain prominent medieval halakhists (e.g., Rabbis Solomon ibn Adret and Nissim Gerondi), mundane legislation must quite generally leave aside the utopian requirements of talmudic law, especially in the realm of criminal justice (and cf. the discussion of "the law of the kingdom" above).

20. See Maimonides's formulation in MT, "Laws Concerning Kings" 3:9.

21. The adjective I rendered "general" is actually *mamlakhti*, a term harking back to the state's first prime minister, David Ben-Gurion. A central theme of Ben-Gurion's ideology, the word suggests a civic consciousness or public-spiritedness grounded in the commitment of citizens to the state. It is used also in the caption of the religious-Zionist section of the public education system, called *mamlakhti-dati*.

Response to Noam Zohar

David Biale

THE RELATIONSHIP between state and civil society in the Jewish tradition is complicated by the factors that make Jewish history in many ways unique. Like Islam, the Jewish tradition is political in nature: its laws are intended to be the laws of the state. On the other hand, since Jews did not possess a state for most of their history, the political character of the tradition was necessarily circumscribed. As Noam Zohar argues in his excellent excursus, the semiautonomous communities in which Jews lived as early as the Greco-Roman Diaspora up until the nineteenth century combined many of the features of a quasi state with features of voluntary communities. The modern state of Israel, which represents an unprecedented development, is riven by tensions that derive from this twofold, contradictory character of Jewish political history.

There is, however, an inherent problem in trying to locate categories like "the state," "citizenship," and "civil society" in historically remote contexts. The very concept of a civil society—a realm of voluntary, noncoercive associations made up of individuals and distinct from the state—is the creation of modern political theory; put differently, it is the rise of the modern state that generated civil society. As Zohar notes, the regnant political concept in the Jewish tradition is not citizenship, but the covenant with God that constitutes the "community of Israel" (*knesset yisrael*). Although the sources at times seem to recognize the autonomous status of the individual, as in Zohar's example of when a person becomes a "townsman," the individual is most commonly defined as a member of a collectivity that in turn is defined by its covenantal relationship to God. Thus, the premise of modern political theory that the state is created by a compact of individuals comprising civil society reverses the fundamental premise of the Jewish tradition according to which it is the collective that defines the individual. In this regard, the Jewish tradition does not dramatically differ from other premodern political theories. For all of these, the source of an individual's identity was his or her corporate, tribal, or familial affiliation, even if these affiliations were not described in the religious language of covenant. It is evident that a "civil society" consisting of voluntary associations is utterly foreign to such a theory, as is the social contract as the source of the state.

Thus, the difficulty with Zohar's argument lies in applying categories from modern political theory to historically anachronistic cases. Several examples, taken from Zohar's chapter, will illustrate my point. Zohar characterizes the period of the Judges as "civil society without a state" and as a condition of "(religious) anarchism." But, in fact, the charismatic system of leadership constituted something like a state (although not in the modern sense), or at least like a form of tribal governance. Moreover, the early kings of Israel (Saul and David) were themselves charismatic judges as much as kings. The two categories overlap, and it was only the redactors of the biblical texts who tried to make them completely distinct: thus, the statement in Judges 21:25 that "in those days there was no king in Israel; everyone did what he pleased" is the ideological judgment of an editor from the Davidic court who wished to justify the system of monarchy against its predecessor. We cannot presume to learn anything historical from this statement about the true nature of politics in the period of the Judges. But in neither the period of Judges or of Kings can one speak of civil society as we understand it.

Zohar is quite correct in identifying a kind of oppositional strain— from the biblical prophets to the Second-Temple Zealots—to the power of the state. This tradition is based on the notion of the Torah as potentially superior to the law of the state. Yet this opposition comes from a messianic perspective: only in the end of time will the Torah become the fully realized law of the state. The degree to which one might oppose the state in favor of the Torah typically hinged on whether one believed the *eschaton* to be imminent. It was their apocalyptic mentality rather than some fundamentally anarchistic impulse that explains the Zealots' opposition to the Romans in the first century of the common era. In any case, it must be emphasized that this messianic stance has nothing to do with choosing civil society over the state.

A second example is medieval associations such as the burial society (*hevre kadisha*), which Zohar characterizes as "elements of civil society." But here, too, the categories are fuzzier. In some communities, such as Prague, the burial society sometimes assumed many of the functions of the communal government, such as the giving of charity. Communal governments (the so-called *kehillah*), whose powers were sanctioned by the non-Jewish state, often look to modern eyes like voluntary associations of the wealthy. In fact, they functioned as semiautonomous, quasi governments in political entities in which power was not centralized. The self-governing Jewish communities were neither states in the modern sense nor were they voluntary associations. For the Middle Ages in general—and not only for the Jews—the diffusion of power among many "corporations" makes it harder to speak of a sharp dichotomy between "state" and "society." The categories themselves do not work.

This kind of fluidity of (modern) categories applies to concepts of citizenship as well. The Bible itself insists on the same law for the *ger* (resident alien) and the *ezrah* (native), as Zohar points out. But the very categories remain substantially unclear, as one example will demonstrate: Uriah the Hittite, a general in David's army, who was married to an Israelite, Bathsheba. Was David's Hittite general a citizen or an alien? Was his marriage an intermarriage (a violation of Deut. 7)? And what are we to make of his name, which suggests that he was a worshiper of the Israelite god? Is this an ancient case of citizenship encompassing several ethnic groups, or was identity understood very differently than in modern terms?

Zohar suggests that the Torah was understood to be a kind of ideal constitution. This contention is definitely borne out for certain thinkers. Moses Maimonides, for example, evidently understood the Davidic kings as something like constitutional monarchs, since their actions were constrained by a divine law. Maimonides distinguished the Davidic kings from the Hasmonean kings, whom he treated as absolute monarchs beholden to no higher law. In this sense, a "theological" regime based on the Torah would be far more constricted than a "secular" regime. Yet, not all traditional Jewish commentators have necessarily understood the Torah to have this political meaning. For example, the contemporary Orthodox Jewish philosopher Yeshayahu Leibowitz adamantly denied that the Torah ought to be used as a political blueprint.

The doctrine that "the law of the Kingdom is the law" was originally circumscribed to the right of the non-Jewish state to levy taxes on the Jews. By the Middle Ages, the dictum had become the foundation of a political theory in which the Jews might justify in their own legal terms their status as a minority community and that would explain the division of political power between the Jewish community and the Gentile state. In modern times, certain Reformers took the doctrine to an unintended extreme: the non-Jewish state ought to possess full political and legal authority, and the Jewish community ought to exercise none at all. This new stance reflected the attempt by these critics of the medieval Jewish community to dismantle what they regarded as a "state within the state." Note, however, that "the state within the state" formulation does not recognize the medieval Jewish community as a voluntary association or as composed of voluntary associations. This very category of civil society did not exist and, indeed, it might be argued that the Reformers were trying to introduce it.

Curiously enough, certain Orthodox authorities in modern times have themselves adopted the dictum that "the law of the Kingdom is the law" to turn the Torah into the codebook for a purely voluntary Jewish association within the non-Jewish state. Faced with the loss of communal authority, some Orthodox sought to salvage a measure of power by embracing the new realm of civil society.

It is in the state of Israel that these shifting relationships between the Jewish community and the state took an entirely different turn. In the earlier years of the state of Israel, most Orthodox Jews such as the Agudat Yisrael (the ultra-Orthodox political party formed in 1912) understood the state in the same terms as a non-Jewish state: its law was the law. In recent years, though, another point of view has emerged, which seeks to turn the state of Israel into a theocracy with the Torah as its constitution. The phenomenon that Zohar mentions of Orthodox Jews threatening to disobey the laws of the state in favor of "higher" laws is curiously only to be found in Israel and not in any of the other, non-Jewish countries in which Orthodox Jews live. Only in Israel, it would seem, do some Orthodox Jews refuse to accept the dictum "the law of the Kingdom is the law." Precisely because Israel defines itself as a Jewish state, the categories that the legal tradition developed over centuries to regulate relations between Jewish communities and the non-Jewish state no longer seem to apply.

Israel has, in fact, become the battleground for conflicting ideas about the relationship between religion and state, perhaps more than any other country in the democratic world (Turkey is another case that comes to mind). Medieval concepts of empowered corporations compete with modern concepts of civil society. On the one hand, religion in Israel has the status that it inherited from the Ottoman Empire in governing personal status (marriage, divorce, and inheritance). On the other hand, since Israel is a democracy, with all power residing in the legislature, this status was conferred on religious authorities by an act of a secular parliament. So those who argue for the Torah as the constitution of the state and who wish to redefine the source of the state's legitimacy must do so using the instruments of democracy. Religious parties and institutions in Israel therefore function at once as part of civil society and as competitors for and beneficiaries of state power. Biblical models appear utterly irrelevant to the present reality, for nowhere can we find there either modern notions of democracy or of civil society. Neither are medieval models particularly useful, since they are drawn from quasi-autonomous minority communities rather than from a state in which Jews held political power. It is therefore both this confusion of categories and the lack of real historical precedents that suggest the great difficulties that Israel has experienced and will no doubt continue to experience in creating the autonomous civil society that most liberal theorists would argue is necessary for a healthy democracy.

Civil Society and Government in Islam

John Kelsay

A FEW COMMENTS on terms seem appropriate. Thus, *civil society*, as seen throughout the essays in this volume, can mean many things. One way to summarize involves tying the term to a specific set of institutions or organizations that are held to "mediate" between private and public life. Churches and synagogues fit, as do labor unions, political parties, and such associations as the People for the American Way, the ACLU, the Rotary Clubs, and the National Organization for Women. For those influenced by Hegel, in particular, organizations like these are critical for the development of the type of people who can participate as full citizens in the political life of a modern state. They "mediate," in the sense that taking part in them helps people to develop loyalties beyond those of kinship. To put it another way, the importance of civil society is that it represents a crucial stage in the development of people who can deal with those who are different from themselves. And this is held to be crucial "practice" in anticipation of the more extensive experience of difference characteristic of the modern state.[1]

For others, influenced more by Anglo-American writers such as Locke, "civil society" seems largely identical with a certain kind of political or governmental regime: namely, constitutional democracy. Churches, synagogues, and the rest of the mediating institutions listed above are important in preserving a balance of power between those holding the reigns of government and ordinary citizens. To put it another way, strong mediating institutions help to keep society "civil." They give ordinary citizens a means to participate in government, as well as to check the power of more specifically governmental institutions, like the various departments that make up the federal bureaucracy. In so doing, they also help citizens to feel that they have had their say. The hope is that in allowing people to express themselves or in providing a balance to governmental power, the issues that (in noncivil societies) give rise to violence may be dealt with. Give people freedom, tolerate different points of view, allow a wide set of opportunities for participation in social life, and thereby limit the tendencies of government toward authoritarianism and of disenfranchised citizens toward sectarian strife—this is the basic idea of the Lockean tradition on civil society.[2]

In contemporary Islamic discussion, those who speak most about civil society do so in ways that resonate with aspects of both Hegelian and Lockean traditions. Yet there are important differences. Thus, President Khatami of Iran, the Egyptian sociologist Saad Eddin Ibrahim, and other Muslim intellectuals emphasize the importance of allowing certain institutions a degree of independence from state control. Free (that is, non-state-controlled) newspapers and television stations, an independent business sector, and less carefully regulated political parties all receive attention; policies that allow an increased range for freedom of speech and association are said to be important because they will increase a sense of "ownership" or participation on the part of the public. This will improve the quality of life in Muslims societies, both in the Hegelian sense of educating people for citizenship and in the Lockean sense of limiting violence, both on the part of elites with authoritarian tendencies and on the part of people who feel compelled to resist tyranny. One notes, however, that the institutions spoken about are not precisely comparable to those in our earlier list. The political contexts of discussions of civil society in contemporary Western and Islamic societies are distinct. While there are shared characteristics—for example in the focus on opportunities for activities that are sub- or nongovernmental—the emphasis of Muslims seems to be on the creation of a sphere of citizen liberty. By comparison, Europeans and North Americans seem focused on citizen participation in specific organizations.[3]

Government, by contrast, seems a less controversial term. For both Western and Muslim analysts, the term indicates the state, with its power of command and control. As Max Weber put it, the modern state is defined as that entity which has a monopoly on the use of legitimate force within a given territory.[4] For purposes of this discussion, "force" extends beyond the power to employ arms or use violence, and includes the power to punish, to tax, and to regulate the life of citizens. Muslims, along with Europeans and North Americans, can identify with this sort of understanding, as well as with the part of Weber's definition that refers to legitimacy.

Just what constitutes legitimate government, by contrast, may be a controversial point. Western analysts presume the legitimacy of constitutional democracy. Muslim advocates of civil society do so as well. The latter, however, speak within a context where a term like *democracy* has a more complicated valence. Thus, Khatami, Ibrahim, and others must respond to those who see democracy as a recipe for the elevation of (purely) human desires and understandings, and who argue that a just society is one ruled according to the "limits set by God." Properly understood, many who argue in this way end up legitimating something like democratic (in the sense of representative) government, by means of the notion of *al-shura* (consultation.)[5] There is thus room for discussion between advocates of constitutional democracy and those who speak of "Islamic government." At the same time, there are differences, most notably in the ways that the latter insist that the makeup of a consultative assembly (what a Western theorist would call a "representative assembly") as well as the process of selection (voting) must be such as to ensure that legislation is crafted in terms that satisfy the Islamic conscience. Consultation is not just a matter of the citizens of a state involved in give-and-take with respect to their various interests; it must have a moral component, which is secured by the notion that those making policy will consult sources of Islamic authority, as well as their fellow citizens.[6]

A Western advocate of constitutional democracy might well say in response that the rights of citizens rest on, and are somehow limited by, the "higher law" spoken of in Christian or natural law circles, or at least by the precedent of common law. Government in a constitutional democracy is thus not simply a matter of the whim of the majority, a fact that Khatami, among others, recognizes.[7] Nevertheless, it is worth recognizing again the distinctive contexts of Western and Islamic discussions of civil society, since they do rest on and call forth somewhat different terminology.

Thus, finally, *Islam*, which my comments on the relationship between Khatami, Ibrahim, and others already suggest, will be a controversial term. I do not say this lightly, for there are certain references that are, for purposes of this essay, more or less constitutive of any "Islamic" perspective on civil society and government. But the meaning or, perhaps better, the interpretation of those references with respect to this topic is clearly a matter of discussion; of this we must take note. Arguments among contemporary Muslims are often cast in terms of the positions of "reformists" (for example, Khatami and Ibrahim) and "revivalists" (like the critics of democracy mentioned above.) Whether such terms are entirely apt is not our concern at the moment; the point is that "Islam" can be taken to indicate a wide variety of judgments about contemporary political practice. Similarly, the term is utilized to identify expressions of political thought that occur in widely disparate historic and geographic contexts. Thus, for example, the terms "Western" and "Islamic" are utilized above to identify two comparable, though distinctive, conversations about civil society and government. In connection with the examples of Khatami (Iran) and Ibrahim (Egypt), these terms serve a useful purpose, particularly as we try to understand some of their particular emphases. Just how the ideas of these two figures relate to the conversations of Muslims in earlier periods or to the judgments of Muslims living in

Europe and North America (and who thus might be considered as participants in the "Western" discussion of civil society) is not an easy matter
to adjudicate. And this is not even to mention questions about the role of
different schools of thought or modes of political conversation within
Islam.[8] Each of these has its own integrity and, depending on which
group of Muslims one is talking about, might be considered "primary."

That said, there are certain sources and themes that are basic to any
presentation of Islamic political thought. I begin with an overview of
some of these, before proceeding to a discussion of specific issues regarding civil society and government.

THE EXAMPLE OF THE PROPHET

Our presentation of Islamic political thought can begin with the example of Muhammad, the Prophet of God.[9] Born circa C.E. 570, Muhammad came to adulthood in the context of a tribal society characterized by
the politics of clan loyalty. His particular clan, al-Quraysh, enjoyed
prominence in Mecca, one of the few urban areas in the Arabian peninsula. In the late-sixth century, Mecca (and thus, the Quraysh clan) knew
increased prosperity as a primary stop for caravans transporting goods
between the old cities of Syro-Palestine and the Arabian Sea (and, from
there, to India.) With increased prosperity came increased status, or at
least the ambition for it; Mecca was the site of an ancient shrine known
as the Ka'ba, and the Quraysh sought to use it, along with the attraction
of trade, to achieve greater cooperation between the disparate tribes of
the peninsula. The notion of a *hajj*, or "pilgrimage," to the Ka'ba in
honor of ancestral deities may have been quite old. For Muhammad's
story, however, it is important only that the Quraysh seem to have per-
suaded at least some of the tribes to observe an annual truce, four
months during which there was to be no fighting, with the correlative
purpose of encouraging the tribes to make the pilgrimage. There, they
would trade—primarily commercial goods, or so we presume, but also
(and rather naturally) in the sorts of things that encourage people to
think cooperatively. The pilgrimage months seem to have become a kind
of large commercial and cultural festival, with the Quraysh as sponsors
and hosts. For the Quraysh, at least, it seems appropriate to consider
the observance as an expression of pantribal or, if one likes, of Arab
consciousness.

There are stories about Muhammad from this period, which are told
in pious biography as a way of showing that he was chosen by God all
along, prepared for the great work he was to do. Those are worth telling,
however, only in the light of what happened during the first third of the
seventh century. According to tradition, in the year 610, Muhammad

understood himself as called to prophecy. Within a few years, he gathered a small band of followers among the residents of Mecca, and gained enough attention that some of the more prominent members of Quraysh sought to counter the new movement, using economic boycotts, acts of torture, and other forms of persecution. Eventually, in the series of events Muslims call the *hijra*, or "migration," Muhammad moved his community to Medina, a city some distance to the north. From this new location, the Prophet led the Muslims in a campaign by which he sought to unite the various Arab tribes, including Quraysh, into a new social entity—an *umma*—which would not only express, but would carry on his sense of mission. By the time of his death, in 632, Muhammad's campaign, which included what we would call diplomatic and military initiatives as well as preaching, succeeded so thoroughly that tradition has him proclaim that "Arabia is solidly for Islam." As the reader is to understand, all the peninsula, and thus all the tribes residing there, were now united under the banner of Islam.

There are important issues for historical-critical understanding of this "founding" narrative. Those are, however, not the point in the current context. Rather, the interesting point to note is the way the Prophet's career encompasses both religious and political leadership. In an oft-repeated phrase, Muslims speak of religion and politics (Arabic *din wa dunya*) as "twins." While the phrase shows the influence of other, surrounding cultures (for example, the Byzantine and Sassanid), many Muslims have also thought of it in connection with Muhammad's life.[10] The Prophet called human beings to faith by means of "beautiful preaching."[11] He also pursued the cause of Islam by means of statecraft, including warfare. Why the Prophet practiced both religion and statecraft is an important question. Some, noting that traditional accounts stress that the latter only begins with the migration to Medina, argue that politics, in particular warfare, is a secondary and derivative aspect of Muhammad's ministry. He becomes a statesman, in other words, under duress, as indicated in the words of Qur'an 22:39–40:

> To those against whom war is made, permission is given to fight, because they are oppressed. Truly, God is most powerful in their cause. Those who have been expelled from their homes in defiance of right, without cause except that they say "God is our Lord." If God did not check one set of people by means of another, then monasteries, churches, synagogues, and mosques in which the name of God is often commemorated would be pulled down. God will help those who help God. Truly God is full of strength, exalted in might.

According to the oldest extant biography of the Prophet, these verses, revealed at the time of the hijra, constitute the first time Muhammad was given an order to fight.[12] And thus some, as indicated, take it that politics is something Muhammad was forced to. The military and diplomatic initiatives of Medina are tactics to which the Prophet had to resort in order to provide security for his fledgling and oppressed community.

Other interpreters, while agreeing that resort to war was a kind of last resort for the Prophet, argue that it was nevertheless a means to what he had in mind all along. In other words, preaching in Mecca and warfare in Medina were both politically oriented activities. While no one should make the mistake of believing that the submission achieved by means of statecraft is equivalent to faith (so this line of thinking goes), it is an important way of spreading the influence of Islam or, to speak in terms of the Qur'an, to "make God's cause succeed."

Thus, if Muhammad's example supports the notion that religion and politics are twins, it does not negate the space between the two. To put it another way, one may speak here of a prominent example of what I shall be calling throughout the *complementarity thesis*—namely, the idea that religion and politics or, more properly, religious and political institutions play complementary roles in the pursuit of human welfare. Complementarity does not indicate identity, however. Indeed, it sets up a certain set of tensions, as the human beings engaged with each type of institution attempt to carry out their assigned tasks. Just where are the limits of religious authority? Of political? These are questions to which I shall return.

For now, one should simply note the example of the Prophet as religious leader and statesman. In the end, Muhammad built a community that challenged the system of clan loyalty characteristic of pre-Islamic Arabia. The solidarity of the umma would lie not in the blood loyalties of kinship, but in the members' consciousness that they were, before all else, Muslims—people characterized by submission to the one true God. As the Qur'an has it,

> O believers! Have regard for God, with true piety, and do not die except as Muslims. Hold together, by the rope of God; do not be divided. Remember God's favor to you, how you were enemies, but God put love between your hearts. By God's graciousness, you became brothers. You were on the brink of destruction, when God rescued you. Even so the signs of God are clear for you, that you should be rightly guided. From you, let there come a community, calling to the good, commanding what is plainly right, forbidding what is plainly wrong. These are the ones who will find happiness. Don't be like those who are divided, or differ after receiving clear signs. Theirs is a dreadful punishment.
>
> On the day that some faces are made bright, while others will be cast down, and the downcast are asked "Did you act as ingrates, after faith came to you? Taste the punishment for ingratitude."

Those whose faces are made bright receive God's mercy, and enjoy it forever.

These are signs from God, brought to you in the cause of truth. God does not will harm to any rational being.

To God belongs everything in the heavens and the earth; and their works return to God. You are a good community, called out from humankind. You command the good; you forbid the evil. You trust in God. (3:102–10)

CLASSICAL ISLAM

The community established by Muhammad soon became a force to reckon with. Following the Prophet's death, the Muslims became a conquering army, making Islam the dominant political reality throughout Egypt, Syro-Palestine, the Iraq, and Iran by 661.[13] And this was only the beginning. As the center of the empire moved, first to Damascus, where the Umayyads held sway from 680 to the 740s, then to Baghdad, where the Abbasid caliphs ruled for nearly five centuries, Islam became the established religion of an imperial state of world significance.[14]

In this setting, Muslims developed types of political practice that may be regarded as "classical," in the sense of establishing precedents that carry a continuing weight. For our interests, the most important of these precedents have to do with working out a version of the complementary relation of religion and politics that establishes a relative independence on the part of two sets of institutions. The one, standing for the independence of religious practice, was constituted by a class of religious specialists known as ʿulama (knowers.) Recognized, as the name implies, for their expertise in the interpretation of certain agreed-upon sources (in particular, the Qur'an, but also of *ahadith*, "reports" of the example of the Prophet), these specialists carried the power to "bind and loose" with respect to the Islamic legitimacy of rulers, government policies, and the answer to such questions as Who is a true Muslim? Their power, which was intrinsically moral, rested in their knowledge—not in their political expertise or their military capacity. Through the associated institutions of the *masjid* (mosque, place of communal gathering), the *madrasa* (religious school), and eventually the *jamiat* (university), the ʿulama established a kind of sphere of influence, politically relevant but not quite "governmental," that limited the power of government officials. *To my mind, this sphere represents the closest analogy in classical Islam to "civil society."* It is aimed, that is, at providing and protecting an institutional setting for citizen expression regarding social and political, as well as religious, affairs. This setting is not identical with that of "government," though it can have an impact on policy, and is thus of interest to government officials. It acts as a kind of protection for the expression of dissent, in a manner reminiscent of the Lockean tradition; at the same time, it helps citizens move out of the sphere of familial relations and establish a set of broader loyalties, as in the Hegelian tradition.

"Government" is correspondingly represented by officials involved in a second set of institutions, the foremost of which was the *khilafat* (caliphate.) By this term, which carries the meaning of "successor," rulers of the Muslim empire established continuity with the example of the Prophet. And, in the manner of rulers throughout the ancient world, those who exercised power in Islam often employed the trappings of religion. The holders of the caliphate, in other words, sometimes led prayers at the great mosques of Damascus or Baghdad. They, or their representatives, might preach from the pulpit of the mosque. They gave financial support to those 'ulama who pleased them and withheld it from those who did not. But when it came to the presumption of legitimacy in knowing the sources of Islam, the caliphs, whether Umayyad or Abbasid (or, in later periods, Ottomans, Safavids, or Moghuls), simply could not compete with the 'ulama. The role of the caliph, as "commander of the faithful," was to preserve and protect the security of the Islamic state. It was his duty to defend and, if possible, to extend the borders of Islam; to maintain the peace of the empire; and to collect taxes and administer the worldly affairs of state in a just manner. Through such governmental institutions as the army, the courts, and the bureaucracy associated with a courtly culture, the caliphs carried on the traditions of Islamic statecraft (they hoped) with the blessings of the 'ulama.

To illustrate something of the way this worked, consider the example of Abbasid policy under the great al-Ma'mun, who held power from 809 to 833.[15] The Abbasids came to power in the 740s, as the result of an uprising against the Umayyad dynasty. One feature of the Abbasid triumph had been their ability to marshal support from a number of pious groups. Abbasid propaganda included promises to rule "by the book of God" (the Qur'an.) Numerous groups, most of which featured prominently one or more persons with the religious expertise of the 'ulama, responded to these promises. Perhaps inevitably, most of the groups in question were disappointed to find that whatever the Abbasid propagandists meant by government "by the book of God," it did not precisely correspond to the understanding of their featured 'ulama.

Correspondingly, Abbasid rulers always worried about the tendencies toward sectarianism within their religious support. Al-Ma'mun, who seems to have been a pious and learned ruler, sought in several ways to deal with this. In 817, for example, he floated publicly the suggestion that 'Ali al-Rida, a leader in Shi'i circles, might rule as successor to al-Ma'mun.[16] The experiment came to nothing when al-Rida died the following year.

Most notably, however, al-Maʿmun decided to regulate the teaching of the ʿulama. In the 820s, following the doctrine of certain Muʿtazili scholars prominent in his court, the caliph declared that all ʿulama should give answer to a question about the nature of the Qurʾan—was it created or not? The answer al-Maʿmun wanted was "created."

The precise theological import of this question need not concern us at the moment; for our purposes, al-Maʿmun's "test" or "inquisition" is an important experiment in the relationship of religious and political institutions in Islam. Extant sources tell us that most of the ʿulama yielded to al-Maʿmun's pressure, affirming that the Qurʾan was indeed created. The most outstanding exception was Ahmad ibn Hanbal, a scholar particularly noted for his knowledge of reports of the Prophet's example, and thus a fine example of the basis of the authority of the ʿulama. Ahmad, we are told, was noteworthy for his insistence on financial independence from the caliph's court. He would not take governmental stipends, and criticized scholars who did. He also, in the instance at hand, became notable for his insistence that al-Maʿmun's test went beyond the rights of a Muslim ruler. From all one can tell, Ahmad probably believed the Qurʾan was uncreated. But his public response to the inquisitors seems simply to have been that they had no right to ask the question. The Prophet had never inquired of anyone about the nature of the Qurʾan; there was no hadith concerning it. Thus, the nature of the Qurʾan was a matter on which the Muslim conscience should be regarded as free.

Now, Ahmad was known as one who stressed respect for government; as I shall indicate below, the general tendency of classical Islam was against revolution, even in the case of an unjust ruler. In a manner consistent with this, his resistance to the inquisition was purely moral. Ahmad gave answers when asked; he accepted imprisonment; finally, he submitted to a public beating. When this led to popular unrest, the architects of the inquisition ceased; Ahmad was eventually released and, in an ironic twist, one of al-Maʿmun's successors (al-Mutawakkil, ruled 847–61) reversed his predecessor's policies and tried to secure Ahmad ibn Hanbal's public support. From what we know, it appears the scholar, quite old by this time, refused to give his support or even to take a stipend from the court, eventually dying in poverty.

Ahmad's example is particularly outstanding in terms of a scholar maintaining a certain independence for the religious in relation to the political. But the principle holds. In classical Islam, as in the example of the Prophet, religion and politics are to complement one another. To exist in complementary relation, however, does not suggest identity. And, particularly once Islam became identified with a large, diverse imperial state, it was rather natural that there be a kind of unpredictability about the relationship of the guardians of the message and the guardians of the borders of the territory of Islam. To restate the judgment above: to my mind, the ʿulama, with their associated institutions of mosque, school, and university, present the closest classical analogue to civil society. In thinking of an Islamic perspective on civil society and government, then, we should think about the relations between ʿulama and khilafat.

MODERN ISLAM

As one moves to more contemporary examples, the first thing to be noted is the falling away of the imperial state. Following the demise of the Abbasid caliphate in 1258, Islamic political power was divided between three great dynasties: the Ottomans, who from Istanbul ruled over south-central Europe, the Middle East, and North Africa; the Safavids (followed by the Qajars), who ruled in Iran; and the Moghuls, who held sway in the Indian subcontinent (inclusive of what we call Pakistan, Bangladesh, Bengal, and parts of Afghanistan, as well as of India.) By the end of the First World War, only the Ottomans survived; within five years after the war, they too were gone.[17]

The abolition of the Ottoman caliphate created something of a crisis for Muslim political thought.[18] Some used the opportunity to wonder whether Islam, as a religious tradition, needed the institution of khilafat at all. The Egyptian ʿAli ʿabd al-Raziq, for example, presented a fascinating argument about religion and politics in Islam, focusing on the uniqueness of the authority exercised by the Prophet. Muhammad, al-Raziq argued, did not so much "combine" the roles of prophet and statesman as he exercised fully the role of prophet. Muhammad's prophetic authority did not so much combine or complement his statecraft as subsume it. Politics, or better, government, is natural to human beings, who need social order to survive. Religion is something more, something beyond politics. Only a prophet can exercise political *and* religious authority. The danger of the classical institution of khilafat, with its religious trappings, was always that it would exceed its proper boundaries, as the example of al-Maʿmun shows. Better to let religion (with the ʿulama) be religion, and government be government, in whatever form.[19]

Al-Raziq was too radical for most. And thus, contemporary Islamic political thought continues to reach for a complementary relation between religion and government, ʿulama and khilafat, with the latter now understood to include constitutional regimes, elected parliaments, an independent judiciary, and the like. The ʿulama, with their power to bind and loose, still provide an entree into civil society in Muslim societies; they represent the dynamic, associational power of religion, and understand themselves as dedicated to the preservation of an Islam that cannot be simply identified with any existing governmental regime. Even the insistent calls of revivalists for Islamic government are often best understood in this light. The idea of the late Ayatollah Khomeini, for example, seems to have been that the record of modern Iranian governments was so dominated by attempts to usurp the proper authority of the ʿulama that the religious specialists would have to take a place within government in order to protect the independence of Islam. In the attempt to maintain complementarity, Khomeini and other revivalists "fudge" the civil society/government relation one way, in order to limit the power of overweaning government.[20]

In modern settings, of course, the ʿulama cannot be identified simply as the whole of civil society. We do have to deal with the concerns of reformers like President Khatami and Saad Eddin Ibrahim. Despite Khatami's strong identification with the ʿulama, calls for strengthening the independence of the press and, more generally, for greater freedom of association and speech might be understood as a way of creating an independent sphere for a new class of people, who judge that their interests and their understanding of Islam are not entirely represented by either existing governments or by the ʿulama. Particularly in Iran, a relatively well educated, highly motivated business and professional class, inclusive of many women as well as men, appears to be reaching for a sphere in which liberty is regulated by neither centralized political nor religious authorities. What this will yield is impossible to predict. One can only note that with respect to this class of people, the relationship of civil society and government in Islam seems an open question.

I now turn to specific issues in the civil society/government relationship.

BOUNDARIES

Islam's emphasis on the complementarity of religion and politics creates a number of possibilities for the relationship between the religious community and state authorities; or more generally, between civil society and government. ʿUlama and khilafat share in a common task, to make God's cause succeed, or to bring about justice in the earth.

I have already suggested that such complementarity does not rule out distinctions in roles; neither should it obscure the fact of recognizable boundaries between the religious community and the state. In particular instances, such boundaries were and are well noted. The state thus has the task of regulating behavior with respect to military and police force; the religious community, with its scholars operating through the associated institutions of mosque and school, has the task of rendering normative judgments about the state's fulfillment of this task. The state, to take another case, has the task of collecting taxes and distributing funds. The religious community passes judgment as to which taxes can be collected and as to whether funds are distributed in accord with Islamic values.

An important test case of such boundaries lies in the duties Muslims are said to have toward their rulers. The following are examples of standard ahadith on the duty to obey the caliph.[21]

Abu Huraira reported God's messenger as saying, "He who obeys me has obeyed God and he who disobeys me has disobeyed God; he who obeys the commander has obeyed me and he who disobeys the commander has disobeyed me. The imam is only a shield behind whom fighting is engaged in and by whom protection is sought; so if he commands piety and acts justly he will have a reward for that, but if he holds another view he will on that account be guilty."

Ibn Umar reported God's messenger as saying, "Hearing and obeying are the duty of a Muslim both regarding what he likes and what he dislikes, as long as he is not commanded to perform an act of disobedience to God, in which case he must neither hear nor obey."

Ibn Abbas reported God's messenger as saying, "If anyone sees in his commander what he dislikes he should show patience, for no one separates from the community and dies without dying like those of pre-Islamic times."

Auf b. Malik al-Ashja'i reported God's messenger as saying, "Your best imams are those whom you like and who like you, on whom you invoke blessings and who invoke blessings on you; and your worst imams are those whom you hate and who hate you, whom you curse and who curse you." They asked God's messenger whether in that event they should not depose them, but he replied, "No, as long as they observe the prayer among you; no, as long as they observe the prayer among you. If anyone has a governor whom he sees doing anything which is an act of disobedience to God, he must disapprove of the disobedience to God which he commits, but must never withdraw from obedience."

The list goes on. Clearly, the idea is that political authority is important to the welfare of the religious community, and is to be respected. One might even say that the duty to respect goes in the direction of forbidding more extreme forms of resistance, as, for example, in the case of revolution or an attempt to depose existing authority. But there is, just as clearly, a delimitation on the authority of rulers. They are primarily "a shield behind whom fighting is engaged in and protection is sought." They are to be obeyed, though one must disapprove of any actions or policies that fall short of God's design. And indeed, further ahadith recommend disobedience and attempts to correct political authority when its departure from God's purpose is severe enough. Thus,

An-Nawwas b. Sam'an reported God's messenger as saying, "A creature is not to be obeyed when it involves disobedience to the Creator."

[Abu Sa'id] reported God's messenger as saying, "The most excellent jihad is when one speaks a true word in the presence of a tyrannical ruler."[22]

Now, it is clear, as previously indicated, that the tendency of classical Islamic political thought presents a picture of rule by one person (some ahadith, in fact, stress that rule should reside in one person, and that if a second presents himself as a candidate, one of the two should be killed!) and of a religious community that considers itself as obligated to respect the "powers that be," at least in the sense that one rarely finds texts that would support a right to armed revolt. In al-Mawardi and other writers, one finds the saying that "a thousand years of tyranny are better than one night of anarchy"; obviously, there was a great worry about the harmful potential of revolutionary activity.[23]

Such a picture should not suggest, however, that opposition was impossible, or that the distinction of roles for the religious and political arms of society is collapsed. Nor can the emphasis on rule by one person (or, more realistically, by a courtly culture having one person standing as the symbol of power) be understood as "Islamic," in any simple sense, given the predominance of imperial models in the world of the sixth through the twelveth centuries. In a more contemporary setting, we find different patterns of political thought emerging, partly as a result of the collapse of the imperial state. For example, both the constitutions of the Islamic Republic of Iran and of Pakistan stipulate the requirement of an elected legislature. The legislature or "consultative assembly" is understood to fulfill the requirement that leadership should be a matter of consultation—in some sense, in both cases, this consultation is understood to include all those living within the boundaries of the state, although the process is decisively weighted toward Muslims. The constitution of the Islamic Republic of Iran understands itself to establish a set of checks and balances between the religious community and political leaders. While its emphasis on the role of religious leaders in supervising elections, legislation, and ultimately all matters of public policy suggests that the balance of power is thrown toward the religious, it is clear from the history of revolutionary Iran that the intent of the framers (in particular, the late Ayatollah Khomeini) was to safeguard the independence of the religious community, and to limit what was understood to be over-reaching by the late shah of Iran or, more generally, by the political leaders of most states. The religious leadership, which is represented first in the person of the "supreme leader" (a religious scholar chosen for excellence in knowledge of Islamic sources, for piety, and for the ability to practice justice), has ultimate oversight in all matters of policy. Together with the supreme leader, a council of guardians, made up of a dozen religious specialists (half chosen by the supreme leader and half by the consultative assembly), effectively carries out the role envisioned in classical thinking for the ʿulama (the power to bind and loose). A president elected by popular vote is able to appoint ministers and, with them, to run the day-to-day affairs of the state, given the supervision of the religious leaders. Constitutionally, at least, the balance of powers is protected by provisions for a free press and other communications or information media, by the delineation of certain sectors of the economy as "public" (owned by the state), "cooperative" (mixed public/private ownership), and "private" (particularly in the area of agriculture), and by the stipulation that everyone, including the supreme leader, is understood to stand in equal relationship before the law. Boundaries are drawn between civil society and government, with the common limitation being the law recognized as the standard for all normative discourse, political or otherwise:

> All civil, penal, financial, economic, administrative, cultural, military, political, and other laws and regulations must be based on Islamic criteria. This principle applies absolutely and generally to all articles of the Constitution as well as to all other laws and regulations, and the religious scholars of the Guardian Council are judges in this matter. (Article 4)[24]

NEEDS

For the classical period, the relations outlined above indicate the general ways in which civil society and government "need" each other. Roughly, the 'ulama lend legitimacy to the caliphate; the caliphate employs legitimate force to protect the independent practice of Islam. Even the duty of the caliphate to call on the people and to carry out the duty of jihad on the "frontiers" of Islamic territory can be seen in this light. The notion of the extension and protection of the borders of the imperial territory known as the territory of Islam should be seen as part of a program to extend and protect the influence of Islamic values in the world, and thus "to make God's cause succeed." The task of the government, working in support of the 'ulama, was to extend the realm within which Islam's influence as the "state religion" could be established. The task of the 'ulama, working with the support of the government, was to spread the message of Islam through "beautiful preaching" or, more prosaically, to convert the hearts of the conquered to Islam. Each institution needs the other; thus the complementarity of civil society and government.

With the demise of imperial Islam, the principle of complementarity is extended, as indicated above, more and more in the direction of participatory democracy: Extended—but not negated. Thus, the constitution of the Islamic Republic continues to see all as united by the notion of God's law.

> In the Islamic republic of Iran, the commanding of the good and the forbidding of the evil is a universal and reciprocal duty that must be fulfilled by the

people with respect to one another, by the government with respect to the people, and by the people with respect to the government. The conditions, limits, and nature of this duty will be specified by law. (Article 8)

The government, as specified in Article 3, is to direct "all its resources" toward, among other things, "the creation of a favorable environment for the growth of moral virtues based on faith and piety and the struggle against all forms of vice and corruption." One notices, of course, that the government is not said to be responsible to secure such growth—that is a matter outside its competence, as more generally one should say about faith. But the provision of an environment where faith can take root—this is language typical of the complementary relationship envisioned in classical sources.

The government also, however, must direct "all its resources" to such goals as "raising the level of public awareness in all areas, through the proper use of the press, mass media, and other means." In connection with Article 175, which stipulates that the power to appoint and dismiss the head of the state radio and television network belongs to the supreme leader, one would be justified in reading "proper use" as opening the door to censorship. It is interesting, however, that the grammar of the article makes possible more than one reading on such a key point; thus one reads that the "freedom of expression and dissemination of thoughts in the Radio and Television of the Islamic Republic of Iran must be guaranteed in keeping with the Islamic criteria and the best interests of the country." Is it that freedom of expression and dissemination of thoughts are goods so important to the well-being of the republic that they are thought to be worthy of guaranteed protection, based on Islamic values? Or is that these are to be guaranteed, insofar as their exercise is in keeping with (that is, within the bounds of) Islamic criteria and the good of the country? If the former, we have an important contemporary expression of the value of an aspect of civil society to the exercise of good government and a recognition of the importance of an independent news media. If the latter, we have a notion that allows civil society to be collapsed or delimited, in the interests of good or effective government.

LIABILITIES

From Michael Walzer and others, one gathers that the associations covered by civil society, resting as they do on loyalties more delimited and more intense that those inspired by the state, pose a kind of sectarian problem. Government, by contrast, poses a threat to civil society, in that its monopoly on the use of legitimate force gives it a means to regulate, and even to eliminate, associations it deems threatening.[25]

One can understand, with slight alterations, much of the Islamic perspective on liabilities in the civil society/government relationship through Walzer's terms. The imperial version of complementarity between civil society and government, as we have seen, supposed that representatives of the former, in particular the 'ulama, might give Islamic legitimacy to those filling the latter's function. Given the limits on this legitimacy, however ("A creature is not to be obeyed when it involves disobedience to the Creator" and "The most excellent jihad is when one speaks a true word in the presence of a tyrannical ruler"), one might expect the recognition of legitimacy to be contentious. The possibilities for such contention are multiplied when one considers the nature of religious authority in Islam. The 'ulama, that is, are specialists who are recognized, carrying a kind of "certification" from one of several persons or institutions whose standing is undisputed. And those who cannot themselves gain such certification—which is to say, practically speaking, nearly everyone—are supposed to attach themselves to an individual specialist or, more generally, to a recognized "school" or "way" of interpreting Islamic sources with which publically recognized specialists are attached.

But there is nothing—that is, in the way of Islamic norms themselves—that keeps one from changing allegiance—from adhering to the judgments of one authority for a time, then changing to follow another. Indeed, on some counts, adult Muslims are allowed to take stock of the judgments of all the recognized "ways," and then to choose the judgment that pleases them. The potential for slippage in the civil society/government relation is clear, I think. In effect, the lack of a full-blown ecclesiastical structure, with its own canon law and methods of punishment, allows a great deal of autonomy in the practice of religion. One could not, on classical Muslim standards, publically criticize certain fundamentals of religion (could not, for example, speak of the Qur'an as a fabrication). One could, however, manage to find a religious scholar and a kind of subcommunity interested in criticizing the courtly culture and, with it, scholars representing establishment Islam; judging from the preoccupation of Muslim scholars with the delineation of sects and stories of conflicts between the followers of very great 'ulama and the courtly culture, one would have to say that many Muslims did exactly that.

We will return to some specific instances of conflict, and to the great attempt of Muslim jurists to craft rules to bring such conflict under the rule of Islam, below. For now, however, it is important to notice that from the governmental point of view, the liability of civil society lies precisely in the notion that religious specialists own the power of binding and loosing. As indicated above, this indicates that the 'ulama have the power to withhold or withdraw legitimacy, as well as to give it. And the lack of a formal regulatory structure, which in one way leaves the ʿulama open to government domination, at the same time inhibits the government's ability to regulate civil society. Al-Maʾmun's infamous inquisition, discussed above, may be interpreted as one ruler's attempt to address this problem.

From the side of civil society, the great fear seems to be that governments will overreach. Correspondingly, the ʿulama of Islam express interest in limiting government's sphere of influence. Thus, in a "creed" attributed to al-Maʾmun's famous interlocutor, Ahmad ibn Hanbal, we read that

> [t]o fight in the jihad, as commanded by rulers, is a valid obligation, whether the rulers act with justice or not. . . . The Friday worship, the Two Feasts, and the Pilgrimage are observed according to the declarations of the rulers, even if they are not upright. . . . Taxes are to be paid to the commanders, whether they deal justly or not. . . . Those to whom God has entrusted your affairs are to be followed . . . and not opposed by your sword. . . . To keep aloof in civil strife is an old custom whose observance is obligatory.[26]

Taking this statement piece by piece, one finds affirmed the basic notion that the duties of government include military action in the interests of the umma; provision for public acts of worship; the collection and administration of taxes; and, in general, affairs important for public order. What is missing, and importantly so, is the notion that the caliph is a religious authority, able to regulate or trump others or both on matters of interpreting sacred texts. In effect, the question of the nature of the Qurʾan could be said to be a matter of conscience, which the caliph has no right to regulate.

As the story of Ahmad, or really of al-Maʾmun's doctrinal test, indicates, the liability of government (that is, from the standpoint of civil society) is its monopoly on legitimate force. Ahmad's understanding of the complementary roles played by religious and political authority is that the latter is not to be opposed by the sword. In effect, the right of arms belongs to government. The strength or duty of each side in the complementary relation is, correspondingly, a threat that it poses to the other.

Similarly, this is true in more contemporary settings. Reading the speeches of Ayatollah Khomeini from the 1960s, one cannot help noticing how often he criticizes the shah of Iran for failing to exercise his constitutional duties to protect the "Islamic people of Iran." The shah is said to pursue private interests, rather than the common good. He is said to undermine the independence of the religious leaders, and thus of Islam. In effect, he is accused of violating the "compact" between religious and political authority, and thus of a kind of default with respect to the complementary relationship between the two.[27]

This kind of criticism is characteristic of much modern Islamic political writing. What is interesting to think about is what complementarity means in a constitutional democracy. The shah, for example, characterized certain changes in policy as giving greater rights in citizenship to minority groups—for example, the Baha'i, who by all account have suffered greatly under the regime of the Islamic republic. By securing the welfare of the people and safeguarding the independence of Islam, must one think of Muslims first? This leads to considerations of groups and individuals, and of citizenship in an Islamic polity.

Groups and Individuals

A.K.S. Lambton, among others, argues that the "individual and the state . . . are broadly at one in their moral purpose, and so the conception of the individual is not prominent, nor the conception of rights. Islam does not in fact recognize the legal personality of the individual in which his rights are secured to him and vested in him by law. The state or the government is both expected and able to exercise a very considerable degree of coercion. . . . In Islam the antithesis between the individual and the state or the government is not recognized, and no need is therefore felt to reconcile and abolish this antithesis."[28] Reading these sentences, one supposes that much hangs on phrases like "not prominent," "very considerable degree," and "antithesis between the individual and state." It certainly seems true that Islamic thinkers do not picture individuals as solitary, or as preexisting society in an apolitical "natural" state, à la the Rousseau of *Emile*, and perhaps even of *The Social Contract*. Nor does the existence of the state require explanation, as in some Christian thinkers' suggestion that without the Fall, there would be no state, or at least no coercive power. So far as I can tell, the notion of a power regulating or ordering social life is simply assumed in Islam. God deals, as indicated above, with peoples or nations; each has a prophet or prophets, who come to remind them, in their personal and collective identities, of the truth which is represented by the phrase *al-islam*.

God deals with peoples; but it is ultimately the individual members of each people who are judged, and sent either to eternal damnation or to Paradise, on a "day about which there is no doubt, when each soul will be paid out what it has earned, and there will be no injustice" (3:25b). Given such an emphasis on persons and their responsibility, it is not strange, then, to find ample evidence that runs counter to Lambton's statements. Thus, in his *Bidayat al-Mujtahid*, Ibn Rushd argues that every person has rights to life, to liberty, and to property.[29] These are not to be violated, unless one acts in ways that mitigate or sacrifice one's claim—for example, by fighting in an unjust cause. The law of property recognizes the right of personal or individual ownership, as does the law of contracts, which is in large part a set of rulings concerning the ways ownership may be transferred, for example, by sale.[30] And finally, one must consider the law of personal status, which to a great extent could also be termed "family" law. It was, in fact, in this regard—that is, the attempt to order human relations in terms of marriage and divorce, the recognition of children, and rights to inheritance—that the state allowed the most latitude for religious scholars. The denizens of courtly culture, that is, tended toward the view that the great matters of policy, such as treaties, wars, and taxes, were "their" concern, while regulating ordinary life was a safe preoccupation for the ʿulama. Judging from the responsa of the scholars on issues "great" as well as "small," one should say that the scholars did not share this delimited view of their power. The relative freedom they enjoyed in the realm of personal or family law, however, did give room for a great deal of practical experience.

As such, government's role with respect to family life seems largely to have been "backing up" the religious leaders. Thus, in the division of tasks characteristic of the complementary relation I have been describing, the jurists understood family life, contracts, and the like, as "their" sphere. Their judgments on these matters form the great bulk of what Muslims call "the branches of comprehension" or "applied religious norms." Thus, in the texts of the ʿulama, we find descriptions of marriage, or *nikah*, as a "contract for the legalization of intercourse and the procreation of children."[31] It is important here, as in commercial settings, to know just what establishes a contract; in general, the "essential requirements are offer and acceptance."[32] Provided these take place before the required number of witnesses and that there are no grounds for a claim of incompetence, offer and acceptance establish a contract by which intercourse becomes valid. If incompetence can be established or if it can be shown that one or both parties did not give consent (for example, in the case of minors married by the agreement of their parents), the contract may be regarded as invalid, or in the latter case, one would better say that it may be repudiated. And, in general, it is inappropriate to speak of the Islamic law regarding contracts like marriage without noting that the judgments pertaining to divorce allow for its dissolution.

Family life, commerce, property holding are all in the sphere of civil society, by long-standing tradition in Islam. This leads to a concern about the possibilities for oppression within civil society, and to questions about a possible role for governments in regulating or transforming civil society. Thus, the classical judgments on marriage follow a pattern that distinguishes between the rights and obligations of men and women, as is well known. A Muslim man may be married to as many as four women at any given time. A Muslim woman, by contrast, may be married to only one man at any given time. Similarly, most judgments indicate that a Muslim man may be married to a non-Muslim woman. A Muslim woman, however, may be married only to a Muslim man. And, regarding divorce, the weight of tradition favors a form that gives the husband the power of initiating the action. While there are forms of divorce recognized by the tradition in which the woman's power to initiate or request divorce is important, these seem to have been less emphasized; indeed, the most prominent of these, the form called *khul*, is so called because the desire to separate comes from the wife—but in legal terms, the divorce is by common consent, and thus implies that the husband has agreed to her request. Much more difficult is the notion that a woman could seek to end a marriage, on her own or without the consent of her husband.[33]

Such judgments regarding marriage and divorce are only a small part of the set of practices approved by Islamic scholars, which appear to run counter to the Qur'an's dictum "Those who do righteousness, male or female, and have faith, will be among those entering the garden and no harm will come to them," or "to men is allotted what they earn, and to women is allotted what they earn."[34] That such practices are, in large part, authorized by the Qur'an itself only complicates the issue. As noted, some argue that this is a point at which an enlightened government ought to intervene in civil society; that, in effect, government has a valid interest in instituting an egalitarian regime with respect to gender relations, whatever the weight of tradition.

In response, it should be said that Muslims often have a different "take" on the traditional precepts than do many who are "on the outside looking in." Thus, for example, Ziba Mir-Hosseini's very interesting study of debates among Iranian 'ulama over the proper understanding of Islamic judgments pertaining to gender makes clear that many Muslim scholars, reformers and traditionalists alike, see the distinctions drawn between men and women in matters of marriage, divorce, and inheritance law as reflecting certain presuppositions about social and economic practice.[35] Thus, the fact that women receive a share of a testee's estate less than that of men, or that the amount of "blood money" required to pay a tort to the family of a deceased victim of deliberate or accidental death is less in the case of a female than of a male victim, is said by Mir-Hosseini's scholar informants to reflect the social fact that men generally carry greater responsibilities for earning. Families losing a male member may thus be considered to have a greater need. As Mir-Hosseini points out in the give and take of her interviews, it may be argued that this kind of social background is no longer to be presumed in contemporary Iran.

The scholars are often willing to admit this, many of them quite evidently struggling for a language that will allow them to move toward a more consistent egalitarianism of the type envisioned in the Qur'anic verses quoted above.

In Mir-Hosseini's own reflections, one finds expressed the dilemma of those who wonder whether governments should intervene to push reforms in gender relations: That is, reform from above is almost always depicted as anti-Islam or as a plot hatched by a West still unwilling to give up colonial aims. Thus, the shah's attempts to reform Islamic laws in ways suggestive of gender equality have been discredited, and it is the 'ulama who, according to Mir-Hosseini, hold the key to new models of gender relations. In some sense, this is unsurprising. If family law has been the sphere of the 'ulama for centuries, one would hardly expect to find them willing to relinquish it to governments; similarly with commercial law. The 'ulama have seen themselves, with some validity, as the guardians of freedom, struggling with an overweening government. The question now is whether some groups of citizens will think it necessary to organize in ways constructed so as to limit an overweening 'ulama. Thus, Mir-Hosseini remarks on the remarkable presence of women in Iranian professional life, and notes that there is now an institution dedicated to educating women in the traditional manner of the 'ulama. She wonders where this can go, and so may we.

CITIZENSHIP

With respect to citizenship, classical judgment, by and large, reflected the pattern evidenced in the famous "Medina Constitution," or agreement between the Prophet and the various groups living in the city. The Muslims and those who "followed them and joined them and labored with them . . . are one community to the exclusion of others."[36] The Jews of Medina are said to constitute a distinct community with their own religion. They are tolerated or, more literally, "protected" by the Muslims, in the sense that they are free to follow their own sacred texts and laws, within limits indicated by the security needs of the Muslims. They are not to run their own foreign policy, for example. Nor are they to engage in public criticism of the Prophet or to attempt to persuade Muslims to drop their allegiance to Muhammad.

Over centuries, the pattern of imperial Islam was governed by this model. Thus, *ahl al-dhimma*, the "protected" peoples, paid tribute to the Islamic government in exchange for the right of limited freedom. Christians, for example, were allowed to govern their own affairs in family and commercial law, provided these created no conflict with Muslims. They were allowed to worship, so long as their public displays did not disturb the peace of Islam.[37]

What Christians and others were not is full citizens in the sense of participants in the enterprise of Islamic government. As we move into the modern period, we do better, in fact, to think of them as recognized minorities. Thus, once notions of representative government appear, we find such groups receiving a certain delimited place in the political process. The constitution of the Islamic Republic of Iran, for example, sets aside one seat in the Consultative Assembly for each of the recognized religious minorities present in the republic. Similar patterns hold in Egypt, where Coptic Christians receive a set portion of representation.

Among other things, it is important to note the persistence of a religious dimension in understandings of citizenship. And it is important that in terms of certain aspects of citizenship, the disabilities for women present in family law seem to be overcome. After some initial opposition from religious scholars, there is now no question about women's right to vote in contemporary Iran—it is established in the constitution and in practice. Similarly, women may hold office in the legislature, though it should be noted that, in the complicated procedure by which candidates are approved to run for president, none of the women applying for certification has been approved for the ballot.

CONFLICT

The religious nature of citizenship, and thus of participation in an Islamic state, shows up in a fascinating set of rules developed by classical scholars for dealing with a variety of intrastate conflicts. *Ahkam al-bughat* are "judgments about rebels," specifically, Muslims who take up arms against an established caliph. These are different from *ahkam ahl al-dhimma*, "judgments about the protected communities," which attempt to guide caliphal policy in cases where religious minorities violate the terms under which they are tolerated. And both are distinguished from the rules for fighting against *al-murtadd* (Muslims who "turn" and are those apostates), as well as those for dealing with criminal bands ("highwaymen," as most translators have it.) Rules pertaining to rebels, in particular, illustrate the attempt of the 'ulama to create a protected space for religious practice; as I have been arguing, this is the classical Islamic analogue to civil society. The rules specify the characteristics of a legitimate rebel group, as opposed to a group of apostates or thieves; correspondingly, there are strict limits on the response of government.[38]

We have already seen that classical Islam viewed rebellion with suspicion. The ahadith cited above are only a few of the reports suggesting the problematic nature of taking up arms against an established government. The ʿulama feared the propensity of zealots to put considerations of purity above the welfare of the community as a whole; they also feared that, whatever the intention of rebels, harm would come to many innocent people. Thus they favored quiet resistance, conscientious refusal to obey unjust commands, or the speaking of a well-placed warning over outright revolt. Better a thousand years of tyranny than one night of anarchy—that summarizes the scholars' general view; one hardly needs to say further that it establishes an anti-revolutionary tone.

Nevertheless, governments are prone to overreach, and the Muslim caliphate provided numerous examples of this. Given this, the ʿulama recognized the import of at least some room for more boisterous forms of resistance. In recognition of the independence of civil society, they drew up a description of the characteristics of legitimate activist groups. Generally speaking, there are three such characteristics: al-khuruj, al-ta'wil, and al-shawka. The first, which draws on the Arabic for "exiting" or "secession," indicates that the group resists an established regime, employing means beyond speech or "merely" expressive activity. "Rebels" must, as a group, clearly violate the laws or policies of the regime.

The second characteristic, al-ta'wil, indicates that the rebels provide public justification for their action. Further, in its ordinary sense, al-ta'wil (interpretation) implies that this justification is offered in terms of recognized Islamic sources. The point is that the rebels provide a demonstration that they are Muslims. They are not apostates, meaning people who have turned from Islam and are rejecting its authority. Nor are they Jews or Christians, whose ta'wil might be expressed in terms that challenge the honor of Islam. The rebels are Muslims—an important way of drawing the lines between legitimate expressions of civil society, and illegitimate activities.

The third characteristic, al-shawka, or "strength," indicates that the rebels must have a following or that the group must be of a certain size. What exactly this entails is a matter of disagreement. Some scholars say ten, others forty, others more. The point is that the rebellion is not "private"—say, the activity of an extended family disenchanted with the government. To be classified as a rebel group, there must be a demonstration of support from the Muslim community.

Provided a group demonstrates the required characteristics, governmental response is limited in important ways. A caliph responding to a rebel group is not allowed to deal with its members as criminals. He must follow the directive of the Qur'an.

> If two parties of believers fall to fighting, then make peace between them. And if one party of them does wrong to the other, fight the one that does wrong until it returns to the way of God; then, if it returns, make peace between them

with justice, and act equitably. Lo! God loves those who act equitably. The believers are brothers: so make peace between your brothers and observe your duty to God, that you may receive mercy.[39]

Reconciliation, rather than punishment, is the goal in responding to rebels. Further, the caliph must exercise extreme care in resorting to armed force against a rebel group. His policy should be set by following the example of ʿAli, son-in-law of Muhammad, viewed as the fourth caliph by most Muslims.

[A contemporary of ʿAli said:] I entered the Mosque of Kufa through the Kinda gates where I met five men cursing [the caliph.] One of theme, covered with a burnus, said: "I have made a covenant with God that I shall kill him." Whereupon, I kept close while his companions dispersed, and I took him to ʿAli and said: "I heard this man saying that he has made a covenant with God that he will kill you." "Bring him nearer," said [ʿAli] and added: "woe to you, who are you?" "I am Sawwar al-Manquri," replied the man. "Let him go," said ʿAli. Thereupon, I said: "Shall I let him go, though he made a covenant with God to kill you?" "Shall I kill him even though he has not killed me?" replied ʿAli. "He has cursed you," [I said.] "You should then curse him or leave him," said ʿAli.

It has been related . . . that, while ʿAli was once making a sermon on Kharijis, from one side of the Mosque, pronounced the formula: "Judgment belongs to none save God." "A word of Truth to which is given a false meaning," said ʿAli [and he added]: "we shall not prohibit you from entering our mosques to mention God's name; we shall not deny you [your share of public funds], so long as you join hands with us; nor shall we fight you until you attack us."

It has also been related . . . that ʿAli said in the Battle of the Camel: "Whoever flees shall not be chased, no prisoner of war shall be killed, no wounded in battle shall be dispatched, no enslavement shall be allowed, and no property shall be confiscated."[40]

By comparison with the rules governing armed conflict with non-Muslims, these examples restrict the caliph considerably. In all, the message is that the government is responding to Muslim groups, who are to be accorded a kind of legitimacy. Formally recognized as "rebels," they must be treated in ways that will foster reconciliation. Or, in terms of the civil society/government relation, one might say they are to be treated in ways that recognize that there are limits on the caliph's right, with respect to the conscience of the Muslim community. Whatever liabilities result, whatever fears the caliph has of the sectarian possibilities implicit in a relatively independent religious sector, the government's response to Muslim rebel groups must be crafted so as to recognize and respect the limits on the claims of khilafat as the successor to the Prophet. The caliph's duties are (primarily) political. The ʿulama safeguard a relatively independent religious sector, within the general model of the complementarity of civil society and government.

In contemporary Islamic societies, it might be argued that the status of rebel groups is the most contentious point in the relationship between civil society and government. In settings where despite constitutional provisions for elections, an independent judiciary, and the like, many citizens consider that their ability to speak and associate freely or to express their conscientious judgments is unfairly restricted, the tendency to form activist, even revolutionary groups whose identity is in some way "Islamic" is very strong. In Egypt, for example, a member of the group of activists accused of conspiracy in the assassination of President Anwar Sadat provided a public justification for such acts in a much-discussed treatise called *The Neglected Duty*.[41] The argument of the treatise was that political leaders who claim to be Muslims but whose policies are not consonant with Islam are apostates or traitors to the Islamic community. Following long-standing tradition, the author said that such people are deserving of death. In the absence of a "real" Islamic government willing to carry out such a sentence, the duty of punishing people who commit crimes against Islam devolves upon the community as a whole. The author's group, one of many bearing the name "Islamic Struggle," simply stood in for the Muslim community against the traitor, Sadat.

The ensuing trial of members of Islamic Struggle featured, among other things, arguments by defense attorneys to the effect that the accused were, in the technical sense of classical Islam, "rebels." In particular, the claim was that the imposition of the death penalty would be wrong and, according to Article 2 of the Egyptian Constitution, illegal. As Khaled Abou El Fadl puts it, "The military tribunal ignored this argument in passing the death sentence on certain defendants."[42]

Certainly activities like assassination go beyond the scope of what is ordinarily considered "civil society." Groups like Islamic Struggle are in one sense outside the scope of that term, as they involve themselves in a kind of ongoing armed conflict with existing political power. The focus on their military or paramilitary activities often leads observers to miss, however, a number of other aspects of such groups. The "duties" the members see government neglecting have to do with the efficient provision of social services, health care, and basic education, especially for growing numbers of urban poor, numbers created by government policies that unsettle traditional rural patterns of life (for example, policies that promote agribusiness.) Groups like Islamic Struggle ordinarily serve multiple purposes, mediating not only between governments and families, but between families and survival. Governments count these groups as liabilities, because their affinity for violence threatens public order, and their public use of Islamic slogans undermines the legitimacy of an established regime. At the same time, governments and, even more, the urban poor need such groups to counter some of the effects of poverty.[43] Currently, the approach to this set of tensions between civil society and government in Muslim societies moves back and forth between several options. One approach attempts to broaden the scope of political participation by allowing activist groups to play an official role—for example, by allowing Islamic groups to function as political parties, who field candidates in elections, bargain for members of their group to hold certain cabinet offices, and in general take part in parliamentary politics. Such parties receive a portion of public funds for patronage purposes, and put them to use by providing social services to the public, or at least to some portion of the public. In return, activist groups lay down their arms, or at least curtail their paramilitary activities. The long-standing part played by the Muslim Brethren in Egyptian politics provides an illustration of this approach.

Difficulties arise, however, in cases where the parties formed by activist groups secure a broad enough following that they threaten to change established patterns of power distribution. In the case of Algeria, where Islamic parties actually won an electoral victory in the early 1990s, those elites used to exercising authority were simply unwilling to transfer power. A military regime was put in place, the election results canceled, and the resulting civil war has yet to play itself out.

If inclusion is one approach, and nullification (as in Algeria) a second, yet a third option is presented by revolutionary Iran. There, opposition to the shah reached such heights during the 1970s that a coalition of ʿulama and reform-minded business and political leaders rallied public support in a successful revolution in 1978–79. The resulting Islamic Republic, the constitution of which has been mentioned in passing at several points in this essay, is an attempt to safeguard the independence of the ʿulama as guardians of Islamic values. In this attempt, it is arguable that the notion of a relatively independent governmental sphere is violated; it is also arguable that the complementarity of civil society and government swings so far in the direction of the ʿulama that their role as guardians of an independent civil sector is undone. Recent elections, in which large numbers of young, relatively well educated voters express their desire for a greater sphere of personal liberty, might be taken to suggest that the ʿulama, or at least those most directly identified with the governing apparatus of the Islamic Republic, are coming to be seen as tyrants in their own right; people who, in the name of protecting Islam, set themselves the role of so regulating the practice of members of the Islamic community that they endanger the freedom of conscience to which every Muslim has a right.

CONCLUSIONS

Throughout this discussion, I have suggested that the complementarity thesis—that is, that religion and politics play distinct, though mutually supportive, roles in the life of a Muslim society—suggests one way to develop an Islamic perspective on the civil society/government relation. Particularly in the classical model of Islamic society, whereby a class of scholars, the ʿulama, have authority as interpreters of Islamic values; and a corresponding class of rulers, advisers, military, and bureacrats have authority under the umbrella of khilafat to secure the peace of Islamic society, I have suggested that one might view the ʿulama/khilafat relation as an analogy to that between civil society and government. I have suggested that throughout the history of Islam, inclusive of more recent developments in the Islamic Republic of Iran and in other Muslim-majority societies, the complementarity thesis holds. Thus, "civil society" becomes a discussion of the ways that Muslims have understood that social life should be organized, so as to protect the relative independence of Islamic values from the authoritarian tendencies of governments. In turn, "government" comes to stand for the set of institutions whose legitimate monopoly on armed force within a given territory must be carried out in ways that respect the relative independence of the religious sphere.

Three points seem to follow.

First, there is a way in which the analogy I have suggested (whereby ʿulama/khilafat stands for civil society/government) might be characterized as uneasy, or even inept. If civil society means, as in the more contemporary versions of the Lockean tradition, that one must think in terms of the ways a society like the United States legitimates a thoroughgoing regime of liberty in religious and, more generally, civil matters, then the concept does not fit neatly with most of Islamic political thinking. Complementarity, in the Islamic setting, has meant and continues to imply some sort of established status for Islam. Governments carry out their political duties with the presumption that they are Islamically legitimate. Leaders give at least lip service to the notion that they form policies based on consultation with the ʿulama. Rights of citizenship are set with religious distinctions in mind; distinctions of gender, insofar as those are thought of as having a basis in authoritative Islamic texts, are also part of the public regime of Islamic societies. A fully developed civil society, in the sense that many analysts presume, has not been, and is not at this time, an aspect of most Islamic political thinking.

Second (however), one must note that complementarity, as a model for the civil society/government relation, provides an indefinite norm. In general, it establishes certain limits on institutions. In the Islamic case, the tradition has been especially to stress the limits on government, with respect to the threat that its officials will overreach their mandate and encroach on the sphere of religious values. If one thinks positively, one might say that complementarity sets civil society and government in a relation of creative tension. Governments will always be worried, given the loose structure of religious authority in Islam, about the sectarian potential of religion. Correlatively, they will always be tempted to regulate religion, to foreclose or delimit the independence of the ʿulama, and to regulate the conscience of Muslims. The ʿulama will always be tempted by the prospect of religious purity. They will be critical of government, particularly insofar as they perceive that the realities of political life often involve officials in activities that leave them with dirty hands. The loose structure of religious authority in Islam will also create problems for the ʿulama. Since every Muslim has the right to read the Qurʾan and ahadith, and to interpret them for him/herself, the idea of a special class of experts rests on somewhat tenuous grounds. As a practical matter, most Muslims have identified themselves with the ʿulama of a particular school. They have, and will continue to, defer to the consensus of these ʿulama. Every Muslim has the right to interpret for him/herself, however; that much is shown, even in the traditional allowance for an adult male Muslim to examine the judgments of ʿulama from a variety of schools on a particular question, and to follow whichever school he likes best. This loose structure has relevance for our discussion of civil society and government in yet another way, as well—for it points to the potential for new judgments. The discussion of Iranian ʿulama concerning traditional judgments about gender is one example of the tendency built into the religious structure of Islam. One consults the sources of Islam; one should be informed by the precedent of earlier generations of interpreters. But new contexts require new judgments. The idea that the thesis of complementarity somehow forecloses reform within Islam should be avoided.[44]

Finally, I want to revisit a question raised earlier in this essay, regarding the place of a professional and business class in Muslim societies. The recent elections in Iran, the results of which clearly favor President Khatami's calls for a greater independence of "civil society," may be analyzed as the expression of desires on the part of such a class for a certain independence, not only from the overreaching of governments like that of the shah, but from the overreaching of certain ʿulama. The business and professional classes of Muslim societies are not themselves religious specialists (at least most are not). Nor are they politicians or government bureaucrats. They *are* citizens, most of them "lay" Muslims, interested in the building of a society in which freedom and justice are respected values. Khatami's speeches and writings articulate a view, which many business and professional types would share, that in the history of Islam the ʿulama have been the protectors of liberty, over against authoritarian, not to say despotic, governments. As Khatami has warned his fellow scholars, however, those who utilize their position as guardians of Islamic values in ways that deny the hopes of citizens for freedom and justice (for example, by closing newspapers and television stations associated with opposition parties) run the risk of undoing this history. The ʿulama, in short, begin to look like the government officials they previously despised.

When Khatami speaks about the importance of civil society, he means to call for a way of organizing an Islamic state that increases freedom for this business and professional class. He does not emphasize so much the role of American-style voluntary associations like the Rotary Clubs or the National Organization for Women. Nor does he imply a society in which religious identity becomes a matter of indifference with respect to citizenship. Khatami means to preserve an Islamic identify for Iran and, by extension, for other Islamic states; this means the complementarity thesis, with its supposition of some sort of Islamic religious establishment, is presumed. By civil society, Khatami does mean a greater role for ordinary citizens in discussions of the policies of an Islamic state. Whether his call will be successful and what it will mean for Islamic political thought are matters on which only time will pronounce a verdict. That a greater role for lay Muslims in Islamic societies would have an impact on the Islamic perspective on civil society and government seems, however, beyond question.

NOTES

1. See the expositions in Shlomo Avineri, *Hegel's Theory of the Modern State* (Cambridge: Cambridge University Press, 1972); and Michael O. Hardimon, *Hegel's Social Philosophy: The Project of Reconciliation* (Cambridge: Cambridge University Press, 1994), in addition to Hegel's own *Philosophy of Right*, trans. (with notes) T. M. Knox (New York: Oxford University Press, 1967).

2. Cf. John Locke, *Treatise of Civil Government and A Letter Concerning Toleration*, edited by Charles L. Sherman (New York: Appleton-Century-Crofts, 1937); also Adam B. Seligman, *The Idea of Civil Society* (Princeton: Princeton University Press, 1995).

3. Cf. Mohammed Khatami, *Islam, Liberty, and Development* (Binghamton, N.Y.: Global Publications, 1999). A second volume, *Hope and Challenge: The Iranian President Speaks* (Binghamton, N.Y.: Global Publications, 1998) contains some of the same material. Saad Eddin Ibrahim's work is well represented in "Civil Society and Prospects for Democratization in the Arab World," in *Civil Society in the Middle East*, ed. Augustus Richard Norton (Leiden: E. J. Brill, 1995), 1:27–54.

The entire collection of essays in Norton's volume are useful, though they are more social scientific and less philosophically oriented than the present essay.

4. Max Weber, "Politics as a Vocation," in *From Max Weber*, trans. and ed. by H. Gerth and C. Wright Mills (New York: Oxford University Press, 1946), 78. Despite Weber's reference to the "modern" state in this oft-quoted remark, the description stands generally for the type of institutions that may be classed as "government" in the present essay.

5. With respect to Arabic terms: In this essay, I follow the practice of the *International Journal of Middle East Studies*, and have thus omitted most diacritical markings in the transliteration. The exceptions are 'ayn (signaled by ') and *hamza* (signaled by '). In addition, I shall use italics for only the first use of a term.

6. Hamid Enayat, *Modern Islamic Political Thought* (Austin: University of Texas Press, 1982) provides an excellent survey of Muslim discussions of democracy, among other issues.

7. Khatami, *Islam, Liberty, and Development.*

8. With respect to "schools of thought," one must at least take note of the great division between Sunni and Shi'i Islam. In surveys of Islam, the former is usually said to be the marker of identity preferred by some 85 to 90 percent of Muslims; the latter would then be preferred by 10 or 15 percent. It is difficult to establish such percentages with precision, but most analysts would agree with the implication that Sunni Islam is "majoritarian," and Shi'i Islam a minority expression within the tradition. Most would also then agree with a gloss on the figures indicating that, in reality, the terms Sunni and Shi'i are broad "umbrella" terms; each school contains multiple groups.

Many texts suggest that the division between Sunni and Shi'i begins almost immediately following the death of the Prophet in 632, and involves a dispute over whether or not the Prophet designated his son-in-law, 'Ali ibn Abi Talib, to succeed him as the ruler of the Islamic community. As things turned out, an older companion of the Prophet, Abu Bakr, in fact served as the first caliph or successor to the Prophet, and 'Ali did not serve in that capacity until the year 656.

Whatever the historical case for the claim of such an early appearance of the two schools (and one must note that, in contemporary Sunni-Shi'i polemics, the dispute over the proper understanding of these early events is very prominent), the terms Sunni and Shi'i gradually came, over several centuries, to identify two schools within Islam, each with its characteristic ways of talking about politics, theology, and piety. With respect to politics, in particular, the Shi'i groups were and are distinguished by their emphasis on the rule of a righteous *imam*, or "leader," who is the "proof" of God's justice on earth. There is one, and only one, such imam on earth at any particular time. That person is designated by God to lead; the imam is characterized not only by piety and learning, in the ordinary sense of the terms, but by special insight into the sources of Islam and by the quality of sinlessness. Politically speaking, right authority or legitimate government exists only when the imam of the age is in charge of the affairs of the Islamic community. Sunni Islam, by contrast, is usually presented as a tradition in which consultation and consensus establish legitimate government.

The importance of this difference, in terms of perceptions of the ultimate purposes of politics, is very great, as it also may be for certain issues in political ethics, for example, the justification and limitation of war. For the issue before us, however, the import seems surprisingly small. This is so, to a great extent, because the largest Shi'i subgroup, the Twelver or Imami Shi'a, holds that the Imam of the Age has been absent, in a state of occultation, since 873 or 874. He will appear at a time of God's designation, and will then establish justice and equity. In the meantime, the Shi'i religious leaders are charged with preserving the integrity of Islamic practice in relation to an established government. They thus occupy a place in Islamic political thought very similar to that of the Sunni scholars (see below). That being the case, I shall move freely between Sunni and Shi'i examples as my argument proceeds, and will not be concerned with the distinctions between the two schools. For more on the Shi'i tradition, I refer the reader to two works by Abdulaziz Sachedina: *Islamic Messianism* (Albany: State University of New York Press, 1981); and *The Just Ruler in Shi'ite Islam* (New York: Oxford University Press, 1988).

With reference to "modes" of political conversation, I have in mind the distinction A.K.S. Lambton drew between legal, philosophical, and "literary" styles in her *State and Government in Medieval Islam* (Oxford: Oxford University Press, 1981).

9. The next few paragraphs contain nothing that would be considered "controversial." Readers may supplement my brief comments by turning to a standard biogaphical study like that of W. M. Watt, *Muhammad: Prophet and Statesman* (London: Oxford University Press, 1961). A more recent study, less biographical but covering much of the same material, is F. E. Peters's *Muhammad and the Origins of Islam* (Albany: State University of New York Press, 1994). Both of necessity draw heavily from pious sources, in particular the biography by Ibn Ishaq (d. 767), which is available as *The Life of Muhammad*, trans. A. Guillaume (New York: Oxford University Press, 1955).

10. For more on the relation between Byzantine, Sassanid, and Muslim notions of statecraft, see Fred M. Donner, "The Sources of Islamic Conceptions of War," in *Just War and Jihad: Historical and Theoretical Perspectives on War and Peace in Western and Islamic Traditions*, ed. John Kelsay and James Turner Johnson (Westport, Conn.: Greenwood Press, 1991), 31–70.

11. Qur'an 16:25. Throughout this essay, I make use of the translation of Yusuf 'Ali, though I have sometimes altered the translation according to my own sense of the Arabic text.

12. The oldest extant biography is that of Ibn Ishaq (see n. 9).

13. Cf. Fred M. Donner, *The Early Islamic Conquests* (Princeton: Princeton University Press, 1981) for a chronology of the spread of Islamic power, as well as a survey and critique of the literature on the "reasons for" the Muslim push out of Saudi Arabia.

14. For details and a penetrating analysis, nothing surpasses Marshall G. S. Hodgson, *The Venture of Islam*, vol. 1 (Chicago: University of Chicago Press, 1974).

15. For the next few paragraphs, see John Kelsay, "Divine Commands and Social Order," *Annual of the Society of Christian Ethics* (1990), 63–80, and literature cited there.

16. According to Shiʿi tradition, ʿAli al-Rida was the eighth imam, in the line beginning with ʿAli ibn Abi Talib.

17. In general, see Marshall G. S. Hodgson's *Venture*, vols. 2 and 3.

18. Here, see Enayat, *Modern Islamic Political Thought*; also, Albert Hourani, *Arabic Thought in the Liberal Age, 1798–1939* (Cambridge: Cambridge University Press, 1984).

19. ʿAli ʿabd al-Raziq's book on "Islam and the basis of government" (*Al-Islam wa usul al-hukm*, published in Cairo in 1925) is excerpted (tran. Joseph Massad) in *Liberal Islam: A Sourcebook*, ed. Charles Kurzman (New York: Oxford University Press, 1998), 29–36, among other places.

20. Cf. the collection of Khomeini's speeches and writings published as *Islam and Revolution*, trans. Hamid Algar (Berkeley, Calif.: Mizan Press, 1981). Cf. also Farhang Rajaee, *Islamic Values and Worldview* (Lanham, Md.: University Press of America, 1983); R. Mottahedeh, *The Mantle of the Prophet* (New York: Simon and Schuster, 1985). My own exploration of Khomeini's thought is "Spirituality and Social Struggle: Islam and the West," published in *What Kind of God? Essays in Honor of Richard L. Rubenstein*, ed. Betty Rogers Rubenstein and Michael Berenbaum (Lanham, Md.: University Press of America, 1995).

21. The following reports are cited from the compendium Muslims know as *Mishkat al-Masabih*, trans. James Robson, 4 vols. (Lahore: Sh. M. Ashraf, 1963–64). *Mishkat* collects representative ahadith on various issues (for example, political obligation) from each of the six collections regarded as authoritative by Sunni Muslims.

22. Ibid.

23. Al-Mawardi (d. 1058) is the author of one of the most authoritative classical treatises on the caliphate. See the translation by Asadullah Yate, *Al-Ahkam as-Sultaniyyah: The Laws of Islamic Governance* (London: Ta-Ha Publishers, 1996).

24. Here and elsewhere, I quote from the official English version, available online at *http://www.iranonline.com*. Article numbers will simply be noted in the text.

25. M. Walzer, "The Concept of Civil Society," in *Toward a Global Civil Society*, ed. Michael Walzer (Providence, R.I.: Bergahn Books, 1995), 7–28.

26. As in W. Montgomery Watt, *The Formative Period of Islamic Thought* (Edinburgh: Edinburgh University Press, 1973), 293.

27. Khomeini, *Islam and Revolution*.

28. Lambton, *State and Government in Medieval Islam*, xv.

29. As in the "chapter on *jihad*," translated in R. Peters, *Jihad in Mediaeval and Modern Islam* (Leiden: E. J. Brill, 1977).

30. Cf., among others, Joseph Schacht, *An Introduction to Islamic Law* (Oxford: Clarendon Press, 1964); N. J. Coulson, *A History of Islamic Law* (Edinburgh: Edinburgh University Press, 1964); Asaf A. A. Fyzee, *Outlines of Muhammadan Law*, 4th ed. (Oxford: Oxford University Press, 1974).

31. Fyzee, *Outlines*, 90.

32. Ibid., 91.

33. It should be noted that it is possible for a provision to be placed in the original contract of marriage, by which a woman's right to initiate divorce is stipulated. This is considered binding in Islamic law. For a discussion of this

provision, see Ziba Mir-Hosseini, *Islam and Gender: The Religious Debate in Contemporary Iran* (Princeton: Princeton University Press, 1999).

34. 4:124, 4:32.

35. Mir-Hosseini, *Islam and Gender*.

36. Ibn Ishaq, *Life of Muhammad*, 651.

37. Cf. Ronald L. Nettler, "Dhimmi," in *The Oxford Encyclopedia of the Modern Islamic World*, ed. John L. Esposito (New York: Oxford University Press, 1995), 1:374.

38. For more extended analysis, cf. John Kelsay, *Islam and War: A Study in Comparative Ethics* (Louisville, Ky.: Westminster/John Knox Press), 77–110; and also Khaled Abou El Fadl, "*Ahkam al-Bughat*: Irregular Warfare and the Law of Rebellion in Islam," in *Cross, Crescent, and Sword: The Justification and Limitation of War in Western and Islamic Tradition*, ed. James Turner Johnson and John Kelsay (Westport, Conn.: Greenwood Press, 1990), 149–78. My understanding of this material is largely due to Abou El Fadl's incisive presentation.

39. 49:9–10.

40. From Muhammad ibn al-Hasan al-Shaybani, *The Islamic Law of Nations: Shaybani's Siyar*, trans. M. Khadduri (Baltimore: Johns Hopkins University Press, 1966), sec. 1372.

41. Trans. Johannes J. G. Jansen (New York: Macmillan Co., 1986). Jansen provides an introduction, and also translates a number of Egyptian responses to the document. I analyze the argument at some length in *Islam and War*.

42. Abou El Fadl, "*Akham al-Bughat*," 168.

43. Cf. analyses presented in the five volumes produced by the Fundamentalisms Project, directed by Martin Marty and R. Scott Appleby (Chicago: University of Chicago Press, 1991–93).

44. This is the place to refer the reader to several works by Muslim intellectuals who advance proposals about the relationship between religion and politics in Islam that suggest a wider sphere for religious liberty. Such a widening of scope for liberty suggests a model of civil society more like that characteristic of the Lockean tradition, in particular. See, among others, Abdulaziz Sachedina, "Freedom of Conscience and Religion in the Qur'an," in *Human Rights and the Conflict of Cultures*, ed. David Little, John Kelsay, and Abdulaziz Sachedina (Columbia: University of South Carolina Press, 1988), 53–90; Abdullahi an-Na'im, *Toward an Islamic Reformation* (Syracuse, N.Y.: Syracuse University Press, 1990); and Khaled Abou El Fadl, *Authoritative and Authoritarian in Islamic Discourses: A Contemporary Case Study*, rev. ed. (Taiba Publishing House, 1997).

Perspectives on Islam and Civil Society

Farhad Kazemi

CONTEXT: CIVIL SOCIETY AND ISLAMIC POLITICS

Civil society has become an important issue in Islamic politics in recent years and a central topic of discourse for scholars, policy makers, and other observers. Its renewed relevance is a reflection of a set of two relatively recent international and domestic developments. On the international side, these developments included the collapse of the Soviet Union, the end of the Cold War, the initial movement toward democratization in several parts of the world, and what appeared to be major progress toward resolving the Arab-Israeli conflict. The external environment seemed to be moving away from a preoccupation with festering international and regional conflicts and, hence, allowing for greater attention to important issues of governance at home.

On the domestic front, the collective impact of internal dynamics in the Islamic world (particularly the Middle East) created significant pressures on the traditional relationship between the state and society in the region. These developments included rapid urbanization; dramatic increases in literacy, especially among females; regular and major movement of population within the region and abroad; increased use of different forms of electronic communication; and other similar factors. The changed environment ushered in more forceful demands for accountability and the rule of law for an ever-expanding segment of the population. The theme of civil society in many ways emerged as a vehicle (especially among the intelligentsia) for expressing the demands for greater freedom for the people and less oppression by the ubiquitous arms of the state.

Civil society as a theme of governance and as a reflection of state-society relations, however, was contentious from the beginning. The thrust of the debate concerned the relevance of the concept to non-Western societies and particularly its applicability to Islam. Some have argued that civil society "does not translate into Islamic terms."[1] It is often argued that civil society developed as an essentially modern phenomenon in the West, while much of the theoretical elements of Islam have premodern roots. The applicability is, therefore, problematic.

Others, including the author, have argued that the concept is eminently applicable to Islamic politics.[2] The premodern features, though occasionally problematic, are not insurmountable barriers. The real task is more one of ascertaining the extent of civil society's presence and its level of autonomy from the state.[3]

The contending views have resulted in a large number of meetings, conferences, and publications in the Middle East and elsewhere. Two other developments brought additional public attention to the topic. The first was Huntington's article, "The Clash of Civilizations?" with its contention that liberal democracy is not compatible with the religious traditions of Islam.[4] This article has received an inordinate amount of attention (both positive and negative) among the Muslim activists on all sides. The second critical development was the enshrinement of civil society (and the corollary themes of pluralism and respect for the rule of law) in the successful presidential campaign of the relatively moderate Iranian candidate, Mohammad Khatami, in 1997.[5] These sharply opposing conceptions further fueled the debate in the Islamic world about the congruence of Islam, civil society, and democracy. The political context for an analysis of Islam and civil society is, therefore, quite clear.

CIVIL SOCIETY

I use the concept of civil society in the classical Western model and contend that it has a direct relevance to Islam and Islamic politics. Following Walzer's usage, I maintain that "the words 'civil society' name the space of uncoerced human association and also the set of relations networks—formed for the sake of family, faith, interest, and ideology—that fill this space."[6] This separation of the state from civil society does not eliminate the state's critical role. The state "lays down laws" that provide the framework for and limits of action. Beyond these constraints, "the actions of individuals and collectivities are freely chosen."[7] The idea of civil society, then, to use Shils's words, is "a part of society which has a life of its own, which is distinctly different from the state, and which is largely in autonomy from it. . . . It lies short of the state."[8]

Several components must be present for civil society to exist. In addition to the space separating the individual from the state, civil society encompasses two other principal components: (*a*) the existence of a complex of autonomous institutions and (*b*) the prevalence of "civility" in the social order and in relations among individuals. The network of autonomous institutions—family, groups, tribes, guilds, unions, clubs, associations, parties—provides the buffer between the individual and the state and allows for the development of a participant society.[9] These institutions permit individuals to express their attitudes, views, and orientations. They allow for participation in civil life.

Civil society, however, is not just a mélange of different groups and associations. As Norton points out, "it also refers to a quality—civility— without which the milieu consists of feuding factions, cliques, and cabals. Civility implies tolerance, the willingness of individuals to accept disparate political views and social attitudes; sometimes to accept the profoundly important idea that there is no right answer."[10] Civility implies not only tolerance of the other, but also "attachment to the institutions which constitute civil society."[11]

To sum up, then, civil society implies the existence of associations autonomous from the state and of individuals tolerant of others and accepting of institutions of civic order. These are institutions that allow for the development of democracy and citizenship in various spheres of life. Among these are institutions of market economy, competing political parties, independent judiciary, free press, and a host of voluntary associations.[12] Ultimately and as Michael Walzer has indicated, "only a democratic state can create a democratic civil society; only a democratic civil society can sustain a democratic state. The civility that makes democratic politics possible can only be learned in the associational networks; the roughly equal and widely dispersed capabilities that sustain the networks have to be fostered by the democratic state."[13]

CRITICAL ISSUES

From my perspective as a secondary commentator on the topic of civil society and Islam, I have selected a few broad issues of special and continuing relevance. In terms of the questions raised in this volume, these issues can be subsumed under two general categories of needs and boundaries, and groups and individuals. I will then use the example of Islamists, who play an important role in the debate on Islam and civil society, to illustrate the problematique of group conflict and citizenship rights from this perspective. In order not to repeat the discussion of the primary reader on civil society and Islam in this volume, I will review the topics in a cursory fashion.

NEEDS AND BOUNDARIES

In the Islamic worldview, a vibrant society needs the state in order to allow for full participation in public life. It is the state that provides protection, maintains legal order, and safeguards rights of individuals and groups. Traditionally Islam has been preoccupied with order and overwhelmingly fearful of chaos (*fitna*). The assumption, then, is that a properly functioning civil society has a basic need for the existence of the state. As Kelsay points out, "the idea is that political authority is important to the welfare of the religious community, and is to be respected."[14] By the same token, a believing Muslim citizen is also expected to be an activist for the faith and involved in civic matters. Mutual need and dependency of state and society is eminently recognized in Islam.

There are several classical Islamic concepts that have traditionally facilitated the state-society relationship. These include the need for the ruler to consult with the elders of the community (*shura*), adherence to the consensus within the community (*ijma*) on relevant legal issues, some degree of allowance for independent inquiry (*ijtihad*), and fidelity to the pact between rulers and the ruled (*bay'a*). The meaning and relative importance of these concepts have been conditioned by historical and sect specificities. On the whole, however, they have had some degree of continued relevance to state-society relationships.

Moreover, Islam has also developed the general notion of a just ruler. A just ruler is one who first and foremost upholds the Islamic law (*shari'ah*), which for all practical purposes functions as the constitution of the Islamic state. In addition, the ruler is expected to defend the community, collect taxes, supervise the conduct of war, consult with leaders of the community, and administer judicial and executive regulations. There are no clear-cut provisions for dismissing a ruler who violates these norms. In fact, concern with order is so strong that classical jurists had even rationalized tyrannical rule at times and judged it to be superior to chaos and social and political disorder. However, such a view has not ever stopped the not-so-infrequent overthrows of political leaders and dynasties or the onset of upheavals, riots, and revolutions. There has not often been a conjunction of theory and practice in this matter.

The complexity and diversity of Islamic civilization, and its multiple cultural and political poles, do not allow for simple generalization on any one issue. There is, however, an enduring pattern in state-society relationship in the more modern and contemporary period that requires some attention. This concerns persistence of authoritarianism in the Islamic world. Why is it that the Islamic world is generally behind other regions in the democratization process and in limiting authoritarian state power?

Authoritarianism

Authoritarianism has been an enduring and common feature of much of the Islamic world and Middle Eastern political systems for some time.[15] Despite the large variety of regime types that the Muslim world has experienced (monarchical, socialist, secular nationalist, Islamist, mobilizational, military junta, and others), authoritarian rule has persisted. Since authoritarianism depends largely on the use of tacit or explicit coercion to secure popular compliance, it also raises questions about the political legitimacy of the regimes and the region's long-term political stability.

What, then, is the problem? Let me start by stating that I reject the purely cultural or essentialist explanations for the persistence of authoritarianism. Although it is quite accurate, for example, to point to patrimonialism and clientelism as critical forces in Islamic politics, it is more accurate to view these as symptoms rather than causes of authoritarianism. Religious explanations, likewise, also fall short for at least two reasons. First, Islam, like all other great religions, embodies elements that can be used instrumentally for both authoritarian or democratic purposes. There is no necessary incompatibility between Islam and democracy. Second, as the not-too-distant elections in secular Turkey, Bangladesh, Pakistan, and other places have shown, open contestation for political office can take place in an Islamic society with Islamic political parties participating fully and responsibly in the electoral system. Moreover, although many regimes in the region have explicit references to Islam in their constitutions, most of the regimes are in fact secular. The source of authoritarianism, therefore, must be found in areas other than simply the religion.

A far better explanation for the persistence of authoritarianism and exclusionary political systems may be found in other realms. There are a number of political and economic factors that have sustained authoritarian control in the Islamic world in general, and in the Middle East in particular. In this regard, the role of the state has been especially problematic. Broadly speaking, the region's states have dominated the economy, manipulated sociocultural diversity to fragment the opposition, used repression to stifle dissent, and promoted different ideological formulas to rationalize nondemocratic regimes.[16] These features are in turn nurtured by both the internal and external environments. Internally, the so-called rentier states—that is, allocation states dependent on either oil or security rents for their revenues—have cultivated governmental nonaccountability and have promoted autonomy of the state from society.[17] Even when pressured by fiscal crises, as in the post–Gulf War era, rentier states of the Middle East have so far been able to adjust and, at least for now, maintain the old patterns of governance. For a variety of reasons, these fiscal crises have not yet played the same role in helping open the political systems as debt crises did for Argentina and Brazil.

The emergence of the rentier state in the Middle East, then, has had a detrimental effect on both economic development and political liberaliz-ation. Its economic impact can be seen in the state's dependency on rents, extracted primarily from oil, as its essential source of revenues. This has in turn discouraged the emergence of an independent bour-geoisie that can engage the state in economic give-and-take. The state has in effect attempted to satisfy the population at large through provi-sion of a host of services and economic activities paid through income received from rents. As long as rent is available, the state will respond only to those concerns of the population which it finds necessary for maintaining its power and position. Moreover, the rentier state's often extensive economic programs tend to engage the bourgeoisie fully and reward it economically in projects conceived and funded by the state. Hence, the bourgeoisie's fortunes come to center on the state and its defined economic goals. It becomes a dependent bourgeoisie unable and unwilling to engage the state in delineation of rights, responsibilities, and obligations.

The rentier state has the additional problem of becoming increasingly autonomous from the society. It can use the income from rent to enlist compliance and to pursue goals not necessarily in the best interests of society. Since most of the state's revenues are not extracted from the population, the corollary sense of obligation and responsiveness to the society does not necessarily develop. Rentier states find themselves in-creasingly reluctant to liberalize their political systems. As Luciani indi-cates, the oil rent becomes "a factor perpetuating authoritarian government."[18] This stands in sharp contrast to what Luciani calls "pro-duction states," where income is based primarily "through taxation of domestic economic activity"[19] In Luciani's view, taxation and the widen-ing of the state's fiscal base are essential inducements for democratiza-tion. He further posits that a state facing fiscal crisis and forced to resort to increased taxation will create demands from within the society for accountability and democratic institutions.

To sum up, then, authoritarianism in the Islamic world is a phenome-non that is intimately tied with the process of state formation and the form of economic and political control that the states have established over the population. These have allowed the state to extend the bound-aries of its control over civil society and to try to enforce one-way depen-dency. These actions of the state have been and are being challenged in much of the Islamic world. The slow but clear emergence of a more vibrant civil society as a counterweight to state domination is simply one of the more positive developments in the region. If ultimately successful, it will bring in a more balanced relationship between the state and soci-ety and help pave the path of reform, accountability, and probable democratization.

GROUPS AND INDIVIDUALS

Islam is, in many respects, a highly communitarian religion. Although individual rights are recognized and the sanctity of the private realm acknowledged, the thrust of Islamic civilization has been essentially group emphasis, not individual rights. Society is categorized into groups of people with legally differentiated rights. The broadest two categories juxtapose the two largest groupings known as the Abode of Peace (*dar a-Islam*) and the Abode of War (*dar al-harb*). The Abode of Peace encompasses all those Muslims who make up the Islamic community (*umma*) and are subject to the rules and regulations of the Islamic state. Those in the Abode of War are further subcategorized into the People of the Book and idolaters. The People of the Book are adherents of monotheistic religions who are also citizens of the Islamic state. Broadly speaking, they are given certain second-class citizenship rights and are expected to pay specified taxes and uphold their expected duties. Idolaters are all others outside the boundaries and jurisdiction of Islam.

This pattern of categorization of people with different citizenship rights and duties extends even to the Islamic community. For example, minors or those with mental disabilities have different rights. Both Islamic criminal and civil codes (personal status laws) make clear differentiation along gender lines in favor of males. Moreover, any Muslim—individual or group—who denies the finality of the Prophet Muhammad's message or rejects Islam for another religious community is viewed to be an apostate. The individual risks not only the loss of civil and political rights but is also subject (at least theoretically) to capital punishment.

There are also certain groups in the Islamic world that have come to acquire privileged positions in the community. Descendants of the prophets are often treated as one such group. This inchoate privilege is institutionalized in Shi'i Islam in the form of special taxation on the faithful for the benefit of the Prophet Muhammad's descendants. Moreover, and in spite of Islam's prophecy to what can be called "priesthood of all believers," the clerics have assumed a privileged position in the social order. Their importance has varied according to time, space, and sectarian fissures in Islam. For example, and due to particular historical and doctrinal developments, the clerics have assumed a far greater institutional importance among the Shi'is (specially the numerically dominant group of Twelver Shi'ism) than among the majority Sunnis.

In spite of these divisions and differences, the overriding group identity in Islam is with the community (umma). Islamic history has frequently taken account of this sense of solidarity and group identity irrespective of time and space. Although the actual operational relevance of group solidarity is subject to dispute, it does serve as a psychological bond that crosses boundaries and historical periods and brings Muslims together under the banner of God's unity (*tawhid*).

Norms and Group Exclusion

It is perhaps appropriate to raise the issue of group exclusion more systematically in the Islamic world. The key question is whether civility and the acceptance of the other is any less prevalent in Islamic traditions than in other great monotheistic religions. The charge here would be that in the Islamic world, norms of exclusion, whatever their origins, are more common than in other regions of the world and are applied more regularly to keep the out-groups at bay. This observation takes into account differences between two principal classes of norms, universalistic norms and norms of difference and exclusion. As Hardin has argued, universalistic norms apply to essentially all members of society, while norms of difference basically benefit a well-defined subgroup in the social order. The force of universalistic norms is their indifferent application. Norms of exclusion, however, are not universally applied; they work to differentiate among ethnic, religious, social class, gender, or other groupings. These norms can succeed depending on their level of support, cost of deviation, and the availability of enforceable sanctions.[20]

In the Muslim world, as in all societies and regions, both universalistic and exclusionary norms operate. What makes the Islamic case different may be the significant role of the state and some social groups in defining and enforcing a set of exclusionary norms. The problem is further exacerbated when norms of exclusion are derived from universalistic religious criteria. In other words, this amounts to invoking a universal norm but particularizing it—that is, applying it to one group only. Such exclusionary postures can benefit only a well-defined in-group and will exclude others. Similar observations can be made about norms of difference that are based on ethnicity, gender, and nationality. All of these serve to exclude the other on the basis of preconceived and unchanging norms.

As alluring as this explanation may be, it has some problems. Can one confidently say that norms of exclusion are more common in the Muslim World than, say, in Africa, Latin America, or Central Europe? I doubt that norms of exclusion are more prevalent in the Islamic world than in other regions. Clearly, the recent history of conflicts and warfare in the Muslim areas, especially the Middle East, has increased the saliency of exclusionary norms because of anger, perceptions of injustice, and the like. It is also true that certain groups, particularly those with fundamental religious orientations, use universalistic norms to exclude the other. But this does not amount to any kind of conclusion asserting that norms of exclusion are more common among the Muslims.

We can, however, say that any analysis of the politics of inclusion in the Islamic world must also take into account the role of values and other cultural artifacts that have become part of the Middle East over time. Some of these are positive and conducive to inclusive politics; some are not. Clearly, when an extremist Islamist group claims that it alone knows the truth, and that you either join them or risk excommunication, then there is a serious problem. This issue is also relevant to extremist groups elsewhere in the Middle East, whatever their religious orientation may be. An immediate and serious consequence of such exclusionary attitudes is to raise legitimate fear among religious minorities and women. Rather than promoting ecumenism, these views perpetuate particularism and deny a proper place for pluralism in politics and social affairs.

I do not deny the relevance of these factors and their bearing on people's attitudes and views. What I am concerned with, however, has less to do with deeply seated views of individuals and groups and more with their behavior in the political arena. And it is in the political arena, in the context of the rule of law, where the inclusion is most applicable to the Muslim world.

Group Conflict and Citizenship Rights: The Islamists

The pressing problem of inclusion-exclusion is particularly relevant to Islamists and their vision of an Islamic polity based on the *shari'ah* (Islamic Law) and religious norms. Historically, the revivalist movements in Islam have generally concerned themselves with two broad themes of reform (*islah*) and renewal (*tajdid*).[21] Their interest has been to reform the existing social order, since it has strayed from the Straight Path, in order to once again renew Islam in public life. Although the form of relationship between renewal and reform has varied from one group of Islamists to another, all groups have dealt with this problem in one manner or another.

An inherent element in the concern with reform and renewal is the reintroduction of some form of traditionalism in the discourse of the Islamists.[22] As Sivan explains, "Islamic Resurgence is to be explained to a large extent by the durability of what one may dub the Islamic 'traditional bedrock', i.e. the persistence through constant adaptation of classical Islam as *living tradition*."[23] Traditionalism requires adoption of certain basic authentic Islamic views and practices borrowed from the past. These include their views on (1) sovereignty and social contract, (2) religious minorities, (3) gender, and (4) lay intellectuals. Although the precise differences among the Islamists on these issues are not always clear, there remain important variations among them on the direct relevance and applicability of these views to the political system. Since the impact of the differential application of these views is potentially profound, it behooves us to underline points of convergence and divergence, as well as several problem areas in the Islamists' use of these norms.

Sovereignty and Social Contract

All Islamist groups maintain that sovereignty belongs to God. It is sacrilegious to hold a contrary opinion. It is the supremacy of tawhid (God's unity) as the essential doctrine that defines an Islamist. The Rousseauian idea of social contract with its explicit acceptance of people's sovereignty has no place among the diehard Islamists. It is, however, possible to move beyond the debate on God's sovereignty and allow for the human agency to have extensive, if not complete, control over the organization of political life, including the legislative domain.[24] Islamic history is a rich depository of precisely this practical form of freedom to legislate in a vast array of fields for the interest of the polity.

It is also possible to conceive of the time-honored concept of bay'a (allegiance to the ruler) as a way to legitimize on theological grounds a form of contract between the ruler and the ruled. In its essential meaning, this is clearly not social contract. In its implementation, however, it can codify and underscore the existence of certain rights and responsibilities for both the rulers and the polity. It can also give rise to a sense of entitlement that is critical for holding regimes responsible and accountable to the citizenry.[25] It is perhaps not too farfetched to think that the more modern notion of pacts between regimes and their adversaries is not unrelated to this practice. Pacts are predicated on agreements, rights, obligations, and entitlement. As Tilly has shown, rights of citizenship have historically developed in Europe as part of bargains in the course of long struggles with the invasive state.[26] Rights do not emerge on the scene overnight. They have to be acquired and then preserved against all odds.

The durability of basic rights is largely dependent on its collective enforcement by the state and its citizens. Hence, the definition of citizenship becomes highly poignant—a murky and problematic area for many Islamists. Again as Tilly says, "citizenship rights belong in principle (if not always in practice) to everyone who qualifies as a full-fledged member of a given state; membership in the category suffices to qualify a person for enforceable claims."[27]

Religious Minorities

Islamists' views of citizenship, and who is entitled to it, have different gradations and important differences. There are those Islamists (e.g., Jihad, Takfir wa al-Hijra) whose view of citizenship is highly exclusionary. Even monotheistic religious minorities are basically denied such rights except as they are granted to them by virtue of benevolence of the Islamists in power. This form of exclusion also extends to the Muslims, rulers and otherwise, who do not fully share the Islamists' view on the organization of the polity.

Introduction of the concept of *jahiliyya* (ignorance) by Sayyid Qutb and some of his followers to modern Egypt is in essence a rejection of the existing society and its particular conception of rights and obligations. Jahiliyya has traditionally been used to refer to Arabia before the rise of Islam. The Prophet eliminated jahiliyya through the force of monotheistic Islam. The term itself was used exclusively for this era until the Pakistani Islamist Abu-al-Aʿla Mawdudi applied it in his writings to the modern period. In Qutb's further application, places such as modern Egypt are reincarnations of pre-Islamic Arabia in their ignorance of divine design and religious norms. As Qutb states emphatically, the jahiliyya society is Godless, subject to its own rules and regulations, and it rejects the central place of divinity in human affairs. The Muslim vanguards should fight this corrupt society until it is overthrown.[28] This is a decisive call to action on behalf of a rigid and exclusionist Islamic state.

Other Islamist groups have also made explicit denunciations of broadly defined non-Islamic groups. In his analysis of some of the Egyptian Islamists and their rejection of the Western culture and ideas, Gilles Kepel refers to a broad set of rejected categories, the Four Horseman of the Apocalypse. They are the Jewry, the Crusade, Communism, and Secularism.[29] Those who adhere to these groups or their ideas are, then, denied citizenship rights in this particular form of an Islamic state. These Islamists do not make a distinction between Judaism and Zionism, collapsing them into one rejected category. The Crusade refers essentially to the Egyptian Copts, whom they denounce for their attributed links with the Western culture. Clearly, neither Communism nor Secularism can have any place in these Islamists' rigid conception of the universe. After all, Communists are Godless and Secularists reject the paramount role of religion in Muslims' political life. They must all be eliminated.

This extreme rejectionist stand is in contrast to many other Islamists who not only have a more liberal conception of citizenship but also extend it to at least some religious minorities. The example of the Islamic Republic of Iran is of interest here. In conformity to the traditional Islamic treatment of monotheistic religious minorities, certain citizenship rights are granted to the Christians, Jews, and Zoroastrians. These include freedom to enact religious ceremonies, religious education, and personal status matters such as marriage, divorce, and inheritance. Although it can be argued justifiably that there is an element of second-class citizenship that defines these rights, it is nevertheless clear that some formal rights have been granted to these religious minorities. The problem is most severe, however, when another religious minority, the Baha'is, is concerned. The refusal to recognize this significant group as a religious minority, and their arbitrary designation of it as a political group, has resulted in the regime's systematic persecution of the Baha'is. In other words, citizenship rights have been denied to the Baha'is because of certain aspects of their doctrinal belief that the theocratic state finds fundamentally unacceptable.[30]

The case of the Coptic Christians of Egypt is also illustrative. Copts and Muslims have lived side by side in Egypt for centuries. Coptic and Muslim traditions have shaped Egypt's culture, and while each community has sustained its unique rites and institutions, there is little to distinguish an individual Christian from a Muslim. Comprising less than 10 percent of the country's population, the Copts have admittedly been circumspect in their practice of religion. A leading Coptic personality, Makram Obeid, once said that we are all Muslims culturally. This was repeated by Adel Hussein, a leading pro-Islamist politician, who noted: "in Egypt, all people are Muslims. Some pray in churches, others in mosques."[31] In recent years, however, the Copts and Christian institutions in Egypt have come under steady attack by Islamic militants. More disturbing, arguably, is the fact that recent Egyptian governments have not generally encouraged Coptic representation in state offices. For instance, none of Egypt's twenty-six governors is Christian.

The right to religious freedom is a serious issue with implications that extend beyond the Islamists. Many Islamic countries do not fully appreciate the meaning of this fundamental right. This problem is evident in the 1990 Cairo Declaration on Human Rights in Islam, issued by the Organization of Islamic Conference, which includes all Muslim countries. Endorsed by Saudi Arabia, Iran, and other Islamic countries, the Declaration (as Mayer points out accurately) falls short of international human rights standards in not designating freedom of religion as "a fundamental and nonderogable right."[32] This failure is potentially detrimental not only to all non-Muslim citizens, but also to those who dissent from the officially imposed constructs of Islam. As Mayer points out,

> The failure to provide for religious freedom also has serious practical implications for Muslims, given the number of Muslim dissenters from officially-imposed constructs of Islam and members of local minority sects who have been mistreated, charged with apostasy from Islam, or subjected to pressures or threats to compel them to abjure nonconforming belief.[33]

The important point here for our purposes is to put the Islamists' view on freedom of religion and religious minorities in proper contextual perspective. Clearly, many militant Islamist groups have negative perceptions of both religious minorities and secularists. This perception is nurtured, however, in a larger environment where even the moderate pro-Western regimes do not fully appreciate the fundamental right of religious freedom. This does not, of course, excuse either the Islamists or the moderate regimes. It only underlines a significant problem that needs to be addressed on a larger scale.

Gender

Another problem area with special application to the Islamists is the issue of equality of women and gender rights and relations. The difficulty here stems from two related sources: first is the essentially discriminatory nature of Islamic personal status laws and the criminal code when applied to women. Second, there is a prevalence of certain fixed attitudes and views, learned through the socialization experience, about women and gender roles.[34] The combination of these two factors places women in a highly disadvantageous position in the Islamists' universe.

All Islamists emphasize the role of family and its critical importance as the backbone of a moral and ethical society. Women are praised as the carriers of virtue and as the key agents of socialization for children. Family values, and women's essential role in their propagation, are recognized and given special praise in the discourse of all Islamists. Nevertheless, and in spite of the recognition given to women, Islamic personal status laws discriminate against women in the areas of inheritance, divorce, and marriage rights. A woman's inheritance from her parents is half that of a male sibling's. Despite certain restrictions, a man can divorce a spouse rather freely, while a woman's rights to do so is substantially more restrictive. Men can engage in polygamy; women cannot. In Twelver Shi'i Islam, marriage based on a temporary contract (*muta'a*) for a specified time is allowed.[35] Although women also partake of temporary marriage, restrictions on them are more stringent. Islamic criminal code based on the concept of talion is dependent on witnesses' testimonies. Testimony of a woman is valued as half of a man's. Additionally, testimonies of women alone, irrespective of their numbers and validity, are not sufficient to convict a murderer. In all cases, a male witness is required for validation.

Closely tied in with legal restrictions are the Islamists' attempts to segregate women in public space. The moral imperative that dictates such a view may be hard to fathom but it is advanced by the Islamists as a justification for enforced separateness. The public space applicable to this form of separateness includes public transportation, all levels of education, even parts of the workplace. The separateness is further reinforced through application of female veiling and the imposition of penalties for its nonobservance. While voluntary veiling is also done for economic reasons for women, and at times as an act of protest, the relevant issue to the Islamists is state-imposed involuntary veiling.

Lay Intellectuals

The intellectuals as a broad category (many of whom are secularists) comprise another potential problem area for the Islamists. Although there are many traditional intellectuals who may not feel necessarily constrained by the Islamists' vision, most intellectuals feel otherwise. Their often individualist and nonconformist postures can create problems, especially if they are accompanied by avowed secularist attitudes. Many recent examples of intolerant attitudes toward intellectuals abound in places such as Egypt, Iran, the Sudan, and elsewhere. The intellectual's propensity to secularism is fundamentally not acceptable to hardline Islamists.

The one hopeful area of mutual acceptance between practicing Muslims and those with secularist orientation is the progressive evolution of Islamic modernism, with its growing acceptance of separate realms for religion and the state. In other words, a religious society does not necessarily require an Islamic state to dictate its course and direction. There have already been some important and influential beginnings in this domain by those who find Islam, popular sovereignty, and democracy compatible. Noted Islamic modernist thinkers of the present Middle East—the likes of Hasan Hanafi, Muhammad Shahrour, and Abdol-Karim Soroush—have already advanced the idea that it is necessary to reorient critical Islamic themes in light of the developments of modern society. Since these thinkers and their followers remain faithful to the essential precepts of Islam, their potential impact can be significant. More importantly, since Islam has never been a static civilization, and has had a rich tradition of modernism, a successful fusion of Islam and modernity can remove the hostile cultural edge from the interaction of the Islamic world with the West.

Conclusion

I have stressed that the concept of inclusion can be a serious problem with the most Islamists' weltanschauung. I have further argued that citizenship disenfranchisement falls most heavily on religious minorities, women, and lay intellectuals. However, I also observe that there are significant ranges of opinions and views among Islamists on fundamental issues of governance. These differences apply even to the operation of such critical concepts as sovereignty, legitimacy, human rights, and the rights of women and religious minorities. More importantly, the problem of exclusion and authoritarianism needs to be put in its proper perspective by comparing it with the record of secularist and authoritarian regimes. Unfortunately, the regimes' record is not all that promising.

There is no simple solution for the foreseeable future, and the Islamists are here to stay. In my view, it is important for us to note their demonstrated differences, recognize those potentially positive views that promote social justice and fair redistribution of wealth, and acknowledge attempts that make human agency dominant while at the same time pay respect to God's sovereignty. All this said, we must also be prepared to expose and denounce exclusionary practices of radical fundamentalists.

As far as the broader theme of Islam and civil society is concerned, it is clear that it has become an important subject of debate and discussion in the Islamic world. The practical applicability of this discourse on issues of governance, civility, and pluralism remain unclear. Islamic politics in the next millennium, however, points to a real ray of hope in the potential impact of its youth. If real change (with greater inclusivity and accountability) does come about in Islamic politics, it will be because of pressures from the youth. Two other factors also support the youth's demands for change and inclusive politics. The first has to do with women, especially the younger generation. Women will become increasingly a force for change and openness. The other will be the vibrancy of civil society and associational life in the region. Although states in the Middle East and other parts of the Islamic world have traditionally tried to control and thwart the development of autonomous civil society, associational life and "social capital" remain important assets in the Middle East. These three interrelated forces are potentially the harbingers of change. They help cement the growing differentiation between the spheres of religion and the state—a differentiation that can only promote the development of civil society. They have the ability to influence, but not dictate, the course of Islamic politics in the direction of accountability, civility, and pluralism.

NOTES

PASSAGES have been excerpted from the following published articles (all cited in full in the endnotes that follow): Farhad Kazemi and Augustus Richard Norton, "Civil Society, Political Reform, and Authoritarianism"; Farhad Kazemi, "The Inclusion Imperative"; Farhad Kazemi and Augustus Richard Norton, "Political Challenges to Middle Eastern Governments in the Twenty-First Century."

1. Serif Mardin, "Civil Society and Islam," in *Civil Society: Theory, History, Comparison*, ed. John A. Hall (Cambridge: Polity Press, 1995), 279.

2. See, for example, the "Civil Society in the Middle East" project at New

York University as reflected in the following publications: Augustus Richard Norton, ed. *Civil Society in the Middle East*, 2 vols. (Leiden: Brill, 1995–96); Jillian Schwedler, ed., *Toward Civil Society in the Middle East: A Primer* (Boulder, Colo.: Lynne Rienner, 1995); Farhad Kazemi, guest ed. "Special Issue on Civil Society in Iran," *Iran Nameh* 13, no. 4 (Fall 1995), and 14, no. 1 (Winter 1996).

3. See John Kelsay, "Civil Society and Government in Islam," in this volume.

4. Samuel Huntington, "The Clash of Civilizations?" *Foreign Affairs* 72 (Summer 1993): 22–49.

5. Said Amir Arjomand, "Civil Society and the Rule of Law in the Constitutional Politics of Iran under Khatami," *Social Research* 67 (Summer 2000): 283–301.

6. Michael Walzer, "The Idea of Civil Society," *Dissent* (Spring 1991): 293. For further discussion see Jean L. Cohen and Andrew Arato, *Civil Society and Political Theory* (Cambridge: MIT Press, 1994); Adam Seligman, *The Idea of Civil Society* (Princeton: Princeton University Press, 1992); John Hall, ed., *Civil Society: Theory, History, Comparison* (Cambridge, UK: Polity Press, 1995). See also the definitions in Norton, *Civil Society in the Middle East.*

7. Edward Shils, "The Virtue of Civil Society," *Government and Opposition* 26 (Winter 1991): 4.

8. Ibid., 4.

9. Augustus Richard Norton, "The Future of Civil Society in the Middle East," *Middle East Journal* 47 (Spring 1993): 211. See also Bryan Turner, "Orientalism and the Problem of Civil Society in Islam," in *Orientalism, Islam, and Islamists*, ed. Asaf Hussain, Robert Olson, and Jamil Qureishi (Brattleboro, Vt.: Amana Books, 1984), 27.

10. Norton, "Future of Civil Society," 214. See Michael Walzer, *On Toleration* (New Haven: Yale University Press, 1998); David Heyd, ed., *Toleration: An Elusive Virtue* (Princeton: Princeton University Press, 1996).

11. Shils, "The Virtue of Civil Society," 11.

12. Ibid., 9–10.

13. Walzer, "The Idea of Civil Society," 302. See also Robert Putnam, *Making Democracy Work: Civic Traditions in Modern Italy* (Princeton: Princeton University Press, 1993).

14. Kelsay, "Civil Society and Government in Islam," 21.

15. See Farhad Kazemi and Augustus Richard Norton, "Civil Society, Political Reform, and Authoritarianism in the Middle East: A Response," *Contention* 5 (1996): 107–19.

16. Jill Crystal, "Authoritarianism and Its Adversaries in the Arab World," *World Politics* 46 (1994): 262–89.

17. See Giacomo Luciani, "Allocation vs. Production States: A Theoretical Framework," in *The Rentier State*, ed. Hazem Beblawi and Giacomo Luciani (London: Croom Helm, 1987).

18. Giacomo Luciani, "The Oil Rent, the Fiscal Crisis of the State, and Democratization," in *Democracy Without Democrats: The Renewal of Politics in the Muslim World*, ed. Ghassan Salame' (London: I. B. Tauris, 1994), 131.

19. Luciani, "The Oil Rent," 131. See also Luciani, "Allocation vs. Production

States." For a somewhat different view, see Yasuyuki Matsunaga, "L'Etat Rentier Est-il Refractaire a la Democratie?" *Critique Internationale* 8 (July 2000): 46–58.

20. Russell Hardin, *One for All: The Logic of Group Conflict* (Princeton: Princeton University Press, 1995); Farhad Kazemi, "The Inclusion Imperative," *Middle East Studies Association Bulletin* 30 (1996): 147–153.

21. John Voll, "Renewal and Reform in Islamic History: Tajdid and Islah," in *Voices of Islamic Resurgence*, ed. John Esposito (New York: Oxford University Press, 1983), 32–47. See Farhad Kazemi and Augustus Richard Norton, "Political Challenges to Middle Eastern Governments in the Twenty-first Century," in *New Frontiers in Middle East Security*, ed. Lenore Martin (New York: St. Martin's Press, 1998), 79–104.

22. Ali Banuazizi, "Social Psychological Approaches to Political Development," in *Understanding Political Development*, ed. Myron Weiner and Samuel Huntington (Boston: Little, Brown, and Co., 1987), 287; and see Said Amir Arjomand, "Traditionalism in Twentieth-Century Iran," in *From Nationalism to Revolutionary Islam* (London: Macmillan, 1984), 195–232.

23. Emanuel Sivan, "The Islamic Resurgence: Civil Society Strikes Back," *Journal of Contemporary History* 25 (May–June 1990): 357.

24. Ahmad S. Moussali, "Modern Islamic Fundamentalist Discourses on Civil Society, Pluralism, and Democracy," in Norton, *Civil Society in the Middle East* 1:70–119. See also Roxanne Euben, *Enemy in the Mirror: Islamic Fundamentalism and the Limits of Modern Rationalism* (Princeton: Princeton University Press, 1999), 49–92.

25. Amartya Sen, *Poverty and Famines: An Essay on Entitlement and Deprivation* (Oxford: Clarendon Press, 1981), cited in Charles Tilly, "Where Do Rights Come From?" (paper presented for the Vilhelm Aubert Memorial Symposium, University of Oslo, August 1990), 1.

26. Tilly, "Where Do Rights Come From?" 2

27. Ibid., 2.

28. Sayyid Qutb, *Milestones* (Indianapolis: American Trust Publications, 1990).

29. Gilles Kepel, *The Prophet and the Pharaoh: Muslim Extremism in Egypt* (London: Al Saqi Books, 1985).

30. See Firuz Kazemzadeh, "The Baha'is in Iran: Twenty Years of Repression," *Social Research* 67 (Summer 2000): 537–58.

31. Interview with Adel Hussein, Cairo, July 11, 1995.

32. Ann Mayer, "Universal versus Islamic Human Rights: A Clash of Culture or a Clash with a Construct?" *Michigan Journal of International Law* 15 (1994): 334.

33. Ibid.

34. For further elaboration, see Farhad Kazemi, "Gender, Islam and Politics," *Social Research* 67 (Summer 2000): 453–74.

35. Shala Haeri, *Law of Desire: Temporary Marriage in Shi'i Islam* (Syracuse, N.Y.: Syracuse University Press, 1989).

Confucian Perspectives on Civil Society and Government

Peter Nosco

LET ME BEGIN by explaining what I mean when I use the terms *civil society* and *Confucianism*, since both terms are used in widely varying ways. I regard civil society as inseparable from voluntary associations, but I view these voluntary associations somewhat more narrowly than do some students of the subject. That is to say, where some[1] would regard civil society as comprised of all voluntary and noncoercive social groups— excluding principally only the family and the state, participation in which cannot be regarded as, under ordinary circumstances, elective—I do not include public religious associations or affiliations, which for most people until relatively recent times have not had the same elective character, nor do I include participation in secret societies with a political character. That the most obvious involuntary (in the sense of nonelective) associations are those of the family or the state—both of which are fundamental and primary from a Confucian perspective—provides us with an immediate suggestion regarding what a Confucian perspective on civil society might resemble.

I shall also exclude the market from our understanding of civil society. Unquestionably, an increasing volume and complexity of transactions both within and without the marketplace characterize early modernity and strengthen the individual's sense of self as a competent and increasingly autonomous actor in an ever more complex social field. However, the historical coincidence of market culture, early modernity, and civil society in Europe and North America appears not to have been a comparable feature of East Asian societies, and so we look not to markets and their culture, except as they contribute to those qualities of competence and integrity that characterize human agency, and are suggestive of the emergence of a relatively autonomous self.

Civil society is often conflated with constitutionally structured society, but this is likewise not helpful in an Asian context, where constitutions and their related institutions have most commonly been understood as conferred from above rather than generated from below.[2] And again, where civil society has often been associated with the public sphere, we are more interested here in the development of a private sphere of the sort that enables individuals to associate in ways potentially destabilizing to the organic society envisioned in Confucian societies.

As with any of the other perspectives offered in this project, the term *Confucianism* has likewise meant different things at different times—even different things, surely, at the same time—and this contributes to making this task particularly challenging. For decades, social scientists with a comparative bent have linked "Confucianism" with economic development—an ironic linkage in view of traditional Confucianism's hostility toward profit and disdain for merchants and commercial activity—and have designated such countries as Singapore and Taiwan as Confucian societies. The principal features of these "Confucian" societies—the "little tigers," as they are often styled—are on the one hand their social cohesion and order, and on the other hand their authoritarian governments, which embrace the mantle of benevolent paternalism. The now discredited economic linkage notwithstanding, any sense of "Confucianism" that privileges, say, Singapore over China would seem quite obviously to merit reconsideration.

We understand that it is largely to the past where one must turn to find "Confucianism," but how far back does one go? The Confucianism of the Four Books—the *Analects, Mencius, Great Learning*, and *Mean*—certainly represents one "Confucianism" and is of course authoritative, but the authors of these works both lived in and posited times in which voluntary associations of virtually any kind simply were not a prominent feature. Further, from, say, the fall of the latter Han dynasty in 220 till the founding of the Sung dynasty in 960, Confucian teachers in China largely relinquished the ontological battlefield to Buddhists. To be sure, so-called Confucian diviners offered insight into how to achieve good and avoid adverse fortune, but they had little to say on classical Confucianism's traditional concerns, such as how one might become a better ruler, "citizen," or family member.

After 960 Chinese Confucian scholars succeeded in refashioning and revitalizing their tradition so as to compete successfully with and eventually displace Buddhism as the intellectual and spiritual orthodoxy of the day. This revitalized Confucianism, commonly called Neo-Confucianism, represents a second "Confucianism," whose tradition was embraced in China, Korea, Japan, and Vietnam in so compelling a manner and to such a degree that it actually contributes to the definition of these lands as belonging to the cultural sphere of East Asia.[3] Neo-Confucianism posited the identity of both natural principles and moral principles, suggesting that analogues of the same principles that inform and govern the material world can be found within the human person in the guise of an originally good human nature or mind. Neo-Confucianism further asserted a twofold praxis intended to recover and reassert these primordial seeds of goodness. On the one hand, orthodox Neo-Confucianism proposed studying the external world around one (the so-called investigation of things) in order to discern the role of principle within it and thereby to acquire objective knowledge concerning the seeds of one's original goodness. On the other hand, Neo-Confucianism also embraced the internal cultivation of one's originally good properties through such exercises as quiet sitting, and through the nurturing of seriousness and reverence, understood in East Asia as dimensions of the same word: *ching* in Chinese, *kei* in Japanese.

One might in comparable fashion identify yet a third "Confucianism" in the form of those institutions and ritual traditions which have played such prominent roles variously throughout the societies of East Asia. These would include an examination system that tested one's mastery of Confucian classical texts and commentaries as a prerequisite for participation in the civil service; institutionalized opportunities for individual remonstrance with the political order, which are examined toward the end of this essay; social regulations governing matters ranging from divorce to inheritance; rituals performed both within and without the home, intended to honor one's ancestors; and of central importance to us as a form of voluntary association, the role of private academies as well as official schools in training potential elites; and so on.

It is, however, the canon that ultimately defines who is or is not a "Confucian," and it is to this canon that we inevitably return for textual insight into the questions that concern us, questions such as: How is one to know if the Way is prevailing? What are the properties of true kingship? What is the role of learning in defining the individual? How does one's activity in individual relationships contribute to the larger goal of peace and order? How is one to cultivate and thereby transform oneself in the direction of pure goodness? Please note in this last regard that to the extent that the Confucian effort to achieve human perfection involves transformation in the direction of a moral absolute such as Heaven (Ch. *t'ien*, Jpn. *ten*), this activity has a manifestly religious character.[4]

The canon and the textual insight it offers are, however, ultimately insufficient for addressing all of the topics and questions that inform and structure this inquiry into civil society and government, and so we must also turn to history for answers to certain quite basic questions. Was there civil society in East Asia? If so, when and where did it develop? And if not—or at least not as the term has been generally understood in Europe and North America—are there perhaps ways in which we can modify the concept of civil society to provide an alternative working model applicable to East Asia?

This chapter attempts to address these questions. It surely goes without saying—but seems prudent to acknowledge nonetheless—that my answers to these questions will necessarily be open to argument by specialists in both civil society and East Asian social and political history. Further, the constraints of space necessarily limit the depth of our inquiry into the topic questions, particularly since I at times try to historicize the issues. I thus fear that the specialist on East Asia will find my characterizations of the historical, social, and textual dimensions of this exercise frustratingly shallow, while the novice in East Asian matters will find them no less frustratingly complex and overly wrought. The specialist on civil societies will likewise surely find much of both a theoretical and practical nature with which to quarrel in my analysis. These reservations and disclaimers notwithstanding, it is evident that, like the other perspectives offered in this exercise, if Confucianism can offer insights on and contribute to the clarification of issues that never developed in the "local cultures" that represent Confucianism's original setting—issues like ecology, human rights, and so on—then it can likewise offer its own perspective on civil society.[5]

BOUNDARIES

The discussion of Confucian perspectives on the boundary between civil society and the state—or, to rephrase the question, Where would Confucianism draw the line between the authority of government and that of other groups in the society?—is thoroughly speculative, for classical Confucianism never envisioned a society inclusive of secular, voluntary associations of the sort suggestive of my understanding of civil society. This kind of society requires not just a sense of the integrity of the individual as an actor capable of negotiating his/her interactions in a responsible and ultimately socially constructive manner—something Confucianism would affirm—but also an acknowledged sphere of privacy granted by the state and society to its individual and corporate members to enable unauthorized voluntary associations, and Confucianism has generally not distinguished between privacy and selfishness in these contexts.[6]

In ancient (Han) China, Confucianism accommodated the clan and village loyalties characteristic of the society of that age by accepting both the family and the community as laboratories in which one learns to progress and measure one's progress in the direction of goodness. And, in classical (T'ang) Chinese and (Heian) Japanese societies, what was known as "Confucianism" of necessity accommodated the widespread individual religious and aesthetic affiliation with Buddhism and was of limited intellectual or spiritual appeal, even as its practical value to the public realm was generally acknowledged. Thus, when we ask where Confucianism would locate the boundary between the authority of government and that of other groups in society, our initial impulse is to visualize this in terms of circles that share a point of tangency, as in illustration 1.

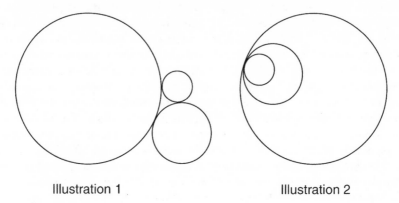

Illustration 1   Illustration 2

This perspective is mistaken, however, since classical Confucianism and its Neo-Confucian variants saw the relationship between the individual, the family group, and the state more as concentric circles, as represented in illustration 2, and as articulated in the following famous passage from the *Great Learning*.

> The ancients who wished to manifest their clear character to the world would first bring order to their states. Those who wished to bring order to their states would first regulate their families. Those who wished to regulate their families would first cultivate their personal lives. Those who wished to cultivate their personal lives would first rectify their minds. Those who wished to rectify their minds would first make their wills sincere. Those who wished to make their wills sincere would first extend their knowledge. The extension of knowledge consists in the investigation of things. When things are investigated, knowledge is extended; when knowledge is extended, the will becomes sincere; when the will is sincere, the mind is rectified; when the mind is rectified, the personal life is cultivated; when the personal life is cultivated, the family will be regulated; when the family is regulated, the state will be in order; and when the state is in order, there will be peace throughout the world.[7]

One goal of Confucianism—and certainly the goal of greatest interest to those in positions of state authority—was to bring order to the state and thereby to spread peace throughout the world, but as this passage indicates the goal has its roots in the moral and spiritual ordering of the individual person and his/her family.

Further, Confucianism in many ways modeled its understanding of the state on its understanding of the family. In Confucianism, the ruler is unambiguously represented as the parent of the people, which reinforces an organic view of society as an enormous quasi family with the ruler as its paterfamilias. This being so, there is no more "space" or boundary between a Confucian ruler and Confucian citizen than between a Confucian father and Confucian son. And, just as the Confucian *Analects* insists that a filial son must never disobey (2:5), one fundamental responsibility of the Confucian "citizen" is to submit to that cosmically ordained authority which represents the incarnate mandate of Heaven to exercise terrestrial rule.

Historically, however, as societies in East Asia acquired the conditions of early modernity, a kind of "space" did indeed open between the state and the citizen, Confucian misgivings toward such space notwithstanding.[8] As elsewhere around the world, though perhaps not to the same degree as in Europe or North America, this sphere has the character of a public space, distinguished from both official and private spaces, and attendant to the emergence of this space is a boundary of sorts between the government and other groups or individuals in the society.

The factors responsible for this development are not unlike those identified with comparable developments in Europe: increased urbanization, with individuals uprooted from traditional village communities, and endeavoring to create new forms of association to combat the anomie and alienation that accompany such changes; an expansion of surplus wealth and the market, with an ever-increasing volume of transactions, including the commodification of a broad range of cultural products; a developed communication and transportation infrastructure, which contributes to the spread of literacy throughout the society, as well as increased opportunities for personal travel; and in religion, one observes the rise of "protestant" movements in East Asia, as in Europe, such as the Pure Land denominations of Buddhism, which privilege the individual's capacity to negotiate salvation on the basis of personal faith, and which at least conceptually diminish the role of the *ecclesia* as a mediating agency in this process. In a variety of ways, these developments reinforce a sense of the individual as competent on the one hand to negotiate the acquisition of an increasingly diverse range of material and cultural products, and on the other hand to enter into elective associations of an ever more variegated sort.

Confucianism cannot be credited with stimulating these changes, but it can be observed to respond to them in at least two noncongruent ways. First, one notes an increasing priority within Confucianism given to those forms of praxis that privilege interiority and self-cultivation, at the expense of the study of either the external world or the traditional classics. "Look inside yourself" becomes the message of much early-modern

Confucian thought, for there you will find all that you need to know in order to become a perfected person. And second, one finds the reemergence and increasing prominence of forms of Confucianism that assert historicist as opposed to naturalist ontologies, arguing that the Confucian Way is not an unchanging set of universal principles, but rather is comprised of social and political practices that are conditioned by time and place.

The relevance of these changes for our understanding of boundaries between the state and civil society in East Asia rests in the rise of voluntary associations that pursued neither wealth nor power, salvation nor charity, but rather cultural identity and personal development. Accompanying the religious, social, and economic changes identified above was the rise of a secular and urban popular culture that for the first time made possible the successful marketing of cultural products—plays, novels and short stories, woodblock prints, and so on—that literally paid for themselves. That is to say, where in earlier times in East Asia the producers of such cultural products required either independent wealth or external patronage, hereafter it became possible for the producers of these cultural products to make an often lucrative living through their marketing. And one part of this cultural revolution was the rise of the private academy, in which forms of academic culture that had previously been restricted to those whose wealth or class entitled them to its acquisition were now made accessible to an altogether new class of enthusiastic cultural consumers.

This, I would argue, is the closest analogue one will find in East Asia prior to the twentieth century to the kinds of voluntary and noncoercive, nonfamilial associations characteristic of the rise of civil society in Europe, and it is here that I would situate the boundary of an admittedly limited public space between the state and individual in East Asia. Furthermore, and for the purposes of the discussion that follows, it is significant that the earliest and most successful private academies in East Asia were those that offered instruction in Confucianism. In China at least as early as the seventeenth century, one finds an intellectual like Huang Tsung-hsi (1610–95) challenging the careerist orientation of much contemporary private and public instruction by arguing that in ancient times, "even the Son of Heaven did not dare to decide right and wrong for himself but shared with the schools the determination of right and wrong. Therefore, although the training of scholar-officials was one of the functions of schools, they were not established for this alone."[9] In a different vein, in Japan where there was no examination system, but where the expansion of private educational opportunities was at least as great as in China, one finds Huang's contemporary, Itō Jinsai (1627–1705), founding a private academy in Kyoto styled the Kogidō, or Hall of Ancient Meaning, where he offered instruction in Confucian textual studies to hundreds of tuition-paying students.[10] This is where I would locate a boundary between the state and one kind of quasi social group, and we shall continue our examination of the private academy and its significance for both popular culture and civil society in the next section.

NEEDS

The question of whether the state and civil society (as understood here, principally in terms of such voluntary associations as the private academy) need each other discloses the unbalanced and nonsymbiotic nature of their relationship in East Asia. Ultimately, voluntary associations are destabilizing to the Confucian ideal of the paternalistic state, just as voluntary associations are dependent in a Confucian society on the state's forbearance. Indeed, from the perspective of a ruler in a Confucian state, the "space" represented by any form of voluntary association—as we saw in the previous discussion of boundaries—is inevitably contingent and revocable, and to disclose this, let us reexamine the social and historical circumstances that fostered the emergence of the private academy in late-seventeenth-century Japan.[11]

In terms of urbanization, Japan at this time was certainly among the most urbanized societies in the world, with at least 10 percent of its population living in settlements of ten thousand or more. Surplus wealth was more broadly distributed across an unprecedented range of social strata. Literacy rates were likely as high as anywhere else in the world, and there was a remarkably well developed communications and transportation infrastructure. The most important feature of this society, however, at least in terms of the emergence of the popular private academy, was the cultural liberality of the Japanese state.

It goes without saying that the term *cultural liberality* is problematic. Charles Frankel used it to refer to "an affirmative interest in the promotion of the diversity and qualities of mind which encourage empathetic understanding and critical appreciation of the diverse possibilities of human life."[12] This sense of cultural liberality was unarguably present in Japan during the last two decades of the seventeenth century and the first decade of the eighteenth, when Japan was ruled by the fifth Tokugawa shogun Tsunayoshi (r. 1680–1709), who styled himself in the guise of a Confucian monarch, sponsored debates among the various schools of Confucianism, and even lectured on the classics before assembled audiences of feudal lords (daimyō) and scholars. In 1690 Tsunayoshi even had a new home, the Shôheikô, or School of Prosperous Peace, built for the orthodox Hayashi school of Neo-Confucianism, locating it in nearby Yushima and awarding its chancellor, Hayashi Nobuatsu (1644–1732), with court rank. Not surprisingly, the shogun's interest in such matters encouraged others to follow suit, and as one early-modern Japanese scholar reflected on these years a century later, "literature and learning flourished widely. Every house read and every family recited [the classics]."[13]

Even more significant for the emergence of the private academy in Japan, however, was the fact that by the end of the seventeenth century, culture was no longer perceived to be the monopolized prerogative of any particular class or privileged group within the society, and that those who would once have been denied access to one or another form of cultural production could now purchase this culture from altogether willing purveyors. It is this sense of cultural liberality that made it possible in the late-seventeenth century for members of the newly ascendant merchant class to purchase, alongside their samurai classmates, instruction in such topics as Confucianism.

But there was still a third sense in which this era was culturally liberal, and it rests in the fact that the Tokugawa state was unconcerned with censoring or otherwise restricting modes of cultural production, so long as these modes were not perceived to be in any way destabilizing to the regime. The example of the government's attitude toward Kabuki drama is illustrative. When Kabuki performers were little more than theatrically skilled prostitutes, the government was indeed concerned over the street fighting that frequently erupted as samurai found themselves competing with one another for the sexual favors of different actresses and boy actors. But once the government mandated that Kabuki be a theater of adult males, the fighting diminished to the point where it was no longer perceived to be a problem, and the government in turn showed itself to be utterly unconcerned about either Kabuki staging or the content of its repertoire.[14]

The Confucian private academy in Japan benefited from these developments, enjoying the blessings of relative peace and prosperity, and flourishing as a result of the state's indifference toward matters of Confucian interpretation throughout most of the eighteenth century. But it cannot be said that Confucianism meaningfully contributed to these developments other than through its affirmative attitude toward a spirit of learning and inquiry. The irony, of course, is that as we have already observed, classical Confucianism would have regarded the rise of such voluntary associations as a private academy with skepticism at best, since Confucianism viewed society as an organic whole in which each person has his/her ordered role—a society that works harmoniously when each of these roles is fulfilled correctly in all circumstances, just as in a vast family. And, just as there is no room for a private sphere within the Confucian view of the family, the Confucian view of society remained one that found privacy ultimately indistinguishable from selfishness.

This is not to say that there was no room for, say, friendship and other similarly elective relationships within a Confucian worldview. Confucianism's five relationships—ruler/subject, parent/child, husband/wife, elder brother/younger brother, and friend/friend—explicitly acknowledge the importance and value of such voluntary and consensual relationships. But it is also abundantly clear that Confucianism gives priority to those relationships that are found within the household, and to those relationships in which there is a clear benefactor and beneficiary,[15] since these are the relationships that prepare one for citizenship and train one in goodness. For all these reasons, Confucianism would have been deeply skeptical, if not actively scornful, of the voluntary associations that comprise civil society, and it is in this context that from a Confucian perspective, all voluntary consensual associations benefited from the forbearance of the state. Consequently, from a Confucian perspective there is nothing that the state can be said to have needed from voluntary, consensual, or communal associations other than their obedient subservience, which in turn begs the question of liabilities.

LIABILITIES

The question of whether from a Confucian perspective civil society and the state pose liabilities for each other—or alternatively, what kinds of liabilities do rulers and ruled pose for one another?—and how these liabilities are to be averted or at least contained likewise represents a challenging speculative exercise. Inevitably we return to the creation of a private sphere—both at the level of the individual person and that of his/ her voluntary associations—without which civil society (as I construe it) is unimaginable. Confucianism will necessarily view the presence of such a private sphere as a challenge to its organic, familylike view of the ideal society, and it will for this reason inevitably regard civil society as a potential liability to the paternalistic state.

To better understand the Confucian perspective, let us examine in some detail the fundamental Confucian tenet known as the rectification of names, which is actually an argument regarding the accuracy of terminology. Its locus classicus is in the *Analects*, where Duke Ching (r. 546– 489 B.C.) of the state of Ch'i questions Confucius about government. Confucius is said to have replied, "Let the ruler be a ruler, the minister be a minister, the father be a father, and the son be a son." This much is well known to students of Confucianism, but less well known is the Duke's response: "Excellent! Indeed when the ruler is not a ruler, the minister is not a minister, the father not a father, and the son not a son, although I may have all the grain, shall I ever get to eat it?"[16]

In the Confucian view of society, and as already observed, each person has an ordered place, and society may be assumed to go well when each individual correctly addresses his/her responsibilities in the context of each situation and relationship. It is the moral duty of the ruler to be the ruler—that is, to rule justly and benevolently and to give priority to the interests of his subjects over his personal profit. In a similar way, it is the moral duty of the father to be a father—that is, to preside over the affairs of his household in a manner that, like the ruler's, ensures not only that the physical requirements of his beneficiaries are met, but also that he fosters an environment in which their capacity to grow in the direction of moral goodness is addressed. Elsewhere in the *Analects* Confucius addresses this in terms suggestive of a modern perspective: "If names are not rectified, then language will not be in accord with truth. If language is not in accord with truth, then things cannot be accomplished."[17]

It would be tempting, though probably mistaken, in this context of a discussion of civil society to regard the doctrine of "rectification of names" as akin to the principle of subsidiarity. To be sure, the devolution to local entities of authority not claimed centrally was historically characteristic of the political orders of all East Asian countries. Nonetheless, from the perspective of Confucianism (as well as history), this is less a political principle than an example of the practical sharing of authority and responsibility in a manner perceived (in theory) to be conducive to advancement of the general good, and (in fact) to be consistent with the realities of power.

In a related vein, there is an element of reciprocity in the ruler-subject relationship (as in all benefactor-beneficiary relationships), and the responsibilities that thus attend it are decidedly mutual, but it is important to note that in the *Analects* these responsibilities begin with the ruler's example: "If a ruler sets himself right, he will be followed without his command. If he does not set himself right, even his commands will not be obeyed."[18] Early Confucianism emphasized the onus borne by the ruler to rule by the example of his own rectitude, and elsewhere in the *Analects* Confucius goes so far as to assert that for the survival of a state, the confidence of the people is ultimately more important than the quality of either the state's military capacities or the people's social welfare.[19] In this respect, it is noteworthy that in later imperial China, as Henry Rosemont has observed in his response to this chapter, the term for the government representative of the smallest (county) level was "father mother official" (*fu mu kuan*).

Mencius (371–289 B.C.), whom the Chinese tradition has endorsed as Confucius's authentic interpreter, restated the perspective of the ruler's responsibility for the people's welfare in a doctrine that has come to be known as the "right of revolution." As it appears in the text that bears his name, King Hsüan of Ch'i questions Mencius regarding whether there are any circumstances under which it is permissible for a minister to murder the king whom he serves. Mencius's answer is redolent of the earlier linguisticality of Confucius in the rectification of names: "He who injures humanity is a bandit. He who injures righteousness is a destructive person. Such a person is a mere fellow. I have heard of killing a mere fellow [like wicked King] Chou, but I have not heard of murdering [him as] the ruler."[20] In other words, a wicked king who injures humanity or righteousness has failed to create the moral environment requisite to his people's growth in the direction of moral goodness and is for this very reason in default of the definition of a true king, making him eligible for replacement even through violence. It is also evidence of an emerging concept of "the people" in early Confucianism, though as Wm. Theodore de Bary has observed, Confucian government is government for the people rather than government by the people.[21]

Later Confucianism, however, tended to tilt the scales in favor of the state by conflating the ruler-subject relationship with that of the parent-child, in which the sense of mutuality is decidedly diminished. "Never disobey," is how Confucius summarized filial piety in the *Analects*,[22] even suggesting in one conversation that uprightness is to be found in a son's concealing the misconduct of his father,[23] and it is this understanding of filial piety that has largely animated Chinese social practice over the last thousand years and more. It is likewise this understanding of filial piety that came to serve as the basis for a Confucian redefinition of the relationship between the individual and the state.

Let us examine how an early-modern state like Tokugawa Japan used Confucian arguments to fashion an ideology in which the state's aspirations vis à vis its constituent members are clearly absolutist, at least during this state's first half-century of rule. As Herman Ooms has demonstrated, the Tokugawa state early on sought ideological support in a variety of places—Confucianism, Buddhism, folk religion, and so on—for the premise that its authority, which of course had its true origins in violence, was rooted in a benevolent paternalism. This ideological construction at once both effaced the contingent properties of the *bakufu's* (central government) genesis, and articulated a rationale for an absolute authority akin to that of the father as head of household.[24] This again also represented an understanding of the state in which there was simply no room for the sorts of voluntary associations that are necessary for our understanding of civil society.

But as we have also seen, historical, social, and economic forces were already at work in seventeenth-century Japan, laying the foundation for the emergence of an individual private sphere that contended successfully with the Confucian perspective and its ideological expression. In the context of a discussion of the seventeenth-century Japanese state's policies toward religious bodies and their members, I have argued elsewhere that the Tokugawa state initially aspired toward absolute authority over the thoughts, words, and deeds of its individual members, and that the "underground" religious movements that arose at this time did so as a defensive practice. By the late 1660s, my argument continued, one also finds evidence of the state's realistic retreat from this absolutist aspiration, at least as far as the religious thoughts of its members were concerned, as it relaxed those policies which depended for their enforcement upon either the confessions of suspects or the fundamentally antisocial act of informing the authorities of the transgressions of one's neighbors. And it is in that retreat, I concluded, that one can locate the genesis of a heretofore unknown measure of individual privacy that was accorded—as privacy always is—by the state to its members for behavior the state eventually recognized as ultimately nonthreatening.[25] Furthermore, and again as I have tried to demonstrate, it was less than two decades later that the social, economic, and cultural forces of Tokugawa society contributed to the sharp increase in the volume and quality of individual transactions in the society, a change attended by the emergence of a richly diverse, commodified popular culture. These factors contributed to the individual person's integrity as a consumer and potential student of both ideology and culture, allowing in the process the formation of such volunteer associations as private not-for-profit study groups[26] and for-profit academies.

Within those study groups and academies, there was an attendant change in the forms of Confucian interpretation that proved to be most popular. Where earlier "orthodox" teachings had emphasized a naturalist ontology in which the Confucian Way was perceived to be ineluctably linked to enduring first principles of both an immanent and transcendent character, by the midpoint of the eighteenth century, the historicist heterodox Confucian perspectives of Ogyū Sorai (1666–1728) win the day with their argument that the Way is simply a convenient comprehensive term for various political, legal, economic, ritual, and administrative practices that proved successful in the past and are inevitably conditioned by the circumstances of time and place.[27]

Again, Confucianism cannot be regarded as meaningfully responsible for the various transformations to Japan's seventeenth- and eighteenth-century polity discussed in this chapter, nor was the rise of the kinds of voluntary associations I have identified necessarily or inevitably destabilizing, but it is relevant to our discussion that Confucian heterodoxy was at least perceived to be part of the problem, and was addressed as such in a series of conservative "reforms" undertaken in the last years of the eighteenth century by the "Confucian" scholar-statesman Matsudaira Sadanobu (1758–1829). As the head of the Council of Elders (Rōjū) and shogunal adviser, Sadanobu addressed his "Prohibition of Heterodox Studies" to the head of the Shōheikō academy, whose commitment to orthodox Neo-Confucian interpretations was accurately perceived to have declined. Sadanobu's reforms, however, did not stop here and included such measures as: censorship of cultural productions deemed offensive to conservative Confucian morality; efforts to enlist the support of entrepreneurs and their guilds in regulating rice and precious-metal markets; the rebuilding and extension of coastal defenses to preserve Japan's isolation from European and North American representatives; a purge of the women assigned to service the shogun's pleasure, or at least those whose loyalties were suspect; sumptuary legislation that forbade the use of barbers and hairdressers and separated the sexes in heretofore mixed bathing facilities; and the sending of spies into bathhouses, brothels, and even barbershops to eavesdrop on potentially subversive discussions. Both the Confucian premises underlying these policies and their incompatibility with features of civil society are unmistakable, which, in turn, brings us to a discussion of how Confucianism would regard groups and individuals as the constituent components of a society at once both complex in its elements yet simple in its informing principles.

GROUPS AND INDIVIDUALS

From a Confucian paternalistic perspective, the state has a fundamental responsibility to interact in a socially constructive and nurturing manner with both individuals and families, but as we have already noted, the Confucian organic perspective on society left little room for the sorts of voluntary associations this chapter takes as characteristic of civil society. Let us begin by examining Confucian perspectives on the interactions between the state and the individual.

First, Confucian humanism places great responsibility on the shoulders of the individual person and regards it as the ruler's responsibility to teach individuals how to be essentially self-governing: "Lead the people with governmental measures and regulate them by law and punishment, and they will avoid wrongdoing but will have no sense of honor and shame. Lead them with virtue and regulate them by the rules of propriety (*li*), and they will have a sense of shame and, moreover, set themselves right."[28] At the same time, Confucianism would reject the notion of the human person as an *individual*, if by this term one means to suggest the presence of a free and autonomous self.

Confucianism fundamentally distrusts such axiomatic propositions in European and North American political culture as the "rule of law," instead preferring to foster a sense of self-worth that, it is assumed, will cause individual persons to regard any misconduct as demeaning and shameful.[29] Nonetheless, Confucianism does not suggest that, for this reason, individuals are in their solitary condition self-worthy, as others in the European classical liberal tradition have suggested. Where classical European liberalism might argue that individual integrity is akin to an inward capacity of the soul, and that persons thus enjoy an inherent measure of self-worth, Confucianism by contrast is uncompromising in its understanding of human worth as something manifested fundamentally in the context of relationship.[30]

Further, there is a clear tension between what we would nowadays regard as elitist and egalitarian principles in Confucianism. For example despite the obvious dignity accorded to individual persons in the previous quotation from the *Analects*, Confucius elsewhere in the same work asserts that commoners "may be made to follow [the Way] but may not be made to understand it," suggesting an unpromising view of the capacities of ordinary individuals.[31] Citizens not in government service "do not discuss its policies,"[32] according to Confucius, and ultimately, "[t]he character of a ruler is like the wind and that of the people is like grass. In whatever direction the wind blows, the grass always bends."[33] That there is also a cosmic dimension to the ruler's responsibilities with respect to benevolent and humane rule is unarguable, but the Confucian ruler nonetheless remains very much the authoritarian parent of the people.

This tension between egalitarian and elitist impulses is perhaps best expressed in the writings of Mencius, wherein we find Confucius's interpreter idealizing benevolent rule with remarkable imagery when he asserts that truly kingly government is found "when men of seventy [have] silk to wear and meat to eat, when the common people [are] neither hungry nor cold."[34] Mencius also clearly privileges the individual in such statements as, "All things are already complete in oneself," suggesting that the human person need not look beyond the self for the requisites of moral growth and even perfection.[35] At the same time, Mencius reinforces the vertical, inegalitarian, and organic Confucian view of the polity when he asserts: "There is the work of great men and there is the work of little men. . . . Some labor with their minds and some labor with their strength. Those who labor with their minds govern others; those who labor with their strength are governed by others. . . . This is a universal principle."[36] As disagreeable a perspective as this represents in the here-and-now, we perhaps need to remind ourselves that it is a perspective consistent with the realities of life in ancient China, as well as a perspective embraced by most enduring forms of premodern Chinese political thought.

Turning to the state's interactions with families, we have already observed the fundamental importance of the family from a Confucian perspective, but let us review the reasons for its importance from the perspective of the state. First, the family is the only social grouping discussed by Confucianism, for it is both the very laboratory in which individuals are to have their first experience with growth in the direction of goodness, and it is the site of those relationships which serve in barometer-like fashion to enable its constituent members to measure their progress (or retrogression) in this direction. We have already observed that of the five relationships on which Confucians focus, three (father/son, husband/wife, elder brother/younger brother) are to be found within the household. These relationships have a universal quality to them, and it is good to remind ourselves that unlike our current perspective on these relationships, classical Confucianism held that each of the three is a vertical and nonconsensual relationship. Second, Confucianism is remarkably specific regarding how each of the relationships is to be used in one's moral growth. Mencius credits the legendary sage Emperor Shun (third millennium B.C.) with appointing a minister of education to "teach people human relations, that between father and son, there should be affection; ... between husband and wife, there should be attention to their separate functions; [and] between old and young, there should be a proper order."[37] Every relationship within the household thus provides one with daily opportunity to grow in specific moral directions. And third, the family is the most fundamental economic unit in society, and indeed from a Confucian perspective there is no context for imagining economic progress apart from that of individual households. In sum, the family emerges as the singular social unit with which the Confucian state proposes to interact.

CITIZENSHIP

Before one can address Confucian perspectives on the prerogatives and duties of citizenship, it is necessary to review the narrow understanding of citizenship in traditional—and, as will be argued, even in modern and contemporary—East Asia. If in European and North American political thought *citizenship* refers to the legal (constitutional) or quasi-legal (by common law or accepted precedent) rights and responsibilities of individuals within a state (understood as the collection of entities having a monopoly on the legitimate use of force), such was never the case with any of the premodern societies of East Asia, and even among East Asia's modern societies—all of which have constitutions of one sort or another—the matter of human, civil, and constitutional rights of citizens remains arguable, at least in practice if not in theory. Accordingly, and for the purposes of our discussion, *citizenship* is used here to refer narrowly to permanent residence in a country and membership in one of what Confucianism regarded as its traditional four classes: the ruling elite (be they intellectual, political-administrative, or military), agriculturalists, artisans, and merchants. When understood in this way, we can begin to identify both the responsibilities and the prerogatives of citizenship, so long as we recognize that the latter are to be understood more as reasonable expectations than as rights per se.

From a Confucian perspective, citizens may reasonably expect that their government will exercise constructive effort on their behalf in several fundamental areas: first, that the state will ensure that their most basic needs of food, shelter, and orderly society will be met, and that their physical well-being will be thereby assured; second, they are justified in expecting that their affairs will be administered justly and in a manner consistent with their interests and personal well-being—that is, those in authority over them will care for them as a father cares for his child; third, citizens are fundamentally entitled to an environment in which they are both encouraged by the ruler's personal example and enabled by the properties of their surroundings to grow in the direction of moral goodness; fourth, just as sons are entitled to remonstrate with their fathers, citizens are entitled to remonstrate with their state when they perceive the state to be defaulting on its responsibilities; and finally, in this early-modern context the Confucian citizen may even be entitled to a subjective measure of happiness.

The first three of these collectively constitute the essence of what Confucianism regards as humane or benevolent (Ch. *jen*) government. Though we have touched on its features variously in our discussions above, let us revisit this idealized expression of the relationship between the citizen and his state, which is perhaps most succinctly represented in Mencius's words to King Hui of Liang (r. 370–319 B.C.): "If Your Majesty can practice a humane government to the people, reduce punishments and fines, lower taxes and levies, make it possible for the fields to be plowed deep and the weeding well done, men of strong body, in their days of leisure may cultivate their filial piety, brotherly respect, loyalty and faithfulness, thereby serving their fathers and elder brothers at home and their elders and superiors at abroad."[38] The idealism is unmistakable, though we observe that it is tempered by the remarkable specificity of such measures as how the weeding and plowing are to proceed. We recall that it was likewise Mencius who defined the evidence of good government in terms of when "men of seventy [have] silk to wear and meat to eat, when the common people [are] neither hungry nor cold."

In a similar vein, Confucius maintained in the *Analects* (1:5) that no country can be regarded as well administered "unless the ruler attends strictly to business, punctually observes his promises, is economical in expenditure, shows affection towards his subjects in general, and uses the labor of the peasantry only at the proper times of year."[39] Here the emphasis on the ruler's effort is similarly unmistakable, indicating that Confucian governance is far more than simply a matter of harboring good intentions. And, as the seventeenth-century Confucian scholar and social critic Huang Tsung-hsi argued, government did not emerge to bring order out of chaos, as Hobbes posited, but rather in order to overcome individual selfishness out of a concern for the common good, as in the following: "In the beginning of human life each man lived for himself and looked to his own interests. There was such a thing as the common benefit, yet no one seems to have promoted it. . . . Then someone came forth who did not think of benefit in terms of his own benefit but sought to benefit all-under-heaven."[40]

In contrast with classical Confucianism, which concentrated on these physical qualities of well-being, seventeenth- and eighteenth-century Confucianism also addressed such matters as remonstrance and happiness. Even though the *Analects* rejected the notion that individuals outside of government could "discuss its policies," later Confucians turned to what the *Analects* said about remonstrance within families to justify its application at the level of the citizen vis à vis the state. The locus classicus for this understanding of remonstrance appears in the context of Confucius's discussion of filial behavior: "In serving his parents, a son may gently remonstrate with them. When he sees that they are not inclined to listen to him, he should resume an attitude of reverence and not abandon his effort to please them. He may feel worried but does not complain."[41] Whether applied within the household or more broadly in the context of the citizen's relationship to the state, the message is unmistakable: when one discerns what one perceives to be wrongdoing on the part of one's superiors, one has the authority—if not actually the duty—to call this to their attention; if they agree and amend their ways, so much the better; but if they are disinclined to alter their course, then one may indeed experience disappointment, but one is not allowed to translate this disappointment into either resentment or opposition.

This principle has been variously expressed in East Asian history. For example, in China every citizen has for centuries enjoyed the right, at least in principle, to petition the government to seek redress, and from the T'ang dynasty (618–907) onward the function of remonstrance was institutionalized within the bureaucracy in the Board of Censors (Yü-shih-t'ai), whose members were "officials of high prestige who had the primary duty of ferreting out cases of treason, misgovernment or maladministration and reporting them directly to the emperor."[42] This right of remonstrance continues, again at least in theory, to this day in China in its Petitions and Appeals Office on the south side of Beijing, though it is clear that for the contemporary petitioner the experience of remonstrance in China remains as frustrating and even dangerous as it was at times in the past.[43]

In Japan, one's experience with remonstrance was, if anything, variegated and inconsistent. During the early-modern period, there was an aggressive expansion of the use of remonstrance boxes at both the local (domainal) and capital levels, especially during the eighteenth century, providing important evidence for the expansion of "public spaces" within the society. Indeed, nearly two-thirds (thirty-five, or 64 percent) of Japan's fifty-five remonstrance boxes instituted prior to the Meiji Restoration of 1868 were established during the years 1721–91.[44] In Japan, just as in China, the boxes provided an opportunity for ordinary citizens in a broad range of matters to offer suggestions, to express complaints, and to present appeals, and they appear to have been used in Tokugawa Japan by members of all social classes. Nonetheless, it remained against Tokugawa law for anyone outside the government to suggest a change in national policy. One of the most extreme examples of this occurred in 1791 to the scholar Hayashi Shihei (1738–93), who proposed that Japan, being an island country, urgently needed to improve its coastal defenses. His punishment for this innocent and self-evident suggestion was a near-fatal six-month sentence in an Edo prison, a sentence meted out as part of the ideological retrenchment implemented in the Kansei "reforms" by the aforementioned culturally and socially illiberal "Confucian" statesman Matsudaira Sadanobu. In other words, "remonstrance" appears to have given one the opportunity to criticize public figures but not to propose public policy—that is, to complain but not to agitate.

Turning to the perhaps unexpected issue of whether happiness may be regarded from a Confucian perspective as one of the prerogatives of early-modern citizenship, let us turn to two examples. Writing in the early-eighteenth century, the Japanese Confucian naturalist Kaibara Ekken (1630–1714) regarded happiness (Jpn. *raku*) as part of the universal human endowment bestowed by heaven and akin to what we would call a sense of contentment.[45] This sense of happiness as a human endowment was strengthened even further by Ogyū Sorai into something akin to a human right. In the context of a discussion of the core Confucian virtue of goodness (Ch. *jen*, Jpn. *jin*), Sorai argued that it was the responsibility of the state to provide the conditions necessary for individual persons to experience "peace and contentment" (*annon*), and he maintained in near-Jeffersonian terms that such a conception of well-being included happiness:

This [*annon*, or peace and contentment] means that [the people] should be free from cold and famine and from molestation by robbers, that they should have feelings of trust in their neighbors, that they should be content to live in their country and their age, that they should find enjoyment in their various occupations, and [that they] should spend the whole of their lives in happiness (*raku*).[46]

Sorai's stance represents a remarkably comprehensive yet succinct statement of the conditions for human well-being from a Confucian perspective, and it is significant for our purposes here that happiness in this context appears to be no less fundamental than hearth, home, community, and vocation as elements that citizens are entitled to expect from their government.

In all of these ways, what we observe is that Confucianism endorses a broad range of expectations on the part of those who are governed. The physical properties of their well-being were the principal concern of classical Confucianism, but during the early-modern period, when public spaces were at the very least opened if not actually broadened, these expectations were expanded to include both the opportunity to express dissent and the prerogative of a fundamentally psychological sense of contentment. Having raised this issue of contentment, let us now turn to its inverse, or conflict.

CONFLICT

Confucianism has little to say about conflict, but this relative silence notwithstanding, it is not particularly difficult to imagine how Confucianism might seek to handle the conflicting demands of citizenship and voluntary membership or participation in associations outside the family or one's community of faith. Because of the benevolent paternalism Confucianism expects from a state, a Confucian perspective will inevitably favor the state in any adversarial proceeding with voluntary associations. We have already seen an example of this from Japanese history in Matsudaira Sadanobu's Prohibition of Heterodox Studies, in which the Japanese *bakufu* sought to exercise ideological censorship over academic enterprises (or at least those that enjoyed the state's patronage) branded as heterodox and hence as potentially destabilizing. It perhaps goes without saying that from a Confucian perspective, such conflict should not arise in the first place, and that the conflict itself constitutes prima facie evidence of the private entity's wrongdoing.

Less clear is how Confucianism would view a conflict between a family and the state. On the one hand, one can find evidence to support the view that a well-ordered family can never be in conflict with a well-ordered state, as when Confucius's student Yu Tzu (538–457 B.C.) is quoted as having said, "Few of those who are filial sons and respectful brothers will show disrespect to superiors, and there has never been a man who is not disrespectful to superiors and yet creates disorder."[47] On the other hand, we have already observed the example of the upright Kung who is condemned by Confucius in the *Analects* (13:18) for having borne witness against his father, who stole a sheep. In this passage, it will be recalled, Confucius applauds the uprightness of fathers and sons who conceal each other's wrongdoing; historically, a major challenge for all states in East Asia has been overcoming the centripetal impulses of clans, villages, and other entities that posit their own interests in juxtaposition with those of the state. Confucianism unambiguously affirms the interests of households as well as the interests of the state, but entities between the two fare less well. Its approach to resolution of such conflict has traditionally been to articulate a commonality of interests expressed in transcendent principles, rather than to seek institutional means to balance conflicting interests.

Finally, like many traditions, classical Confucianism postulates the existence of an idealized realm in the remote past—a kind of ancient unconflicted terrestrial paradise characterized by universal harmony and peace from which humankind has fallen but that can nonetheless be resurrected in the here and now—and in such concepts as the rectification of names, one sees an implicit acknowledgment of the imperfect nature of society. It is the nature of this process of rectification that all individuals engage in an ongoing collective effort to improve society one person at a time, one household at a time, and eventually one state at a time. Thus from a Confucian perspective, all private and voluntary associations will necessarily be subordinate to the broader goal of creating a kind of heaven on earth.

Confucianism and Civil Society in Present-Day East Asia

By way of conclusion let us revisit the question asked at the outset, of whether one can discern even now in East Asia the kinds of voluntary associations that so prominently characterize civil society in its European and North American settings. As it happens, the question is by no means simple, and there is a vigorous and lively debate on this topic going on at this very moment.[48]

In a recent and important study of Japanese civilization, the sociologist S. N. Eisenstadt has suggested that more than other (post-)modern societies, Japanese society coheres as a result of the remarkably high levels of trust that exist horizontally at the level of the community, and vertically in terms of one's relationship with the state, with one's employer, and so on.[49] And like many other observers of contemporary Japan, Professor Eisenstadt locates the roots of this trust in the priority Confucianism attaches to maintaining correct relationships, both horizontally between persons and vertically between rulers and their subjects.

Nonetheless, events such as the Kōbe earthquake of January 1995, the sarin gas attack in the Tokyo subway system in March of that same year, and the Japanese government's inability during the 1990s to effect those economic reforms necessary to pull Japan out of the most prolonged recession in its modern history have combined to undermine the citizen's confidence in the state, and have made the citizen a far more discerning and discriminating consumer of state ideology than even just a decade ago. In the case of the earthquake, the state appeared to many Japanese citizens curiously inept in fulfilling its most basic responsibilities toward those who suffered loss, hardship, or injury.[50] Similarly with the sarin gas attacks of that same spring, the inability of Japan's civil and military forces of order to provide reasonable assurances of safety to commuters, shoppers, students, and the like suggested to many persons in Japan uncomfortably clear limits in a heretofore seemingly omnicompetent state. And in the economic realm Japan's prolonged economic slowdown as well as the government's apparent paucity of plausible ideas in the realm of either political economy or possible solutions to its micro-managed economy have undermined many citizens' confidence in the government's long-standing exhortation to sacrifice the needs of the present to the hopes of tomorrow. These factors have contributed to a crisis of confidence and breakdown of trust in Japan at the turn of the millennium that are all the more striking when we recall Ogyū Sorai's Confucian sense of *annon*, whereby the people "should be free from cold and famine and from molestation by robbers, . . . should have feelings of trust in their neighbors, . . . should be content to live in their country and their age, . . . should find enjoyment in their various occupations, and . . . should spend the whole of their lives in happiness."

Though sources of information for China are more limited than for Japan, it is evident that comparable phenomena are likewise contributing to a breakdown in whatever remains of the citizen's confidence in government to assure personal well-being. Probably the most dramatic examples of this at the level of the ordinary citizen are the widely reported instances of environmental degradation, which have apparently become common throughout rural China, and the breakdown in the Maoist social safety net as the modernization effort sacrifices the interests of individuals to the interests of the state.

At the same time, however, issues such as the environment are serving as catalysts for the formation of not-for-profit citizen movements, including philanthropic enterprises, watchdog groups, grass-roots organizations and so on, in both Japan and China, and are thereby further opening the space that I have argued in this chapter was initially opened by such entities as the private academy.[51] Whether this is further evidence of the end of history, as some would argue, it does suggest that as the integrity of the individual person is being buttressed on various fronts throughout the world, and as the private sphere of individual persons allows for their greater participation in public spaces, then the most basic features of civil society are likely to become increasingly common in formerly Confucian societies, just as they have elsewhere.

NOTES

I WISH to thank Professors Marshall Cohen, Richard Madsen, Henry Rosemont, and Conrad Schirokauer, as well as the members of the Columbia University Seminar in Neo-Confucian Studies, for exceptionally helpful comments on earlier drafts of this essay.

1. For a more expansive perspective on civil society, see Michael Walzer's liberal-egalitarian perspective on civil society in *Alternative Conceptions of Civil Society*, ed. Simone Chambers and Will Kymlicka (Princeton: Princeton University Press, forthcoming). My differences with Professor Walzer notwithstanding, I have found his perspectives on civil society especially helpful in shaping my own.

2. See Sannosuke Matsumoto, "Nakae Chōmin and Confucianism," in *Confucianism and Tokugawa Culture*, ed. Peter Nosco (Honolulu: University of Hawai'i Press, 1997), 251–66. For a richly nuanced discussion of Confucian perspectives on Chinese law, especially dynastic law, and their implications for civil society in China, see Wm. Theodore de Bary, *Asian Values and Human Rights: A Confucian Communitarian Perspective* (Cambridge: Harvard University Press, 1998), esp. 90–117.

3. The other defining characteristics of East Asia as a cultural sphere are the use of Chinese characters, a tradition of Mahayana Buddhism, and an appreciation for China's centrality within the region.

4. See Rodney L. Taylor, "The Religious Character of the Confucian Tradition," *Philosophy East and West* 48, no. 1 (1998): 80–107.

5. See, for example, Wm. Theodore de Bary and Tu Weiming, eds., *Confucianism and Human Rights* (New York: Columbia University Press, 1997); and Mary Evelyn Tucker and John Berthrong, eds., *Confucianism and Ecology: The Interrelation of Heaven, Earth, and Humans* (Cambridge: Harvard University Press, 1998).

6. Alida Brill argues that privacy is inevitably "*granted* to an individual only when others agree to honor [it], be it by compliance with the law or community custom" (emphasis added). *Nobody's Business: Paradoxes of Privacy* (Reading, Mass.: Addison-Wesley Publishing Co., 1990), xvi.

7. Wing-tsit Chan, ed., *A Source Book in Chinese Philosophy* (Princeton: Princeton University Press, 1963), 86–87.

8. For a wide-ranging discussion of early modernity, see "Early Modernities," a special issue of *Daedalus* 127, no. 3 (Summer 1998). On Japan's early-modern transformation in the seventeenth and eighteenth centuries, see John Whitney Hall, introduction to *The Cambridge History of Japan*, vol. 4, *Early Modern Japan* (Cambridge: Cambridge University Press, 1991), esp. 1–6.

9. In Wm. Theodore de Bary, *Waiting for the Dawn: A Plan for the Prince—*

Huang Tsung-hsi's Ming-i-tai-fang lu (New York: Columbia University Press, 1993), 104.

10. On Itō Jinsai's Kogidō, see Richard Rubinger, *Private Academies of Tokugawa Japan* (Princeton: Princeton University Press, 1982), 49–56. Indeed, there was such a proliferation of private schools in Japan during the late-seventeenth and eighteenth centuries that the humorist Ihara Saikaku (1642–93) inveighed against the ease with which untutored "crooks" could pass themselves off as experts and establish private schools where they duped the unwitting. See Ihara Saikaku, *Some Final Words of Advice*, trans. Peter Nosco (Rutland, Vt.: Charles E. Tuttle Publishing Co., 1980), 131.

11. The following argument is developed in greater detail in my *Remembering Paradise: Nativism and Nostalgia in Eighteenth-Century Japan* (Cambridge: Harvard University, Council on East Asian Studies, 1990), 15–40.

12. See the transcript of his lecture "The Foundations of Liberalism," in *Seminar Reports* 5, no. 1 (1976), Columbia University Program of General Education in the Humanities.

13. From the *Sentetsu Sōdan* of Hara Masaru (1760–1820), quoted in Masao Maruyama, *Studies in the Intellectual History of Tokugawa Japan*, trans. Mikiso Hane (Tokyo: Tokyo University Press, 1974), 115.

14. See two articles by Donald H. Shiveley, first his *"Bakufu* vs. *Kabuki"* in *Studies in the Institutional History of Early Modern Japan*, ed. John W. Hall and Marius B. Jansen (Princeton: Princeton University Press, 1968); and second, "Popular Culture" in Hall, *The Cambridge History of Japan* 4:749–61.

15. I am indebted to Henry Rosemont for this perspective on Confucianism's five relationships, which have more commonly been expressed in terms of superiors and subordinates. See his "Classical Confucianism and Contemporary Feminist Thought: Some Parallels and their Implications," in *Culture and Self*, ed. Douglas Allen (Boulder, Colo.: Westview, 1997).

16. Chan, *Source Book*, 39 (*Analects* 12:11).

17. Ibid., 40 (*Analects* 13:3).

18. Ibid., 41 (*Analects* 13:6).

19. Ibid., 39 (*Analects* 12:7).

20. Ibid., 62 (*Mencius* 1B:8).

21. Quoted with permission. For a related discussion, see also Wm. Theodore de Bary, *The Trouble with Confucianism* (Cambridge: Harvard University Press, 1991), 17–21, 37–38, 94–103.

22. Chan, *Source Book*, 23 (*Analects* 2:5).

23. Ibid., 41 (*Analects* 13:18). In this passage, Confucius is discussing with the Duke of She the merits of a man named Kung who bore witness against his father for stealing a sheep. Confucius is quoted as having said, "The upright men in my community are different from this. The father conceals the misconduct of the son and the son conceals the misconduct of the father. Uprightness is to be found in this."

24. See Herman Ooms, "Neo-Confucianism and the Formation of Early Tokugawa Ideology: Contours of a Problem," in Nosco, *Confucianism and Tokugawa Culture*, 27–61.

25. See my "Keeping the Faith: *Bakuhan* Policy towards Religions in Seven-

teenth-Century Japan," in *Religion in Japan: Arrows to Heaven and Earth*, ed. P. F. Kornicki and I. J. McMullen (Cambridge: Cambridge University Press, 1996), 135–55. For the distinction between privacy and secrecy, see Carol Warren and Barbara Laslett, "Privacy and Secrecy: A Conceptual Comparison," in *Secrecy: A Cross-Cultural Perspective*, ed. Stanton K. Tefft (New York: Human Sciences Press, 1980), 25–34.

26. Itō Jinsai's (1627–1705) Dōshikai (Society of the Like-Minded), which later grew into his Kogidō academy, would be just one example.

27. This, of course, is a much simplified version of the argument found in Maruyama's *Studies in the Intellectual History of Tokugawa Japan*. For a sophisticated and sensitive engagement of the Sorai school, see Tetsuo Najita, ed., *Tokugawa Political Writings* (Cambridge: Cambridge University Press, 1998).

28. Chan, *Source Book*, 22 (*Analects* 2:3).

29. Again, see de Bary, *Asian Values and Human Rights*, esp. 30–40.

30. I wish to thank Professor Steve Scalet for his help with this insight.

31. Chan, *Source Book*, 33 (*Analects* 8:9).

32. Ibid., 34 (*Analects* 8:14).

33. Ibid., 40 (*Analects* 12:19).

34. Ibid., 61 (*Mencius* 1A:7).

35. Ibid., 79 (*Mencius* 7A:4).

36. Ibid., 69 (*Mencius* 3A:4).

37. Ibid.

38. Ibid., 61 (*Mencius* 1A:5).

39. *The Analects of Confucius*, translated and annotated by Arthur Waley (New York: Vintage Books, 1989), 84.

40. de Bary, *Waiting for the Dawn*, 91.

41. Chan, *Source Book*, 28 (*Analects* 4:18).

42. Edwin O. Reischauer and John K. Fairbank, *East Asia: The Great Tradition* (Boston: Houghton Mifflin, 1960), 168. Charles O. Hucker has argued that the functions of remonstrance and surveillance were conflated during the Ming dynasty in China. See his "Confucianism and the Chinese Censorial System," in *Confucianism in Action*, ed. David Nivison (Stanford, Calif.: Stanford University Press, 1959), 182–208.

43. See Erik Eckholm, "Please, Mr. Bureaucrat, Hear My 20-Year-Old Plea," *New York Times* (national ed.), December 7, 1998, A-4.

44. On remonstrance boxes, see Luke S. Roberts, *Mercantilism in a Japanese Domain: The Merchant Origins of Economic Nationalism in Eighteenth-Century Tosa* (Cambridge: Cambridge University Press, 1998), 103–33.

45. On Ekken, see Mary Evelyn Tucker, *Moral and Spiritual Cultivation in Japanese Neo-Confucianism: The Life and Thought of Kaibara Ekken, 1630–1714* (Albany: State University of New York Press, 1989).

46. J. R. McEwan, *The Political Writings of Ogyū Sorai* (Cambridge: Cambridge University Press, 1962), 9; and Sakimoto Seiichi, *Nihon keizai taiten* (Tokyo: Meiji Bunken, 1969), 9:213.

47. Chan, *Source Book*, 19–20 (*Analects* 1:2).

48. See, for example, the website http://www.us-japan.org/dc/cs for papers

presented in a series of workshops titled "Civil Society in Japan (and America): Coping with Change."

49. S. N. Eisenstadt, *Japanese Civilization: A Comparative View* (Chicago: University of Chicago Press, 1996). For the contrarian perspective, i.e., that the "general level of trust is higher among Americans than among Japanese" (130), see Toshio Yamagishi and Midori Yamagishi, "Trust and Commitment in the United States and Japan," *Motivation and Emotion* 18, no. 2 (June 1994): 129–66.

50. Bureaucratic paralysis "was blamed for needlessly inflating the death toll of 6,425." See the Associated Press report at cnn.com/world/asiapcf/9904/04/am-Lessons of Kobe.ap/index.html.

51. See, for example, the papers by Victoria Lynn Bestor, Katsuji Imata, and Masayuki Deguchi posted to the "Civil Society in Japan (and America)" website (above, n. 48).

Commentary and Addenda on Nosco's "Confucian Perspectives on Civil Society and Government"

Henry Rosemont, Jr.

IN THESE REMARKS I should like to both compliment and complement Peter Nosco's good chapter, "Confucian Perspectives on Civil Society and Government."

First, importantly, I believe Professor Nosco correctly and incisively reads the classical Confucian canon as describing the ultimate goal of human life as developing oneself most fully as a human being, to become a *junzi* or, at the pinnacle of development, a *sheng ren*, or sage. And he is equally correct in maintaining that treading the path (*dao*) of this human way (*ren dao*) must ultimately be understood as a *religious* quest, even though the canon speaks not of God, nor of creation, salvation, an immortal soul, or a transcendental realm of being. (And no prophecies will be found in its pages either.)

The importance of the ultimately *religious* nature of Confucianism must, I believe, be underscored, for several reasons. First, it has often been claimed that Confucianism is not a religion at all, but merely a code of deportment, and an elitist one at that. Kant is perhaps not atypical here: "Confucius teaches in his writings nothing outside a moral doctrine designed for the princes . . . and offers examples of former Chinese princes. . . . But a concept of virtue or morality never entered the heads of the Chinese."[1]

More charitably, others have maintained that Confucianism can be seen as a "civil religion," but this, too, does not get at the core of what the classical writings are about.

And a second reason for emphasizing the religious nature of Confucianism is that it brings together what the Master and his successors have to say about the aesthetic, sociopolitical, and moral dimensions of our all-too-human lives. Even a cursory reading of the classical tests show clearly the importance of our leading *integrated* lives as we tread a spiritual path.[2]

To further appreciate Nosco's insight, I would add to it by suggesting that classical Confucianism is very probably the most socially oriented of all philosophical or religious traditions, East or West. Humans develop their humanity and strive to achieve sagehood only through their interactions with other human beings. For Confucius I am not a free, autonomous, individual self; rather am I a son, husband, father, friend, teacher, student, neighbor, colleague, and so forth. And I am *living*, not *playing*, these roles. When all of the human relationships in which I stand with others have been specified, and their interrelationships have been made clear, then I have been fully described as fundamentally a comember of several overlapping communities. Such a person, clearly, will have little left over with which to piece together a free, autonomous, individual self.

Of course it would be absurd to claim that we are not social beings, but our sociality plays virtually no role in modern Western political and moral theory: From Hobbes to Rawls, the ultimate grounding for the major philosophical arguments is that we are rational, autonomous individuals. Our actual lives as deeply embedded social beings are equally ignored in the search for universal moral principles. In calculating the greatest happiness or ascertaining a generalizable maxim, I must *not*, as a moral agent, take into account the concrete particularity of the moral patient(s) toward whom I may have an obligation; they are one and all simply other rational, autonomous individuals.[3]

Now if it is free, autonomous individuals who come together in voluntary association—and thus form civil society—it follows that there will not be any voluntary associations of this kind in early Confucian thought (although there were some in practice, a point to which I will return).

Thus far my remarks pertain only to the classical Confucian tradition, not its Neo-Confucian successor, nor to the interpretations made of Neo-Confucian thinkers by their later Tokugawa counterparts in Japan. It is highly useful to essay a sweep of several of the historical dimensions of the Confucian tradition as Professor Nosco has done, but both the Neo-Confucians and Tokugawa thinkers were very different from their classical predecessors, and it is the latter, I believe, who are most different from ourselves, and hence—to my mind at least—of greatest interest in considering the topics of this book.

One example of these differences from each of the former interpretations: Nosco both quotes and comments on Ogyu Sorai's reading of Confucianism as leading to happiness. Now, this may well be a legitimate construal of the canon, but it is a stretch, because happiness is not described or discussed in the classical texts, it is not a goal toward which we strive, and it certainly was not a goal of the early Confucians to acquire property (although they could do so), which is what Jefferson was about when he replaced Locke's "Estates" with "the pursuit of happiness." (Sorai's predecessor, Kaibara Ekken, was closer to the mark when he discussed the human ability to achieve a sense of contentment).

For the Neo-Confucians, Nosco says of them that they "posited the equality of both natural principles and moral principles," and he is correct on this score. But Zhu Xi, the most famous and influential of the Neo-Confucians, lived a millennium and a half after Confucius, and his China was very different from the land of the Master. It had grown greatly in size and population, had developed economically and politically, had many urban centers, and had been deeply influenced for nine hundred years by the originally alien tradition of Buddhism. This tradition does speak of deities, of creation, salvation, a transcendental realm of being, and a free, autonomous self (or, more strictly speaking ontologically, non-self).

Buddhism is replete with principles, and Zhu Xi formulated other principles to counter the Buddhist challenge. And he had interpretive license to do so, but he, too, had to stretch, because, in the sense of the term "principle," as used in contemporary political theory and moral philosophy, there are few, if any, principles to be found in the classical canon. The term *li*, usually translated as "principle," is central to Neo-Confucianism, but it rarely appears in any of the Classics, and when it does, it has more of its original meaning of "pattern," not "principle." In order to justify their interpretations, the Neo-Confucians equated *li* with *dao*, and while it may well be philosophically legitimate to do so, it was not done by the early Confucians.

Thus, while Kant surely gave the Confucian writings a stalwartly wooden reading, he was correct in saying the Master "knew nothing of morality," if morality is defined as requiring universal principles for action. The early Confucians did not do this, instead instructing us in how to learn how to do what was fitting, or appropriate, for the situation at hand; but contra Kant, this, too, might be considered as belonging to the moral realm, perhaps all the more so as the instructions were also spiritual in nature. Again, then, it is the early Confucians who challenge most basically many common assumptions of modern Western liberalism; hence my focus on them.

I will elaborate on this point below, but against this too-hurried background sketch, let me turn briefly now to each of the six focuses of this book.

BOUNDARIES

Professor Nosco is right, I believe, in maintaining that the question of drawing bounderies between civil society and the state is not a meaningful one for classical Confucians. I would quarrel with his statement, however, that there were no voluntary associations in ancient China, and hence no civil society distinct from a government.

There were such voluntary associations, one of which is clearly reflected in the *Analects* itself: the association of Confucius and his disciples, who lived, studied, worked, and traveled together. After his death, at least three of the disciples formed associations of their own, as did several of their disciples in turn. And there were associations—schools—of Daoists, Legalists, and Mohists as well. Moreover, beginning at least as early as the Former Han, Daoist-inspired secret societies were forming, surely as voluntary associations (and potential threats to the throne; the great majority of later rebellions in Chinese history had their genesis in secret societies).

But Professor Nosco's point remains, because while there were indeed some voluntary associations in ancient China, the canon is absolutely silent about any philosophical or religious import they might have.

NEEDS

If the goal of human life is to develop one's humanity to the utmost, and this is to be done through enhancing and extending human relationships, then we have a clear criterion for measuring the worth of those groups to which each person belongs (family, clan, village, school, state [and human race]): to what extent does each of these groups conduce to everyone's efforts to fully realize (make real) their potential? The several groups to which each of us belong need one another: the state cannot perform many of the functions conducive to human development that the family, clan, and village perform (most relationships are familial or collegial), but there are necessary ingredients—especially economic—of material and spiritual well-being that small groupings cannot realize on their own: repairing dikes, ditches, and roads, distributing grain from bumper harvest to famine areas, establishing academies, and the like. As a semi-aside, the idea that groups are to be evaluated by the criterion of enabling personal growth lets us see how Confucians might condemn the present Chinese government for incarcerating dissidents, and do so without recourse to the language of human rights. We rightly deplore the treatment of dissidents, but do so on the grounds that the government has violated the basic human rights of free, autonomous individuals. A Confucian, however—assuming that the dissidents are indeed patriots and neither self-seeking nor traitorous—would condemn the government on the grounds that remonstrance is obligatory, and that preventing the dissidents from interacting with their fellows denies them the opportunity of continuing to develop toward the goal of *ren*; rights language would not be needed.

LIABILITIES

If the boundaries question is not one addressed within the Confucian tradition, then neither is the liabilities question. Professor Nosco is correct in this section of his chapter when he says that Confucianism describes "an organic, familylike view of the ideal society." Indeed, in later imperial China, the term for the government representative at the smallest (county) level was "father mother official" (*fu mu guan*).

I would quarrel, however, with Professor Nosco's claim that Confucians would necessarily see voluntary associations as a challenge to their views of the ideal society. If such an association provided a means for interactively furthering one's humanity in ways that other groups did not, I believe they would endorse such an association (my reading on this score is of course speculative, as is Nosco's; the classical texts are altogether silent on the matter).

I would also quarrel with respect to Professor Nosco's translation of *Analects* 12:11 on the rectification of names. The use of the copula, and the italics with it, strongly suggests a stative orientation. But there are no copulas in classical Chinese, and hence a more accurate translation of the passage would read: "The ruler [must] rule, the minister, minister, the father, father, and the son, son." (This, too, is strictly speaking inaccurate, because there are no definite articles in classical Chinese either).[4]

This is not a minor point. Some general philosophical views are not made explicit in any tradition, but are rather sedimented in the grammar of the language used to articulate those views. Apart from context, Chinese graphs cannot be put into standard grammatical categories of noun, adjective, verb, adverb, and so on. It is more a language of relations and events than a language of things and states. In English we fully understand "rulers must rule," and "ministers minister." There is a shift of meaning for "fathers must father"—where the verb means "to sire" rather than "to parent"—and "son, son" is positively ungrammatical.

For myself, "The son [must] son" gives us an insight into what Confucius was about, its grating character in English notwithstanding. A theme that permeates the entire *Analects* is filial piety, and Confucius insists that his disciples must always engage in the activity of "sonning"—even after their parents have died; the religious quality of their lives depends on it.

GROUPS AND INDIVIDUALS

Throughout his chapter, Professor Nosco rightly emphasizes the centrality of the family in the Confucian tradition, as when he says, "[The family] is . . . the laboratory in which individuals are to have their first experience with growth in the direction of goodness." I would, however, replace his "individuals" with "persons," because of our reading of individuals as free, autonomous selves, none of whom can be found in the classical texts. If I am the sum of the roles I live, then I am not truly living except when I am in the company of others. As Confucius himself said, "I cannot herd with the birds and beasts. If I do not live in the midst of other persons, how can I live?" (18.6).

While this view may seem strange to us, it is actually straightforward: in order to *be* a friend, neighbor, or lover, for example, I must *have* a friend, neighbor, or lover. Other persons are not merely accidental or incidental to my achieving personhood and struggling for goodness. They are essential therefore; indeed, they confer personhood on me, for to the extent that I define myself as a teacher, students are necessary to my life, not incidental to it. The most succinct statement of this view was given by Herbert Fingarette: "For Confucius, unless there are at least two human beings, there are no human beings."[5] (Note in this regard also that while Confucianism is, in my opinion, correctly characterized as religious, there are no monks, nuns, anchorites, or hermits to be found in the tradition.)

To summarize this woefully brief account of Confucian perspectives on groups and individuals I would borrow a phrase Professor Rosenblum employs several times in her contribution to this volume: for Confucians, it is relationships within groupings "all the way down."

Citizenship

With voluntary associations and civil society playing no role in Confucian thought, issues surrounding citizenship cannot arise; there is no term in classical Chinese that has anywhere near the range of meanings as the English *citizen*, or its Latin root, *civis*. I believe Professor Nosco agrees, for in this section on citizenship, he focuses on the concept of happiness, and on this theme I have little to say beyond what I said in adumbrated form earlier.

We can, however, perhaps see citizenship somewhat differently if we attend to a passage in the *Analects* that Nosco cites earlier, a passage wherein Confucius says that uprightness in a son requires that he conceal the misconduct of his father from the authorities. He (Confucius) is thus unequivocal in answering the vexing question of whether one's highest loyalty is to the family or the state; the state loses every time. Similarly, we might also note that Socrates accepts straightforwardly that Euthyphro is going to prosecute a case at law but is astonished when he finds out the accused is Euthyphro's father.[6] But for Confucius, the question does not seem to be vexing at all; nor do we find anywhere else in the

Analects or other early Confucian texts a discussion of a conflict situation, the final topic to be discussed herein.

CONFLICT

If, as I earlier claimed, there are no universal principles—especially moral or political principles—given in the classical texts, then obviously there cannot be any moral or political principles that conflict with one another (there is no term in classical Chinese that is even roughly analogous to *dilemma*). There is always an answer to the question What should I do? but it will vary from situation to situation, and it will not invoke principles.

In order to make progress along the *ren dao*, human Way of the Confucians, we must fulfill the manifold obligations attendant on the roles we live. To be filial, I must son; to be a good friend I must friend; and to be a teacher, teach. It is by way of doing, and by the use of exemplars, that I progress. Principles are not necessary for this progress, for the more I mature, the more able I will be to do what is fitting or appropriate in my interpersonal relationships. As Professor Nosco correctly observes in this connection "Confucianism has little to say about conflict."

I am pleased that Professor Nosco has abandoned the terms "superiors" and "subordinates" when describing the basic Confucian relationships, using "benefactors" and "beneficiaries" instead, which deepens our insight into the classical Confucian vision of human flourishing. I am largely beneficiary of my teachers, benefactor to my students (although these situations can work in reverse as well; I often benefit profoundly from my students). When young I was beneficiary of my parents; when old, my brother and I became benefactors. And although there is not time or space to elaborate here, this notion of benefactor/beneficiary can also be used to analyze relations between neighbors, siblings, colleagues, friends, and much more.[7]

Now, one untoward way of construing the Confucian vision on this score has been to allow persons, when they are in a benefactor position, to be not only authoritative in fulfilling their responsibilities, but authoritarian as well, and to use beneficiaries for one's own ends. Chinese history is no less replete with despotic rulers, corrupt or incompetent officials or both, exploitative parents, dull pedants, and so forth, than the West. But these kinds of people are uniformly condemned in the classical texts, and just as we lose aesthetic, moral, and spiritual insight from the Bible if we focus solely on the Crusades, Inquisition, and Thirty Years' War, so too will we lose the aesthetic, moral, and spiritual insights of the early Confucian canon if we focus solely on its subversion by authoritarians.

Naively perhaps, the early Confucians do not seem to have worried overmuch about abuses of the benefactor relation, but they did have a theoretical reason for the lack of concern: I only make progress along the Way by fulfilling my roles, and a part of that fulfillment must be to assist the other in making progress along the Way, too. And because I am defined by my relationships, then, to whatever extent I help you flourish, I flourish as well; and hence, by exploiting you I diminish you, and hence I diminish myself. On this point if no other, Confucius would concur with Kant (although for very different reasons) that we are never to use another human being as a means only.

There is much more to say on behalf of studying the classical Confucius tradition in order to illuminate contemporary problems of morals, politics, and religion. I have said nothing in detail about spiritual progress or the importance of ritual, for example. And I have been altogether silent on the thoroughgoing sexism that characterized classical and imperial China, and the homophobia that characterizes the country right down to the present. But there is much that could be said on these matters if time (and space) permitted; classical Confucianism is, to my mind, of great relevance today, especially as a viable alternative to the modern Western liberal tradition, so deeply grounded in individuals that communities are always suspect.

My claim that classical Confucianism is of great relevance today will surely and correctly be challenged by everyone who believes the modern nation-state, more or less as it exists in the capitalist industrial democracies, must be taken as a given in any realistic theorizing about politics or morality. Given the multiethnic nature of most nations today, and given the awesome power the governments of these states can exercise over their citizens, it is essential to have, for example, universal principles, human rights language, and more, to serve as conceptual checks on majority or governmental oppression.

But one may also come from the other way: if there is much in Confucianism that speaks to the human condition; if it provides a way to lead an integrated life while contributing to the integration of the lives of others; if it cherishes what is good from the past yet is attentive to the needs of the present; if it shows us how the secular can become sacred; if it does these things *and* if it is true that such lives are not possible in contemporary individualistically oriented capitalist nation-states, then another conclusion follows: we must significantly change the economic and political structures of contemporary nation-states.

Now, it may seem that in order to make this argument I, too, must appeal to universal principles, or human rights language, or the concept of the rational, autonomous individual, or to all three, none of which is to be found in the Chinese texts. Let me therefore conclude with one final example of the Confucian persuasion, one that poses (seeming) conflict, with respect to government.

One obligation of the Confucian *junzi*—exemplary person—is to assume an official position if called upon to do so, after which the ruler becomes second in importance only to one's parents; unswerving loyalty is demanded. Hence we can easily construct a seeming conflict situation: What is a moral minister to do when serving an evil ruler? If we are seeking principles—universal principles—to answer this question, then we are indeed in conflict.

But let us follow Confucius in his insistence that we look to moral exemplars from the past for guidance in our progress along the way. Two such culture heroes were King Wen and his son, King Wu. King Wen—his name means "polished," "cultured," "decorative," and now means "literature"—was a vassal of a thoroughly rotten Shang Dynasty emperor. He remained loyal, regularly remonstrating with the Emperor (at some risk) to change his ways. He died unsuccessful in his efforts. King Wu—the name means "martial"—thereupon overthrew the Shang and established the most long-lived of all Chinese dynasties, the Zhou (1050–256 B.C.E.).

Thus the canon resolves the conflict. If it does not seem to, we must keep in mind that there are no universal moral or political principles in classical Confucianism, and keep equally in mind that we are always acting, either as benefactors or beneficiaries, with specific others; then we can appreciate that for Confucians, the moral challenge question is never simply What did you do? but rather is What did you do with whom, when? I am always to do what is appropriate with respect to the person(s) I am interacting with at a particular time. The unit of moral analysis in Confucianism is never the action, but the interaction between two or more human beings temporally situated.

Hence, I better live my roles as I better get to know the others with whom I interact, and the more interactions there are, the more I will get to know about myself.

Now, as a moral minister, I must ask myself, Just how bad is this ruler I am now serving? Is he beyond the pale? Might he be reformable? If so, do *I* have the requisite qualities necessary to reform him? Depending on which way the answers are given, my responsibility in my role as minister will be to continue to serve, with King Wen as my exemplar, or my responsibility as a follower of the Way will oblige me at the least to resign, or at the most to raise the flag of rebellion, following King Wu. Either way, there are neither moral principles nor moral conflicts; but in both cases there is appropriate behavior, which we could consider moral—and as leading to the spiritual.

Professor Nosco concludes his chapter with the observation that contemporary events, especially the internalization of the market, will inevitably buttress the integrity of the autonomous self, to paraphrase him. He may be right in this, but I hope not. The U.S. political, economic, and legal systems have been buttressing the autonomous self of American citizens to the point that it is becoming increasingly difficult even to think of ourselves as anything but consuming atoms, whose primary obligations are to do work we do not enjoy in order to buy things we do not need, and to do all of this in a world of increasing economic inequality. This sense of *anomie* is not altogether new; the poet A. E. Houseman captured its essence with the lines "And here am I / alone and afraid / in a world/I never made." If we should lose the vision of human beings as relational selves, it will be a great loss indeed, which no civil society, voluntary associations, or government, will ever be able to replace. And it is on this basis that I commend the texts of classical Confucianism to all people of goodwill concerned about the human condition in its present forms.[8]

NOTES

ILLNESS prevented me from attending the Conference at which these remarks were read. I am sure they would be better—and better integrated with the other essays in this volume—had I been able to profit from the conference discussions; my apologies for the essay's shortcomings. I am grateful to editor Nancy Rosenblum for helpful comments, and to Ms. Mary Bloomer of St. Mary's College for preparing a readable manuscript from my chaotic, handwritten, scrawled pages.

1. H. von Glasenapp, *Kant und die Religionen des Osten* (Holgne-Verlag, 1954), trans. and cited in Julia Ching, "Chinese Ethics and Kant," *Philosophy East and West* 28, no. 2 (April 1978): 169.

2. I have developed this theme further in "Tracing A Path of Spiritual Progress in the *Analects*," forthcoming in *Confucian Spirituality*, ed. Mary Evelyn Tucker and Tu Weiming (Crossroads Publishing Company, 2001).

3. For more detailed arguments, see my "Which Rights? Whose Democracy? A Confucian Critique of Modern Western Liberalism," in *Confuctian Ethics: A Comparative Study of Self, Autonomy, and Community*, ed. Kwongloi Shun and David Wong (Cambridge: Cambridge University Press, 2000).

4. References and translations from the *Analects* are all from Roger T. Ames and Henry Rosemont, Jr., *The Confucian Analects* (New York: Ballantine Books, 1998), which also treats issues of translation and interpretation.

5. Herbert Fingarette, "The Music of Humanity in the Conversations of Confucius," *Journal of Chinese Philosophy* 10 (1983).

6. Socrates, *Euthyphro* IV.4.

7. See also my "On Confucian Civility" in *Civility*, ed. Leroy Rouner (Notre Dame, Ind.: University of Notre Dame Press, 2000).

Overview: The Virtues and Vices of
Civil Society

Richard B. Miller

AMONG THE ISSUES discussed in these pages, three stand out for comparative commentary. First is the issue of human flourishing and the role that civil society or the state play in achieving that good. The second concerns whether the attitudes and practices that materialize in civil society are civil and civilizing, and how we are to distinguish civilizing attitudes and practices from those that are not. Third is whether norms that should direct the attitudes and practices of civil society properly materialize from within it, or whether they should be imposed (directly or indirectly) by the state. Lying behind these concerns are basic queries about the promise and problems of civil society. Given the idea that the modifier *civil* in *civil society* might refer to laudable sentiments and activities, what can civil society contribute to a common life? In what sense is civil society commendable, and in what sense is it morally, politically, and/or existentially incomplete or subversive of important values?

However these issues are sorted out, our traditions share the view that civil society is, at best, ambiguous. It possesses the potential for virtue or vice, is potentially progressive or regressive, and is potentially self-correcting or in need of outside correction. Civil society is an arena of moral formation and deformation. According to its more favorable descriptions, it is a space in which liberations are partial, utopias are relative, personal fulfillment is unfinished. On less favorable accounts, civil society is potentially subversive of social order, social justice, and/or individual well-being. The norms implied by such judgments invite comparison and commentary.

The three issues to which I have referred are, of course, related. Ideas about human flourishing imply a set of goods in which persons can stake an interest; those interests, in turn, presuppose and/or affect civility in interpersonal interactions. Whether such interactions are civil and civilizing requires second-order evaluation and, perhaps, state intervention to remedy aberrations or mistakes. Some forms of intervention may be direct (as in legal sanctions) or indirect (as in state-sponsored education that aims to cultivate civic virtues and social responsibility). Judgments about intervention, moreover, raise questions of paternalism and its (possible) justification. In any event, examining the relevant goods, interests, and institutions of civil society and government requires us to tack between ethical and political thought, theory and practice, and individual and social life.

How our various traditions approach these questions depends in part on how each conceives of civil society; it is not a univocal category. Complicating matters further is the task of determining which aspects of a tradition to isolate and examine from its history of thought and practice, for traditions usually change in response to other traditions or new developments in social life. If any insight emerges from this commentary, it is that the idea of civil society is theory-dependent and is subject to permutations within traditions. There is no conceptually innocent or static category of civil society in relation to government. That fact suggests caution about any comparative insights that might be garnered from this book.

With that caveat in view, I will devote my comments to the three issues that I have mentioned: The role that civil society and government might play in individuals' experience of human flourishing, however that is conceived; the kinds of interests that animate the institutions of civil society and government, and the second-order norms that inform assessments of civility; and the generation of those norms by citizens, mediating institutions, and the state.

The Good of Human Flourishing

The intuition that humans need moral direction in order to flourish animates several if not all of the traditions surveyed in this book. Disagreements emerge when we look more closely at how each tradition considers the respective roles to be played by civil society and the state in the realization of that good, and how each tradition conceives of the groups comprised by civil society and government. Premodern religious traditions, especially Confucianism, mark the outermost boundary of paternalistic direction on one side; classical liberalism marks the outermost boundary of antipaternalism on the other.

For Confucians, the state—not civil society—is to direct human flourishing, in which self and society are rightly ordered by principles of (internal) psychology and (external) role relations. Civil society is generally seen as subversive of that good insofar as it includes activities that presume independent knowledge of *ren dao*, the way of wisdom and well-being. As a sphere (or set of spheres) of private initiative, civil society denotes a range of action that occurs outside the relationships that properly shape society, which is organically and hierarchically arranged around the roles of ruler/subject, parent/child, husband/wife, elder brother/younger brother, and friend/friend. The ideal society is modeled on the family, patriarchally conceived. Central to this model is the idea that relationships are ordered by the virtue of munificence: Leader and citizen are related as benefactor and beneficiary. On this view, humans will flourish when they adhere to their role relations and submit to the philanthropic conduct of the state's political hierarchy, which is responsible for producing social order and harmony. Civil society, as a realm of voluntary initiative, privacy, and pluralism, suggests independence rather than political subservience. For that reason, the attitudes and practices of civil society are viewed with caution and perhaps suspicion. As Peter Nosco remarks, civil society suggests a "sphere of privacy granted by the state and society to its individual and corporate members, and Confucianism has generally not distinguished between privacy and selfishness."

On Nosco's account, Confucianism began to open itself to some aspects of civil society in the late-seventeenth century, with the advent of urbanization, small markets, an ascendant merchant class, cultural liberality, and private academies in Japan. Confucianism experienced the beginning of something like civil society as a result of the liberalizing impact of increasingly complex market relations. Therein lie the seeds of social activity that was not easily coordinated by or integrated into traditional social relationships, the "wisdom of the ancients."

Yet if we take a view of civil society as referring to more than voluntary associations, then Confucianism may have more to report than Nosco's account suggests. Here we do well to pick up a strand from Henry Rosemont's commentary. Confucian thought, Rosemont observes, presupposes a thoroughly social view of the self. We are the "sum of our relationships" in Confucian thinking, tied to others in a network of overlapping and ongoing connections. Society is a skein of harmoniously arranged solidarities, linking immediate families, villages, clans, friends, and political leaders. This aspect of Confucianism puts it nearer to themes of this anthology than either Nosco or Rosemont suggests. Broadly described, civil society refers to the associations of ordinary life, the local solidarities that shape human loyalties and the pursuit of happiness. If we focus less on the volitional and more on the associational features of civil society, Confucian thought (and perhaps, as Rosemont suggests, practice) can be seen as less alien to Western readers than it might first appear. That is not to say that Confucianism presents a theory of civil society on analogy with Western models, which typically view civil society as operating in dialectical relation with autonomy and individuality.[1] It is rather that Confucian thought embraces one of the key values that often lends moral weight to civil society, namely, a (social) view of the self that discovers happiness in relationships.

Judaism also has a difficult time conceptualizing civil society, but for different reasons. For Confucians, civil society is problematical for moral reasons: Civil society refers to a realm of "selfish" activity that proceeds independently of traditional roles or authorities. For Jews, civil society is not problematical because it might suggest selfishness, but for reasons that blend sociology with theology. As David Biale remarks, Jews understand themselves first and foremost as members of "a collectivity which in turn is defined by its covenantal relation to God." While this idea echoes other premodern notions of the self, including the Confucian idea of the self as constituted by relationships "all the way down," it fails fully to endorse the value often assigned to civil society insofar as it generates little space for seeing persons in "individualistic" terms.

The challenges posed by modernity also differ for each tradition. The challenge to Judaism was posed less by the advent of small merchants and the commodification of culture, as in Confucianism, than by the development of the nation-state and the need to protect rights that are typically associated with modern democracies. Complicating the issues is the fact that in parts of the biblical tradition, the state had moral legitimacy only insofar as its monarchs heeded the commands of God. These collectivist and premodern theocratic aspects of Jewish tradition seem to have little to contribute to modern discussions of civil society and the state, premised as they are on notions of individual freedom, rights, and responsibilities.

More might be said, however, if we look at Jewish communities as parts of a wider civil society and state. For Jews, civil society and/or the state have value insofar as they allow for the study of Torah and enable Jews to pursue their vision of human flourishing as a people covenantally called by God. The state might be valued to the extent to which it prohibits regressive groups in civil society from obstructing this pursuit of the good. Alternatively, civil society might be valued insofar as it involves progressive movements and aspirations that contribute to the protection of religious freedom. In this way, Judaism (as minority religion) may adopt a pragmatic approach to civil society and the state, assessing each in light of its contribution to pluralism and tolerance.

A Jewish nation-state, as Biale observes, is another matter. Here the dilemma turns on the fact that "religious parties in Israel . . . function at once as part of civil society and as competitors for and beneficiaries of state power." As such, the boundary between civil society and the state is less than clear, leaving to each some responsibility for facilitating the pursuit of freedom and human flourishing. That boundary remains ambiguous given the (also less-than-clear) synergism between Jewish belief and practice, on the one hand, and modern traditions of democratic politics, on the other.

Islam also presupposes an understanding of human flourishing that is premised on religious values and beliefs; Muslim thought often presumes political arrangements in which Islam is the established creed. But the complementarity thesis to which John Kelsay refers assigns role responsibilities to two main groups—the ʿulama and the caliphate—and thereby allows for greater social differentiation than we see in Confucianism. The ʿulama are scholars who provide authoritative interpretations of Islamic values; the caliphate are governmental officials responsible for securing public welfare and for deploying the coercive institutions of government in the service of Islamic beliefs. In this way, "religious and political institutions play complementary roles in the pursuit of human welfare." In Kelsay's mind, there is a rough analogy between the ʿulama and caliphate, on the one hand, and civil society and government, on the other.

While this parallel does not include reference to voluntary associations and mediating agencies such as we see in Western democracies, it does suggest limits on what an Islamic government may do and provides for considerable latitude in how lay Muslims may seek out authoritative interpretations of their tradition. Like classical liberals (as we shall see), traditional Islam is wary of how government can overreach, and the ʿulama are understood as providing an important barrier to the caliphate's power in matters of faith and interpretation. As Kelsay notes, the idea of civil society in Muslim contexts is about how "Muslims have understood the ways that social life should be organized, so as to protect the relative independence of Islam from the authoritarian tendencies of government." On that account, government would seem to pose a liability to human flourishing insofar as it is largely coercive and prone to excess when seeking to secure proper conduct from citizens.

As I noted, classical liberalism suggests an immediate contrast with some premodern traditions, especially Confucianism, for classical liberalism and Confucianism hold opposite views as to whether civil society or the state poses the main liability to human flourishing. If Confucians view the good of human flourishing as residing in a preordained path that is marked out by familial and political authority, classical liberals see human flourishing as residing in unfettered freedom and in relationships that have no presumptive reason to heed traditional patterns or state authority. For Confucians, the pursuit of flourishing relies on a maximal, paternalistic state; for classical liberals, flourishing relies on a minimal, "night watchman" state, responsible for protecting the plural pursuits of human well-being rather than for ensuring organic harmony. Confucians, moreover, view relationships as constitutive of human identity and welfare "all the way down." Classical liberals see relationships in instrumental terms, growing out of private pursuits of economic and other interests. For Confucians, civil society exists at the forbearance of government, receiving permission "from above." For classical (and other) liberals, government exists by virtue of the powers that have been delegated to it "from below."

Classical liberals and Confucians must thus view each other as anathema. But this opposition should not obscure the fact that both traditions are committed to ideals of human flourishing. Classical liberals view the promise of civil society precisely where Japanese Confucianism experienced various civilizing tendencies: as products of increasingly complex cultural and social interactions brought on by urban and market relationships. In this regard, what is notable is classical liberalism's claims about the relative merits of civil society vis à vis the state to produce civilizing tendencies. According to Steven Scalet and David Schmidtz, classical liberalism is premised on the wager that government is inherently expansionist and does more harm than good when trying to facilitate human flourishing. Therein lies the "pessimism" of classical liberal thought: It is skeptical about the competence and goodwill of government bureaucrats and optimistic about the ability of extrapolitical associations to produce human well-being. On this reading, classical liberalism is less a tightly argued philosophical doctrine than a practical philosophy that is premised on what it judges to be observed facts about state-sponsored attempts to further citizens' goods.

It is important to add that this account of flourishing excludes considerations of distributive justice to guide pursuits of the human good. "Classical liberals deny that justice requires any particular distribution of economic goods," Schmidtz and Scalet write. Because "civil society does not guarantee any particular distribution," then the good that resides in voluntary association must rest on the value of unrestrained activity and not on qualitative assessments of that activity or its outcomes.

Classical liberals thus conceive of equality in terms of negative freedom, and in this they connect with Enlightenment contributions to the natural law tradition. As Fred Miller indicates, that tradition is shaped by a fundamental tension between the classical theories of Aristotle and Aquinas, on the one hand, and modern theories, deriving from Locke and his liberal successors, on the other. What holds this broad tradition together is the claim that human activities are to be regulated by nature-based norms. Its internal tension rests on the fact that those norms derive from either a teleological vision of virtue, community, and the human good (as they do in the classical account), or from a less determinate vision that valorizes authenticity, freedom, self-preservation, and material acquisition (as they do in the modern account).

Miller also notes various shifts that have occurred within the classical account as it has adjusted to modern social formations. Principal among those changes is the (post-Aristotelian) distinction between society and the state, in which the former is made up of groups and activities commonly associated with civil society. But what keeps this "traditional" account coherent over time—from Aristotle through Aquinas to Pius XII and Jacques Maritain—is the idea that human beings are finite and need others to achieve completion and self-fulfillment. In this regard, civil society and the state share important humanizing functions. By providing material and spiritual means for a common life, they enable humans to overcome an ontological lack. The activities of civil society and government are thus open to evaluation according to their ability to provide the goods that human nature requires for its fruition.

Aristotle's critique of Plato's *Republic* provides reasons for understanding the city-state as an arena that coordinates various pursuits of the good into a common good, redounding to the benefit of all citizens. By rejecting the idea that society is organized around a hierarchically arranged set of role relations, Aristotle paved the way for the idea of *subsidiarity*, hoping to prevent the state from assuming the kind of paternalistic, heavy-handed provision of goods that classical liberals (and others) fear. At the same time, the principle of subsidiarity does not identify human initiative as the sole device for supplying human goods or for generating a common good. In that regard the classical approach to natural law theory and its modern reformulation attempt to craft a middle way between the extremes of maximal and minimal government. As John Coleman writes, subsidiarity involves a "limited state," not a "minimal state."

Subsidiarity is a principle that leaves to lower-order associations the presumptive responsibility of providing for human needs and the common good. In that respect the principle heeds the valuation of freedom found in classical liberal and modern natural law thinking. But subsidiarity reflects less pessimism than does classical liberalism about state bureaucrats' competence and goodwill in providing for human needs when the market fails to do so. Or, more precisely, the principle of subsidiarity presumes that social justice constrains the value of market freedom.[2] Flourishing is not equated with freedom, and the latter is esteemed only to the extent to which it can ensure that a floor of justice provides support for private economic pursuits. The goal of such state activity, on this account, is equality and empowerment: It must aim to provide resources that make participation in the common good available to those who would otherwise enter civil society at a considerable social, cultural, or economic disadvantage.

The tradition of social Catholicism, as Coleman indicates, likewise embraces this presumptive principle. But perhaps because he focuses on the place of subsidiarity within a tradition of faith, Coleman is able to understand how the principle bears upon matters of identity, loyalty, and commitment. Seen in this way, the implications of the principle are as metaphysical as they are material. According to Coleman, civil society and the principle of subsidiarity are based "on the social nature of the human person whose sociality is not exhausted by citizenship in the state." Value is presumptively assigned to the associations that make up civil society because civil society marks out a realm in which human beings can freely find meaning, community, and solidarity. In our various associations and interactions, we experience goods that are unavailable to us in the experience of citizenship. For this reason, social Catholicism can be open to the idea that civil society provides an arena of shifting involvements and the experience of pluralism that helps us negotiate complex moral psychologies and needs.[3] The boundary between civil society and the state marks out a sphere of friendship and agency. In the sphere of civil society, the human appetite for loyalty and commitment generates needs that participation in the state cannot satisfy.

The fact that civil society involves extrapolitical commitments is an idea around which Max Stackhouse develops an important amendment to Coleman's account. Stackhouse reminds us that the loyalties animating civil society may generate or derive from solidarities that go beyond the state—that civil society is in one sense local and in another sense cosmopolitan. In this respect we can see a tension in Christianity that parallels tensions within Stoicism and classical natural law tradition, as William Sullivan points out. Sullivan reminds us that, in classical Stoicism, a cosmopolitan orientation derives from the effort to disembed "the sacred from particular civic cults." Similarly, Stackhouse sees the need to avoid parochialism, echoing a concern about what earlier American Protestants called "cultural religion"—the tendency of religions (including Protestantism) to baptize particular cultural, national, or social interests.[4] Stackhouse writes that contemporary civil groups "are likely to spill over national, social, and religious borders in ways that no political or religious authority can, or should be able to, control. . . . People from these various areas of the common life may form overtly political associations . . . with links to people in other places and with various religious convictions, to construct or deconstruct political regimes, to bend or block political policies toward what they care about in civil society and around the world." As such, the principle of subsidiarity is inadequate in marking out spheres of motivation and commitment, for it focuses only on the border between state and society *within* a political regime. Stackhouse rightly calls attention to allegiances that go beyond the boundaries of a state, pointing to groups that seek to constitute a global civil society.[5]

The idea that we must not view civil society and the state according to a "part-whole" model lies at the heart of Stackhouse's critique, and its cosmopolitan implications for viewing the pursuit of human flourishing find parallels in critical theory, liberal egalitarianism, feminist theory, and, as I have mentioned, Stoicism and the natural law. Stackhouse's point is premised on the fact that Christianity holds out a vision of universal community that transcends any particular political or social arrangement. Similarly, various modern theories conceive of civil society as independent of the state and the market, and place normative constraints on the operation of each by imagining civil society in cosmopolitan terms. On these accounts, civil society may involve values and practices within a state and will depend on the political and legal structures of that state. But it also may be evaluated by principles and aspirations that draw from wider solidarities. For many modern theorists, civil society can provide critical resources for transforming some of its own (more localized) formations.

Critical theory is perhaps most noteworthy for maximizing the emancipatory potential of cosmopolitanism, although that potential exists in liberal egalitarianism and feminism as well. All of these theories express an ambivalence toward civil society and the state insofar as each can be progressive or regressive. For Habermas, as Kenneth Baynes indicates, that regressive potential is realized when the state or market succeeds in imposing its juridical or consumerist values on other pursuits. Civil society is to be celebrated only on the condition that it provides the arena for deliberative democracy and reflective communication. Therein lies its potential to promote human flourishing. For the earlier Frankfurt school, as Stephen White notes, that potential requires philosophical analysis that aspires to uncover invisible modes of oppression, especially where anonymous forces both intensify and conceal the suffering of others. Yet in either its earlier or more recent articulations, the same general point holds for critical theorists: Civil society requires not only political and moral norms, but also a philosophical attitude of criticism that seeks continually to expose how the market, state, and various civil associations work to undermine the values of civility, fairness, toleration, and reasonableness. As Baynes remarks, critical theory involves a commitment to these values as well as "a commitment to extending the core ideas of liberalism, especially the idea of a free and rational society, to a critique of the institutions and practices of liberal society itself."

Habermas's distinction between strong and weak publics reflects an effort to capture different aspects of public life, and perhaps to complicate liberals' distinction between public and private spheres. I want to note here that Habermas's distinction resembles the principle of subsidiarity in the natural law tradition, for in each case there is an attempt to mark out an arena of extrapolitical activity that nonetheless has public significance for citizens. What is a "weak" public for Habermas is a "lower-order association" for natural law theory and social Catholicism.

In his recent work, as Baynes observes, Habermas argues that democratic theory and practice must "respect the boundaries of the political-administrative and economic subsystems that have become relatively freed from the integrative force of communicative action and are in this sense 'autonomous.'" For Habermas, however, it is not the case that weak publics enjoy a pride of place when compared to strong publics. There is the danger of the latter colonizing the former with their juridical and bureaucratic values, but there is also the danger that civil society can be irrational and anarchic. Like traditional natural law thinkers, and unlike classical liberals, Habermas is unwilling to valorize freedom (and the market) unconditionally or conceive of the state as incapable of relieving human suffering. But unlike natural law theorists, Habermas is more suspicious of weak publics, owing to their potential for antideliberative and inegalitarian practices.

Baynes notes that Habermas's theory needs greater attention to practices and institutions that mediate between strong and weak publics, pointing to the value of civic norms and "liberal virtues" to amend Habermas's political theory. Those norms—civility, reasonableness, toleration, and fairness—have strong parallels in liberal egalitarianism, as represented by Will Kymlicka. Once again, we are reminded of the virtues and vices of civil society and the need for independent resources for social and political criticism.

Kymlicka argues that if civil society refers in any meaningful way to activities that occur in the public sphere, then it must generate dispositions of public-spiritedness. Civil society comprises not only private voluntary associations, but also attitudes and practices that affect others in a complex skein of social interaction. Citizenship, then, is to be understood more broadly than is suggested in Coleman's account, requiring actions and sentiments that go beyond voting behavior and support for political institutions. On Kymlicka's formulation, citizenship in a healthy democracy also involves

> qualities and attitudes of citizens; for example, their sense of identity, and how they view potentially competing forms of national, regional, ethnic, or religious identities; their ability to tolerate and work together with others who are different from themselves; their desire to participate in the political process in order to promote the public good and hold political authorities accountable; their willingness to show self-restraint and exercise personal responsibility in their economic demands and in personal choices that affect their health and the environment.

And, although Kymlicka fails to say so, it seems correct to add that such dispositions are good for those who embody them insofar as they enable citizens to pursue private, more particular goods. At a minimum, public-spiritedness enables individuals to enjoy the goods of a robust democracy, in which individuals assume responsibility for their collective life.

As Kymlicka and William Galston observe, what civic virtue demands is no simple question to resolve, for requiring such dispositions appears to run contrary to the value of liberty and toleration so important to the liberal tradition. Herein lie the questions of whether to require liberal virtues "all the way down" and where to expect such virtues to be cultivated. For present purposes, note how Kymlicka draws on the language of virtue to amend liberal egalitarianism's prior emphasis on social institutions in theories of justice as well as classical liberalism's celebration of market freedom. For Kymlicka, civil society provides an arena for cultivating civility and social responsibility, imposing on citizens the task of treating others according to the demands of liberal duties. In that way, life in civil society can shore up the dispositions necessary for people to experience the broader goods of democracy, self-government, and equality in public culture. As Galston observes, a healthy civil society "enhances a political community's overall capacity for self-government." Insofar as the latter is seen as a human good, the dispositions nurtured in civil society contribute to aspects of human flourishing.

While feminism draws much from the traditions of critical theory and liberal egalitarianism, it argues that the language of public-spiritedness relies on a distinction between public and private spheres that is historically conditioned by patriarchy. As Nancy Rosenblum observes, the distinction between civil society and the state is less important than (1) the boundary between public and private realms, and (2) the way each realm is constituted by gendered assumptions. If the language of civic virtue is to have any meaning at all for feminists, it must refer not to public-spiritedness in a gender-neutral way, but to the disposition to support policies and institutions that track the requirements of feminist social justice and to resist policies and institutions that have contributed to the ongoing oppression of women.

That means that feminism's pursuit of human flourishing must step back from civil society and the state in order to determine which institutions in each measure up to feminist concerns. By focusing on the private/public distinction and its gendered formulations, feminists employ an independent norm for assessing civil society and government, for each is implicated in different ways in the oppression of women as well as in advancing feminist justice; hence a studied ambivalence among feminists about civil society in relation to government. Thus, to take one example from our readings, feminists would be less impressed by whether the 'ulama in Islamic societies "holds the key to new models of gender relations" (as Kelsay writes) than with whether either the 'ulama or caliphate can initiate reforms that move gender relations in an egalitarian direction.

Reservations about civil society and government are not unique to feminists; I have mentioned them elsewhere in this commentary. But feminists differ from others (e.g., those who embrace the principle of subsidiarity) in that feminists are averse to assigning any presumptive priority to activities "from below" on behalf of advancing progressive aims. In this respect feminists ally themselves in a general way with the intuitions of critical theory. But even this alliance is nuanced, for feminists also seek to draw distinctions within civil society by asking how power and opportunity might be asymmetrically distributed for the sake of advancing gender justice. As Susan Moller Okin's examples illustrate, feminists will view some "exclusive" groups in civil society in asymmetrical terms: the Jaycees' former discriminatory practices are morally and politically different from admissions criteria at women's colleges. Accordingly, feminists draw on considerations of gender justice to evaluate the potential of governmental and nongovernmental institutions to promote equality, and they critically examine the potential of different nongovernmental associations "beneath" the umbrella of the state to advance or inhibit feminists' interests.

Feminists' caution about celebrating civil society as an arena of liberation and justice might be explained in part by women's prior experience as actors in various voluntary associations. That experience involves an irony that might be overlooked in discussions of civil society, not least by those who wish to amend liberal egalitarianism along the lines of a theory of civic virtue. As Okin points out, American women were actors in the civic sphere during the eighteenth and nineteenth centuries in part because they were disenfranchised. Far from reflecting a tendency to broaden our understanding of active citizenship, women were coerced into a set of political choices in part because they were denied voting rights. Turning to the example of women's political action cannot overlook this problematic fact. Those who deploy the history of women's activism as a model for civic virtue must not read that history as morally innocent.[6] Rather, women's activism emerged as a necessity, given their limited options for participation. Perhaps because women's activism is implicated in a larger politics of exclusion, feminists are sometimes cautious about assigning presumptive priority to civil society or "weak publics" as an arena in which to pursue the good of gender equality.

INTERESTS, NEEDS, AND NORMS

A second issue that runs through this book concerns the particular interests that enliven the attitudes and practices of civil society, and whether those interests are in fact civil and civilizing. Debates about civil society invite us to examine the dispositions that animate the institutions of civil society and government, as well as the norms that shape assessments of those dispositions. I have already mentioned the idea of civic virtue and some of the issues it poses. Here we can focus more carefully on the promise and problems of civic virtue, by which I mean the disposition to support institutions and practices that aim to secure public justice.

Once again, premodern traditions appear to be the most cautious, with Confucianism occupying the outermost extreme at one end. Modern traditions appear to be the most permissive, with classical liberalism occupying the other outermost extreme. That is to say, premodern traditions tend to be suspicious about whether civil society provides the proper resources for civilizing and virtuous behavior. Modern traditions, with varying degrees of confidence, view civil society as providing associations and institutions that can properly moralize habits of fairness and civility.

For Confucians, as we have seen, the interests that guide civil society must be viewed with suspicion insofar as the institutions of civil society are conceived along Western views of *voluntary* associations. Civil society's interest in freedom, not its interest in human relationships, is problematical from the Confucian perspective. More precisely, what is important about relationships for Confucians is not whether they are freely created, but whether they are rightly ordered. Herein lies the importance of norms that are independent of civil society, provided by classical Confucian texts. As defined by Confucius, Mencius, and other classical authors, the way of wisdom requires subordinating one's interests to the duties of role morality and the common good of the state. Interests that proceed outside of those norms are delusory, setting individuals on the path toward unhappiness and self-destruction, and society on the path of disharmony. Civility is a matter of abiding by properly ordered roles, and its virtues include filial piety, right-mindedness, attentiveness, benevolence, and moderation, among others.

Classical liberals provide the obvious point of contrast. For them, civility will evolve on the premise that individuals left to their own initiatives will forge cooperative relationships, especially in the market but also in extrapolitical associations. In this respect, classical liberals go beyond Galston's account of libertarian civic virtue, according to which citizens' "only civic obligation is to respect the liberties of others." Scalet and Schmidtz see the promise of civic virtue more robustly: "Those who see markets as classical liberals do—as places where people voluntarily exchange the products of their labor on mutually agreeable terms—will see markets at the heart of civil society, and essentially so. They believe voluntary exchange is a central part of our moral education: an indispensable part (albeit only a part) of the process by which people become civilized." Herein lies the core of classical liberalism's optimism. Classical liberals "believe that in a free society people are not only willing to help each other; they believe that in a free society (albeit only in a free society) people love to help each other—that freely helping others, including bringing to the market products that other people want and need, is one of life's greatest joys."

On that account, the market provides an arena in which individuals come together for mutual advantage. Associations arise spontaneously, classical liberals aver, in order to meet basic human needs. That appears to be classical liberalism's account of civility and the morally educative aspects of market exchange. Norms and coercive mechanisms that constrain activity in civil society must "secure a framework that encourages productive competition within the private sector." Moreover, the state's role in relation to the market is constrained by the need to ensure an arena of cooperative activity: "The government's proper role is to construct and enforce the rules of a cooperative game so that people win by helping each other win. Civil society provides the players and more or less defines a field of opportunities. Government provides the referee, trying to deter those who would seek to win at the expense of other players."

For several traditions surveyed in this volume, the critical question about classical liberalism is whether the needs satisfied by the market are real or artificial, the product of the market's attempt to expand itself. In this regard all the traditions discussed in these pages, premodern as well as modern, would consider classical liberalism's attempt to provide a robust account of civility to be underdetermined How this is so is worth exploring.

Cultures in which Islam is the established religion provide an immediate contrast. For Muslims, social life is civil and civilizing to the extent that it is directed by Islamic values. Freedom is less to be celebrated than to be disciplined according to religious beliefs, as interpreted by authoritative scholars and institutionalized by governmental officials. At the same time, however, modern Islamic societies appear to be wrestling with this arrangement. According to Kelsay, contemporary Iran may be developing a "space" for various liberties as a result of a growing and increasingly influential business and professional class; hence increased attention in modern Islam for "free (that is, non-state-controlled) newspapers and television stations, an independent business sector, and less carefully regulated political parties." Contemporary Islam may be experiencing the same kinds of social pressures that Japanese Confucianism experienced in the seventeenth century. In each case, commercial (and other) interests call for new associations and greater liberties than traditional social arrangements have imagined. Given the fact in modern Islamic societies that economic interests may be tainted with Western values, the call for greater liberties may generate deep cultural tensions between traditionalists and reformers.

Feminists would argue that classical liberalism's celebration of the market as an arena of moral education and cooperative activity overlooks the extent to which women have either been excluded from the market or have been exploited when included. On the first point, feminists would return to the public-private distinction and note how market activity located outside the domestic sphere has typically excluded women and is thus unreliable as a domain of civilizing practices and moral education. On the second point, feminists would argue that when women have been included as participants in the market, they have been undervalued at best and exploited at worst. Creating conditions that "deter those who would seek to win at the expense of other players" requires a more robust form of state action than classical liberals typically endorse. In any event, whatever promise civil society holds as a space of civilizing activity must be critically scrutinized in light of feminist norms and women's experience.

Rosenblum notes that feminists' social criticism allows for a mixed review of civil society's claim to civilize social practices and attitudes. That is to say, feminists' studied ambivalence toward civil society and government carries over into their account of civic virtue. On the one hand, even the best description of civic virtue raises feminists' concerns, for much of what passes as civic virtue reflects gendered assumptions. As Rosenblum writes, "The expansion of duties like neighborliness and other exhibitions of caring have historically fallen to women." Given the gendered way in which selflessness and care are frequently institutionalized in role expectations, a celebration of civic virtue may only mask efforts to encumber women unfairly with additional moral and social responsibilities. Historically, the moralization of citizenship has been distributed inequitably. Compounding this problem is gender injustice in the family. So long as injustice continues in domestic relations, proper civility in more public domains will remain elusive.[7] Expecting the market to provide the kind of civil education that might lead to reforms in the domestic sphere overlooks the extent to which the family is important for moral formation and the construction of attitudes toward women in the public domain.

On the other hand, civil society can work to the advantage of feminists' interests by providing a seedbed of democracy. This point has two facets. Voluntary associations provide arenas in which individuals hone their deliberative virtues and enter into discursive politics according to the general requirements of public reason. Equally important, Rosenblum writes, civil society enables feminists to "sharpen areas of conflict, shape rhetoric, form organizations, weld effective alliances, raise money, negotiate concessions, using political methods that often have little to do with deliberation." Civil society involves civilizing practices insofar as it helps to cultivate deliberative virtues, and it provides arenas in which feminists can develop tools to negotiate conflict when those virtues are insufficient to advance feminist social justice. Accordingly, civil society is civilizing less as a function of market interactions, as classical liberals aver, and more as a function of equipping citizens to enter democratic politics as equal and effective participants.

Classical natural law theorists would offer a more general critique of classical liberalism's emphasis on the market as a sphere of moral education. In part that is because, as Miller points out in his account of Aristotle, we must not overlook other social formations within civil society and see how their respective goods require friendships and dispositions that cannot be captured by the virtues of economic provision. Civil society includes a cluster of diverse associations whose ends require individuals to relate to each other in ways that cannot be fulfilled by economic interactions. Our needs and the virtues required to address them are too diverse.[8] Moreover, classical liberalism's turn to the market as the primary arena of civilizing activity is troubling because it fails to distinguish between the real needs that the market might serve and the artificial needs that it tends to create. For classical natural law theory, classical liberalism lacks a critical principle for distinguishing between those different needs and for evaluating them on terms that are independent of the value of negative freedom. Insofar as civil society emerges from humans' need to meet the needs of others, it may or may not be civilizing. What is essential from the natural law point of view, and from the point of view of religious traditions that have incorporated natural law, is to determine whether those needs are authentically human. Civil society as a domain of civilizing activity and moral education can be celebrated only to the extent to which it enables individuals to achieve their true ends. As such, it is always subject to evaluation according to nature-based norms.

A similar point appears to animate Habermas's concern about the role of the market as a colonizing force in the public sphere. Like natural law theorists, Habermas sees the market as involving values and corresponding power structures that require normative assessment. That is to say, the market is not a neutral arena in which moral associations spontaneously materialize and in which associations of mutual advantage emerge. Rather, the market is itself a "moral" domain insofar as it favors only certain kinds of interactions by valorizing persons and relationships as commodified and instrumentalized. For modern critical theory, such values represent counterfeit freedom. At most, whether the market can be an arena of civilizing activity will depend on the extent to which its participants meet the test of deliberative and reflective norms. Herein lie resources in Habermas's theory for distinguishing between real and artificial needs.

As I noted earlier, Baynes adds to this Habermasian line of social criticism some remarks about virtues that are necessary for resisting the colonizing forces of market commodification and state bureaucracy. Baynes offers the kind of corrective to critical theory that parallels Kymlicka's amendment to liberal egalitarianism. In both cases, emphasis falls on the principled dispositions necessary for individuals to live together in modern democracies. For Baynes, critical theory's "almost exclusive attention to questions of institutional design and discursive procedures" needs to be supplemented by attention to "liberal virtues," especially the duty of reasonableness. Individuals who abide by such virtues coexist on terms that go beyond a mere modus vivendi. Instead, social cooperation can rely on a principled commitment to the goods of civility, toleration, fairness, and reasonableness.[9] Although Baynes does not say so, one implication seems clear: Citizens disposed along the lines of liberal virtues have moral resources for resisting the (colonizing) effects of the state and market, for these are corrosive of interactions among citizens in their various lifeworlds, and contribute to terms of social cooperation that are less principled than instrumental or utilitarian.

Baynes's engagement with Habermas suggests that critical theory's traditional attention to ideological and cultural formations overlooks some basic issues of moral agency. Baynes suggests that we can address the potential dangers of "weak publics" in civil society—their tendency toward anarchic or regressive politics—by articulating how broad requirements of public reason and a sense of justice can translate into specific habits of moral and political psychology. The idea is not to abandon the critique of market and bureaucratic forces, but to shore up that critique by pointing to habits of liberal democracy that must be both presupposed and strengthened in the design of social institutions.

In order to deepen the critique of classical liberalism's account of how the market provides an arena for morally educative and civilizing activity, various traditions emphasize a core intuition of feminist, natural law, and Habermas's critical theory. The general idea would be to recall feminism's attention to oppression, natural law theory's attention to fundamental human needs, and Habermas's emphasis on the market as itself a bearer of (counterfeit) value as pointing toward a basic intuition about the market's capriciousness in assisting disempowered groups. In this respect, White's discussion of the early phase of critical theory is instructive. White isolates the theme of human suffering as an important target of critical analysis. (Religious traditions such as social Catholicism that emphasize the "preferential option for the poor" echo this idea.)[10] The general complaint is that civil society provides an arena of civilizing and educative action only to the extent to which it helps to meet the needs of those who are most disadvantaged for natural or social reasons. Providing goods in market exchanges is no grounds for individuals to feel joy until the structural barriers that contribute to human suffering and disenfranchisement are effectively removed. If civil society provides an arena of spontaneous moral activity, it must first mark the differences in power and opportunity that divide society into distinct classes.

Kymlicka's account of liberal egalitarianism devotes considerable attention to the topic of civic virtue. Like Baynes, he sees debates about civil society as an occasion to address matters of moral psychology, the tenor of voluntary associations in liberal democracies, and the second-order norms that are to guide citizens' dispositions. Liberal citizenship requires "that a substantial number of citizens be willing to participate politically, and that they do so in a publicly reasonable way." Public reason requires citizens "to justify their political demands in terms that fellow citizens can understand and accept as consistent with their status as free and equal citizens." Underlying that notion, of course, is a theory of political legitimacy and justified coercion: Policies that constrain liberty will be unfairly coercive, and undeserving of democratic consent, if they are premised on claims that are presumptively private or sectarian.[11]

Perhaps most distinctive about Kymlicka's account is his attempt to derive the virtue of civility from second-order norms of nondiscrimination. Familiar to citizens in liberal democracies, these norms entail a set of dispositions that should supplement liberalism's attention to the design of social institutions. According to Kymlicka, the obligations of liberal citizenship must be extended into relations between nonintimates in the civic realm. "The norms of nondiscrimination," he writes, "entail that it is impermissible for businesses to ignore their black customers, or treat them rudely, although it is not always possible to legally enforce this. Businesses must in effect make blacks feel welcome, just as if they were whites." Nondiscrimination as a civic virtue means that "liberal citizens must learn to act in everyday settings on an equal basis with people for whom they might harbor prejudice."

How might such virtue be cultivated? This is no small issue for liberals, for it may require imposing the good of civility on those who reject it. No less than tolerating the intolerant,[12] cultivating civility among those who prefer prejudice and incivility is no small challenge in liberal societies. Kymlicka understands the theoretical aspects of this challenge to liberal egalitarianism, noting that the value of equality may limit the value of freedom of expression (and vice versa). (On how liberal egalitarians are to weigh and balance these values, Galston records a substantive disagreement with Kymlicka, allowing for what might be experienced as insufficiently respectful conduct in the "zone of indeterminacy" between equality and liberty in particular cases.) At a practical level, Kymlicka enjoins liberal egalitarians to consider public institutions as proper locuses for cultivating the broad demands of civic virtue. Liberal democracy relies on what John Rawls calls "a sense of justice"[13] among citizens, and civility is one habit that nurtures and expresses that sense. Public institutions in liberal democracies thus have a valid claim to cultivate civility in various socializing processes. Nonetheless, the problem of imparting civic virtue raises difficult practical questions at the margins. The disagreement between Kymlicka and Galston points to a general conundrum for liberals, aptly summarized by Rosenblum: Does civil society provide the "seedbed" of liberal virtue, or does it comprise a "boot camp" of liberal morality?

Christianity—or at least its modern, liberal incarnation—can accept much of what Baynes and Kymlicka describe as ingredients of civic virtue while insisting that Christians have something distinctive to add to the moral quality of public culture. As if to echo Baynes, Coleman points out that the market and the state "depend upon [a] prior vivid experience of reciprocity, duty, responsibility, and solidarity." Such virtues are entirely compatible with Christian notions of "natural equity." Thus, in contrast to classical liberalism, social Catholicism will assess the putative civilizing features of market interactions on norms that operate independently of the negative rights protected by the state.

Moreover, many (but not all) Christians embrace the broad requirements of public reason as an important ingredient of civic virtue. As Coleman avers, "The church can garner public support for the freedom it demands for itself in fidelity to Gospel warrant only if it states its case *simultaneously* on secular warrant." In this respect, liberal Christians are bilingual, believing that justice and reciprocity require them to justify their arguments by drawing on their own idioms while also seeking terms that can be shared with nonbelievers.[14] It seems fair to say that public reason comprises what might be called an "intellectual civic virtue" for modern, liberal Christians, disposing them to argue for policies on terms that nonbelievers can share, at least in principle.

Coleman's account of postconciliar Catholicism devotes considerable attention to religious freedom and tolerance as aspects of civic virtue. It is important to understand why that is so. As Coleman shows, John Courtney Murray laid the groundwork for Catholicism's embrace of religious freedom and the corresponding demands of tolerance, pluralism, and liberal politics. Arguments justifying liberal civic virtue and its corresponding duties had less to do with moral psychology than with a composite of theological, juridical, political, and moral considerations. The idea of religious freedom thus produced a pivotal shift in Catholics' relation to civil society and government, a shift that marshaled a cluster of discourses to pave the way for a new self-understanding. For modern Catholics, civic virtue as including toleration, pluralism, and liberal freedom is not one political virtue alongside others. It is foundational to modern Catholicism's self-conception. In this respect, attention to civic virtue and the duties of citizenship has as much to do with how Catholics view others as it does with how modern Catholics have come to view themselves—hence the importance to which Coleman assigns those topics in his essay.

Yet the idea of civic virtue as allowing for religious diversity and requiring public reason does not exhaust what Christians have to contribute to the civil sphere, which they (like others) construe more broadly than the public-political sphere. Matters of public justice and liberal politics mark a moral minimum. As Coleman notes, Christians "must go beyond that humane minimum to try to inject some wider ideal of neighbor love into the social fabric." The idea is to draw on what are traditionally called the theological virtues to deepen and extend human dispositions toward others.[15] In this way, Christians "might add to the wider repertoire of citizenship such notions as a countercultural vision of a more ideal community and of forgiveness." Herein lies a potential source of ambivalence among Christians about civil society and civic virtue: Civil society provides an arena in which natural equity is practiced, but in which it is sometimes challenged by the more demanding virtue of selfless agape. Indeed, as Coleman briefly notes, Christians of an Augustinian persuasion are likely to believe that local solidarities and voluntary associations are corrupted by parochialism and sin. The countercultural vision of Christianity will distance those Christians from other citizens, raising questions about the compatibility between religion and liberal politics.

In Judaism, it makes sense to speak of the civilizing and moralizing aspects of civil society in terms that relate indirectly or analogously to liberal, Western idioms, since, as Zohar and Biale point out, the idea of civil society as an arena of voluntary associations is foreign to traditional Judaism. In this respect, Judaism bears some similarity with Confucianism. In each case, the associative aspects of civil society, not the voluntary aspects, are important. However, unlike Confucians, Jews do not view this association as structured by the state (Zionism being a notable exception). Judaism emphasizes identity in covenantal membership, which can cut across political and cultural boundaries. Yet no less than liberal egalitarians and critical theorists, Jews must presuppose some dispositions on which the design of social institutions relies. Without such civilizing dispositions, the civilization to which Israel is called would have little on which to secure itself. Torah study, central to the formation and education of the Jewish community, presupposes the disposition to educate and the corresponding embrace of learning as a basic good. In this respect, commitment to covenantal values, broadly conceived, includes the virtue of instruction and the transmission of tradition as central to how one generation nurtures civility in the next. Moreover, burial societies and sick-care societies discharge obligations to past or infirm members of the covenant, suggesting dispositions to minister to those at the margins of the community.

More generally, the idea that Jews derive their identity as members of a covenant with God implies what might be called, on analogy with Rawls's "sense of justice," a sense of covenant. The parallel suggests that life as a covenant people involves covenantal habits, which aim to nurture social responsibility toward vulnerable individuals and the collectivity as a whole. In this way Judaism draws on biblical resources to question classical liberals' confidence in the market as a space of civilizing behavior. Basic requirements of human equity are classically spelled out in prophetic literature, in which the community's social critics call their fellow Israelites back to foundational principles of Israelite law, history, and self-understanding.[16] In that way, biblical prophets articulate principles for civic virtue. If we view civic virtue as (generally) referring to dispositions to support the institutions and practices that aim to secure social justice, then Jewish tradition offers resources for speaking in such terms.

GENERATIVE SOURCES

Given the importance of human flourishing and the dispositions necessary to secure social justice, where can we find sources to generate and support these goods? What role do civil society and government play in the realization of these ends and dispositions? Can we be confident that civil society possesses resources for self-correction, or does it need the state's direct or indirect steering?

Drawing on what we have learned from Nosco and Rosemont, it would seem that traditional Confucianism presumes that the state, and not lower-order associations or weak publics, is responsible for directing citizens' aims and nurturing virtues that are appropriate to the end of perfection. Insofar as lower-order groups emphasize voluntariness rather than rightly ordered association, they appear subversive of the pursuit of personal transformation and the state's common good. At the same time, however, Confucianism places great emphasis on the family as an important school of virtue and right-mindedness. Of special importance is the father's cultivation of his own virtue as a condition of rightly ordering his family. Virtuous fathers bring good order to their families, which contributes to peace and well-being in the state. In this way, the state relies on the activities and practices of a lower-order group—families—to generate habits that contribute to human flourishing and political cooperation.

The patriarchal values embedded in Confucianism find no support from feminism. But in one important respect the two traditions share the idea that the family cannot be omitted from discussions of government and civil society, if only because the family is critical to the development of citizens' social morality. Confucians generally deny a boundary between public and private realms, believing that the movement from the family to the state is relatively seamless insofar as virtues cultivated in the former contribute to the peace and good of the latter. Feminists neither deny the public-private boundary nor assume that the movement from one to the other is, or ought to be, seamless. Rather, as Rosenblum notes, they patrol that boundary, noting how attitudes relegated to the private sphere can thwart feminists' pursuit of equality in the public sphere. Confucians maintain that rightly ordered families contribute to social justice. Feminists often argue that the norms of social justice must shape the internal ordering of domestic life. However different their standards and procedures, Confucians and feminists concur that the family cannot be viewed as an arena of unfettered privacy.

Of course, the family is not the only extrapolitical institution to which feminists direct their attention when thinking about generative sources. Here we do well to recall feminists' ambivalence toward civil society and the state: Although both have provided a space for advancing feminists' interests, the record of each is blemished. (Rosenblum describes civil society as a utopia for women, but that verdict requires some qualification.) Historically, the associations of civil society have furnished ways for women to advance their interests, but that work was required in part by women's inability to participate fully in the public sphere. Moreover, civil society can be an arena of gender inequality. Legal interventions by the state that aim to rectify inequality in civil society have been effective at times, but they have been slow in arriving and inconsistent in application. For these reasons, in feminist theory the state and civil society must each be assessed according to standards of gender equality.

Recent critical theory echoes this ambivalence and takes it to a more general level. It begins with some general presumptions about the respective roles of civil society and the state. The core idea is that there is an important division of labor between weak and strong publics. Weak publics are responsible for identifying social problems; strong publics are responsible for making political decisions and filtering reasons via formal parliamentary procedures. Ambivalence derives from the fact that weak publics do not guarantee deliberative democracy and/or communicative freedom. For Habermas, as Baynes observes, there is the recurrent fear that weak publics are "wild," "anarchic," and irrational. As such, there is the ongoing need to transform "preferences in response to the considered views of others and the 'laundering' or filtering of irrational and/or morally repugnant preferences in ways that are not excessively paternalistic." What is important for Habermas is "that public opinion be formed on the basis of adequate information and relevant reasons and that those whose interests are involved have an equal and effective opportunity to make their own interests (and reasons for them) known."

Habermas develops his views in opposition to classical liberal accounts of freedom and civil society, pointing to an important difference between critical theory and classical liberalism regarding matters of generative sources. Classical liberalism's view of freedom as negative liberty and its conception of law as a restriction on such liberty necessarily imply that civil society, and not the state, will enjoy pride of place as the generative source of human flourishing. The state is limited to setting the proper terms for cooperation between parties that freely seek their mutual advantage. Critical theory, in contrast, is premised on a view of liberty as communicative freedom, "a basic moral capacity of individuals to be bound only by obligations generated through the exchange of mutually acceptable reasons." Freedom for Habermas is counterfeit if it is not governed by rational, deliberative principles. Accordingly, protecting liberty as communicative freedom is likely to require a larger role for the state than classical liberals permit.

We should note, however, that the traffic between strong and weak publics is not one way. Weak publics and public opinion can make themselves "effective in the 'strong public' of the formal political system without either supplanting its functions or ... becoming merely an arm or extension of the formal political system." As such, critical theory privileges neither weak nor strong publics as generative sources of welfare, social justice, or democratic practice. Habermas's division of labor between strong and weak publics allows for synergism between them.

As Baynes observes, Habermas leaves open the question, What institutions or mechanisms properly mediate between civil society and government? While the distinction between weak and strong publics aims to provide a clearer picture of the public realm than the private-public distinction permits, Baynes suggests that a more fine-grained understanding of generative sources and mediating associations is part of critical theory's future agenda.

Kymlicka takes up this concern about mediating between weak and strong publics. For liberal egalitarians, as for Baynes, liberal virtues are important for the health of civil society and the justice of public institutions. How or where might such virtues be generated? According to Kymlicka, herein lies the value of public education for liberal democracies. Among other things, schools "must teach children how to engage in the kind of critical reasoning and moral perspective that defines public reasonableness." In this and other ways, public education can instill the virtues that correct the inegalitarian or antiliberal features of civil society and the state. (The extent to which a democratic society ought to require common schooling is a matter that Kymlicka finally leaves open; he prefers some common schooling for children of cultural or religious groups that have a history of active citizenship.) Insofar as public institutions and civil society both rely on citizens' sense of justice, the state has a legitimate interest in regulating public institutions to foster civil dispositions.

A clear presumption in favor of civil society as a generative source of moral goods and dispositions is provided by social Catholicism and the natural law tradition, although these traditions likewise express important qualifications about the limits of lower-order associations. Social Catholicism, Coleman avers, sees civil society as an "independent source of moral authority." That is a practical rather than a philosophical judgment, drawing on general observations about the experience of freedom, community, and mutuality in political life. For classic natural law theorists as well as social Catholics, civil society provides the occasion for local solidarities, the experience of which generally requires liberty from state interference. As Miller writes, "Civil society, in which the citizens cooperate and interact in many different associations for a wide array of purposes, is thus a sphere in which they can learn to trust and rely on one another." Civil society can thus be a seedbed of friendship and mutuality. Such friendships generally (but not categorically) require freedom from state intervention in order to develop. Moreover, insofar as reliance on government might breed a "culture of dependence," a presumptive turn to the state for direction and welfare threatens to compromise the good of individual responsibility.

For natural law theory and social Catholicism, the principle of subsidiarity implies a presumption in favor of assigning to civil society, not the state, the task of providing moral order and economic justice. The state is authorized to intervene on behalf of basic human welfare only when it is clear that civil associations and the market fail to provide a basic minimum. In this respect, natural law theory and social Catholicism express greater confidence in lower-order associations as a source of justice and virtue than do feminism and critical theory.

Natural law theory and social Catholicism thus provide a useful point of comparison with several theories. They contrast with Confucianism insofar as the latter operates according to a presumption that the state, not civil society, provides the primary source for norms to direct human action. Classical natural law and social Catholicism contrast with classical liberalism's restriction of government to the night watchman state because the principle of subsidiarity allows for more robust interventions by the state when civil society fails to provide material and other conditions for human welfare. Further, natural law theory and social Catholicism contrast with feminism and critical theory insofar as the principle of subsidiarity begins with a presumption in favor of civil society as a source of moral authority, in contrast to those other theories' studied ambivalence about whether the state or civil society should enjoy pride of place as a generative source of moral norms and civilizing interactions.

In Islam the complementarity thesis suggests a relationship of interdependence between the ʿulama and the caliphate when it comes to generating values in Muslim societies. The ʿulama provide authoritative interpretations of Islamic values, to which the caliphate are, in principle at least, accountable when seeking to institutionalize various features of Muslim law and belief. Mosques, schools, and universities perform an important educative and religious role in generating norms for governmental authorities. Perhaps this arrangement might be seen as a kind of synergism between strong and weak publics in Habermas's sense. As Kelsay notes, however, this arrangement is undergoing stress in countries such as Iran. That is because the ʿulama are becoming increasingly associated with the government whose power they are supposed to limit; weak publics are becoming too strong. Hence the emergence of a new source of value and pressure, the business and professional classes, to correct for what is perceived to be an imbalance in how values and norms are interpreted and enforced.

Judaism poses an interesting contrast with all of our traditions for reasons that are more historical than philosophical. Whether civil society or the state functions as a generative source depends in large part on which phase of Jewish tradition one focuses on. Exilic Judaism will look to civil society insofar Jews are to rely on their communities as sources of duty and virtue, communities that are part of larger social and political formations. At other times it is more appropriate to look to the role of either the monarch or the rulers of a Jewish state to provide the direction for virtue and social responsibility. In either case, Jewish attitudes and practices are to be normed by divine teaching as presented in Torah. Instruction from that source is mediated either by the Jewish community within a state or by the Jewish state, depending on more comprehensive political formations. As such, Judaism's testimony is that considerations of civil society in relation to government cannot be approached ahistorically.

Conclusion

Recent attention to civil society and government has generated a series of important topics in political theory and comparative religious and philosophical ethics. Hence the two Ethikon volumes devoted to the subject, along with other recent studies.[17] Many of the reigning categories of political thought in either premodern or modern formulations do not "map" onto the dynamics of civil society in a straightforward fashion. Kelsay candidly notes this difficulty when thinking about Islam; Rosenblum reminds us that this challenge also exists for feminists. For Kelsay, whatever parallel exists between the ʿulama and caliphate, on the one hand, and civil society and government, on the other, must be handled with care. For feminists, the challenge lies not in the substantive differences between premodern and modern categories (as they do in Islam), but in whether modern categories that are used to analyze civil society and government are politically and morally innocent. As Rosenblum notes, feminists have generally patrolled the distinction between private and public spheres. While that hermeneutics of suspicion might instruct discussions of civil society and government, the categories in question (private/public; civil society/government) are not clear analogues.

That said, the apparent novelty of civil society in relation to government should not be exaggerated. How political theory handles the issues posed by civil society and government is a function of more fundamental ideas about freedom, pluralism, social justice, and political virtue. At its core, civil society raises basic questions of how individual interests can find expression and support in social life, and how public institutions are properly to relate to individual needs and corresponding social formations. Whether the attitudes and practices of civil society are to be commended or critiqued depends on terms and distinctions that enjoy a long pedigree in the traditions included in this volume. Whether and to what extent we are to commend the activities in civil society will depend on traditional and modern categories regarding liberty, fairness, and virtue.

Moreover, civil society and its relation to government involve questions that are moral and political. They are moral insofar as civil society involves dispositions that have normative implications for individuals and their associations. They also involve normative judgments about the proper role of the state in relation to those dispositions and associations. They are political insofar as civil society is vulnerable to and potentially subversive of concentrations of power. Whether such concentrations are themselves conducive to a good society depends on a broader account of human freedom and well-being, and invites discussion about the role of individual liberties, local solidarities, public institutions, and their complex interactions.

Notes

I am grateful to Judith Granbois for comments on an earlier draft of this paper.

1. See the discussion in Adam B. Seligman, *The Idea of Civil Society* (Princeton: Princeton University Press, 1992).

2. In this respect natural law thinking echoes the broad contours of a theory of justice, as espoused by John Rawls, *A Theory of Justice* (Cambridge: Harvard University Press, 1971).

3. I have argued as much in *Casuistry and Modern Ethics: A Poetics of Practical Reasoning* (Chicago: University of Chicago Press, 1996), chap. 3. For a more general discussion, see Nancy L. Rosenblum, *Another Liberalism: Romanticism and the Reconstruction of Liberal Thought* (Cambridge: Harvard University Press, 1987).

4. See, e.g., H. Richard Niebuhr, *The Social Sources of Denominationalism* (1929; reprint, Cleveland, Ohio: World Publishing, 1957).

5. For recent discussions, see Michael Walzer, ed., *Toward a Global Civil Society* (Providence, R.I.: Berghahn Books, 1995).

6. In making this remark, I do not mean to suggest that Kymlicka implies such a reading of feminist civic virtue.

7. Susan Moller Okin, *Justice, Gender, and the Family* (New York: Basic Books, 1989).

8. See, as well, Michael Walzer, "The Idea of Civil Society" *Dissent* (Spring 1991): 293–304.

9. Rawls is the clearest exponent of the difference between social cooperation premised on principled agreements as opposed to a modus vivendi. See John Rawls, *Political Liberalism*, 2d ed. (New York: Columbia University Press, 1994). Kymlicka's discussion of civic virtue as providing a basis for social cooperation that is based on liberal principles rather than on a *modus vivendi* may not cohere with his acceptance of the latter in matters of multicultural politics. See Will Kymlicka, *Multicultural Citizenship: A Liberal Theory of Minority Rights* (New York: Oxford University Press, 1995), 154, 168, 182.

10. See, e.g., U.S. Catholic Bishops, *Economic Justice for All* (Washington, D.C.: United States Catholic Conference, 1986).

11. John Rawls, "The Idea of Public Reason Revisited," *University of Chicago Law Review* 64 (Spring 1997): 765–807.

12. See Rawls, *A Theory of Justice*, 216–21.

13. Ibid., 46, 177, 312, 567–77, and passim.

14. See Jeremy Waldron, "Religious Contributions in Public Deliberation," *San Diego Law Review* 30 (Fall 1993): 817–48.

15. Thomas Aquinas, *Summa Theologiae*, 1a-2ae, QQ. 62, 109.

16. For a discussion, see Michael Walzer, *Interpretation and Social Criticism* (Cambridge: Harvard University Press, 1987, chap. 3.

17. In addition to works cited above, see Charles Taylor, "Invoking Civil Society," in his *Philosophical Arguments* (Cambridge: Harvard University Press, 1995), 204–24; John Ehrenberg, *Civil Society: The Critical History of an Idea* (New York: New York University Press, 1999); Michael G. Schechter, ed., *The Revival of Civil Society* (New York: St. Martin's Press, 1999); Frank Trentmann, ed., *Paradoxes of Civil Society* (New York: Berghahn Books, 2000); Robert Wuthnow, *Christianity and Civil Society: The Contemporary Debate* (Valley Forge, Penn.: Trinity Press International, 1996).

KENNETH BAYNES is Associate Professor of Philosophy at the State University of New York at Stony Brook. He is coeditor of *After Philosophy: End of Transformation?* and author of *The Normative Grounds of Social Criticism: Kant, Rawls, and Habermas.*

DAVID BIALE is Emanuel Ringelblum Professor of Jewish History at the University of California at Davis. He is the author of *Power and Powerlessness in Jewish History* and editor of *Insider/Outsider: American Jews and Multiculturalism.* He is currently editing a three-volume cultural history of the Jews.

JOHN A. COLEMAN, S.J., is the Charles Casassa Professor of Social Values at Loyola Marymount University, Los Angeles. For twenty-three years he taught in the graduate program in religion and society at the Graduate Theological Union, Berkeley. Among his many books are *An American Strategic Theology, One Hundred Years of Catholic Social Teaching,* and *Religion and Nationalism.*

WILLIAM A. GALSTON is Professor, School of Public Affairs, and Director, Institute for Philosophy and Public Policy at the University of Maryland. His writings include *Liberal Purposes,* "Two Concepts of Liberalism," and "Value Pluralism and Liberal Political Theory."

FARHAD KAZEMI is Professor of Politics and Middle Eastern Studies and the Vice Provost of New York University. His most recent publications include *Peasants and Politics in the Contemporary Middle East* (edited with John Waterbury), *Civil Society in Iran* (two special issues of *Iran Nameh*), and articles on the politics of reform in the Middle East in professional journals and edited volumes.

JOHN KELSAY is Richard L. Rubinstein Professor of Religion at Florida State University. He also serves as Department Chair. Kelsay's publications include *Islam and War: A Study in Comparative Religious Ethics* and (as coeditor) *Cross, Crescent, and Sword* and *Just War and Jihad.*

WILL KYMLICKA is the author of five books published by Oxford University Press: *Liberalism, Community, and Culture; Contemporary Political Philosophy; Multicultural Citizenship; Finding Our Way: Rethinking Ethnocultural Relations in Canada;* and *Politics in the Vernacular: Nationalism, Multiculturalism, and Citizenship.* He is a Professor of Philosophy and Political Science at Queen's University, and a visiting professor in the Nationalism Studies program at the Central European University in Budapest.

FRED D. MILLER, JR., is Professor of Philosophy and Executive Director of the Social Philosophy and Policy Center at Bowling Green State University. He is associate editor of *Social Philosophy and Policy*. In addition to numerous articles, he is author of *Nature, Justice, and Rights in Aristotle's Politics* and coeditor with David Keyt of *A Companion to Aristotle's Politics*. He is current President of the Society for Ancient Greek Philosophy.

RICHARD B. MILLER is Finkelstein Fellow and Professor in the Department of Religious Studies at Indiana University, where he currently serves as departmental Chair. He is the author of *Interpretations of Conflict: Ethics, Pacifism, and the Just-War Tradition* and *Casuistry and Modern Ethics: A Poetics of Practical Reasoning*. He has edited *War in the Twentieth Century: Sources in Theological Ethics* and has written essays on war and peace, multiculturalism, casuistry, and medical ethics. He is currently writing a book on pediatric medical ethics, drawing on a fellowship year in the Program in Ethics and the Professions at Harvard.

PETER NOSCO is Professor of East Asian Languages and Cultures, and History at the University of Southern California. A specialist in the intellectual and social history of early-modern Japan, he is the author of *Remembering Paradise: Nativism and Nostalgia in eighteenth-Century Japan* and the editor of *Confucianism and Tokugawa Culture*.

SUSAN MOLLER OKIN is Marta Sutton Weeks Professor of Ethics in Society and Professor of Political Science at Stanford University. She is the author of *Women in Western Political Thought; Justice, Gender, and the Family*; and *Is Multiculturalism Bad for Women?* She is currently working on issues of gender, economic development, and women's rights in the less-developed world.

TOM G. PALMER is Fellow in Social Thought at the Cato Institute in Washington, D.C., where he also directs Cato University, the Institute's educational program. He is Senior Editor of *Encyclopedia of Libertarianism* and writes frequently on property and moral theory.

ROBERT POST is Alexander F. and May T. Morrison Professor of Law at the University of California, Berkeley. He is the author of *Constitutional Domains: Democracy, Community, Management*.

HENRY ROSEMONT, JR., is George B. and Willma Reeves Distinguished Professor of the Liberal Arts at St. Mary's College of Maryland. He is the author of *A Chinese Mirror* and the forthcoming *Rationality and Religious Experience*. He has edited and translated many works, most recently *The Analects of Confucius* (with Roger T. Ames).

NANCY L. ROSENBLUM is Professor of Government at Harvard University. She is author most recently of *Membership and Morals: The Personal Uses of Pluralism in America* and editor of *Obligations of Citizenship and Demands of Faith: Religious Accommodation in Pluralist Democracies*.

STEVEN SCALET is Assistant Professor of Economics and Philosophy at Binghamton University, State University of New York, and the Assistant Director of the Program in Philosophy, Politics, and Law. He writes about the link between liberalism and skepticism, and liberalism and conceptions of individual responsibility.

DAVID SCHMIDTZ is Professor of Philosophy and joint Professor of Economics at the University of Arizona. He has edited *Robert Nozick*, forthcoming from Cambridge University Press, and coedited (with Elizabeth Willott) *Environmental Ethics: What Really Matters, What Really Works*, forthcoming from Oxford University Press.

MAX. L. STACKHOUSE is Stephen Colwell Professor of Christian Ethics, Princeton Theological Seminary. He is the author or editor of twelve books, including *Religion and the Powers of Common Life; God and Globalization; Covenant and Commitments: Faith, Family, and Economic Life; On Moral Business; Christian Social Ethics in a Global Era*; and *Public Theology and Political Economy*.

WILLIAM M. SULLIVAN is a Senior Scholar at the Carnegie Foundation for the Advancement of Teaching. He is coauthor of *Habits of the Heart: Individualism and Commitment in American Life* and *The Good Society*. He is author of *Reconstructing Public Philosophy* and, most recently, *Work and Integrity:The Crisis and Promise of Professionalism in American Life*.

STEPHEN K. WHITE is Professor of Government at the University of Virginia and Editor of the journal *Political Theory*. His most recent book is *Sustaining Affirmation: The Strengths of Weak Ontology Political Theory*.

NOAM ZOHAR is Senior Lecturer, Department of Philosophy, Bar Ilan University, Israel; Director of its Graduate Program in Bioethics; and Senior Research Fellow, Shalom Hartman Institute, Jerusalem. His publications include essays in Rabbinics, Applied Ethics, and Political Philosophy, often involving a dialogue between the Western and the Jewish moral traditions. He is author of *Alternatives in Jewish Bioethics* and coeditor of the four-volume *The Jewish Political Tradition*.

between civil society/state in Judaic thought, 276–78; common good in resolution of, 199; critical theory perception of, 133–39; dealings of liberal egalitarians with, 101–3; feminist theory perception of, 170–73, 184–85; between government and civil society, 197–98; in Israel between state and religion, 283; liberal-egalitarian perspective on, 101–3, 120–21; liberal perception on state/civil society demands, 44; natural law theory about society/state, 206–8; rules under Islam about intrastate, 305; among women's groups, 163
Confucianism: boundary between civil society and the state, 337–41, 371–73; meaning of, 335; Neo-Confucianism, 335–36; rectification of names doctrine, 343–44; response to modernity, 339–40; in societies of East Asia, 336
congruence: as accommodation between government and civil society, 14; advocacy of, 13–14; government creation of, 14; logic of (Rosenblum), 12–13, 97–98, 121; unremitting, 16
Constant, Benjamin, 55–56
constitutions: in Asian context, 334; Islamic Republic of Iran, 296–98, 305, 309; of modern East Asian societies, 349; Torah seen in Israel as, 282–83
corporatism, 37–38
critical theory: commitment to certain values, 378; described, 123; Frankfurt School of, 123, 146
Cuddihy, John Murray, 89

de Bary, Wm. Theodore, 345
Delors, Jacques, 239
democracy: citizenship in, 379; classical liberals' support of, 29; dependent on actions of civil society, 16–19; Habermas's model of, 125–39; idea of citizenship in modern, 202; justice in, 84–87; virtues of liberal, 85–87
Dietz, Mary, 91
Dignitatis Humanae, 231, 232
Dillistone, F. W., 256
Dorr, Donal, 247
Durkheim, Emile, 240
duty toward community: Aquinas's view of, 204; as element of social capital, 196

Eberly, Don, 56–57
education: of citizens, 204–5; in Israel, 268–69, 277–78; public system of (Aristotle), 205; role of civil society in moral, 204–5
egalitarianism, liberal: distinct from libertarianism, 101, 111; equality of resources view of, 79–80
Eisenstadt, S. N., 354
Ekken, Kaibara, 352
Elshtain, Jean, 91
Eötvös, Josef, 65–67
equality: in classic liberalism, 175; developed in civil society, 53; feminist groups can advance, 164, 182; government norms of, 13; inequalities within civil society, 6; institutions hostile to women's, 183; moral and distributional, 111, 113–14; under natural law (Locke), 190; in Rawls's theory, 112; women's formal, 168
equality, liberal. *See* egalitarianism, liberal
Evans, Sarah, 170

family, the: Christian concept of, 224; as part of civil society, 28; Confucian view of, 348–49, 364–65, 372; feminist theory of, 153; under Hebrew biblical law, 271–72; relations in 'ulama, 301–4
feminists: distrust distinct public and private spheres, 38–39; group participation to advance equality, 164; handling of conflicts by, 170–73; in the military, 182
feminist theory: about associations of women, 173; benefits provided by government, 155–68; dissenters, 161, 182; on function of civil society, 159; public/private boundary in, 152–55; on values imparted by civil society, 162; view of citizenship, 168–70; view of public space and civil society, 153–54
Ferguson, Adam, 192
Finnis, John, 194
Forster, E. M., 206, 207
Frankel, Charles, 141
Frankfurt School, 123, 146, 378
Fraser, Nancy, 128
freedom: of association, 18, 22; civil society as zone of, 3; in Locke-Hume notions of liberalism, 221
Friedman, Milton, 148
Furet, François, 16